Y0-BDB-685

快感

Sensual
Phrase

Sensual Phrase

Vol. 11

Shôjo Edition

Story & Art by
Mayu Shinjo

English Adaptation/Kelly Sue DeConnick
Translation/Joe Yamazaki
Touch-up & Lettering/Rina Mapa
Cover & Graphic Design/Izumi Evers
Editor/Eric Searleman

Managing Editor/Annette Roman
Director of Production/Noboru Watanabe
Vice President of Publishing/Alvin Lu
Sr. Director of Acquisitions/Rika Inouye
Vice President of Sales & Marketing/Liza Coppola
Publisher/Hyoe Narita

© 1997 Mayu SHINJO/Shogakukan Inc. First published by
Shogakukan Inc. in Japan as "Kaikan Fure-zu." New and
adapted artwork and text © 2005 VIZ Media, LLC. The
SENSUAL PHRASE logo is a trademark of VIZ Media,
LLC. All rights reserved. The stories, characters and incidents
mentioned in this publication are entirely fictional.

No portion of this book may be reproduced or transmitted in
any form or by any means without written permission from
the copyright holders.

Printed in the U.S.A.

Published by VIZ Media, LLC
P.O. Box 77010
San Francisco, CA 94107

Shôjo Edition
10 9 8 7 6 5 4 3 2 1
First printing, November 2005

For advertising rates or media kit, e-mail advertising@viz.com

www.viz.com
store.viz.com

PARENTAL ADVISORY
SENSUAL PHRASE is rated M for mature
readers. This volume contains strong
language and sexual themes.

快感 Sensual Phrase

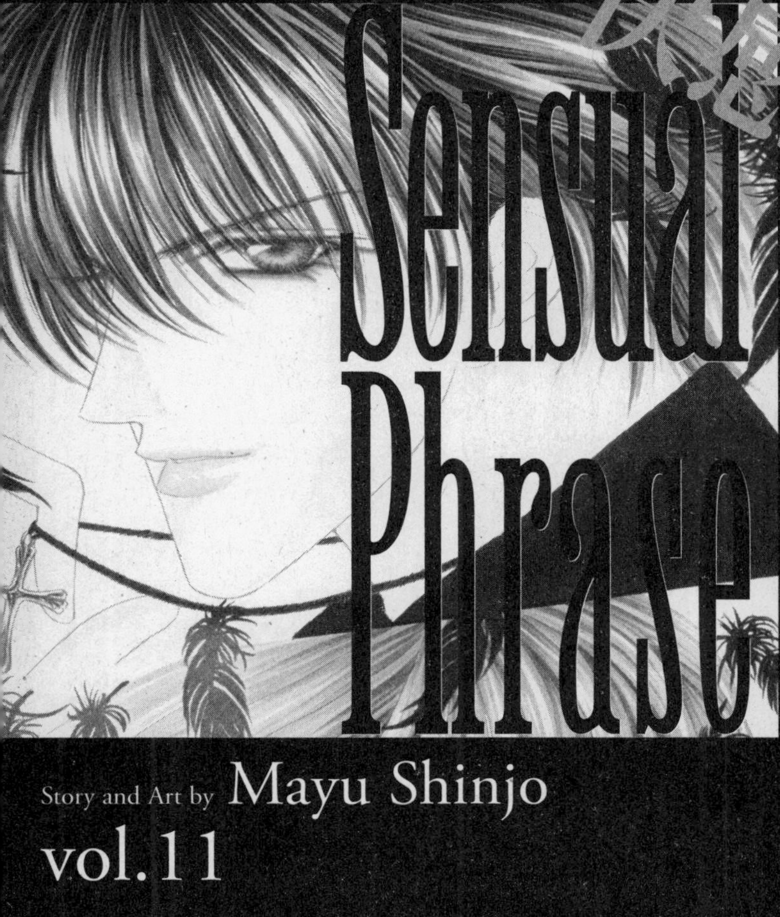

Story and Art by Mayu Shinjo

vol.11

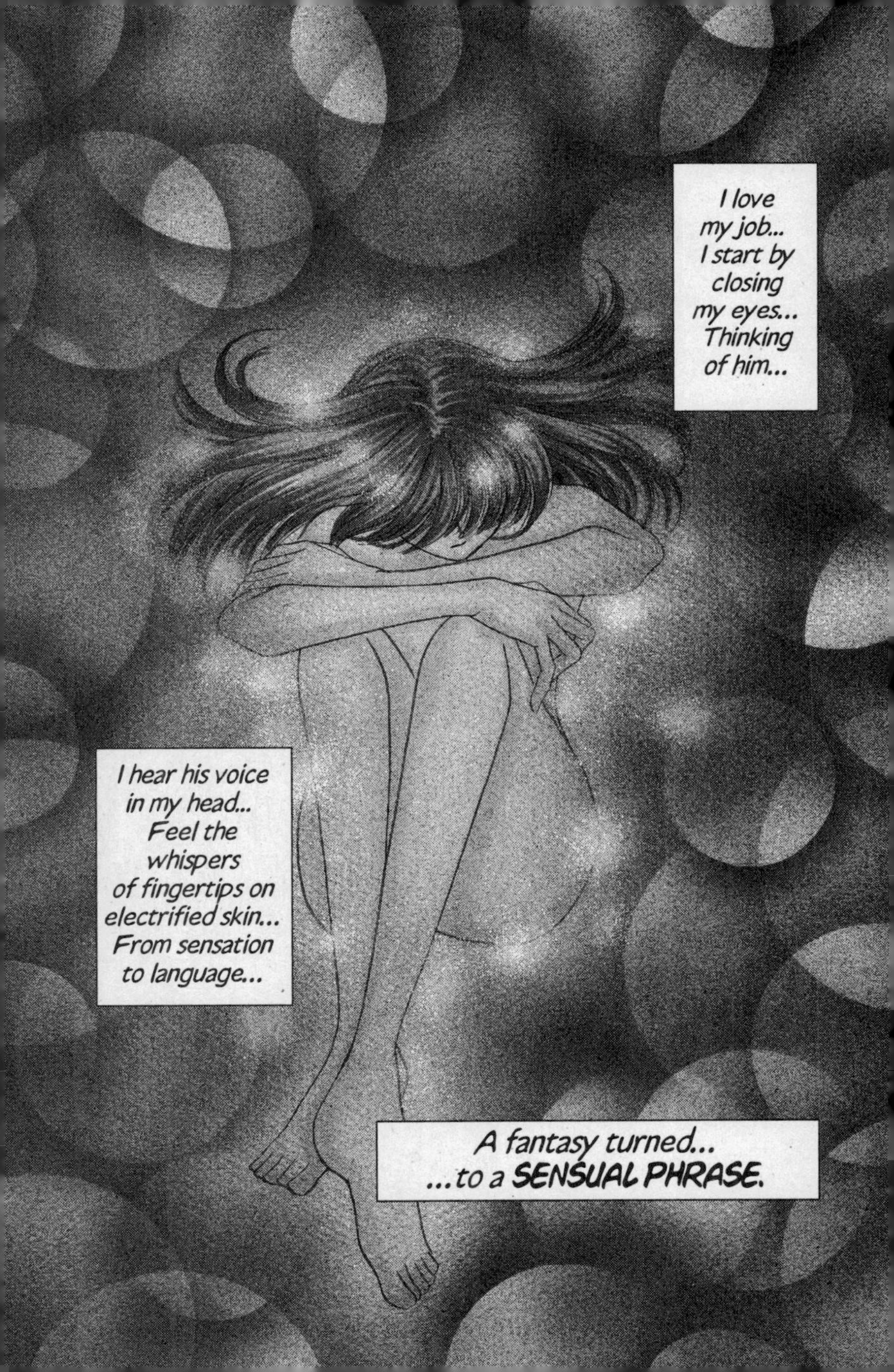
I love my job... I start by closing my eyes... Thinking of him...
I hear his voice in my head... Feel the whispers of fingertips on electrified skin... From sensation to language...
A fantasy turned... ...to a SENSUAL PHRASE.

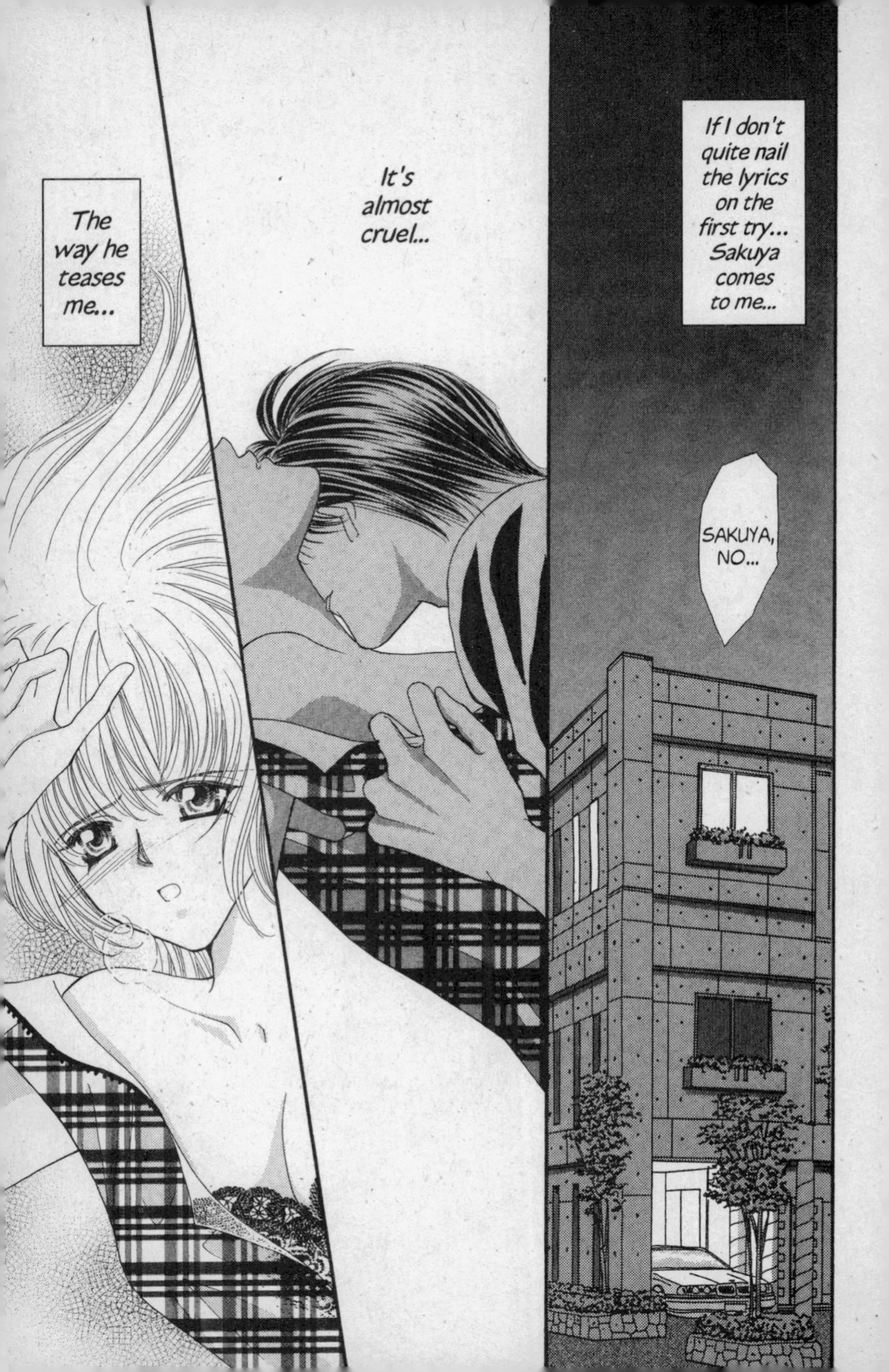
If I don't quite nail the lyrics on the first try... Sakuya comes to me...
SAKUYA, NO...
It's almost cruel...
The way he teases me...

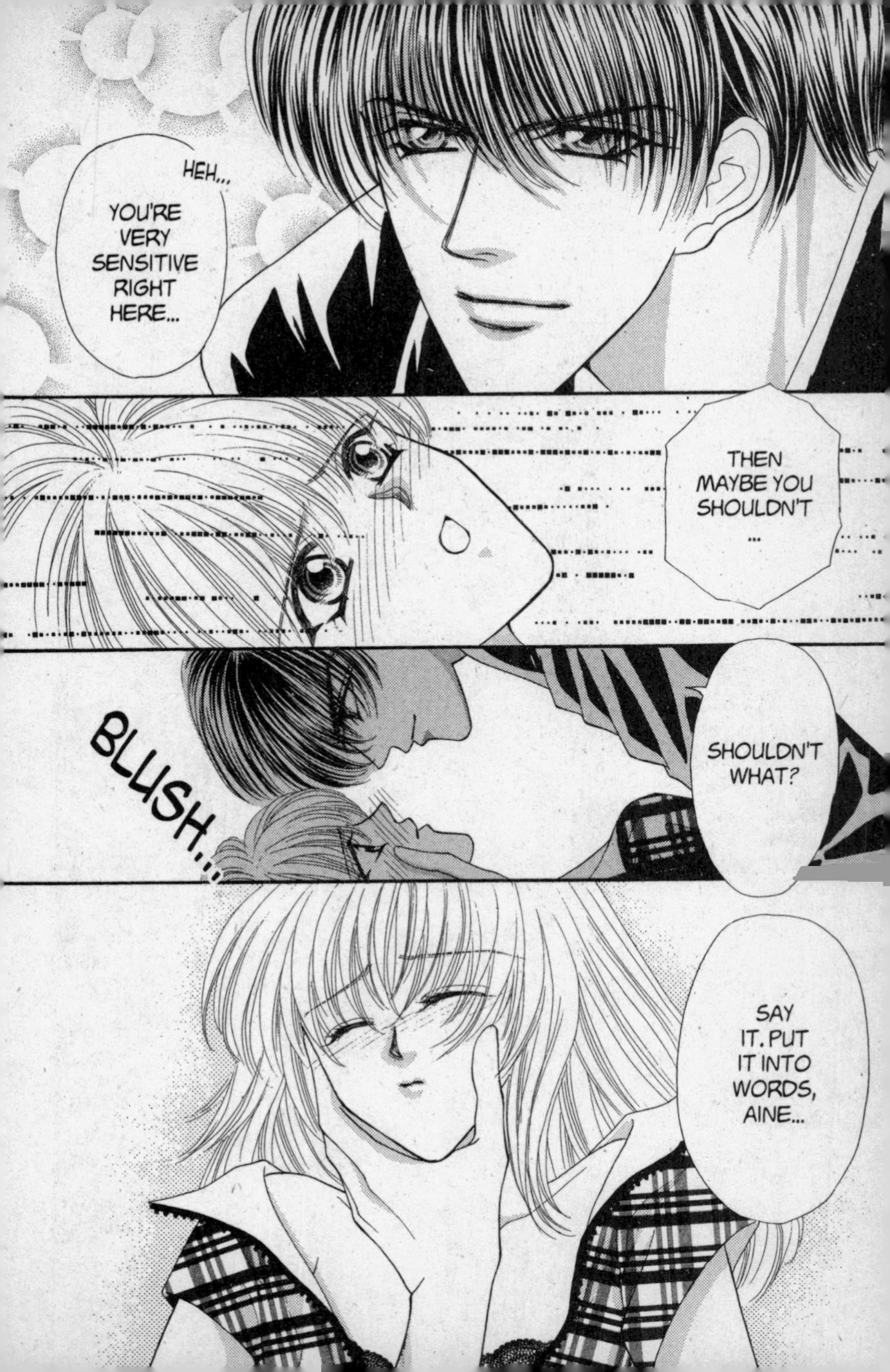
HEH... YOU'RE VERY SENSITIVE RIGHT HERE...
THEN MAYBE YOU SHOULDN'T ...
SHOULDN'T WHAT?
BLUSH...
SAY IT. PUT IT INTO WORDS, AINE...

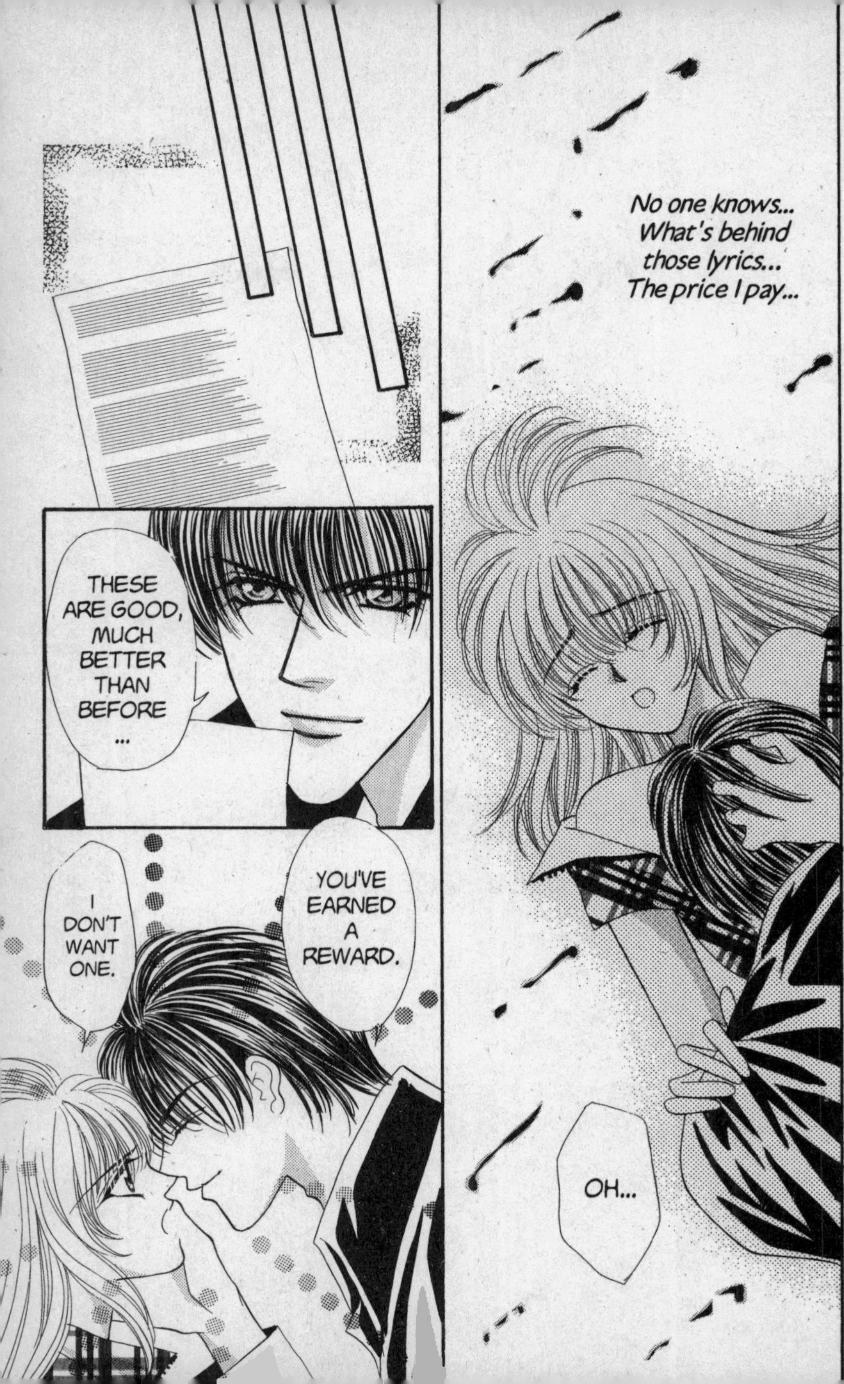
No one knows... What's behind those lyrics... The price I pay...
OH...
THESE ARE GOOD, MUCH BETTER THAN BEFORE ...
YOU'VE EARNED A REWARD.
I DON'T WANT ONE.

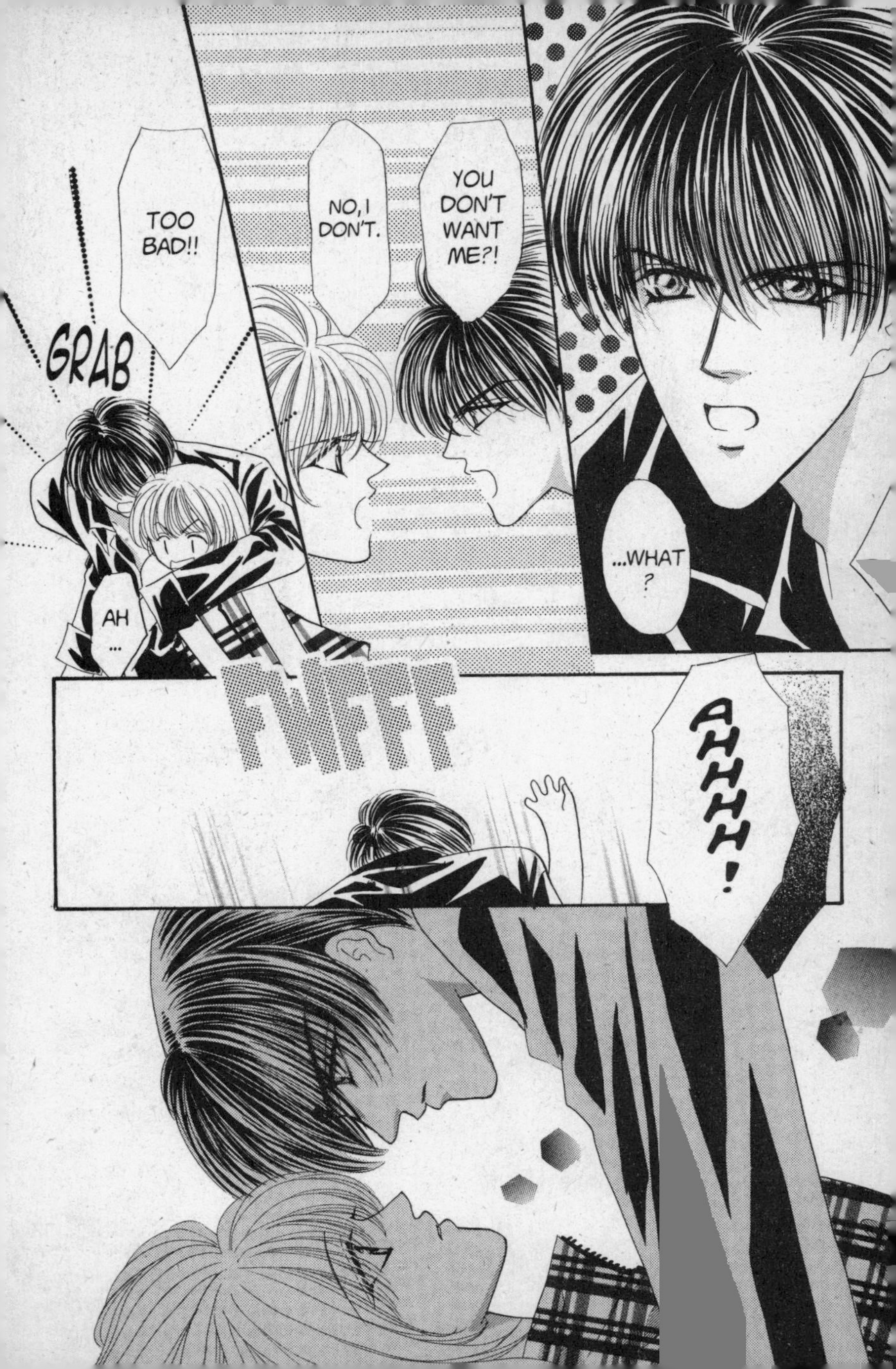
...WHAT?
YOU DON'T WANT ME?!
NO, I DON'T.
TOO BAD!!
GRAB
AH ...
AHHHH!
FWFFF

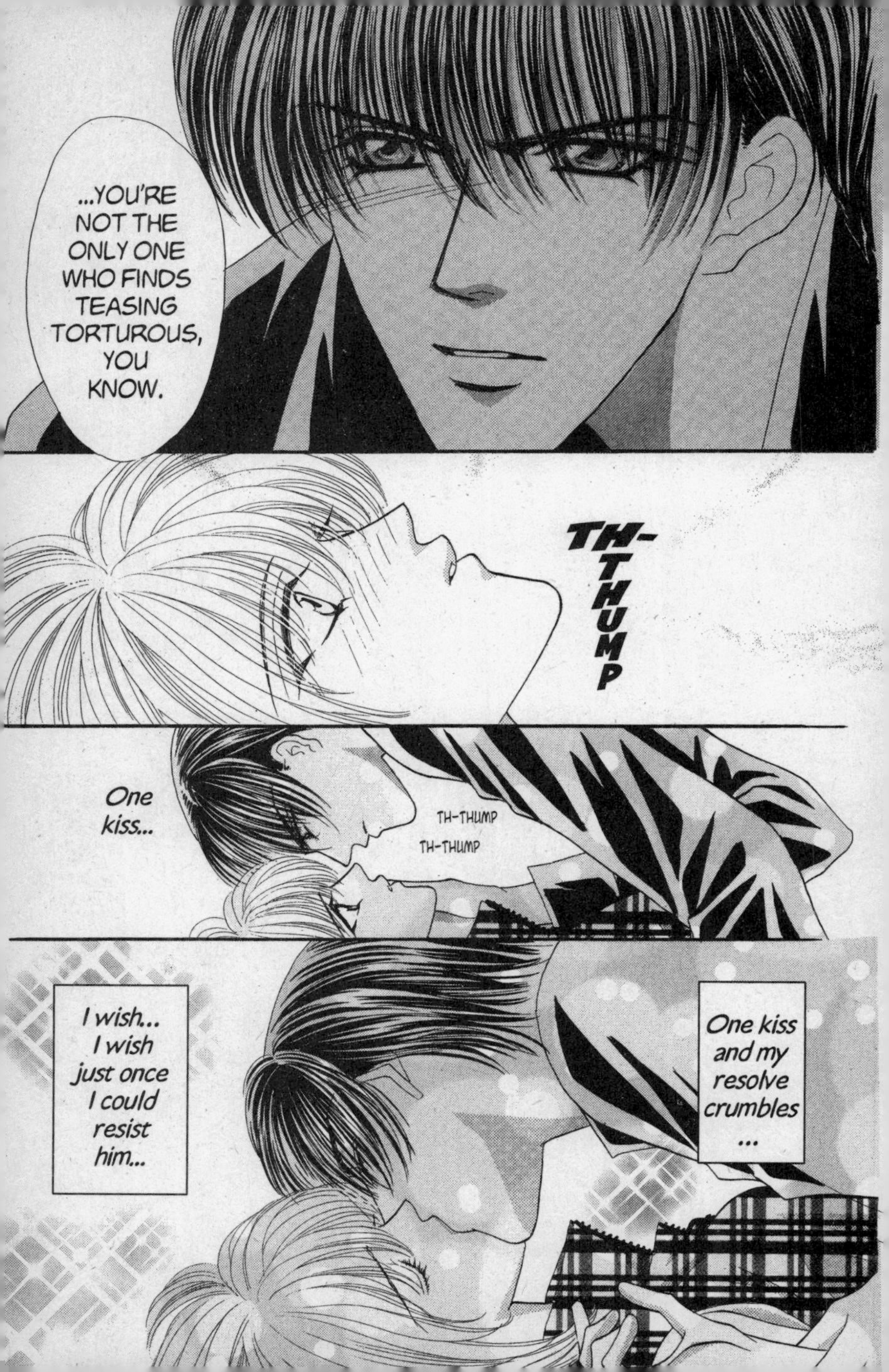
...YOU'RE NOT THE ONLY ONE WHO FINDS TEASING TORTUROUS, YOU KNOW.
TH-THUMP
TH-THUMP
TH-THUMP
One kiss...
One kiss and my resolve crumbles ...
I wish... I wish just once I could resist him...

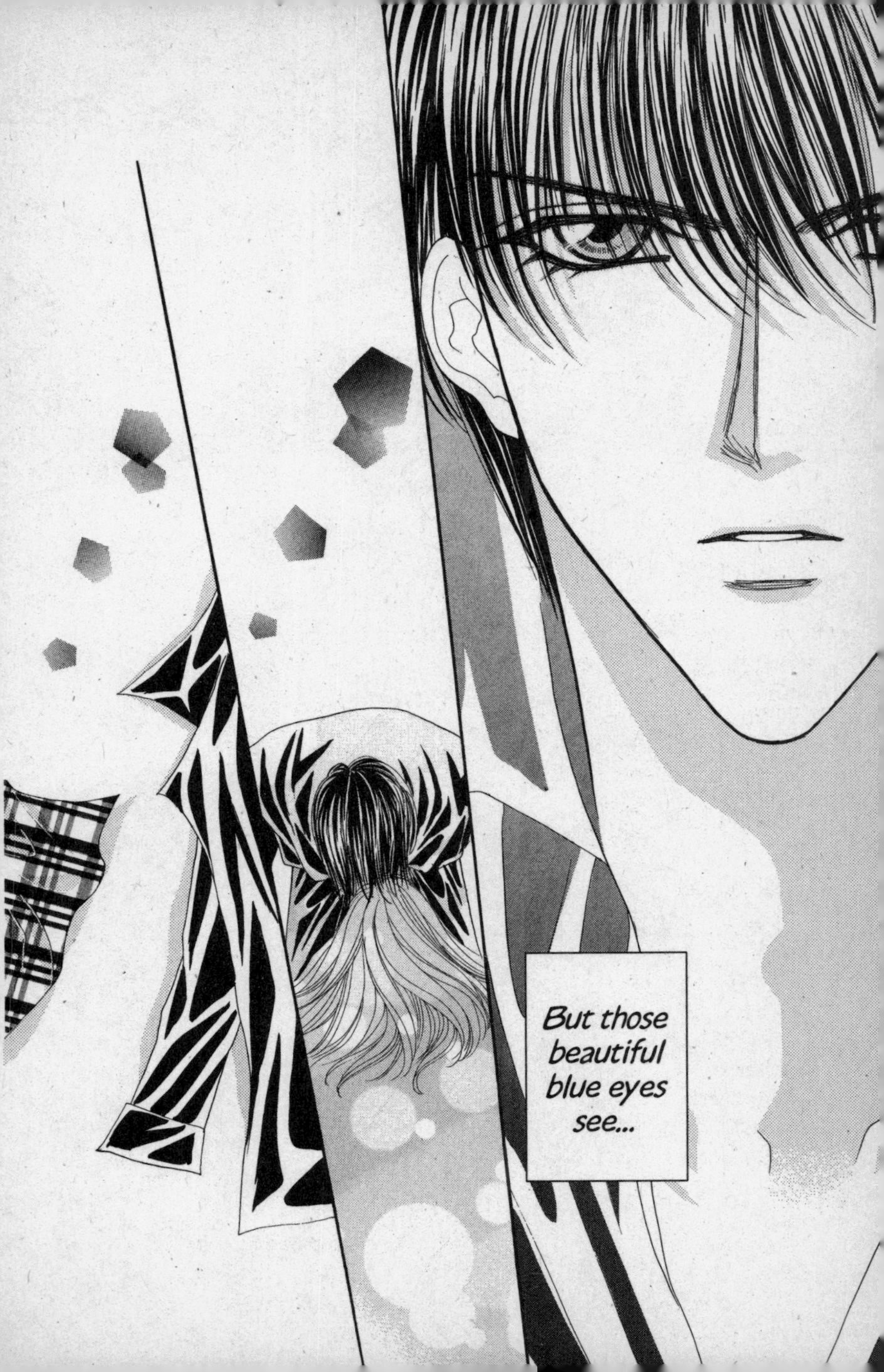
But those beautiful blue eyes see...

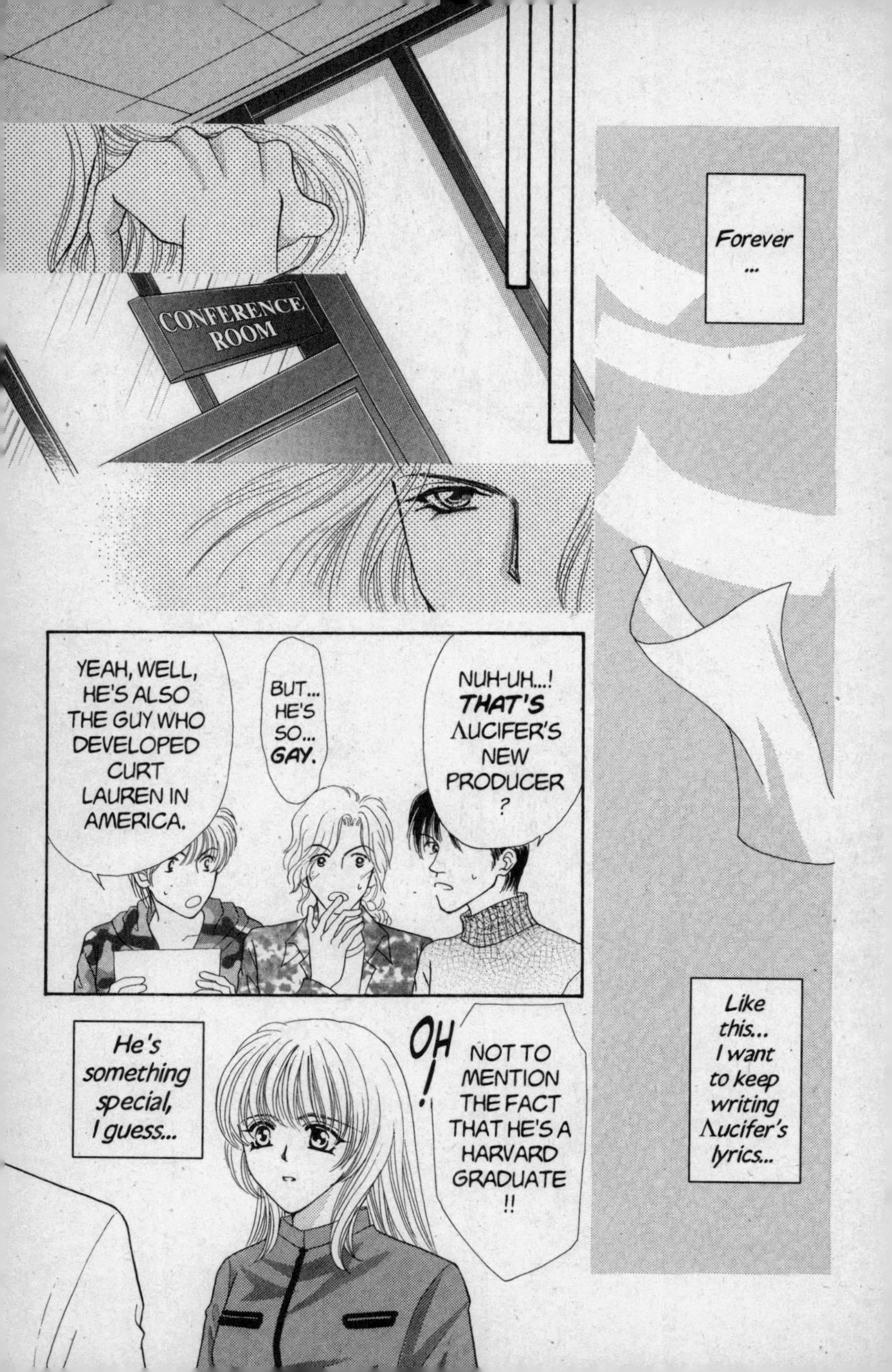
Forever ...
Like this... I want to keep writing Λucifer's lyrics...
CONFERENCE ROOM
NUH-UH...! THAT'S Λucifer's NEW PRODUCER ?
BUT... HE'S SO... GAY.
YEAH, WELL, HE'S ALSO THE GUY WHO DEVELOPED CURT LAUREN IN AMERICA.
OH !
NOT TO MENTION THE FACT THAT HE'S A HARVARD GRADUATE !!
He's something special, I guess...

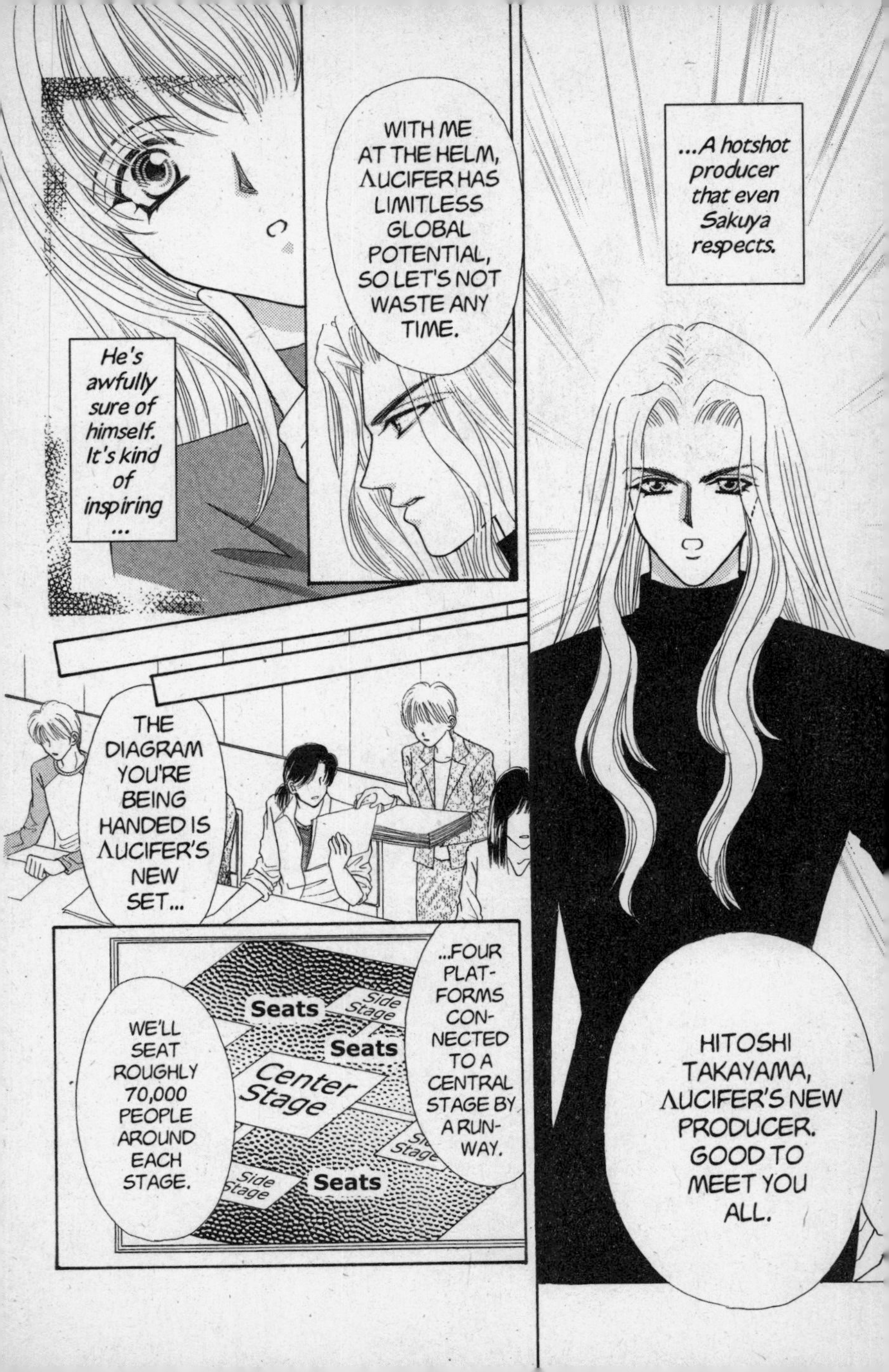
...A hotshot producer that even Sakuya respects.
HITOSHI TAKAYAMA, ΛUCIFER'S NEW PRODUCER. GOOD TO MEET YOU ALL.
WITH ME AT THE HELM, ΛUCIFER HAS LIMITLESS GLOBAL POTENTIAL, SO LET'S NOT WASTE ANY TIME.
He's awfully sure of himself. It's kind of inspiring...
THE DIAGRAM YOU'RE BEING HANDED IS ΛUCIFER'S NEW SET...
...FOUR PLATFORMS CONNECTED TO A CENTRAL STAGE BY A RUNWAY.
Seats
Side Stage
Seats
Center Stage
Side Stage
Side Stage
Seats
WE'LL SEAT ROUGHLY 70,000 PEOPLE AROUND EACH STAGE.

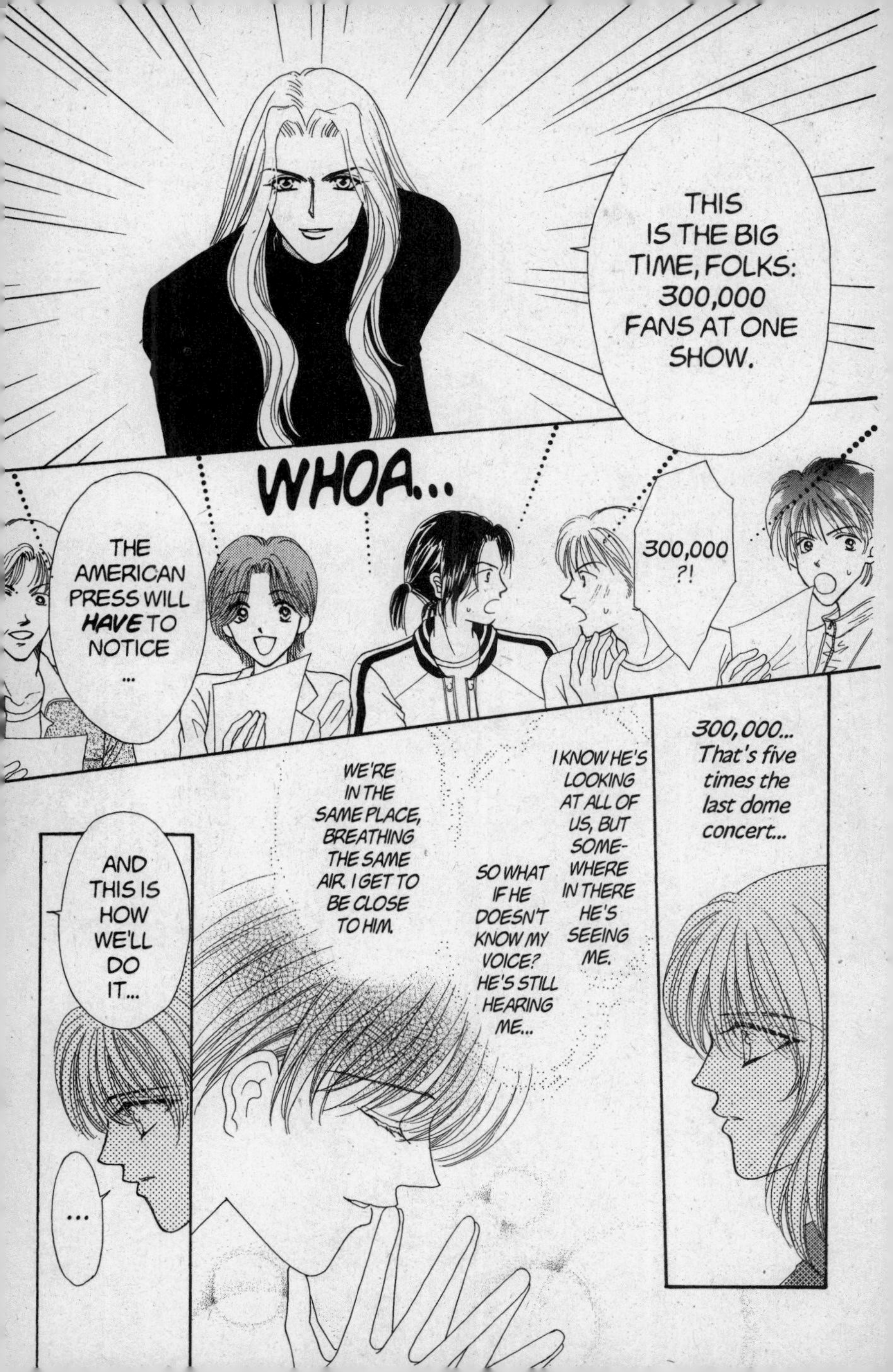
THIS IS THE BIG TIME, FOLKS: 300,000 FANS AT ONE SHOW.
300,000?!
WHOA...
THE AMERICAN PRESS WILL *HAVE* TO NOTICE...
300,000... That's five times the last dome concert...
I KNOW HE'S LOOKING AT ALL OF US, BUT SOME-WHERE IN THERE HE'S SEEING ME.
SO WHAT IF HE DOESN'T KNOW MY VOICE? HE'S STILL HEARING ME...
WE'RE IN THE SAME PLACE, BREATHING THE SAME AIR. I GET TO BE CLOSE TO HIM.
AND THIS IS HOW WE'LL DO IT...
...

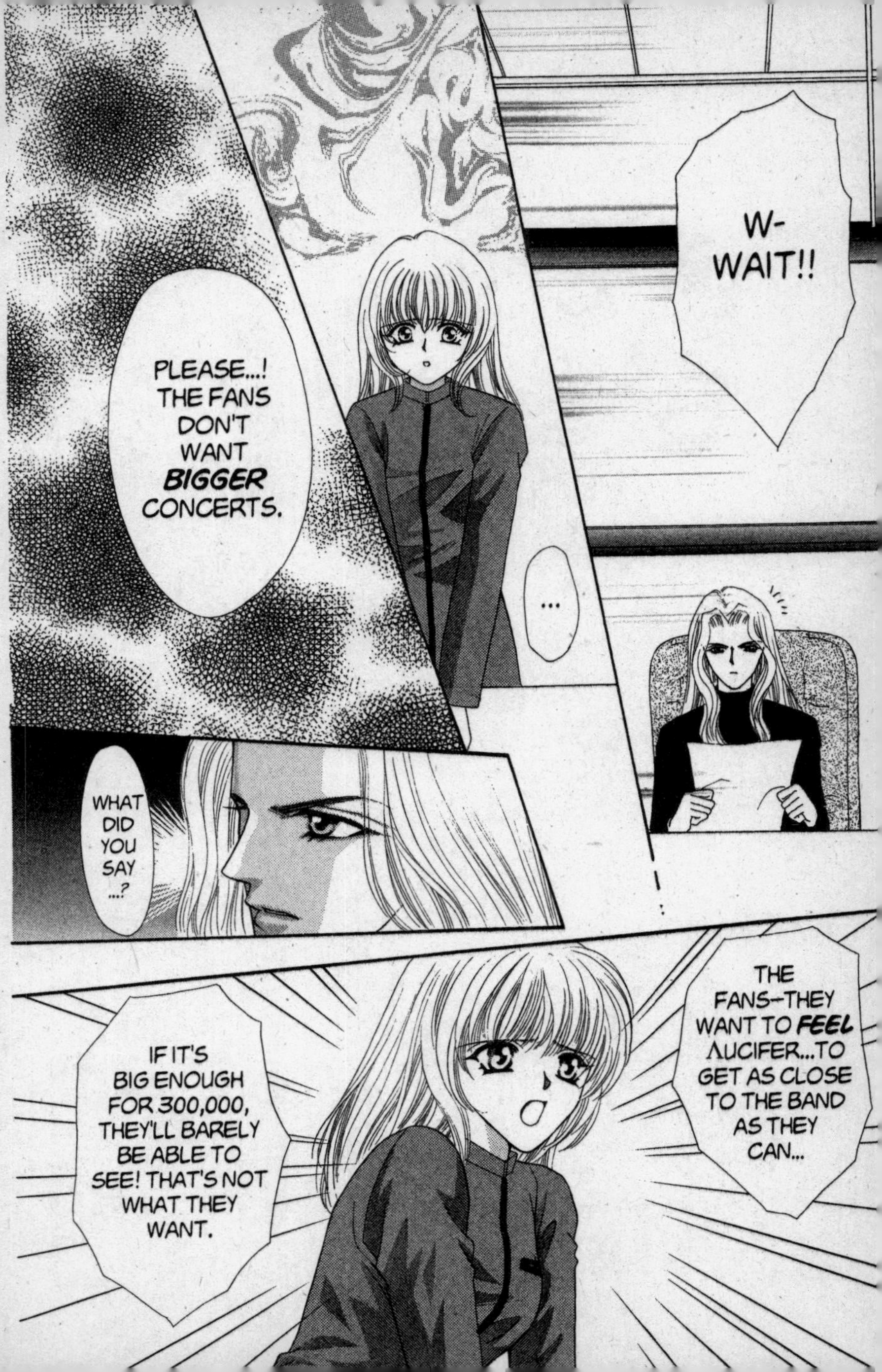
W-WAIT!!
PLEASE...! THE FANS DON'T WANT BIGGER CONCERTS.
...
WHAT DID YOU SAY ...?
THE FANS—THEY WANT TO FEEL ΛUCIFER...TO GET AS CLOSE TO THE BAND AS THEY CAN...
IF IT'S BIG ENOUGH FOR 300,000, THEY'LL BARELY BE ABLE TO SEE! THAT'S NOT WHAT THEY WANT.

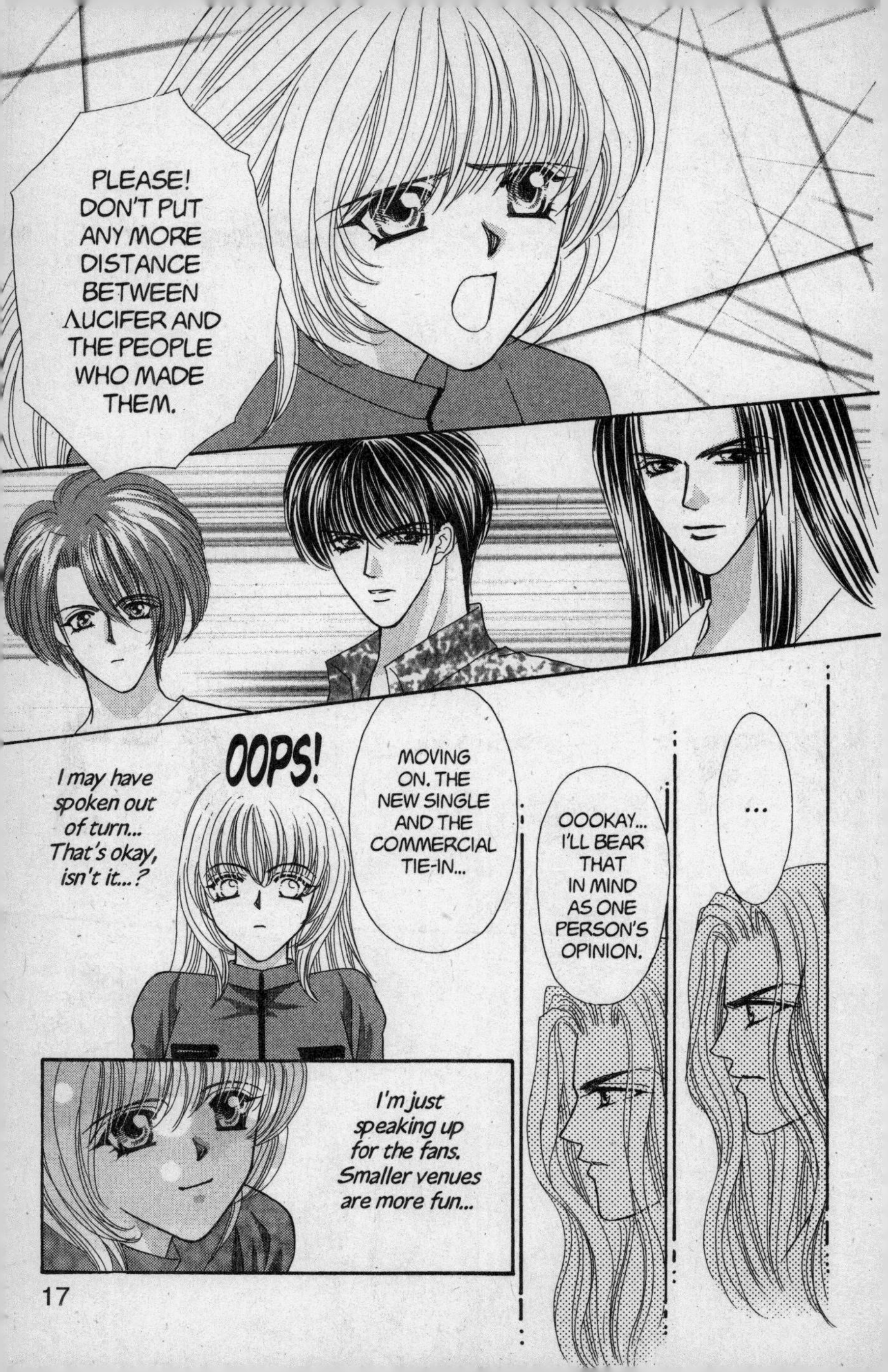
PLEASE! DON'T PUT ANY MORE DISTANCE BETWEEN ΛUCIFER AND THE PEOPLE WHO MADE THEM.
...
OOOKAY... I'LL BEAR THAT IN MIND AS ONE PERSON'S OPINION.
MOVING ON. THE NEW SINGLE AND THE COMMERCIAL TIE-IN...
OOPS!
I may have spoken out of turn... That's okay, isn't it...?
I'm just speaking up for the fans. Smaller venues are more fun...

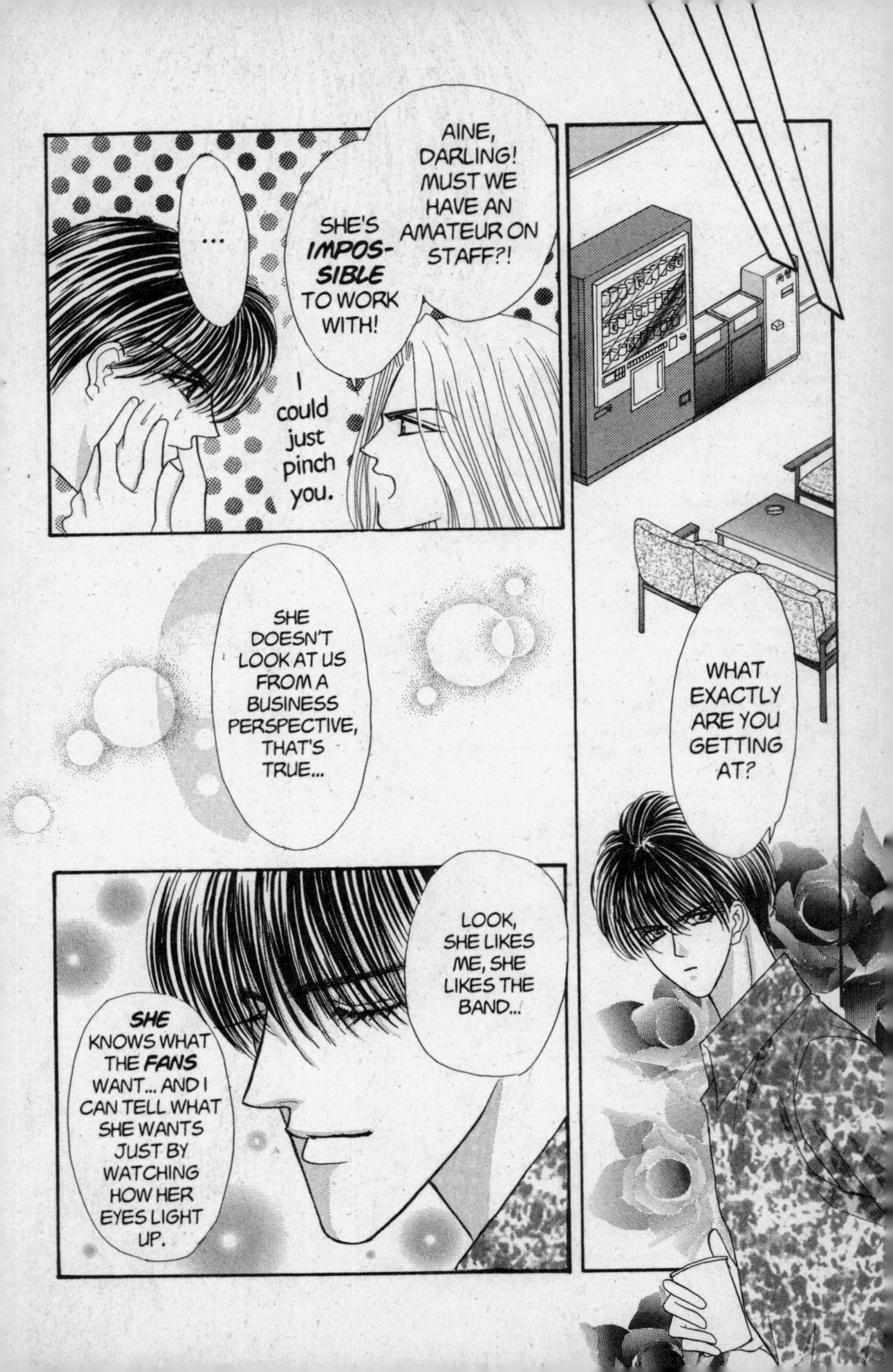
WHAT EXACTLY ARE YOU GETTING AT?
AINE, DARLING! MUST WE HAVE AN AMATEUR ON STAFF?!
SHE'S IMPOSSIBLE TO WORK WITH!
...
I could just pinch you.
SHE DOESN'T LOOK AT US FROM A BUSINESS PERSPECTIVE, THAT'S TRUE...
LOOK, SHE LIKES ME, SHE LIKES THE BAND...
SHE KNOWS WHAT THE FANS WANT... AND I CAN TELL WHAT SHE WANTS JUST BY WATCHING HOW HER EYES LIGHT UP.

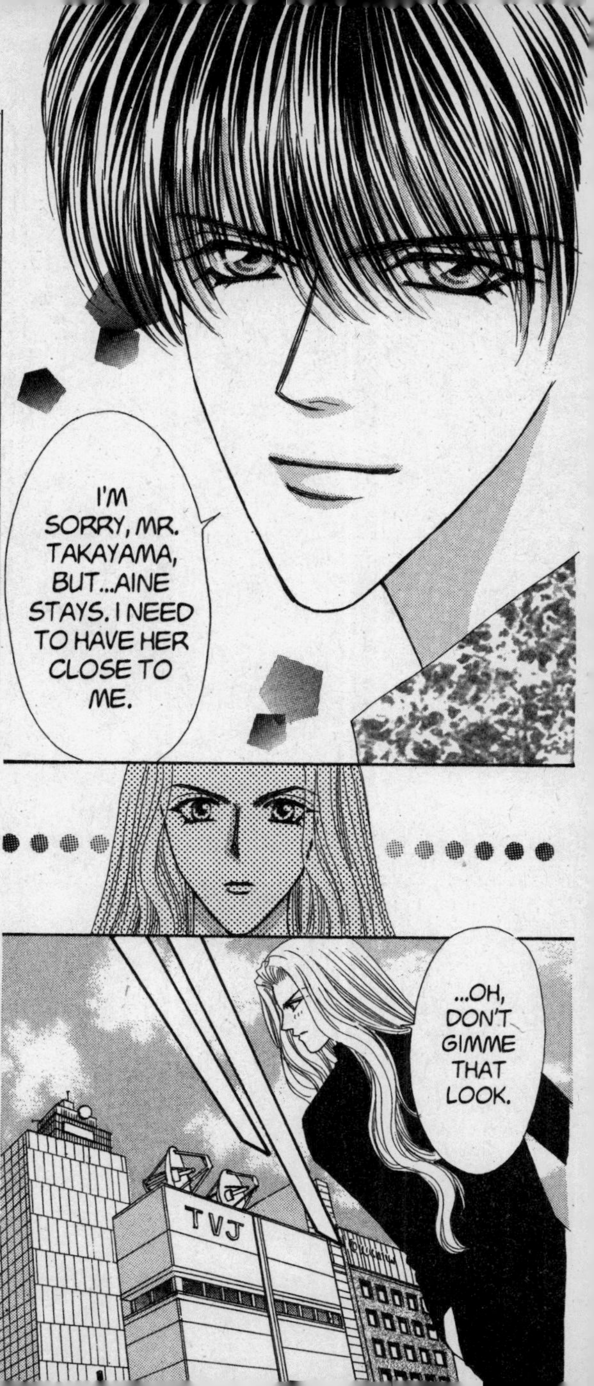
I'M SORRY, MR. TAKAYAMA, BUT...AINE STAYS. I NEED TO HAVE HER CLOSE TO ME.
...OH, DON'T GIMME THAT LOOK.
TVJ

Hi, again! Shinjo here.

So, are you guys watching the anime? Λucifer has finally debuted!! I can't believe it. Am I dreaming? The promo video is BEAUTIFUL. The song is "Fallen Angel Blue," did you guys go buy it? "Silent Melody" is played a lot on the anime so I'm sure you've heard that one. It might be my favorite. If you haven't picked it up yet, you're missing out.

I've been getting a lot of messages for Λucifer in my fan mail recently, too. I love it! Λucifer's official fan club is up and running, and it'll be even more active in the coming months. There are a few private fan clubs, too! They're mostly on the Internet, but they get information even before I do sometimes, so they must be doing something right.

Aine finally appeared in the anime! It's funny, you and I are in the same boat...I have no idea what's gonna happen next either, so I'm looking forward to it just as much as you are.

What's new on the personal front? By the time this volume comes out, I should have moved into a new place. I'm really busy right now, trying to clean up my office for the move. I just don't know where to start!! I did manage to find time to buy some new furniture. Oh, and I'm also getting ready to go to the southern island Maldives on a feng shui trip with my friend. I hope I meet a cute guy...

(The men involved in Sensual Phrase are all so cute that my standards are getting too high...!!)

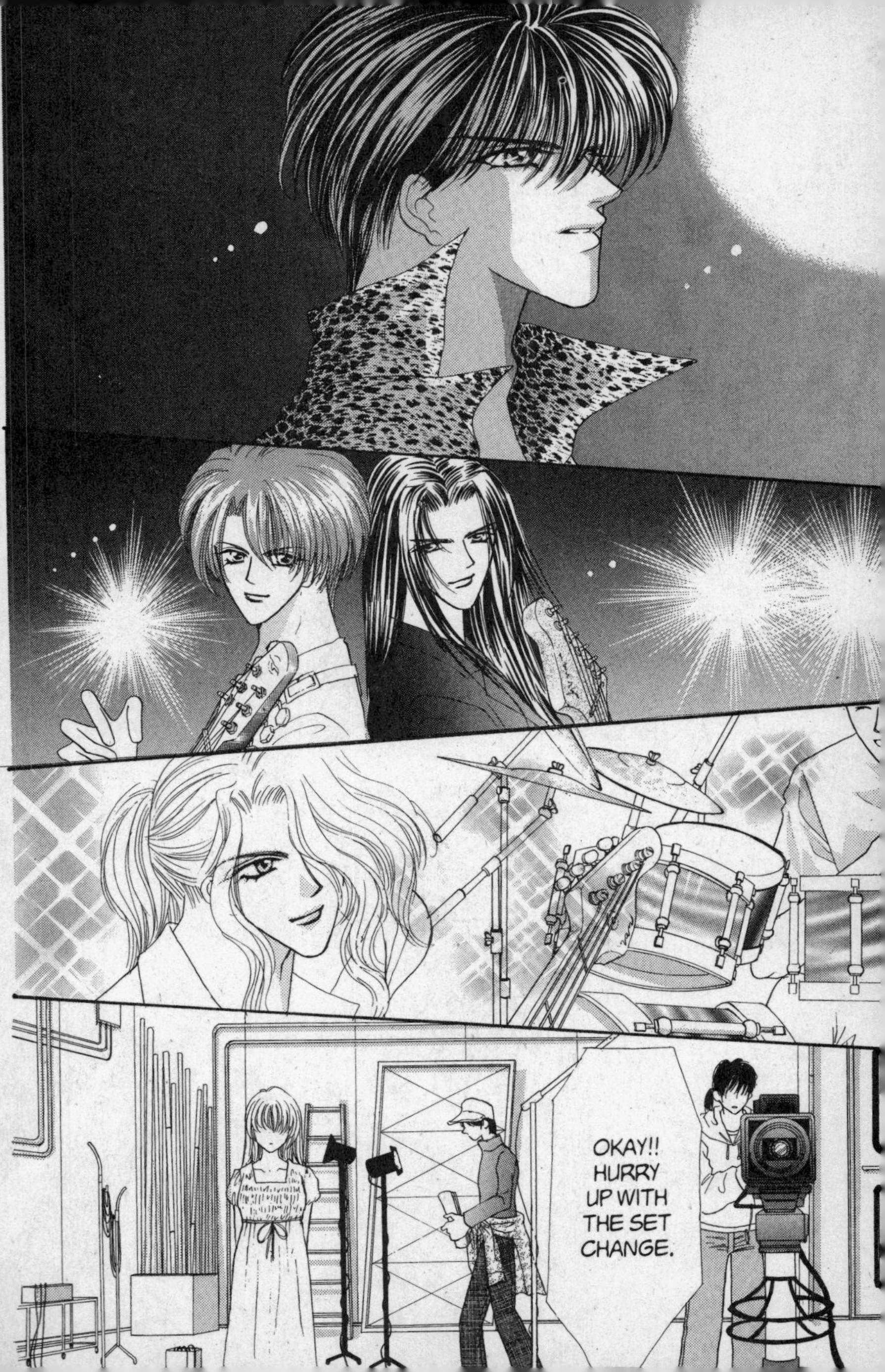
OKAY!! HURRY UP WITH THE SET CHANGE.

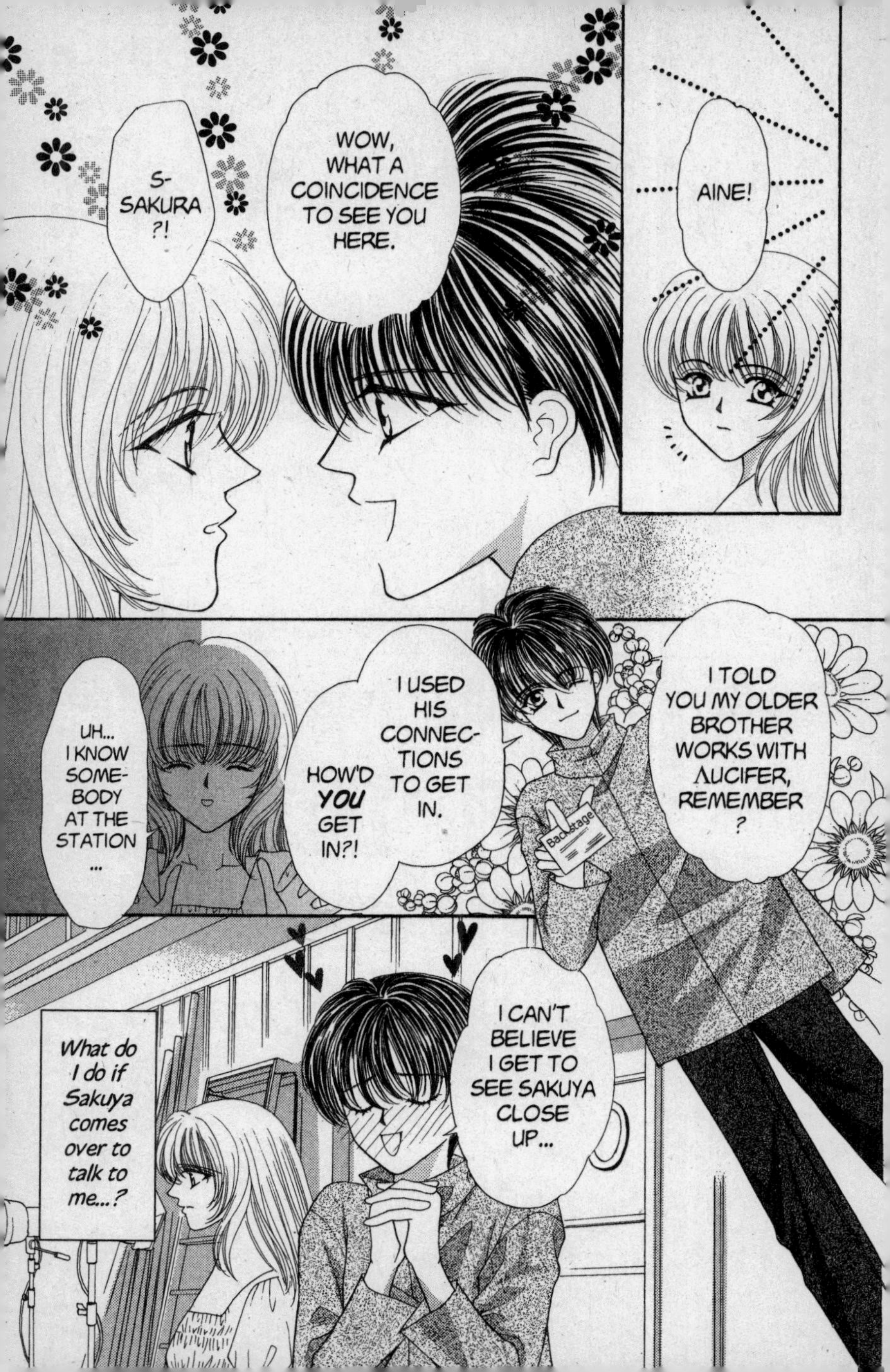
AINE!
WOW, WHAT A COINCIDENCE TO SEE YOU HERE.
S-SAKURA ?!
I TOLD YOU MY OLDER BROTHER WORKS WITH ΛUCIFER, REMEMBER ?
Backstage
I USED HIS CONNECTIONS TO GET IN.
HOW'D YOU GET IN?!
UH... I KNOW SOMEBODY AT THE STATION ...
I CAN'T BELIEVE I GET TO SEE SAKUYA CLOSE UP...
What do I do if Sakuya comes over to talk to me...?

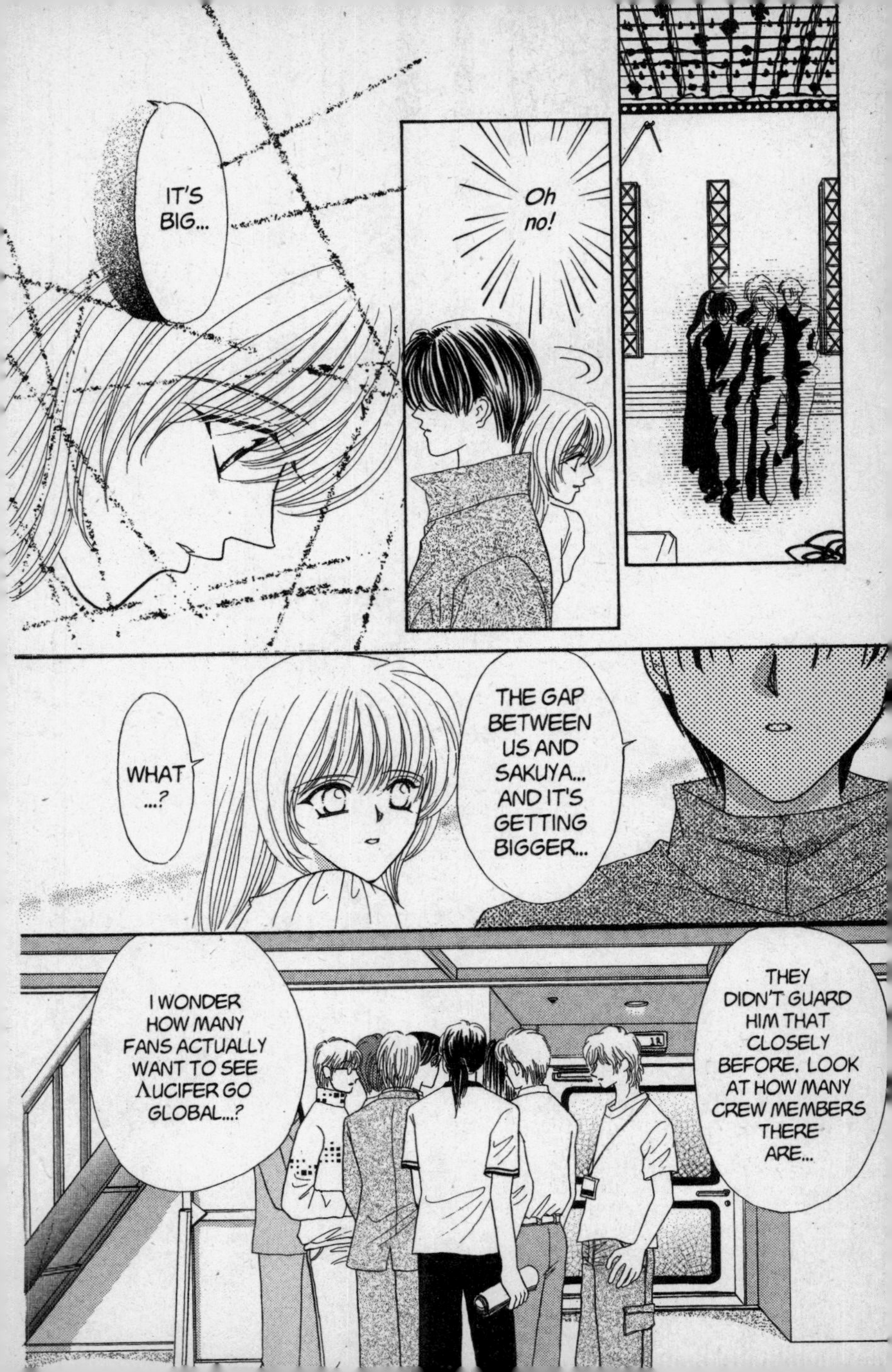
Oh no!
IT'S BIG...
THE GAP BETWEEN US AND SAKUYA... AND IT'S GETTING BIGGER...
WHAT ...?
THEY DIDN'T GUARD HIM THAT CLOSELY BEFORE. LOOK AT HOW MANY CREW MEMBERS THERE ARE...
I WONDER HOW MANY FANS ACTUALLY WANT TO SEE ΛUCIFER GO GLOBAL...?

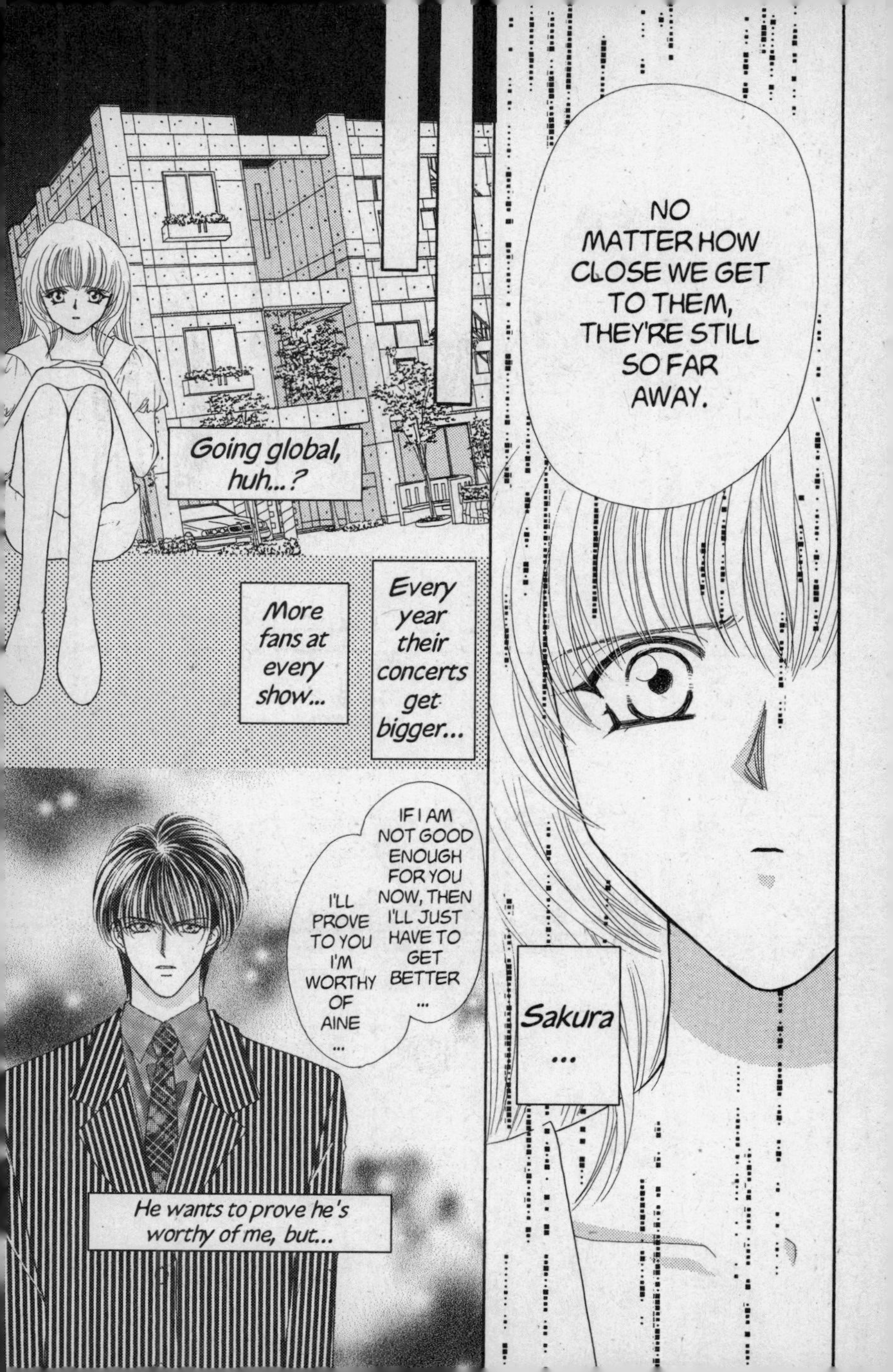
NO MATTER HOW CLOSE WE GET TO THEM, THEY'RE STILL SO FAR AWAY.
Sakura ...
Going global, huh...?
Every year their concerts get bigger...
More fans at every show...
IF I AM NOT GOOD ENOUGH FOR YOU NOW, THEN I'LL JUST HAVE TO GET BETTER ...
I'LL PROVE TO YOU I'M WORTHY OF AINE ...
He wants to prove he's worthy of me, but...

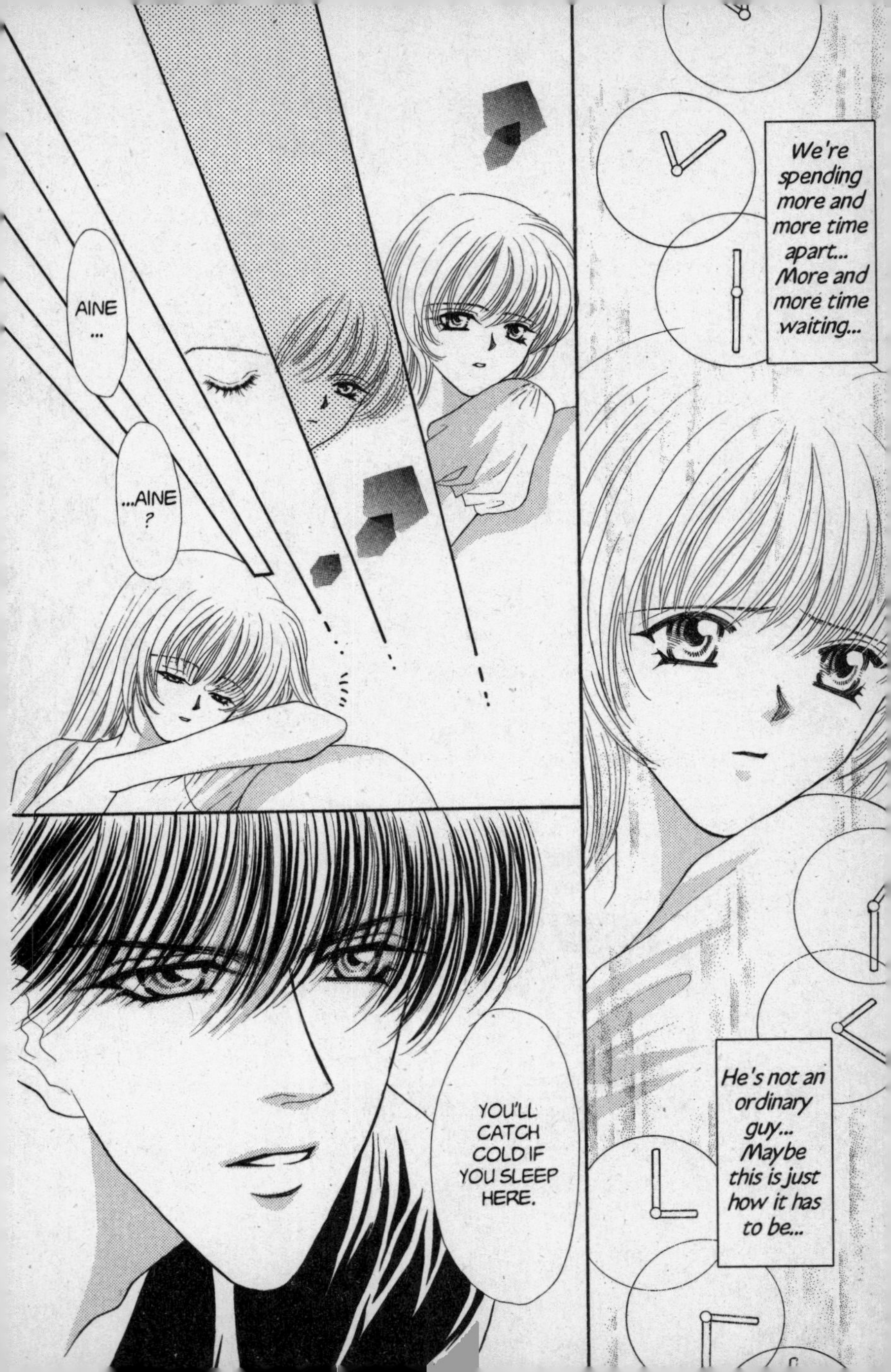
We're spending more and more time apart... More and more time waiting...
He's not an ordinary guy... Maybe this is just how it has to be...
AINE ...
...AINE ?
YOU'LL CATCH COLD IF YOU SLEEP HERE.

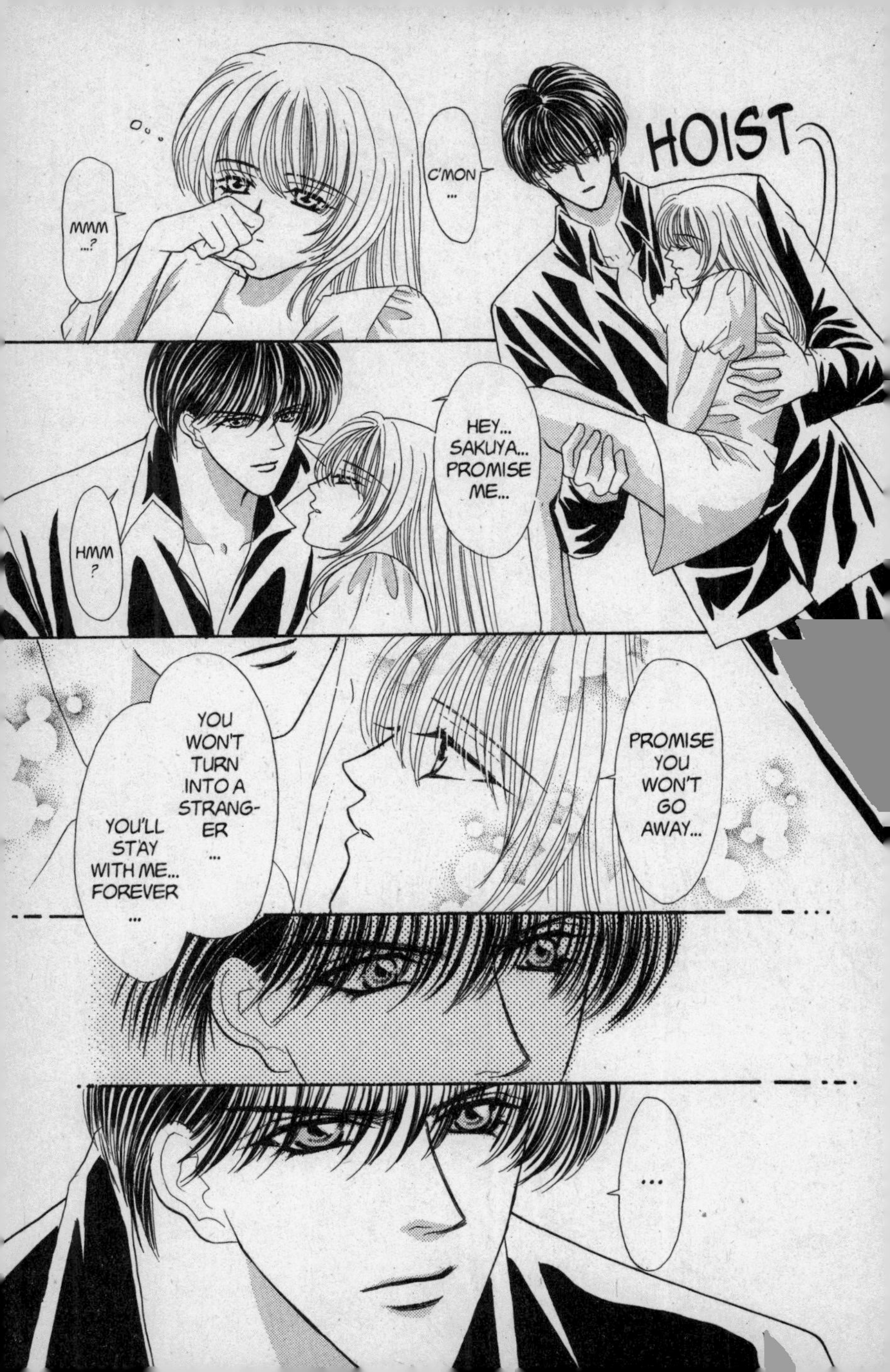
HOIST
C'MON ...
MMM ...?
HEY... SAKUYA... PROMISE ME...
HMM ?
PROMISE YOU WON'T GO AWAY...
YOU WON'T TURN INTO A STRANGER ...
YOU'LL STAY WITH ME... FOREVER ...
...

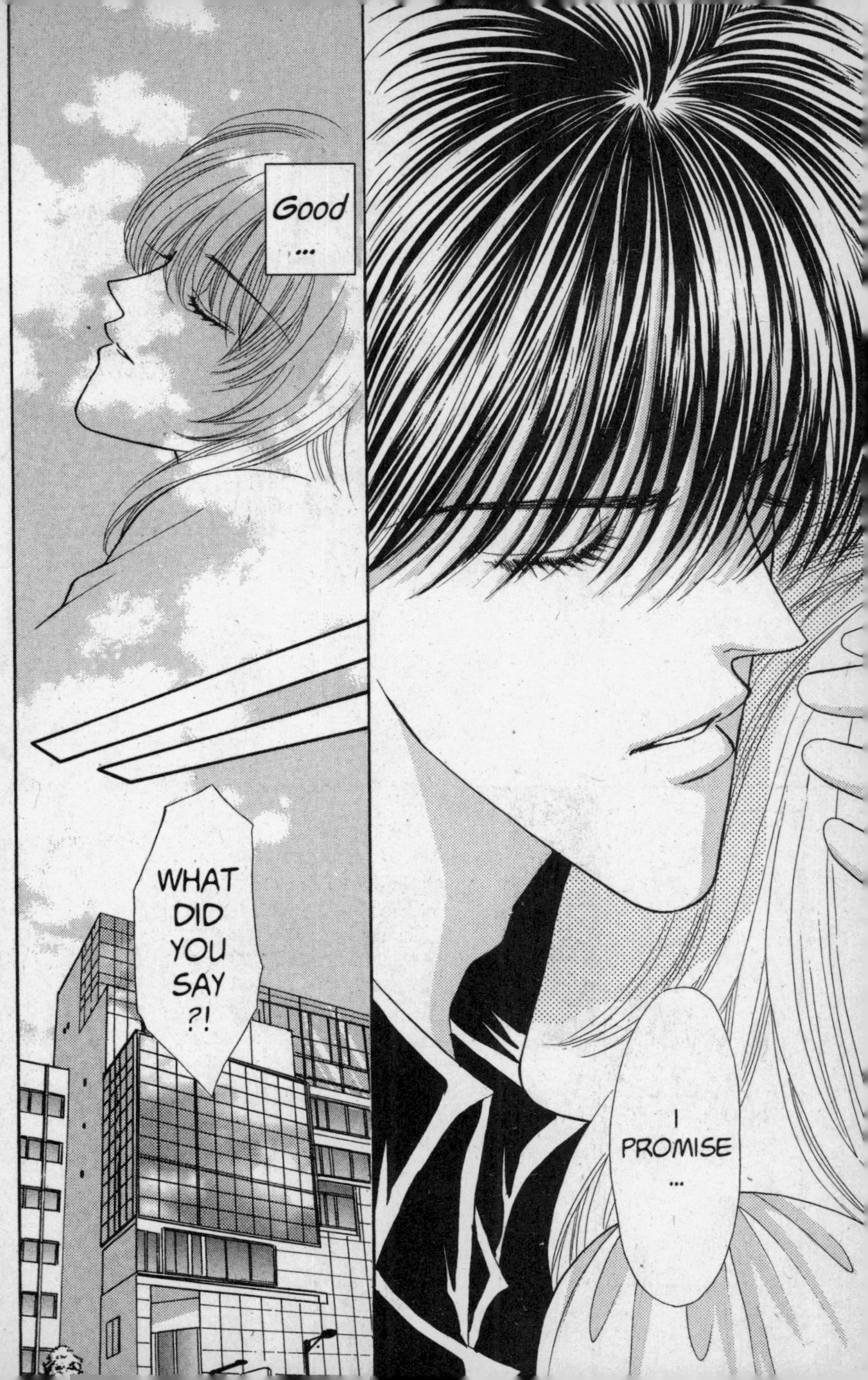
I PROMISE ...
Good ...
WHAT DID YOU SAY ?!

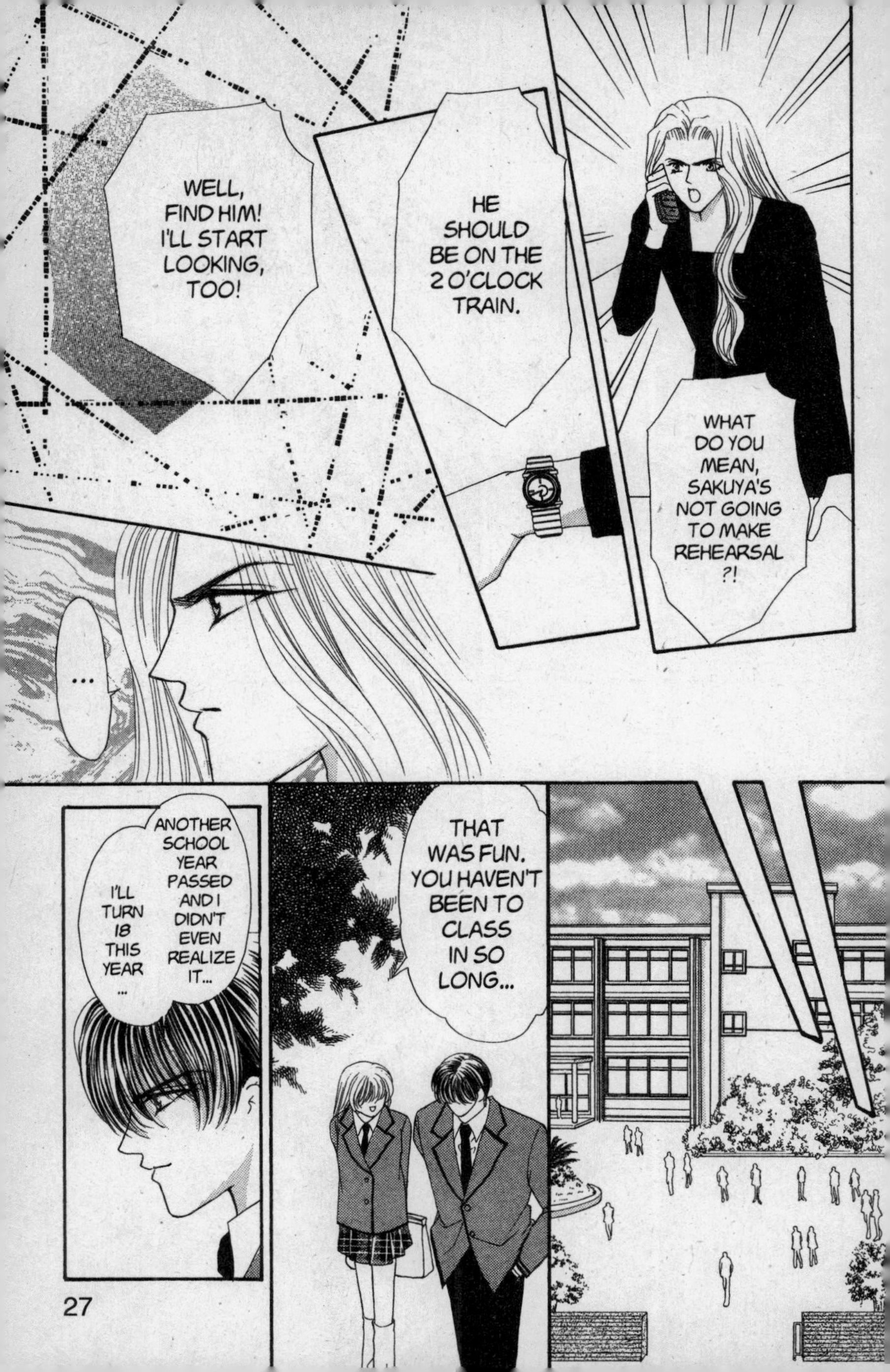
WHAT DO YOU MEAN, SAKUYA'S NOT GOING TO MAKE REHEARSAL ?!
HE SHOULD BE ON THE 2 O'CLOCK TRAIN.
WELL, FIND HIM! I'LL START LOOKING, TOO!
...
THAT WAS FUN. YOU HAVEN'T BEEN TO CLASS IN SO LONG...
ANOTHER SCHOOL YEAR PASSED AND I DIDN'T EVEN REALIZE IT...
I'LL TURN 18 THIS YEAR ...

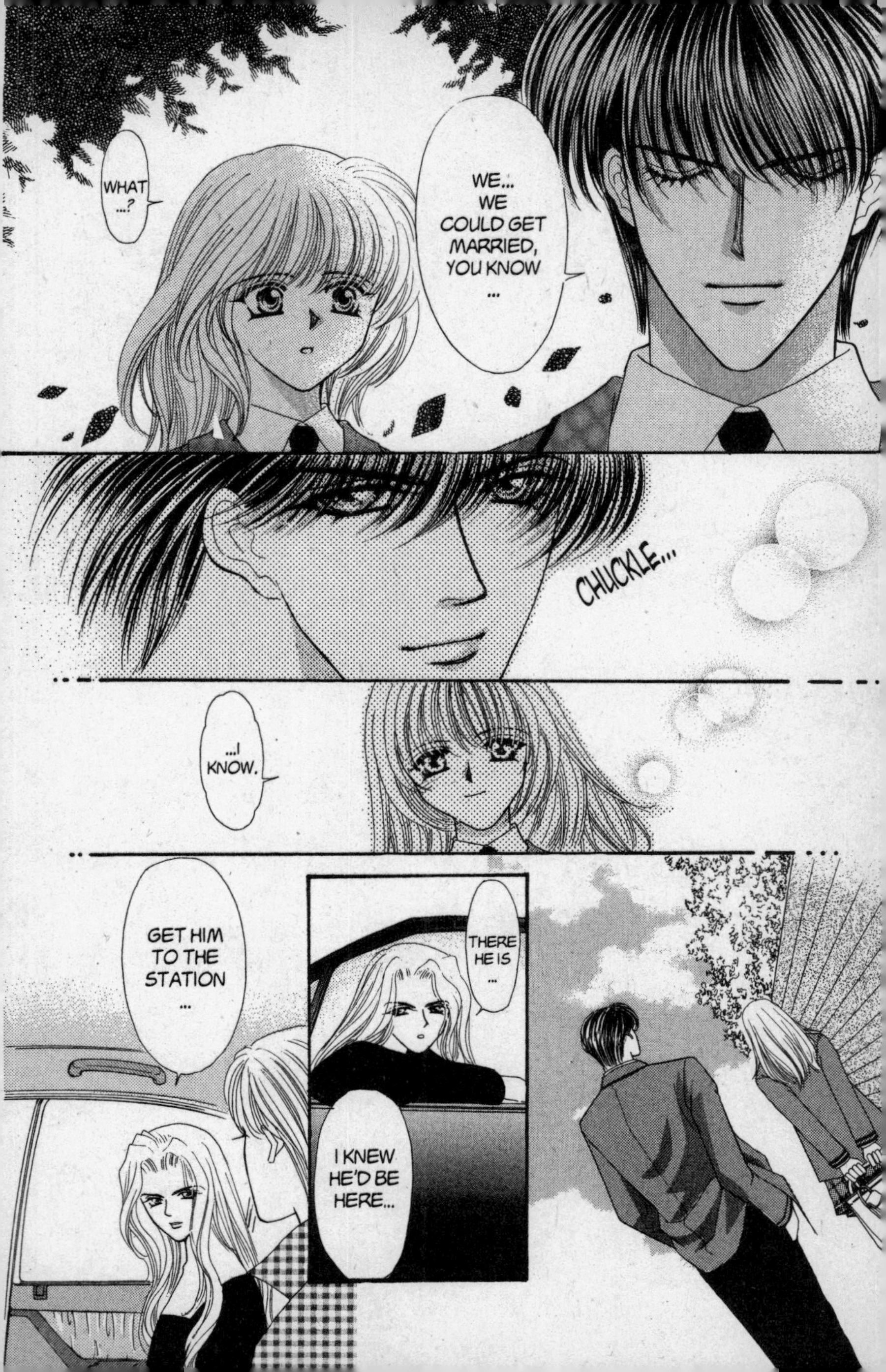
WE... WE COULD GET MARRIED, YOU KNOW ...
WHAT ...?
CHUCKLE...
...I KNOW.
THERE HE IS ...
I KNEW HE'D BE HERE...
GET HIM TO THE STATION ...

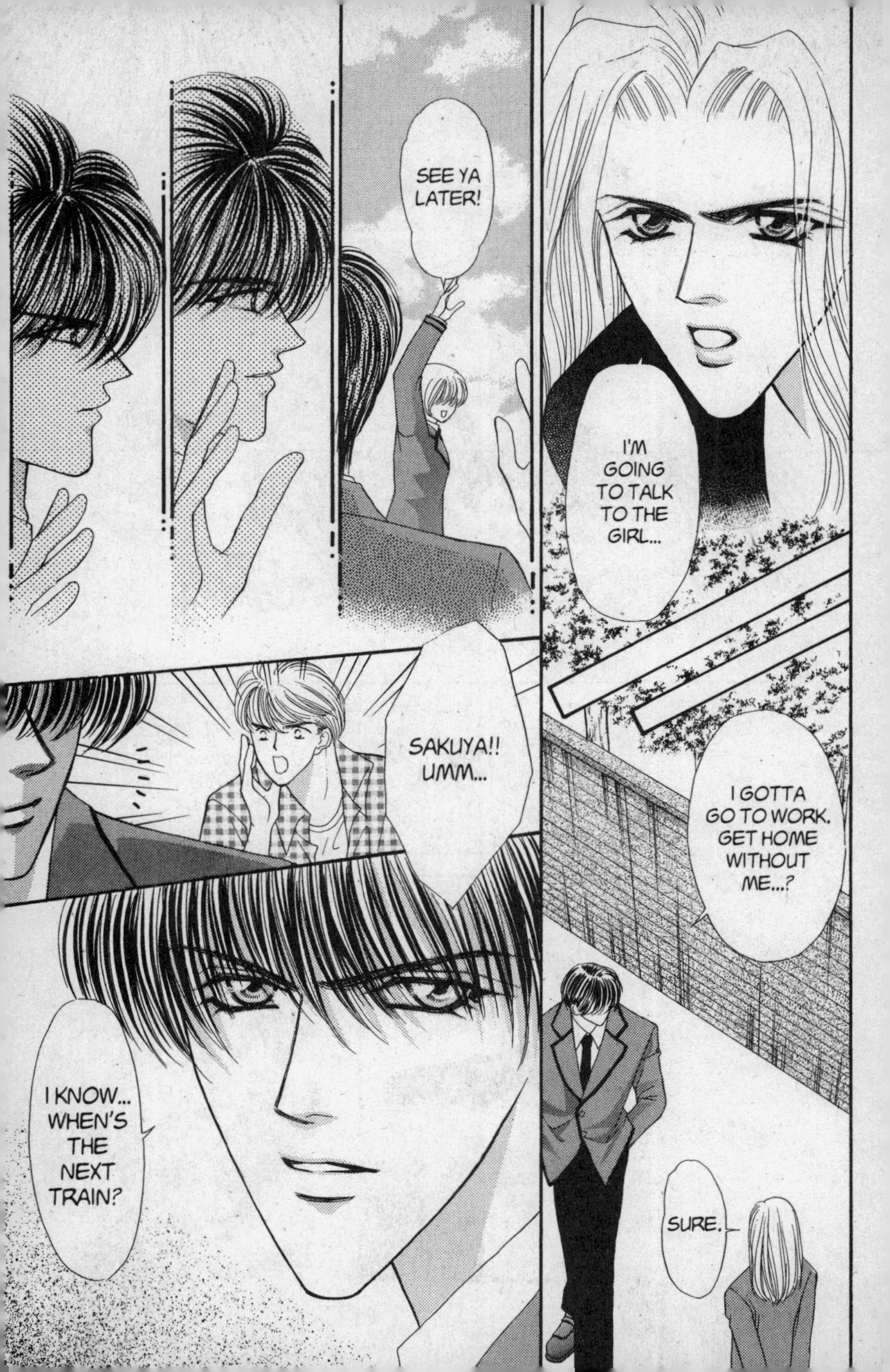
I'M GOING TO TALK TO THE GIRL...
I GOTTA GO TO WORK. GET HOME WITHOUT ME...?
SURE.
SEE YA LATER!
SAKUYA!! UMM...
I KNOW... WHEN'S THE NEXT TRAIN?

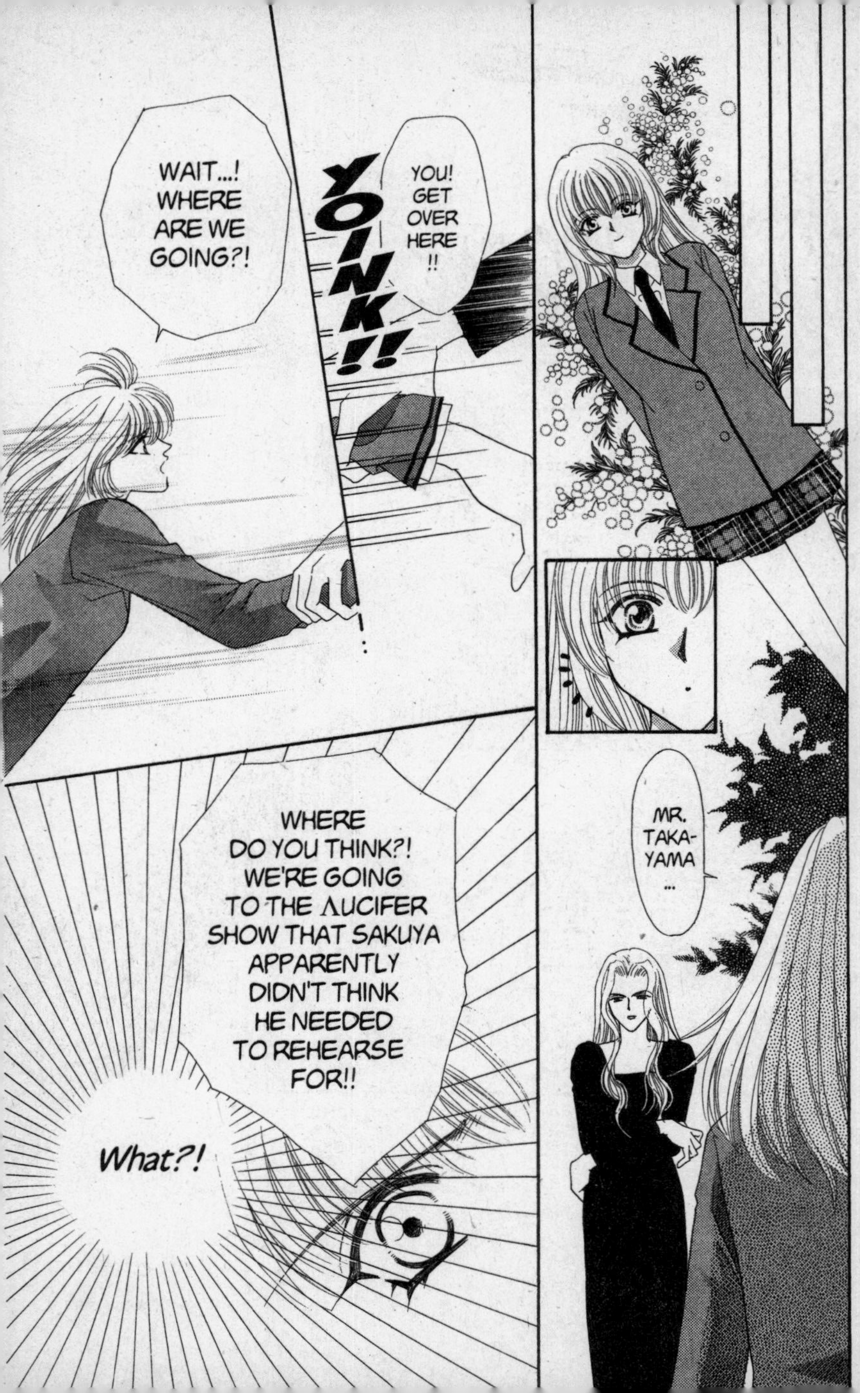
MR. TAKA-YAMA ...
YOU! GET OVER HERE !!
YOINK!!
WAIT...! WHERE ARE WE GOING?!
WHERE DO YOU THINK?! WE'RE GOING TO THE ΛUCIFER SHOW THAT SAKUYA APPARENTLY DIDN'T THINK HE NEEDED TO REHEARSE FOR!!
What?!

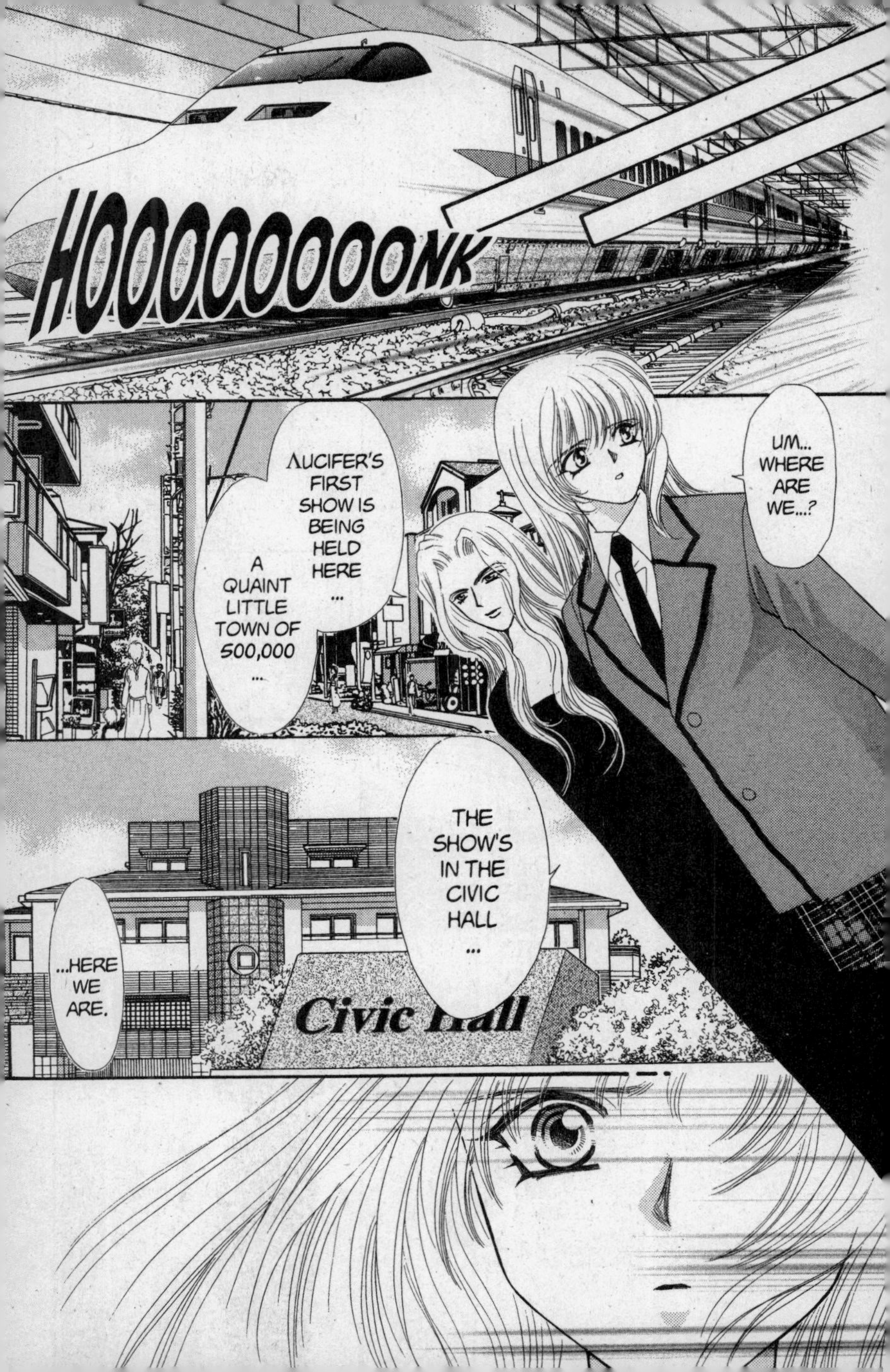
HOOOOOOONK
UM... WHERE ARE WE...?
ΛUCIFER'S FIRST SHOW IS BEING HELD HERE ...
A QUAINT LITTLE TOWN OF 500,000 ...
THE SHOW'S IN THE CIVIC HALL ...
...HERE WE ARE.
Civic Hall

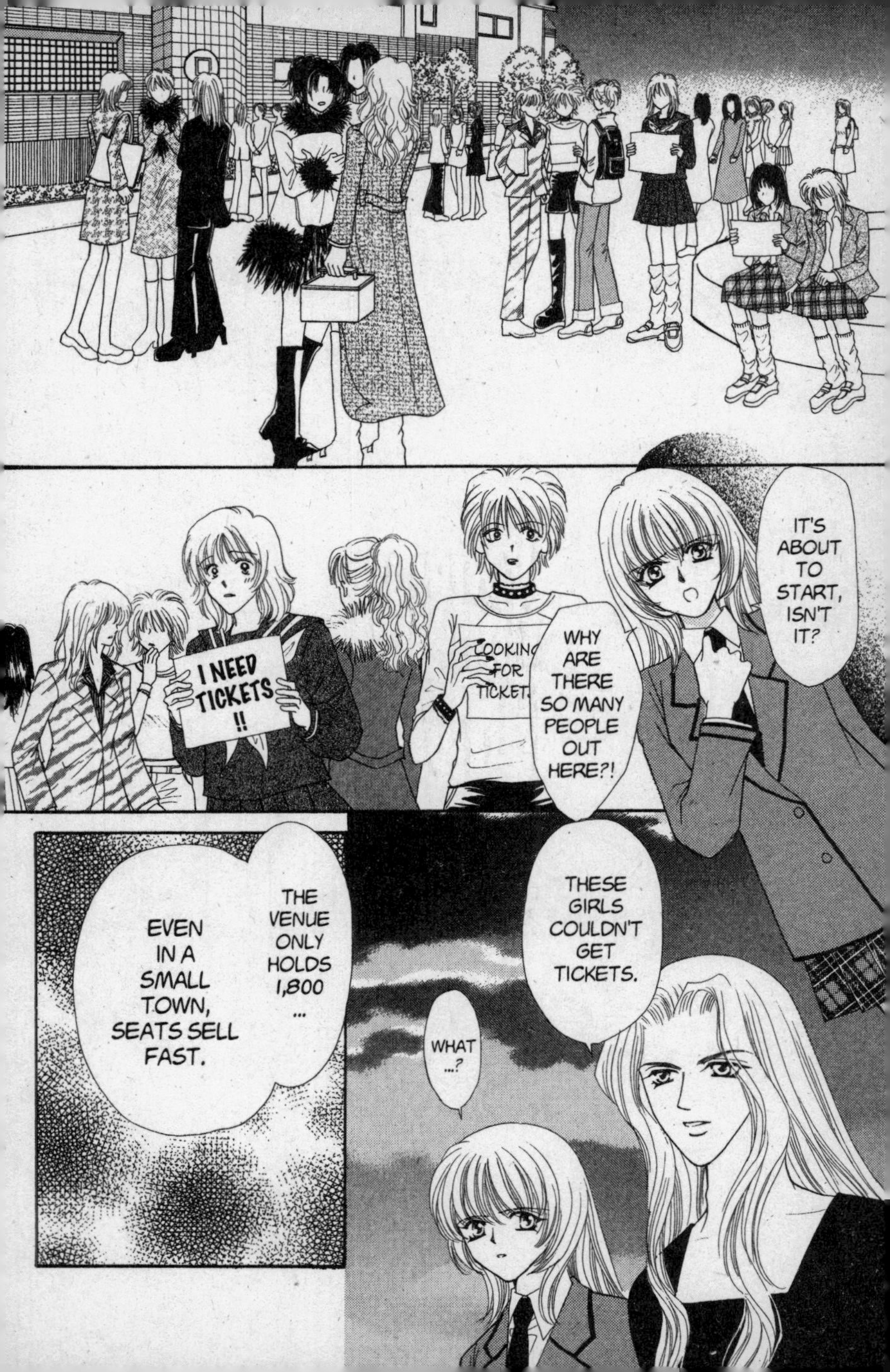
IT'S ABOUT TO START, ISN'T IT?
WHY ARE THERE SO MANY PEOPLE OUT HERE?!
LOOKING FOR TICKET
I NEED TICKETS !!
THESE GIRLS COULDN'T GET TICKETS.
WHAT ...?
THE VENUE ONLY HOLDS 1,800 ...
EVEN IN A SMALL TOWN, SEATS SELL FAST.

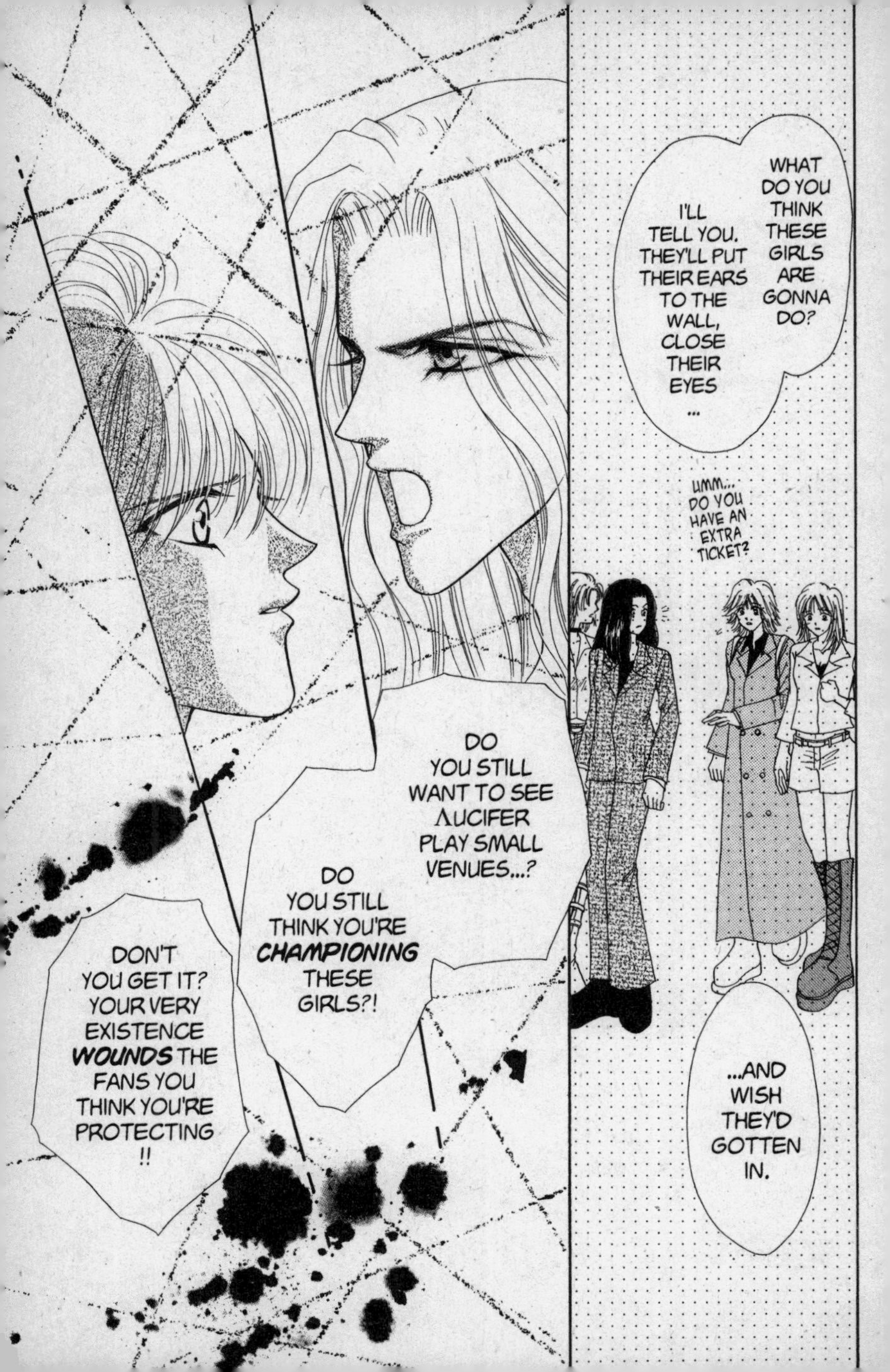
WHAT DO YOU THINK THESE GIRLS ARE GONNA DO?
I'LL TELL YOU. THEY'LL PUT THEIR EARS TO THE WALL, CLOSE THEIR EYES ...
UMM... DO YOU HAVE AN EXTRA TICKET?
...AND WISH THEY'D GOTTEN IN.
DO YOU STILL WANT TO SEE ΛUCIFER PLAY SMALL VENUES...?
DO YOU STILL THINK YOU'RE CHAMPIONING THESE GIRLS?!
DON'T YOU GET IT? YOUR VERY EXISTENCE WOUNDS THE FANS YOU THINK YOU'RE PROTECTING !!

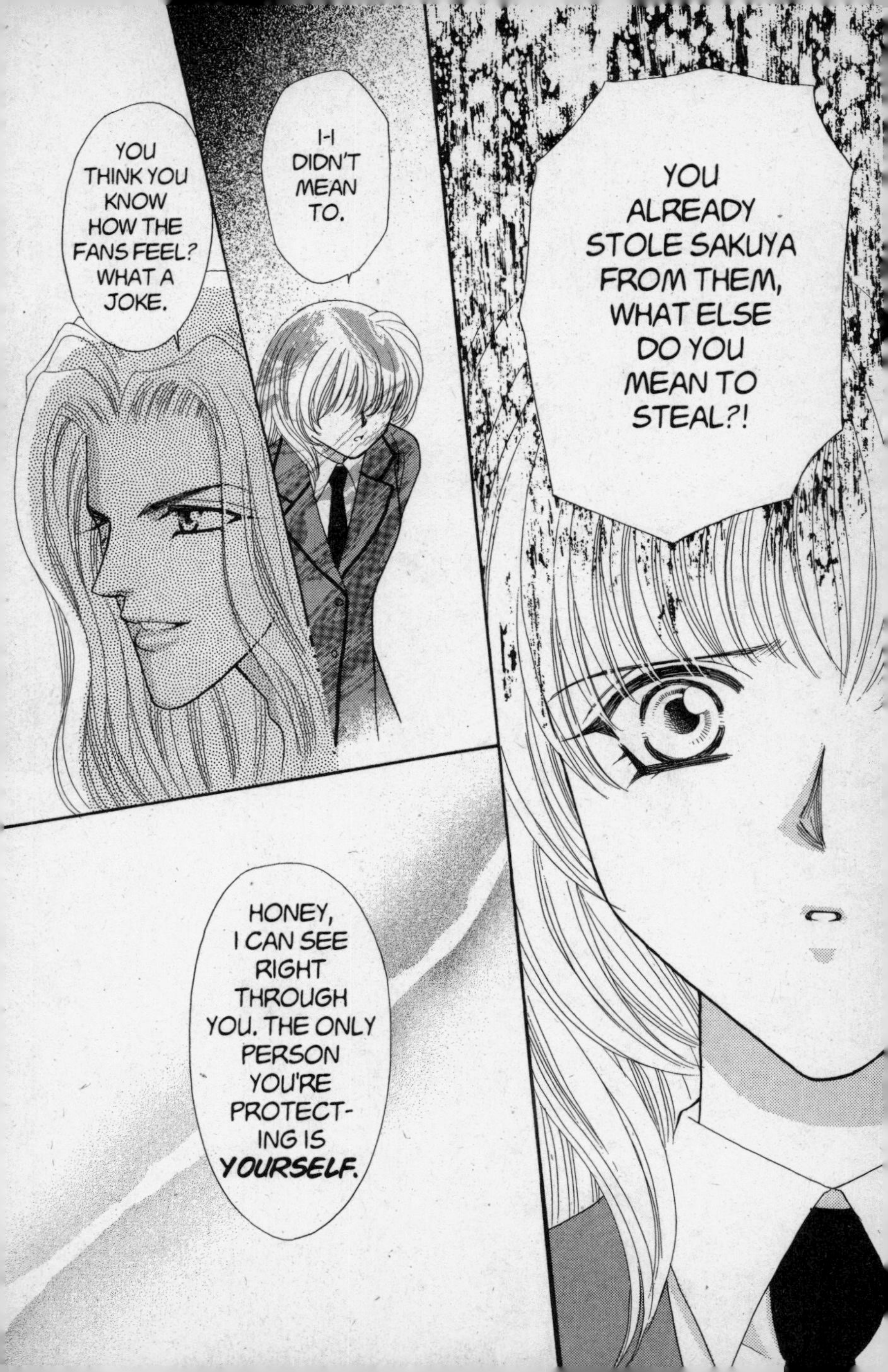
YOU ALREADY STOLE SAKUYA FROM THEM, WHAT ELSE DO YOU MEAN TO STEAL?!
I-I DIDN'T MEAN TO.
YOU THINK YOU KNOW HOW THE FANS FEEL? WHAT A JOKE.
HONEY, I CAN SEE RIGHT THROUGH YOU. THE ONLY PERSON YOU'RE PROTECT-ING IS *YOURSELF*.

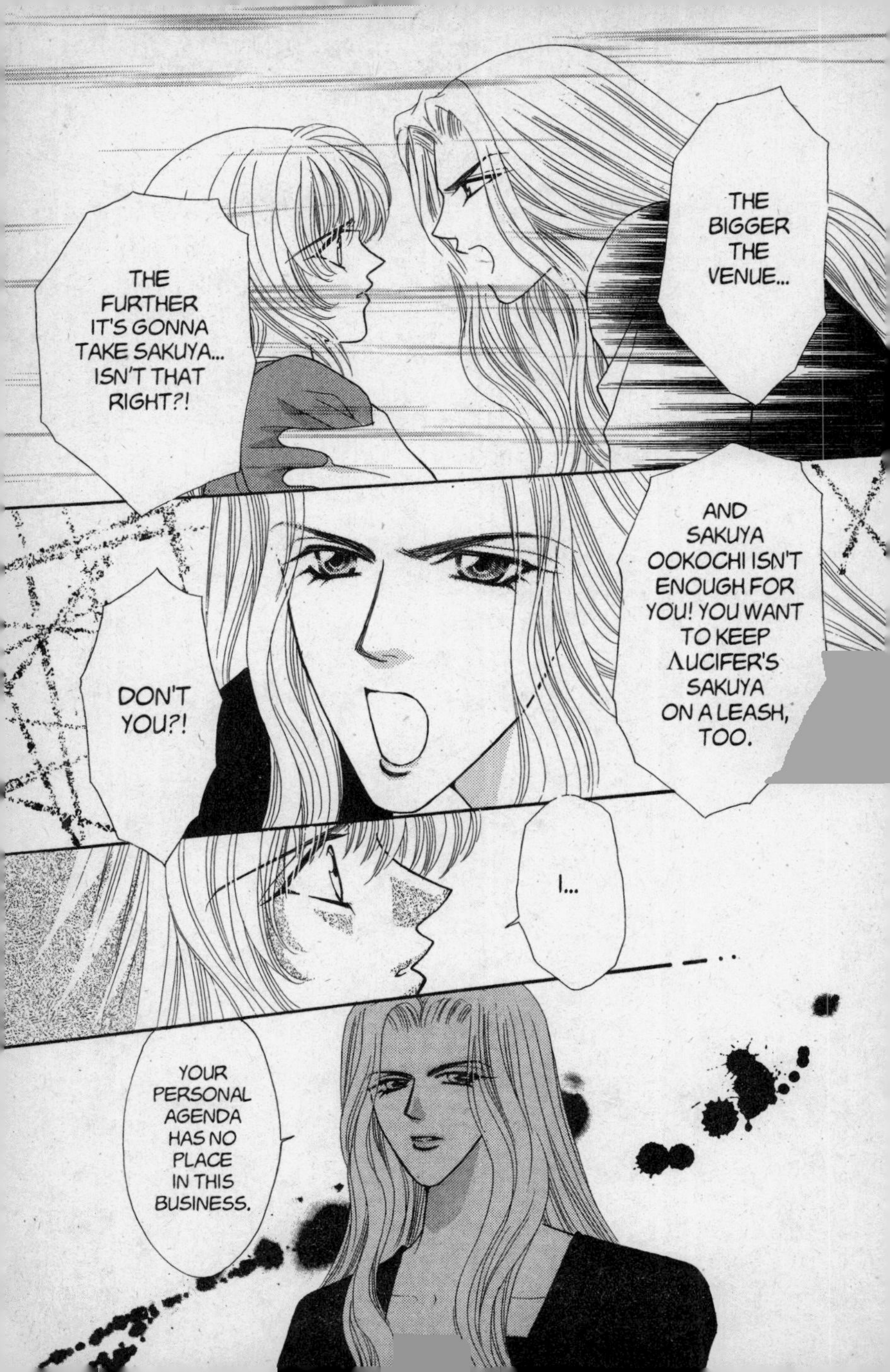
THE BIGGER THE VENUE...
THE FURTHER IT'S GONNA TAKE SAKUYA... ISN'T THAT RIGHT?!
AND SAKUYA OOKOCHI ISN'T ENOUGH FOR YOU! YOU WANT TO KEEP ΛUCIFER'S SAKUYA ON A LEASH, TOO.
DON'T YOU?!
I...
YOUR PERSONAL AGENDA HAS NO PLACE IN THIS BUSINESS.

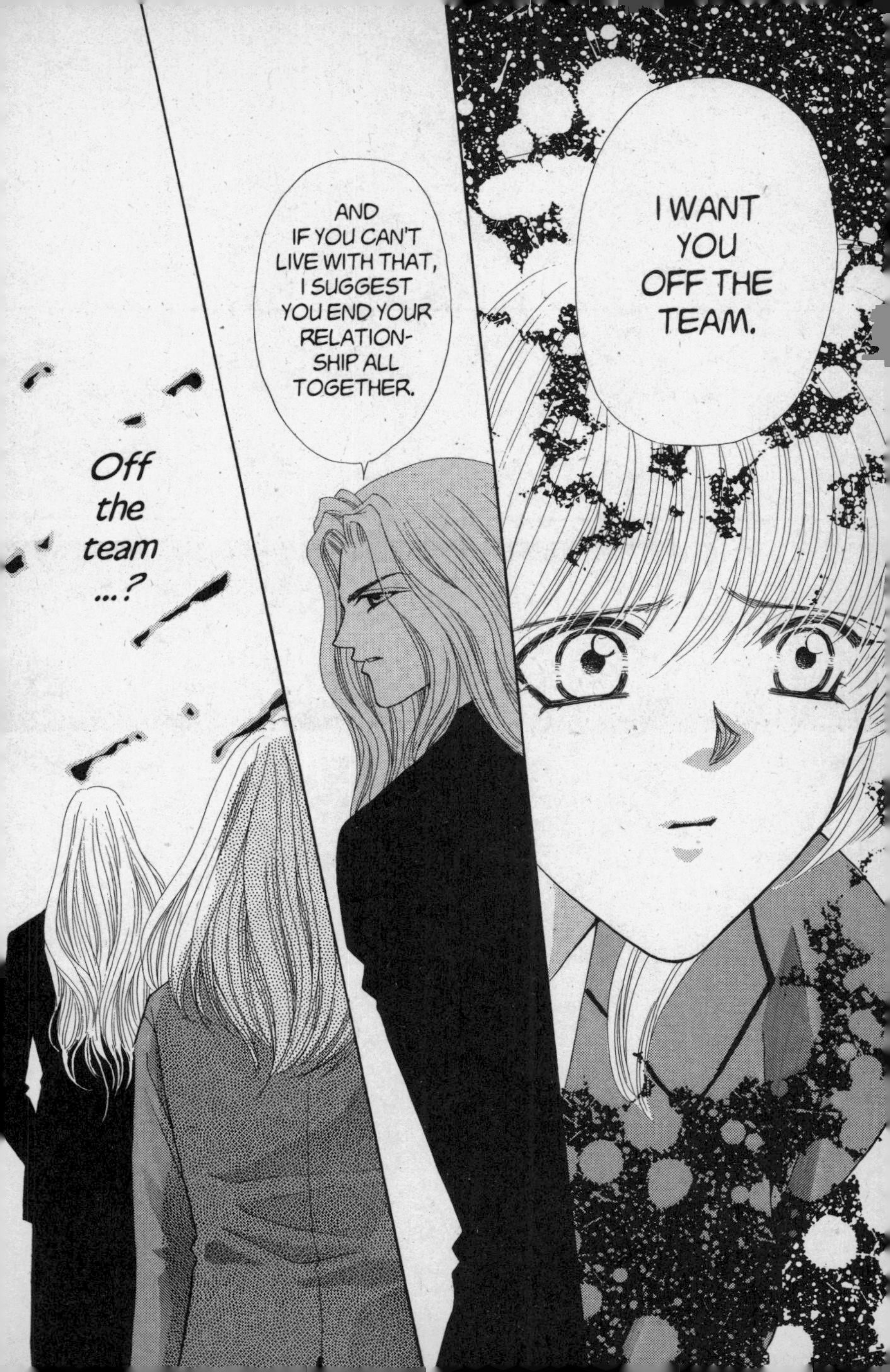
I WANT YOU OFF THE TEAM.
AND IF YOU CAN'T LIVE WITH THAT, I SUGGEST YOU END YOUR RELATION-SHIP ALL TOGETHER.
Off the team ...?

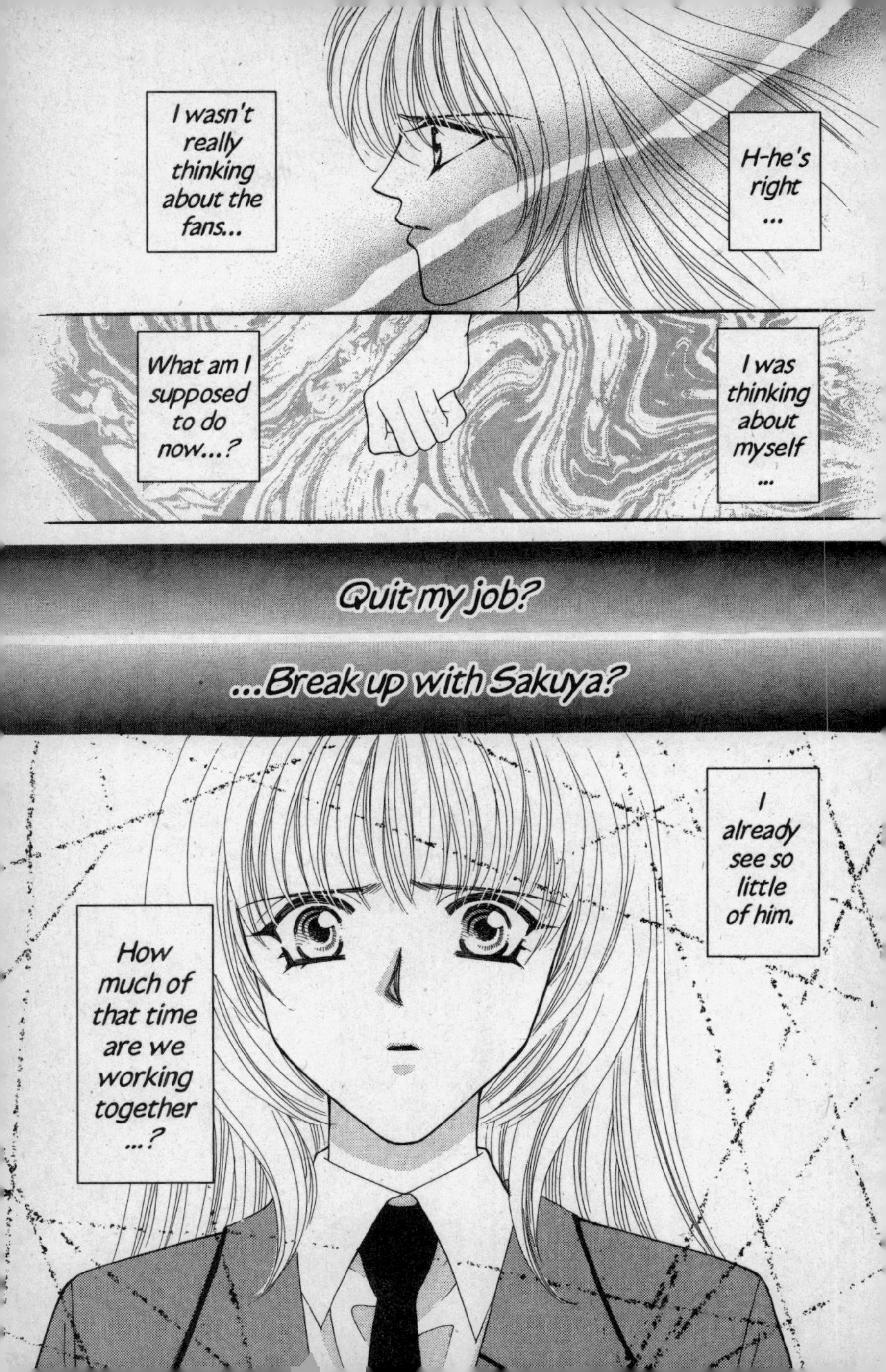
H-he's right ...
I wasn't really thinking about the fans...
I was thinking about myself ...
What am I supposed to do now...?
Quit my job?
...Break up with Sakuya?
I already see so little of him.
How much of that time are we working together ...?

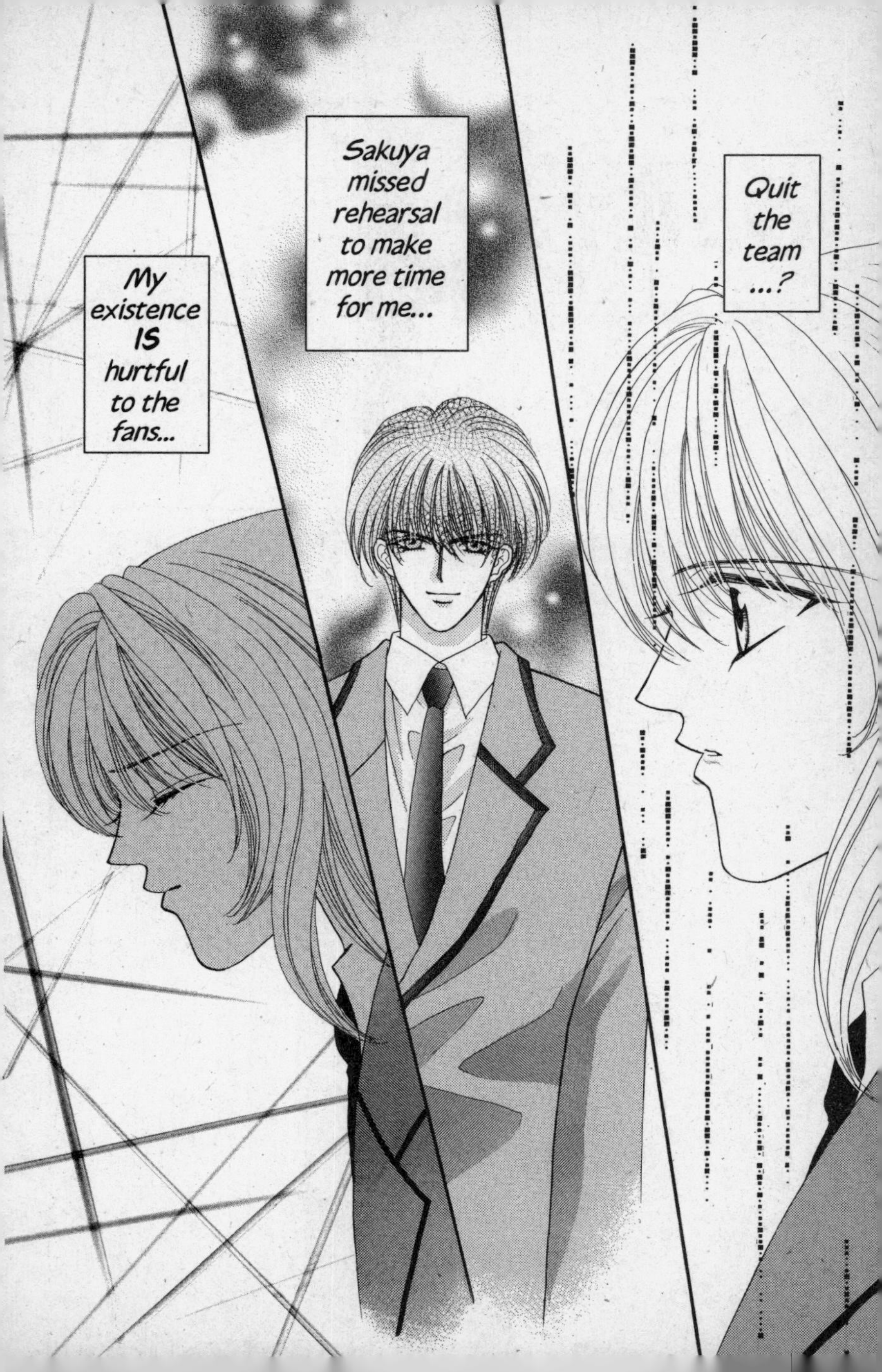
Quit the team ...?
Sakuya missed rehearsal to make more time for me...
My existence IS hurtful to the fans...

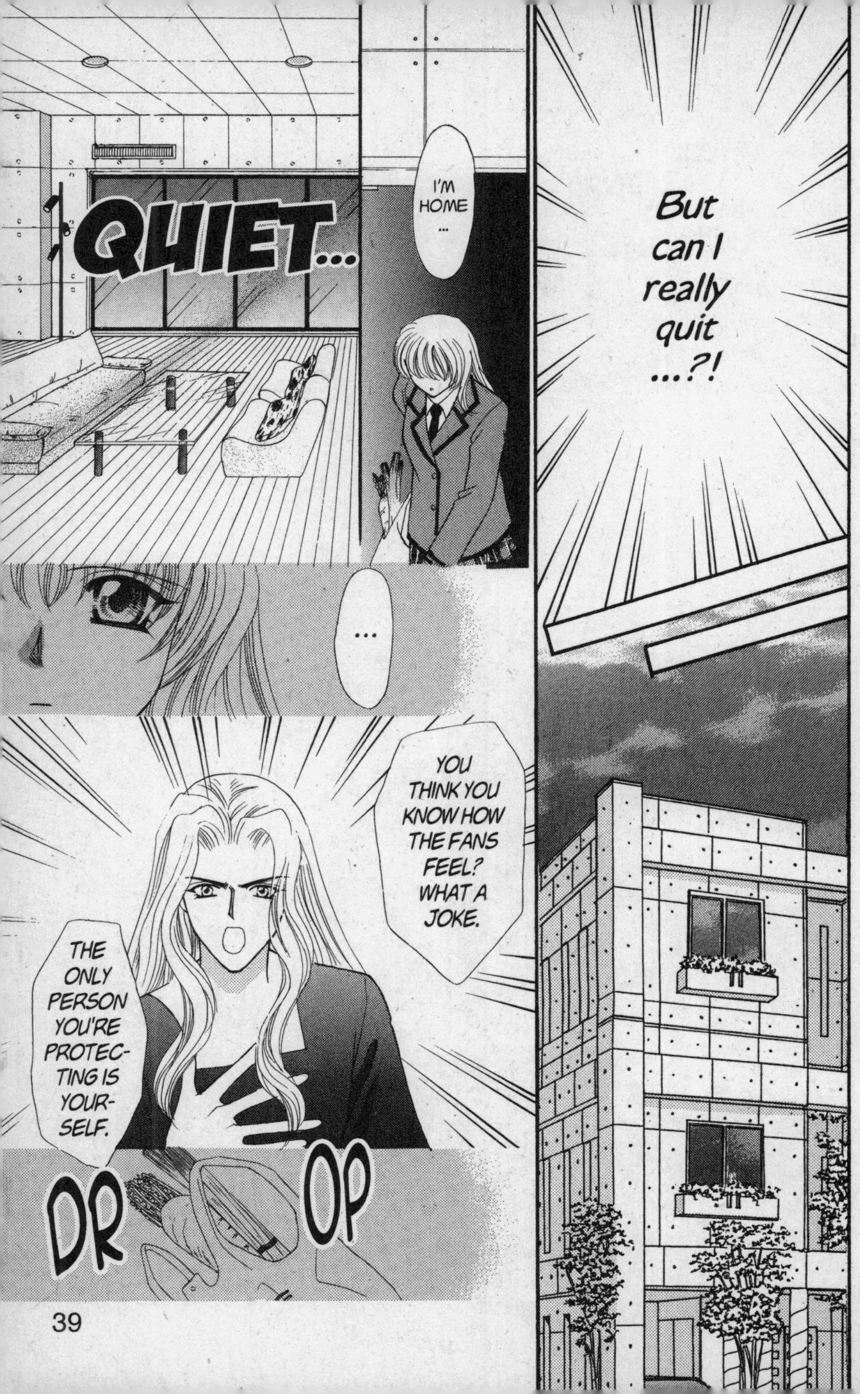
But can I really quit ...?!
I'M HOME ...
QUIET...
...
YOU THINK YOU KNOW HOW THE FANS FEEL? WHAT A JOKE.
THE ONLY PERSON YOU'RE PROTEC-TING IS YOUR-SELF.
DR OP

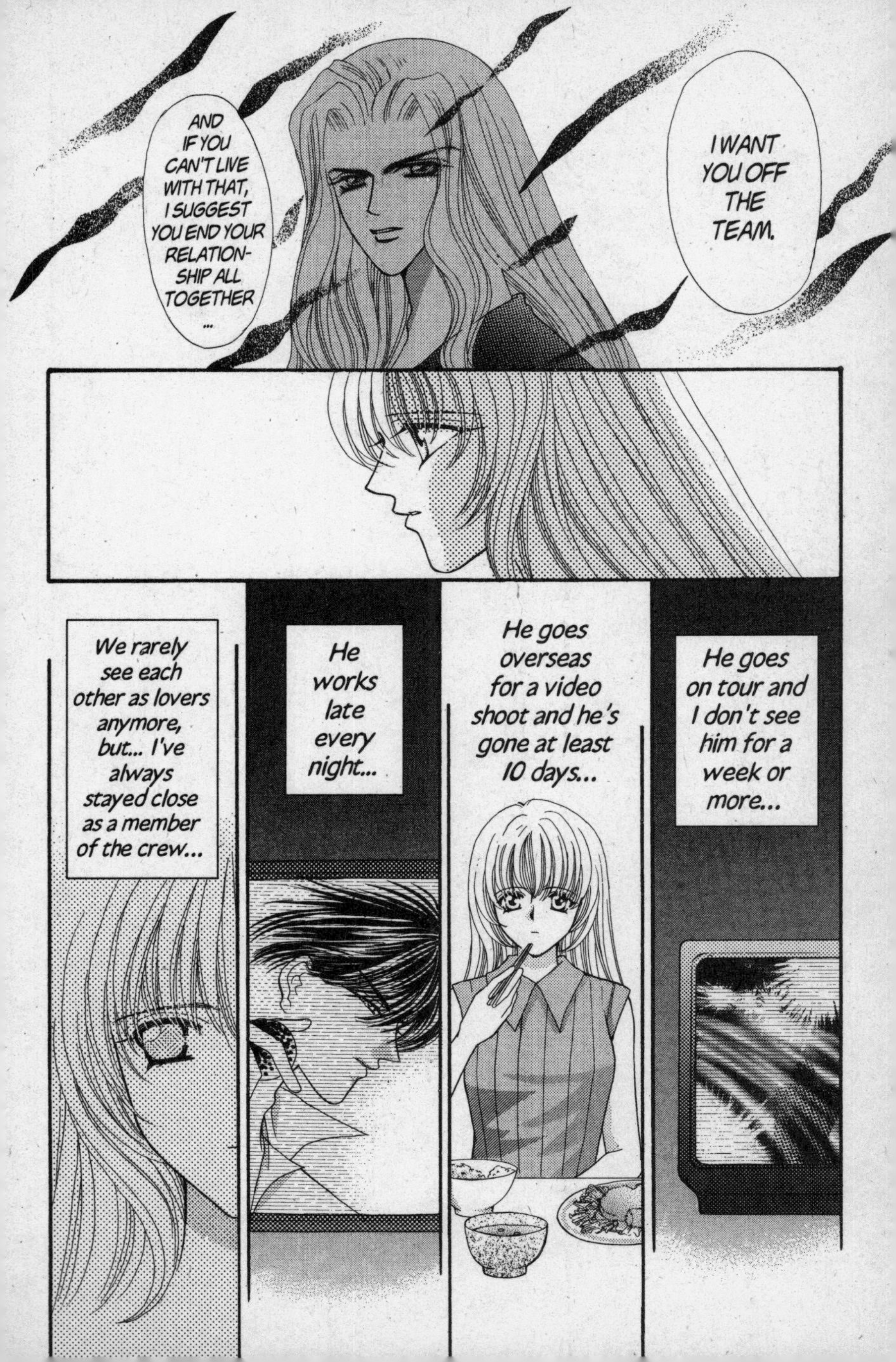
I WANT YOU OFF THE TEAM.
AND IF YOU CAN'T LIVE WITH THAT, I SUGGEST YOU END YOUR RELATION-SHIP ALL TOGETHER ...
He goes on tour and I don't see him for a week or more...
He goes overseas for a video shoot and he's gone at least 10 days...
He works late every night...
We rarely see each other as lovers anymore, but... I've always stayed close as a member of the crew...

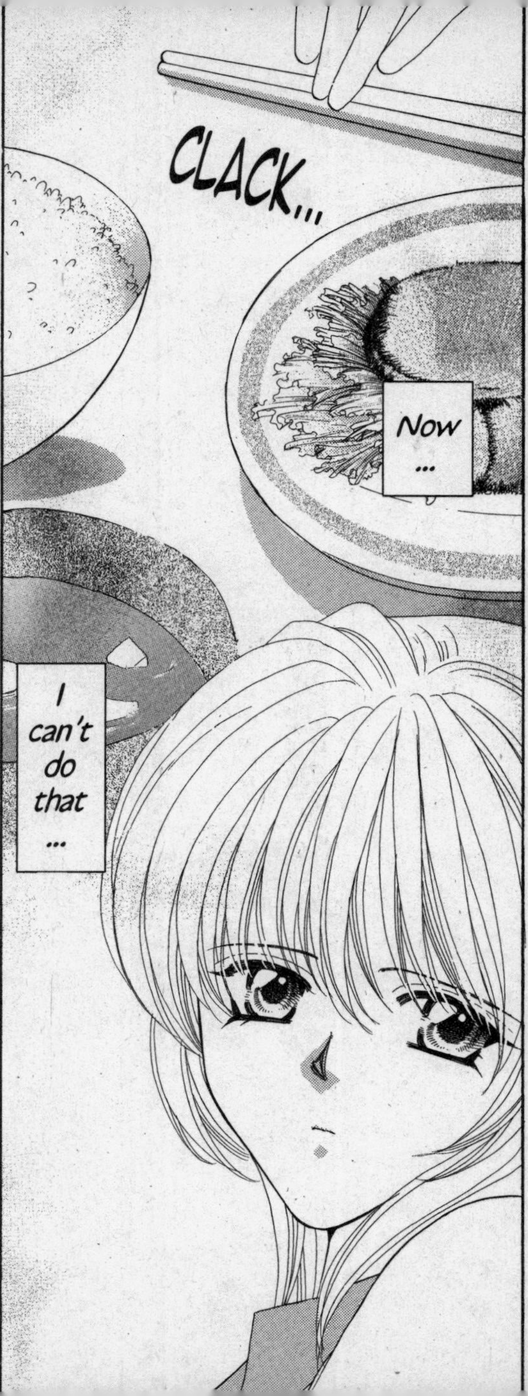
CLACK...
Now ...
I can't do that ...

ΛUCIFER:

MAKOTO
Λucifer's vocalist. I don't get to talk to him much these days. Mommy is sad (ha ha)!! I like his face, but it's his voice that makes him great!! He's a charmer, too. Unlike many of the young guys today (I sound old, huh?... (Eek!)), he's very together and very manly. Like Sakuya, don't you think? They don't make them like that anymore.

ATSURO
Oofah!...His red hair KILLS me! He's got a really youthful face. He's crazy popular at their shows, too. Every time I see him, I keep telling him he's a cutie. He looks good in photos, but if you've never seen him in person you must go check him out. Oh, my! A sweet face like that and a nice lanky build...So cute!! His cheeks...I swoon!

YUKI
Yuki's the one they're always talking about on the Internet. He's got sharp features and GREAT guitar technique—and tons of fans already! I can't believe they found this guy, he's perfect! (Have you noticed how tall Λucifer is...?)

TOWA
He's close to Yuki in the original comic. They told me he had a 'nicely structured face.' They weren't kidding! Very deep features. My assistants are BIG Towa fans.

SANTA
When I heard his drum solo, I seriously got the chills. He's really, really good. One of the guys at the editorial office who used to play praised him very highly.

...Can you tell how happy I am?

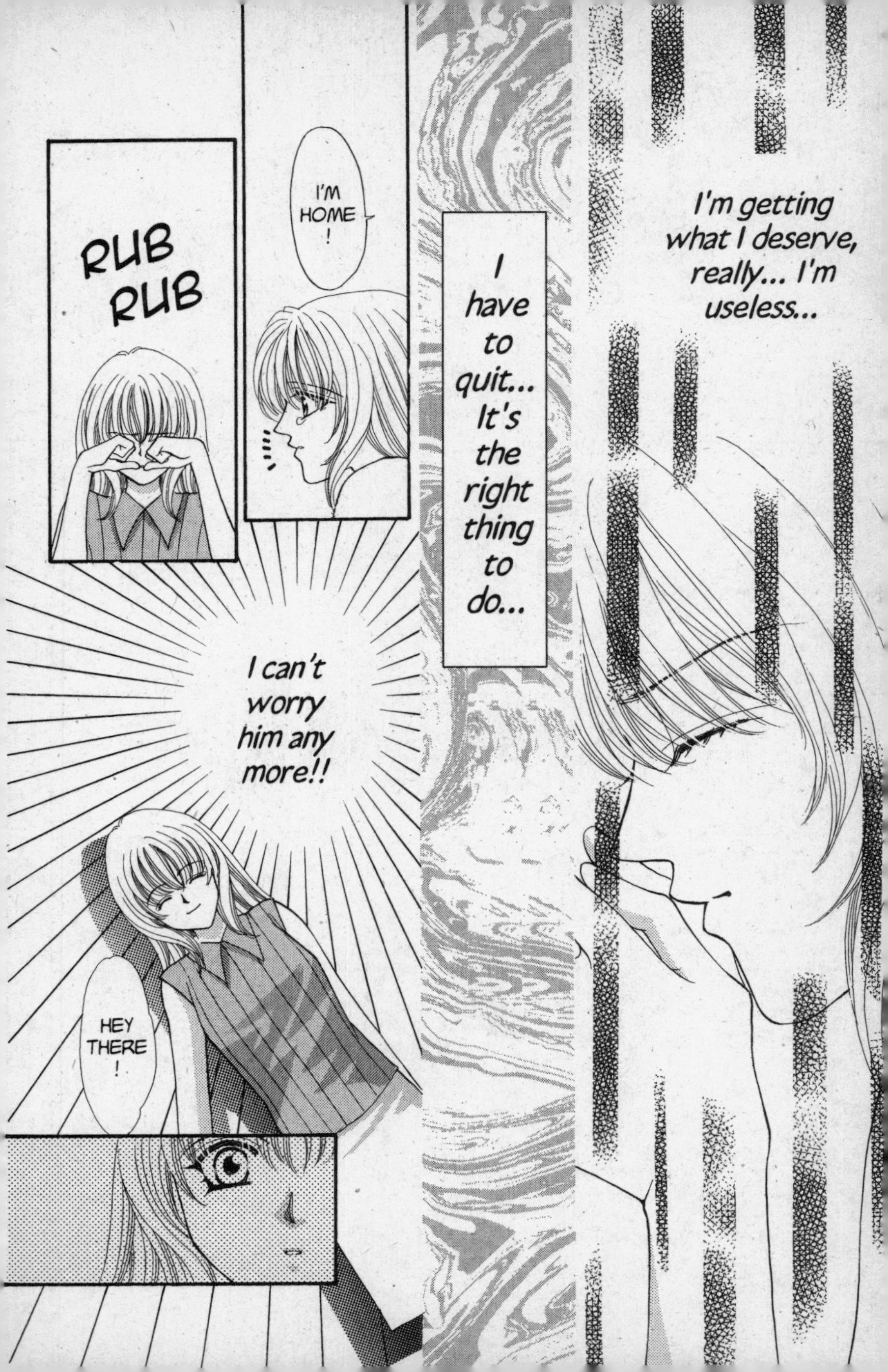
I'm getting what I deserve, really... I'm useless...
I have to quit... It's the right thing to do...
I'M HOME!
RUB RUB
I can't worry him any more!!
HEY THERE!

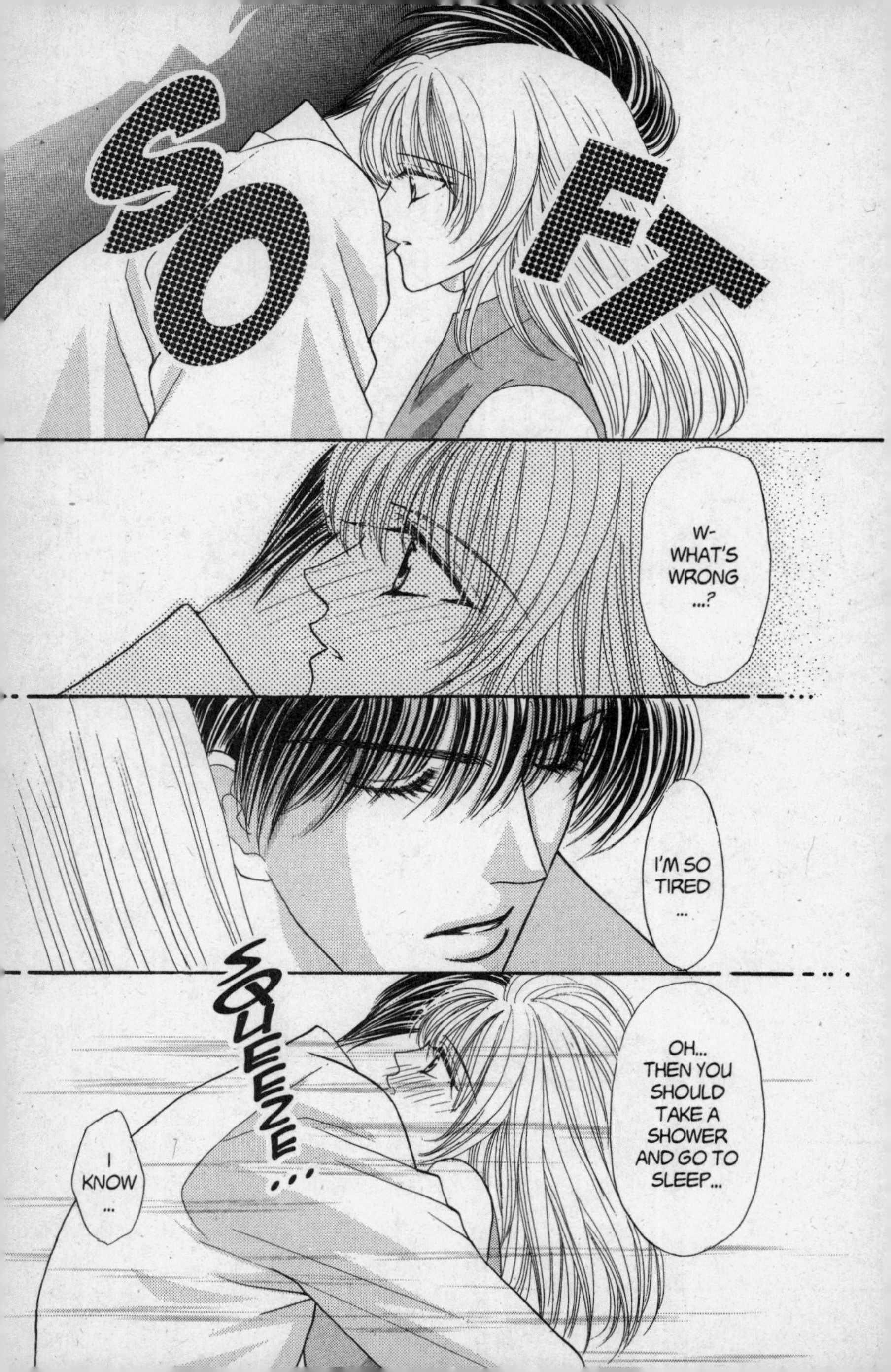
SOFT
W- WHAT'S WRONG ...?
I'M SO TIRED ...
SQUEEZE...
OH... THEN YOU SHOULD TAKE A SHOWER AND GO TO SLEEP...
I KNOW ...

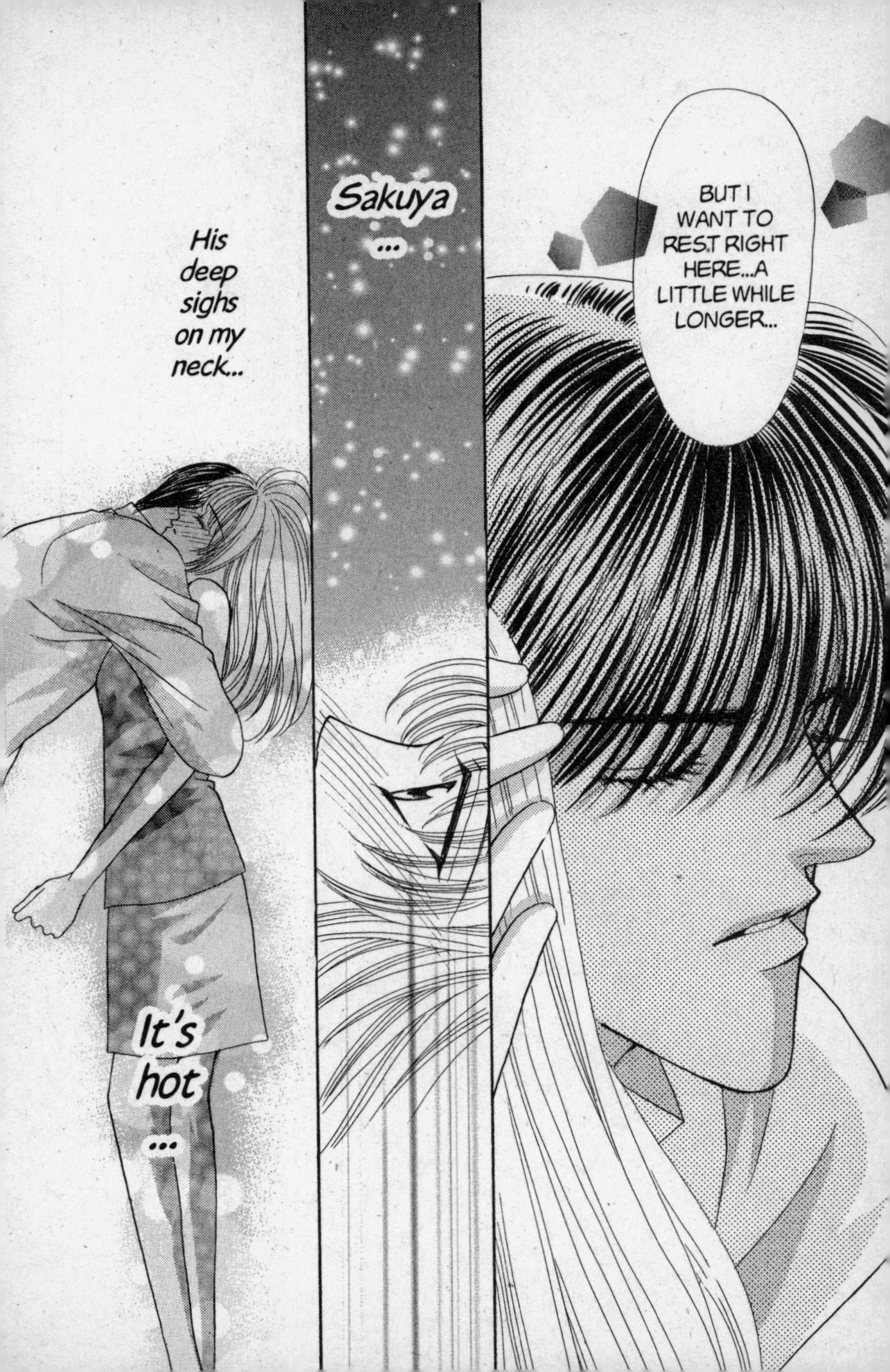
BUT I WANT TO REST RIGHT HERE...A LITTLE WHILE LONGER...
Sakuya ...
His deep sighs on my neck...
It's hot ...

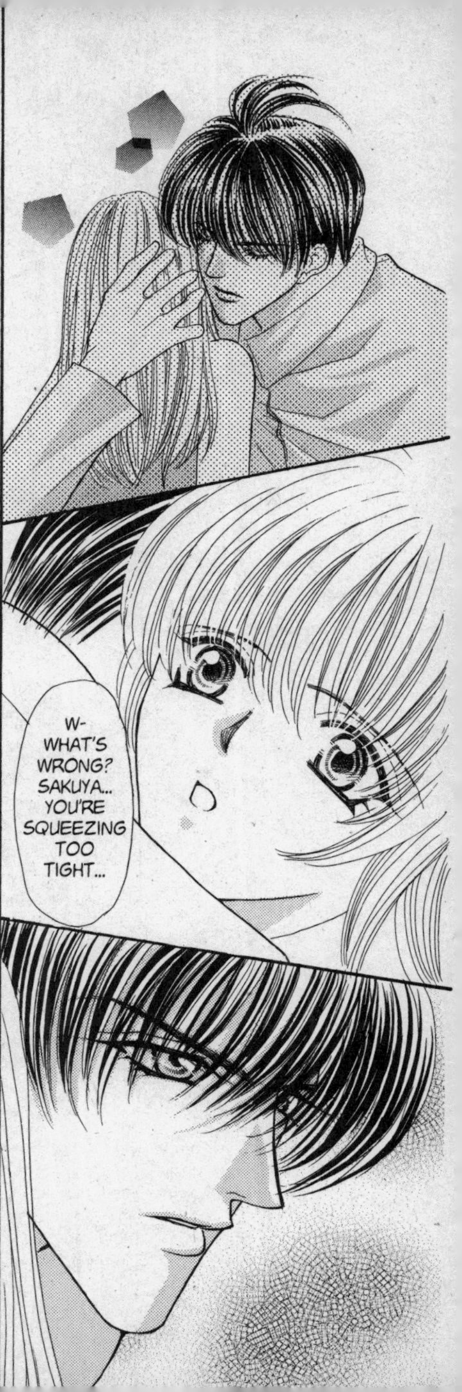
W-
WHAT'S
WRONG?
SAKUYA...
YOU'RE
SQUEEZING
TOO
TIGHT...

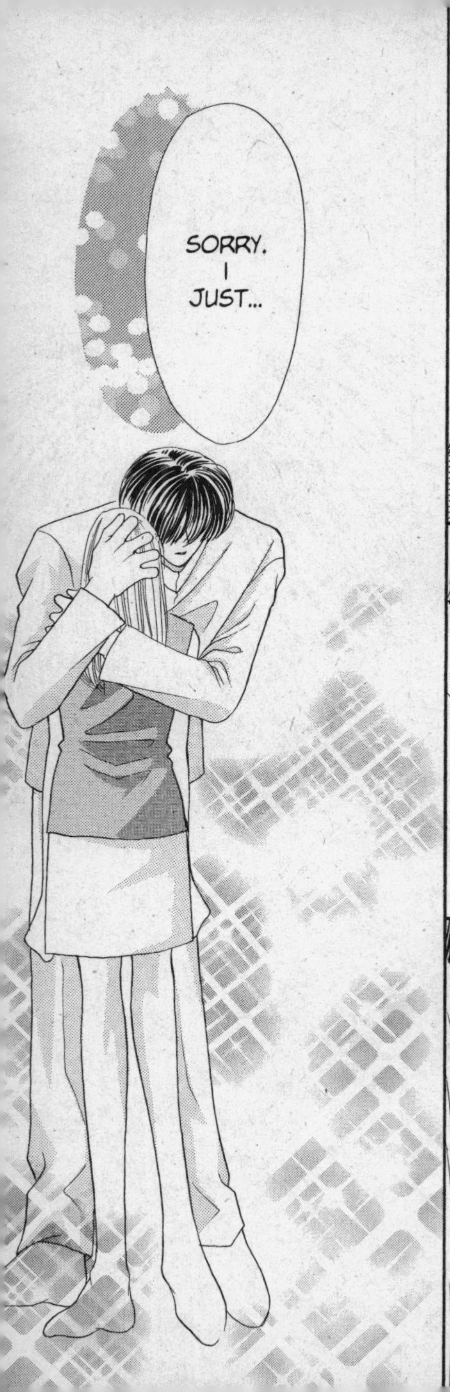
SORRY.
I
JUST...

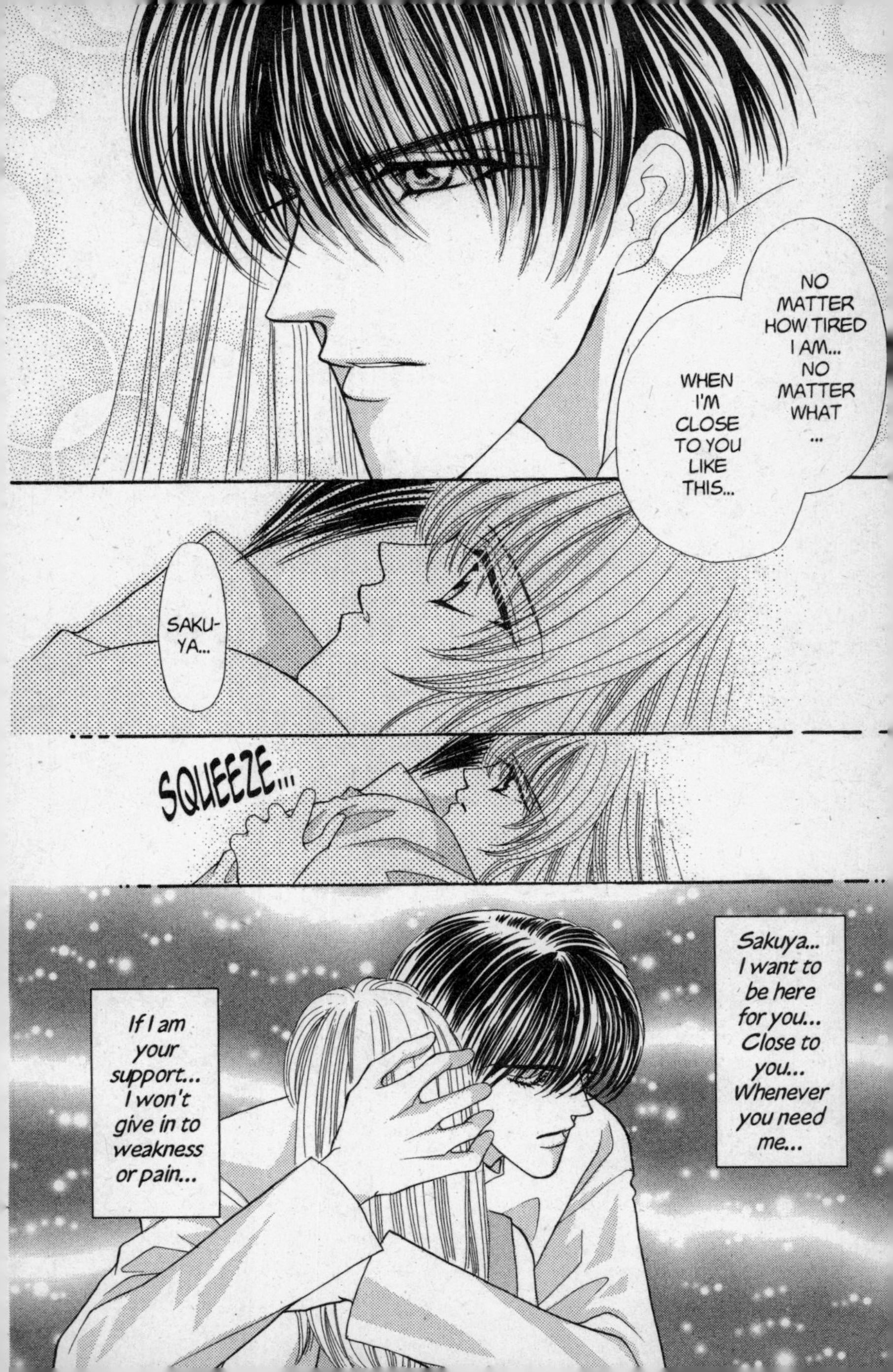
NO MATTER HOW TIRED I AM... NO MATTER WHAT ...
WHEN I'M CLOSE TO YOU LIKE THIS...
SAKU-YA...
SQUEEZE...
Sakuya... I want to be here for you... Close to you... Whenever you need me...
If I am your support... I won't give in to weakness or pain...

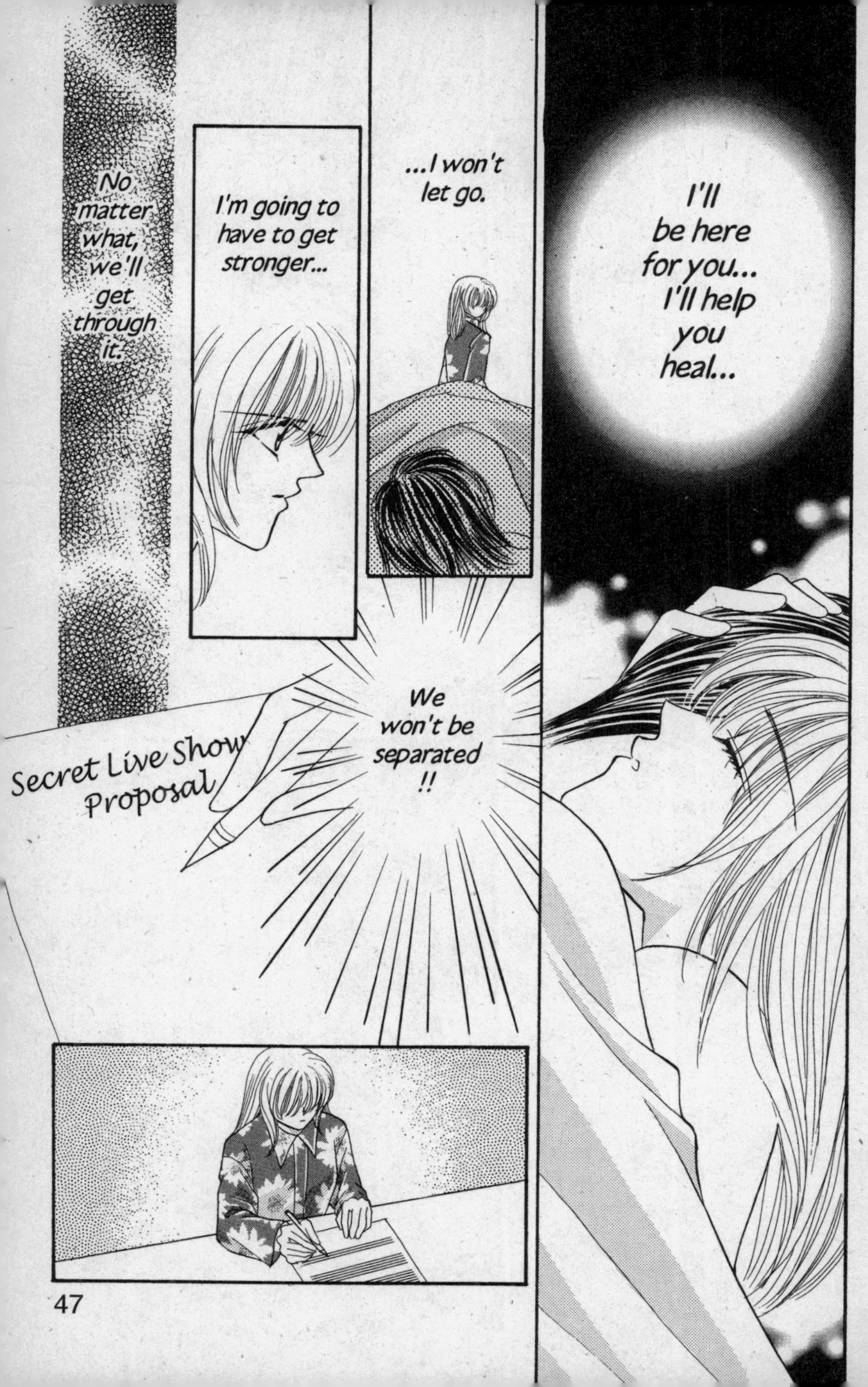
I'll be here for you... I'll help you heal...
...I won't let go.
I'm going to have to get stronger...
No matter what, we'll get through it.
We won't be separated !!
Secret Live Show Proposal

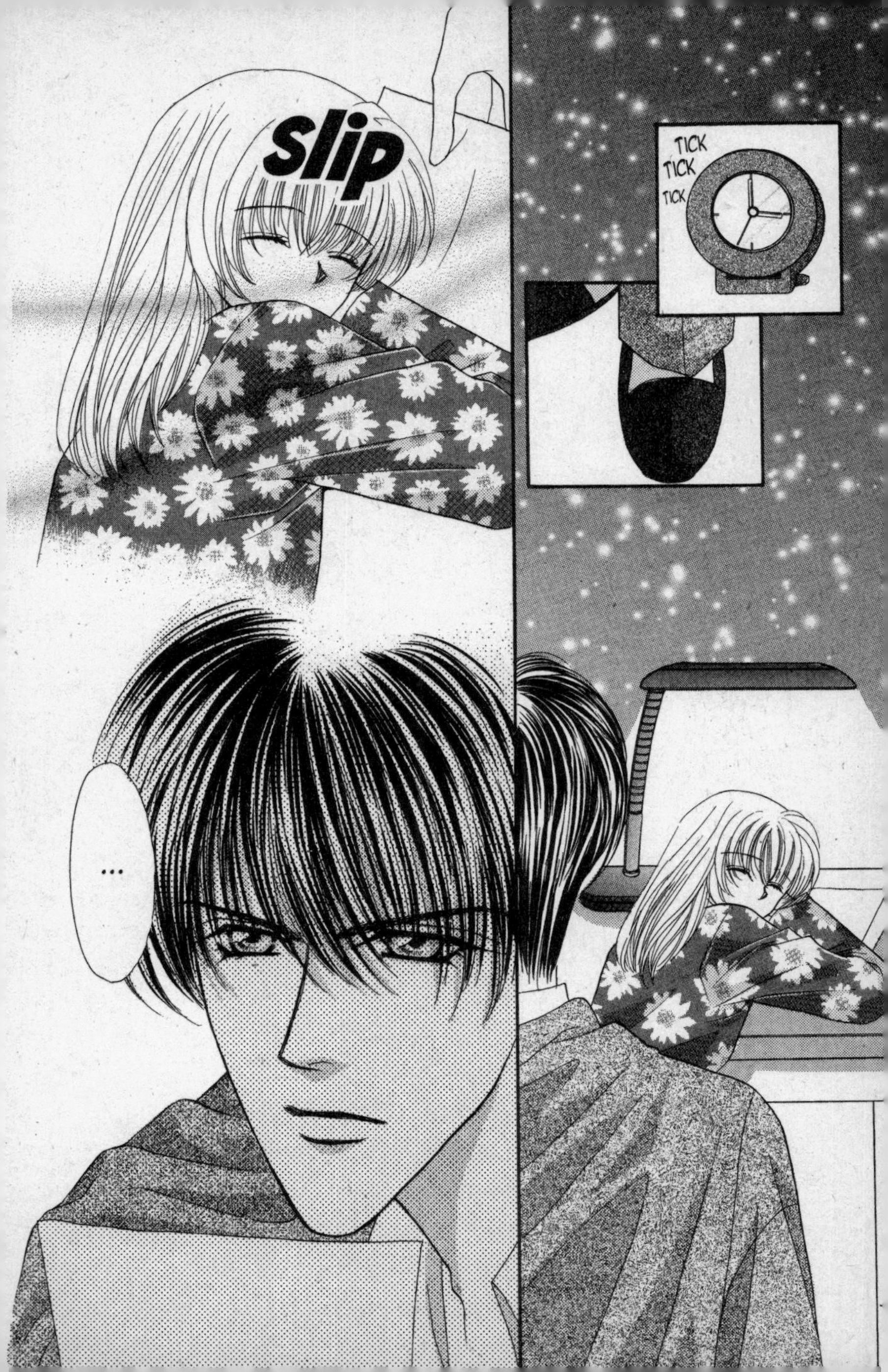
TICK
TICK
TICK
slip
...

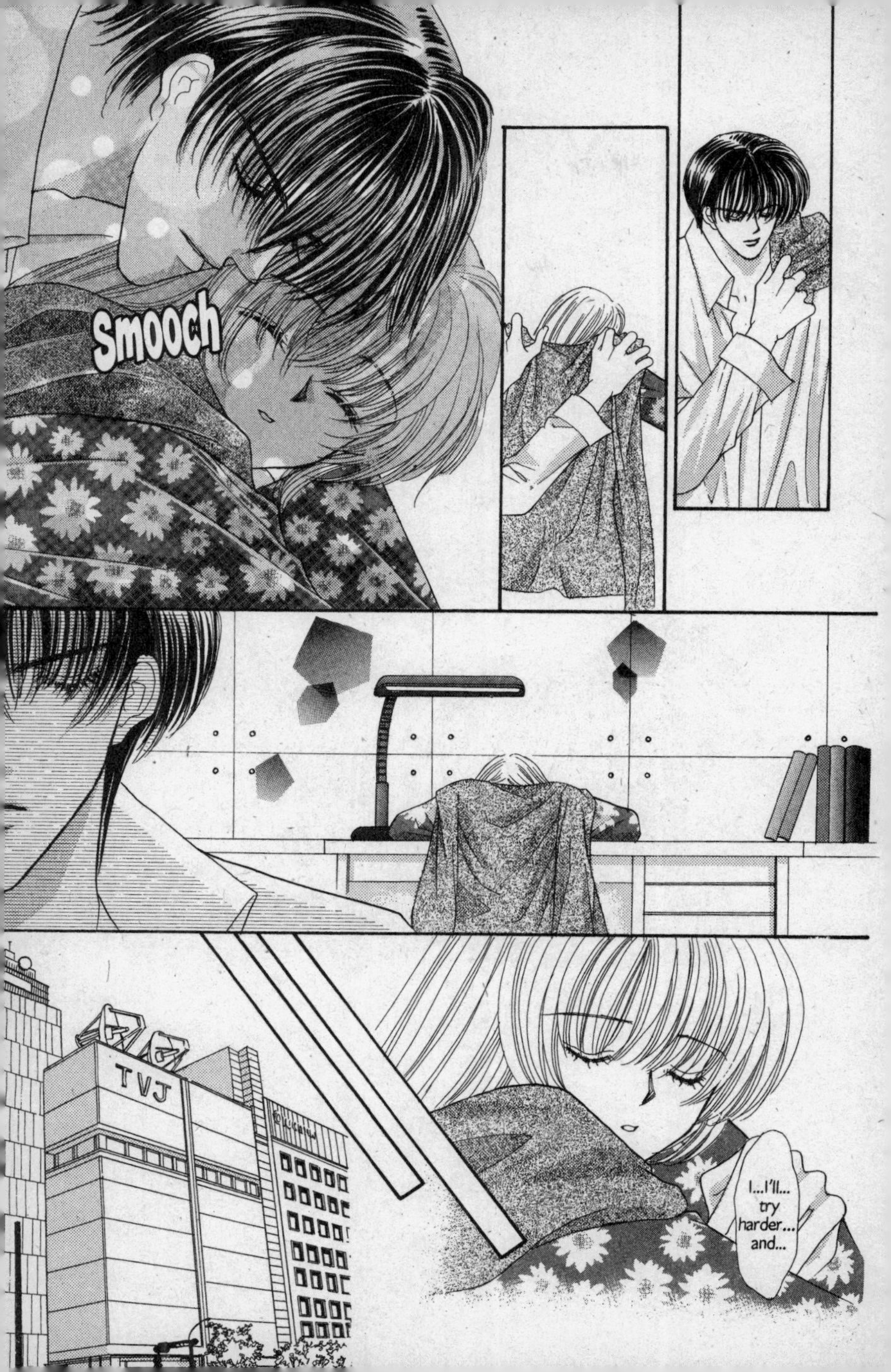
Smooch
I...I'll... try harder... and...
TVJ

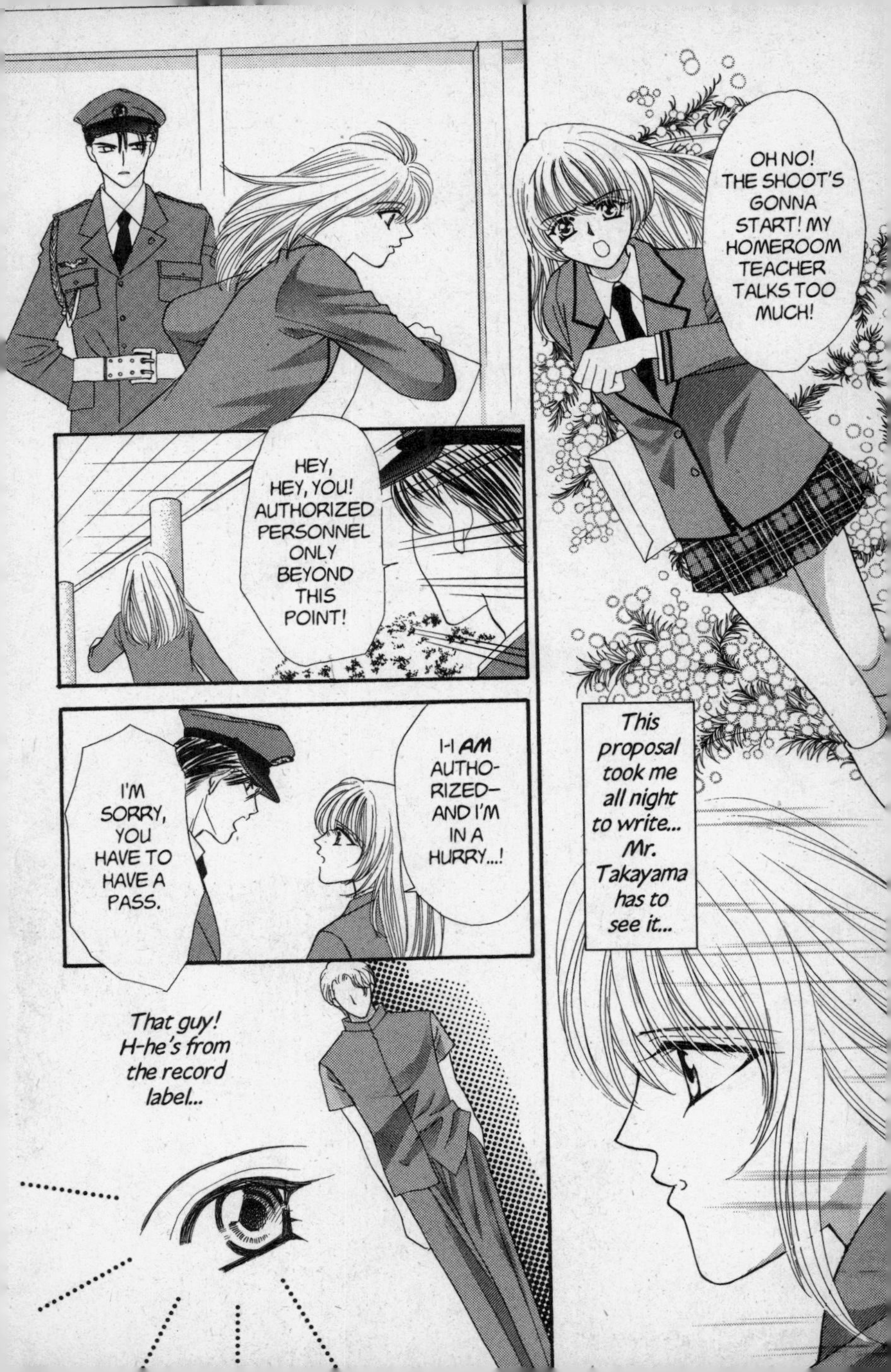
OH NO! THE SHOOT'S GONNA START! MY HOMEROOM TEACHER TALKS TOO MUCH!
This proposal took me all night to write... Mr. Takayama has to see it...
HEY, HEY, YOU! AUTHORIZED PERSONNEL ONLY BEYOND THIS POINT!
I-I AM AUTHORIZED— AND I'M IN A HURRY...!
I'M SORRY, YOU HAVE TO HAVE A PASS.
That guy! H-he's from the record label...
....

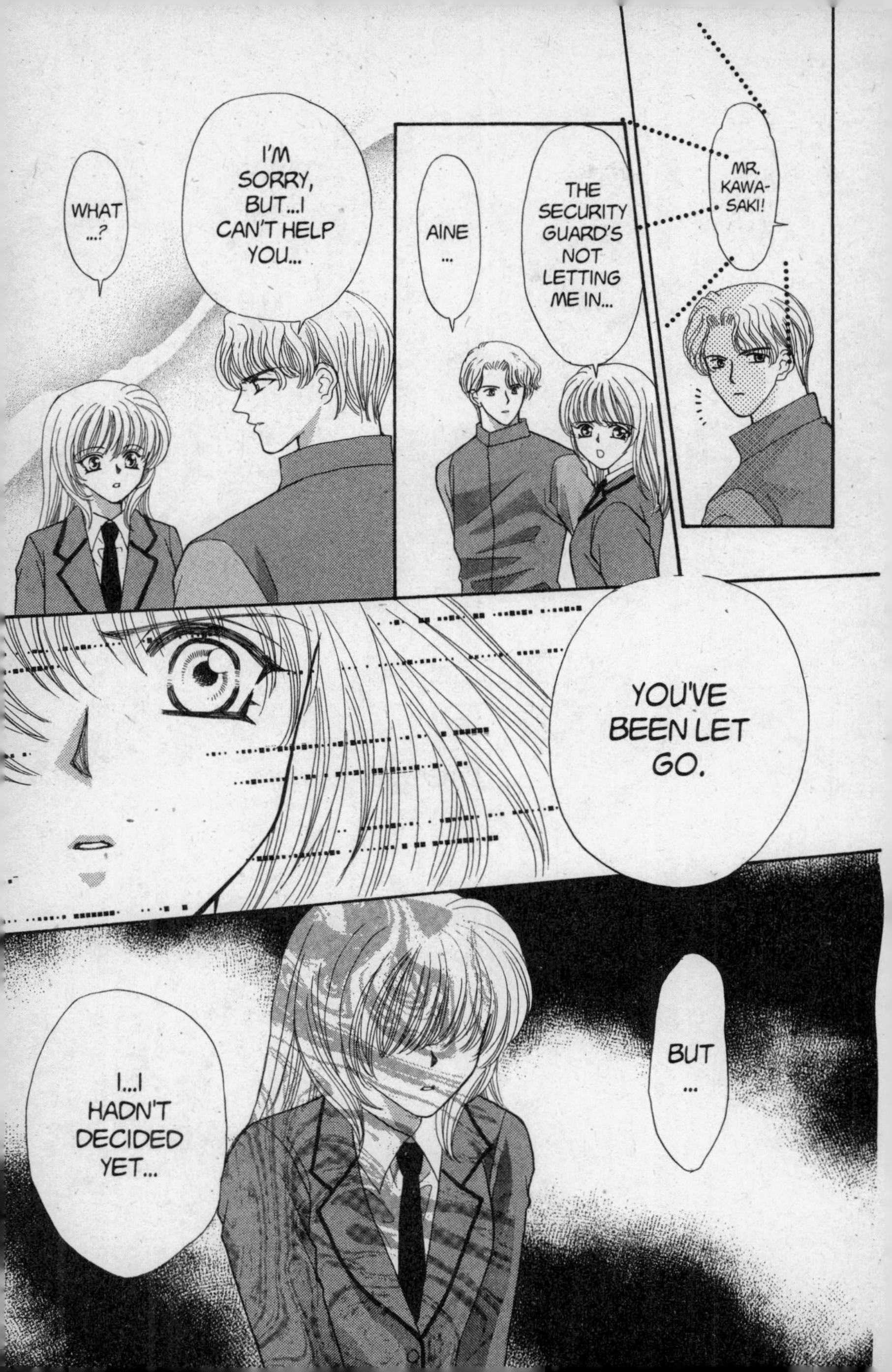
MR. KAWA-SAKI!
THE SECURITY GUARD'S NOT LETTING ME IN...
AINE...
I'M SORRY, BUT...I CAN'T HELP YOU...
WHAT...?
YOU'VE BEEN LET GO.
BUT...
I...I HADN'T DECIDED YET...

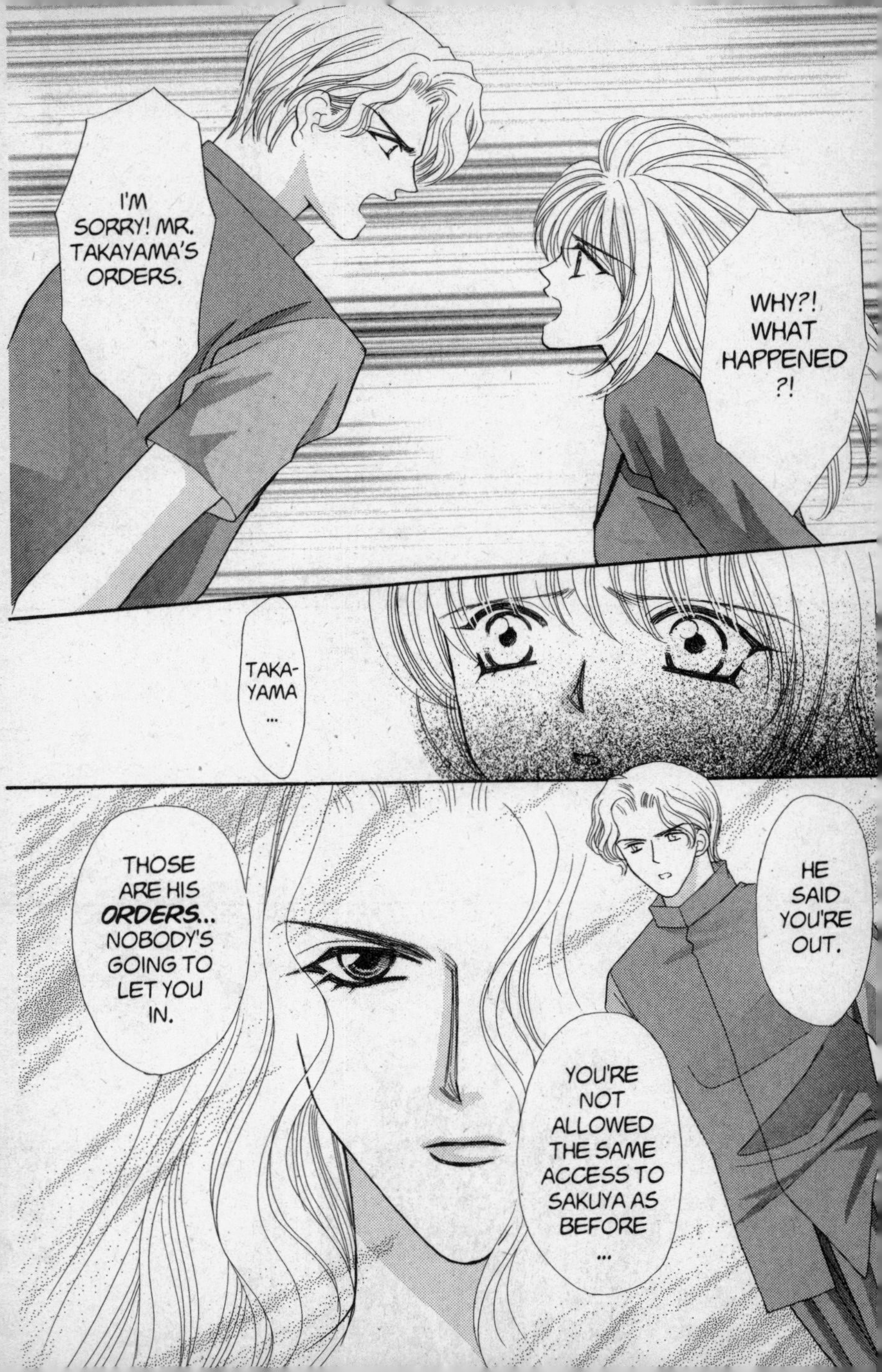
WHY?! WHAT HAPPENED ?!
I'M SORRY! MR. TAKAYAMA'S ORDERS.
TAKA- YAMA ...
HE SAID YOU'RE OUT.
YOU'RE NOT ALLOWED THE SAME ACCESS TO SAKUYA AS BEFORE ...
THOSE ARE HIS ***ORDERS***... NOBODY'S GOING TO LET YOU IN.

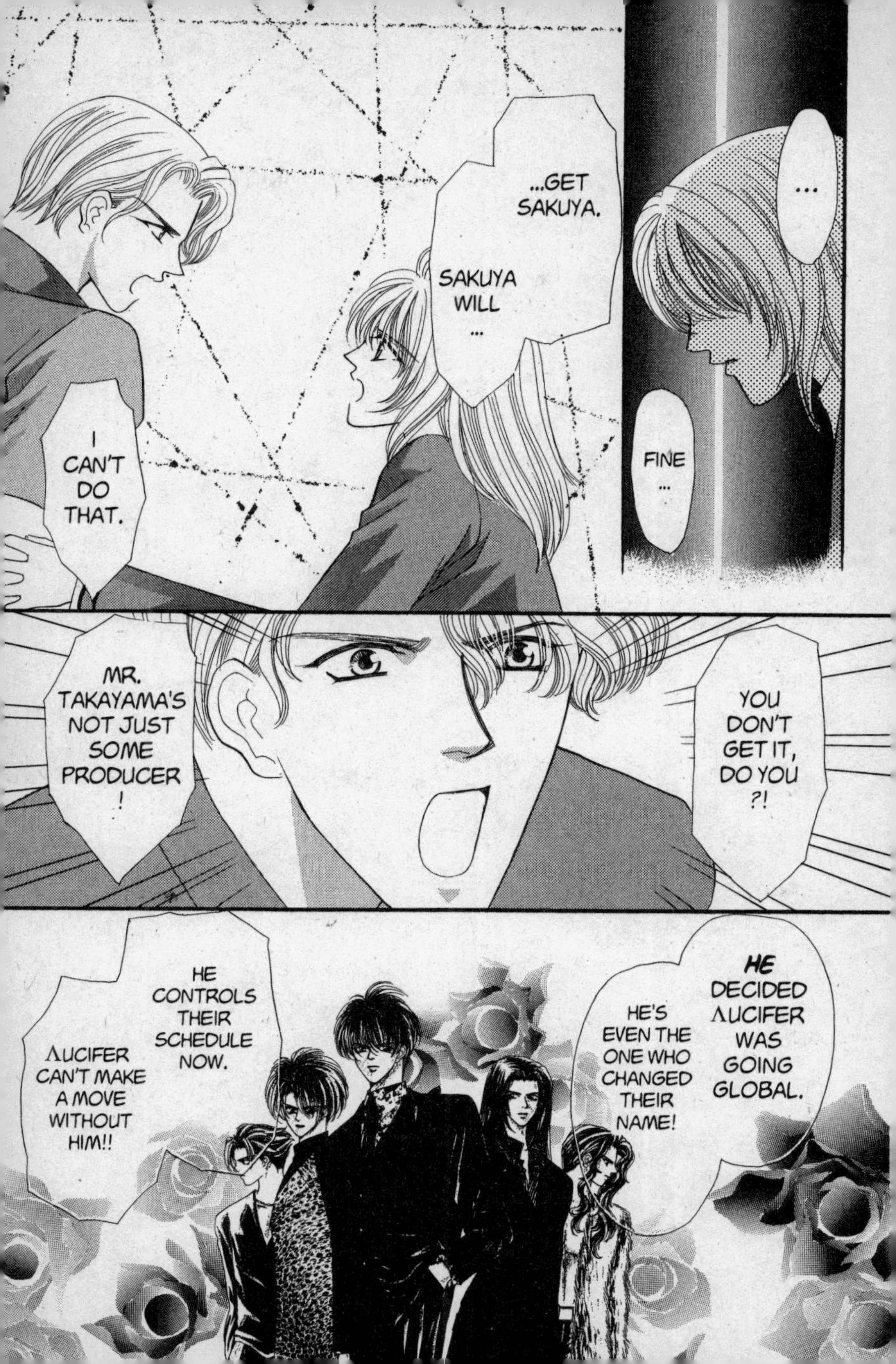
...
FINE ...
...GET SAKUYA.
SAKUYA WILL ...
I CAN'T DO THAT.
YOU DON'T GET IT, DO YOU ?!
MR. TAKAYAMA'S NOT JUST SOME PRODUCER !
HE DECIDED ΛUCIFER WAS GOING GLOBAL.
HE'S EVEN THE ONE WHO CHANGED THEIR NAME!
HE CONTROLS THEIR SCHEDULE NOW.
ΛUCIFER CAN'T MAKE A MOVE WITHOUT HIM!!

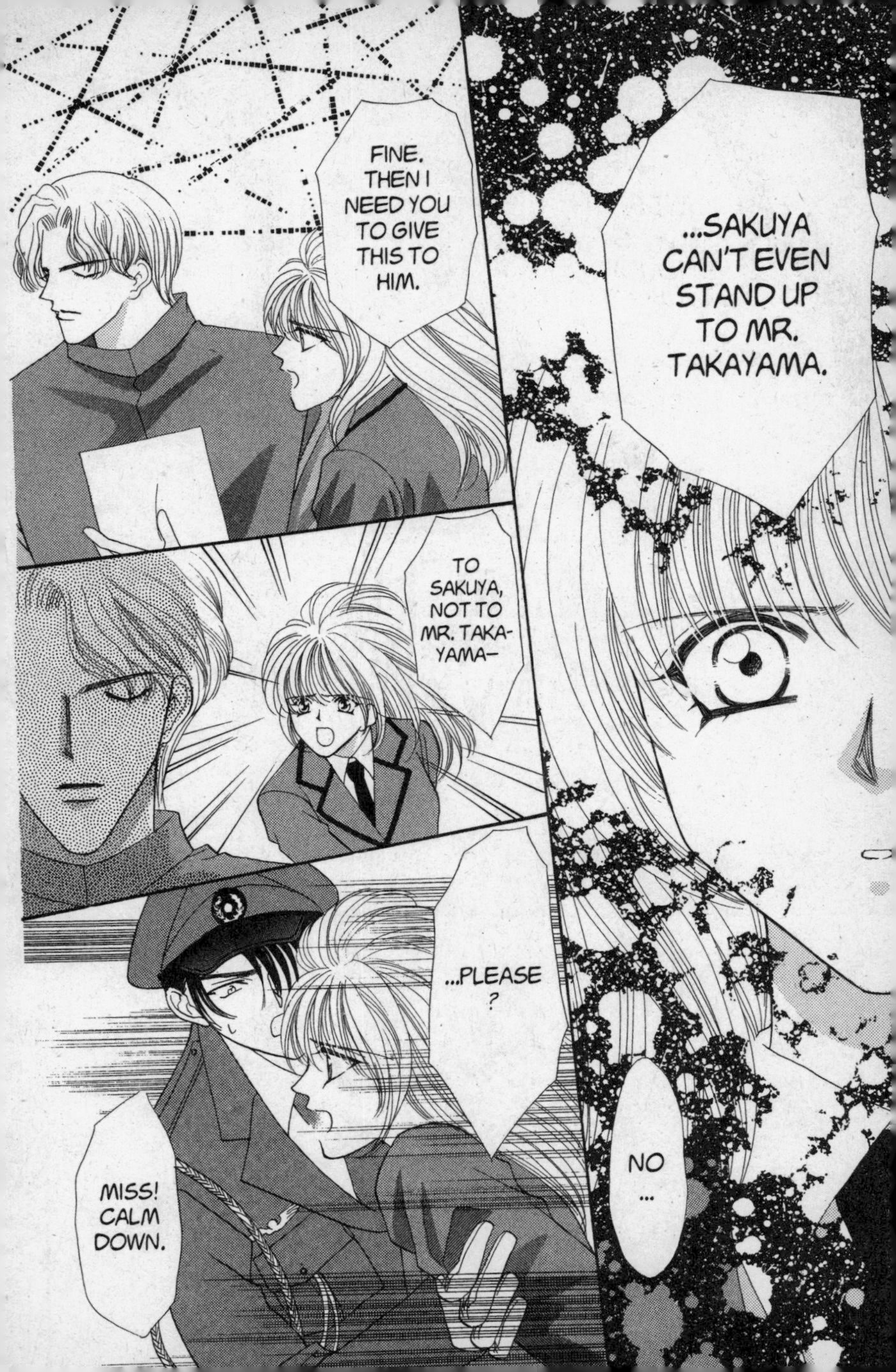
...SAKUYA CAN'T EVEN STAND UP TO MR. TAKAYAMA.
NO ...
FINE. THEN I NEED YOU TO GIVE THIS TO HIM.
TO SAKUYA, NOT TO MR. TAKA-YAMA—
...PLEASE ?
MISS! CALM DOWN.

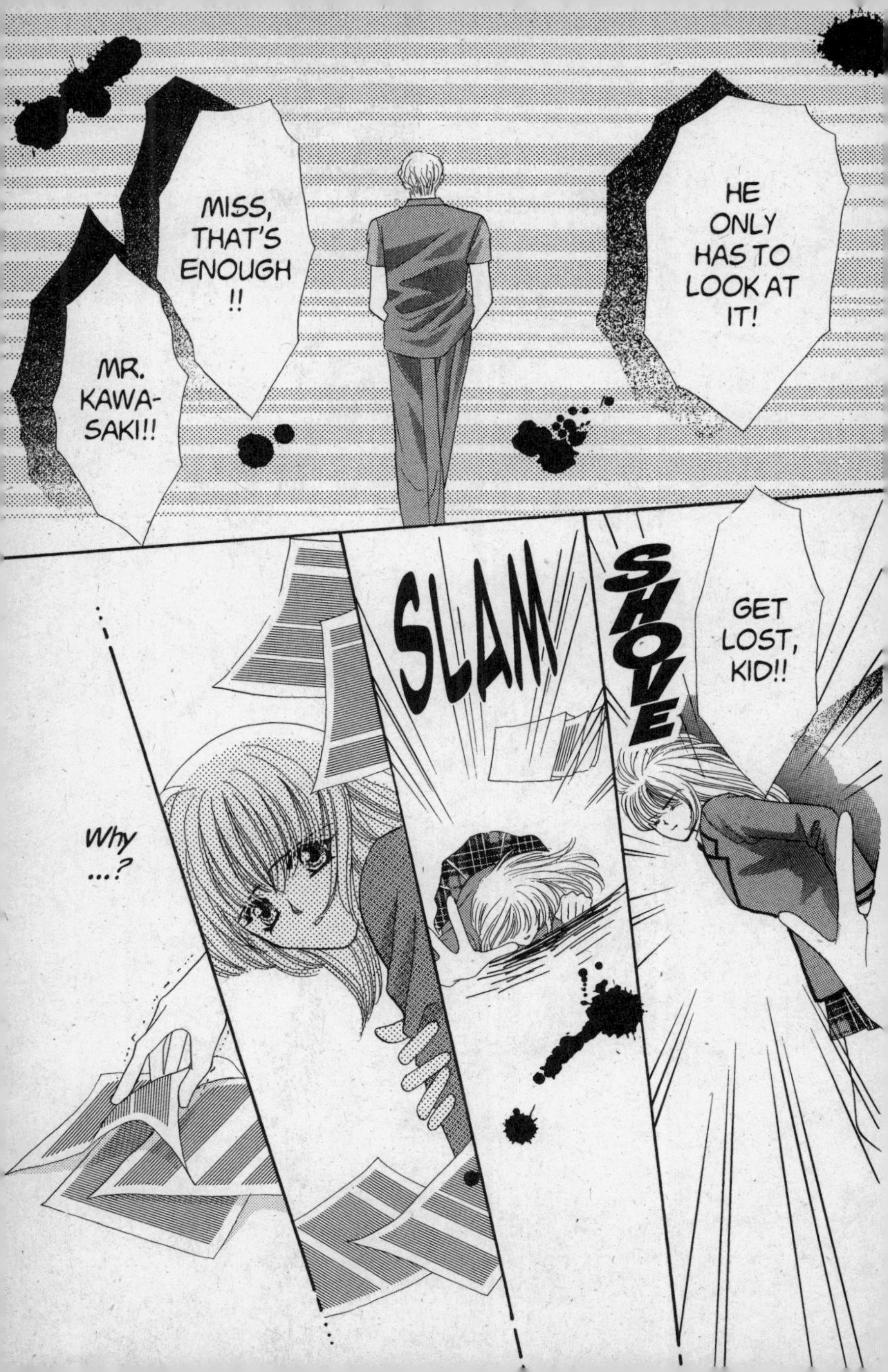
HE ONLY HAS TO LOOK AT IT!
MISS, THAT'S ENOUGH !!
MR. KAWA-SAKI!!
GET LOST, KID!!
SHOVE
SLAM
Why ...?

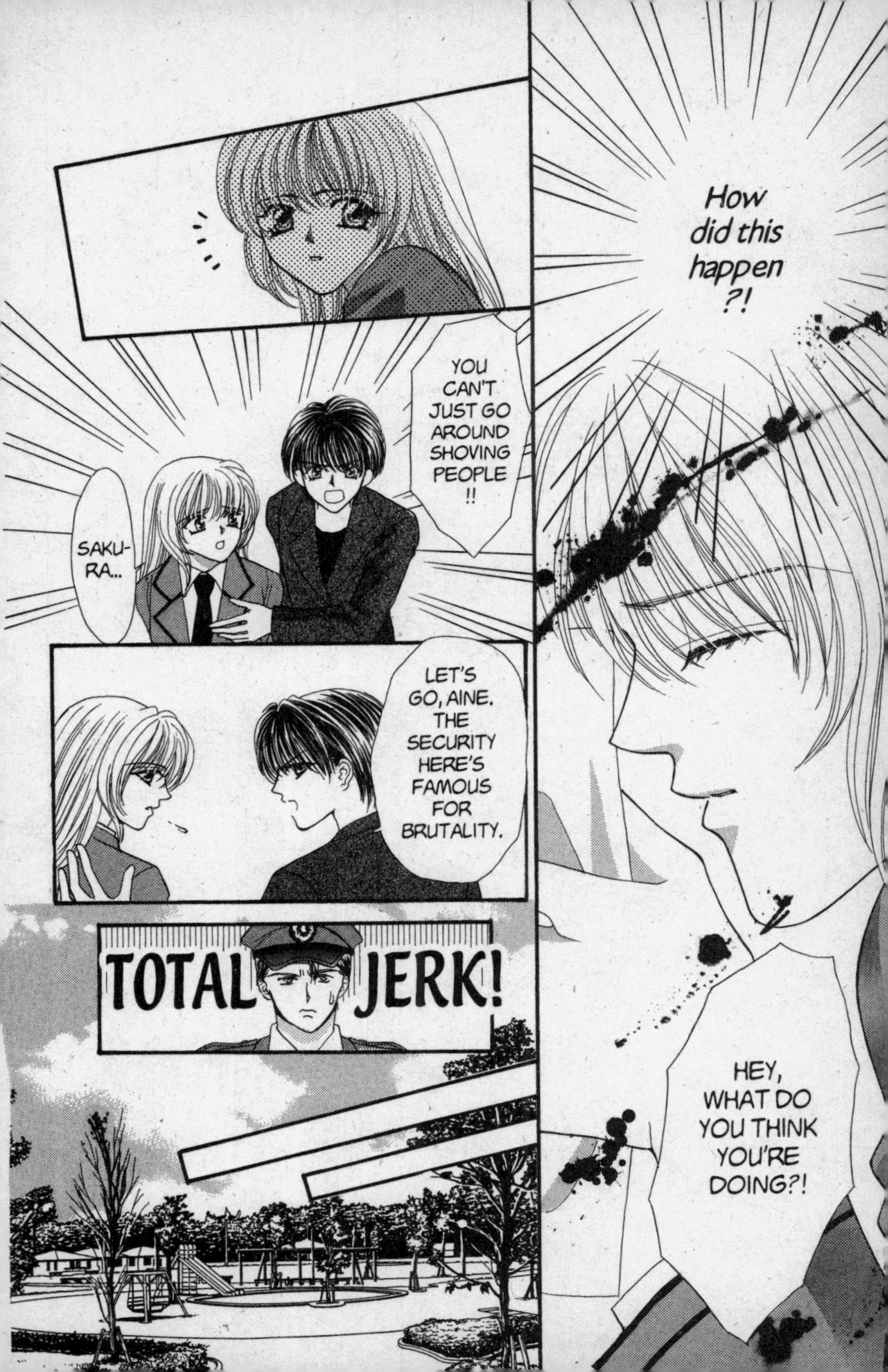
How did this happen ?!
HEY, WHAT DO YOU THINK YOU'RE DOING?!
YOU CAN'T JUST GO AROUND SHOVING PEOPLE !!
SAKU-RA...
LET'S GO, AINE. THE SECURITY HERE'S FAMOUS FOR BRUTALITY.
TOTAL JERK!

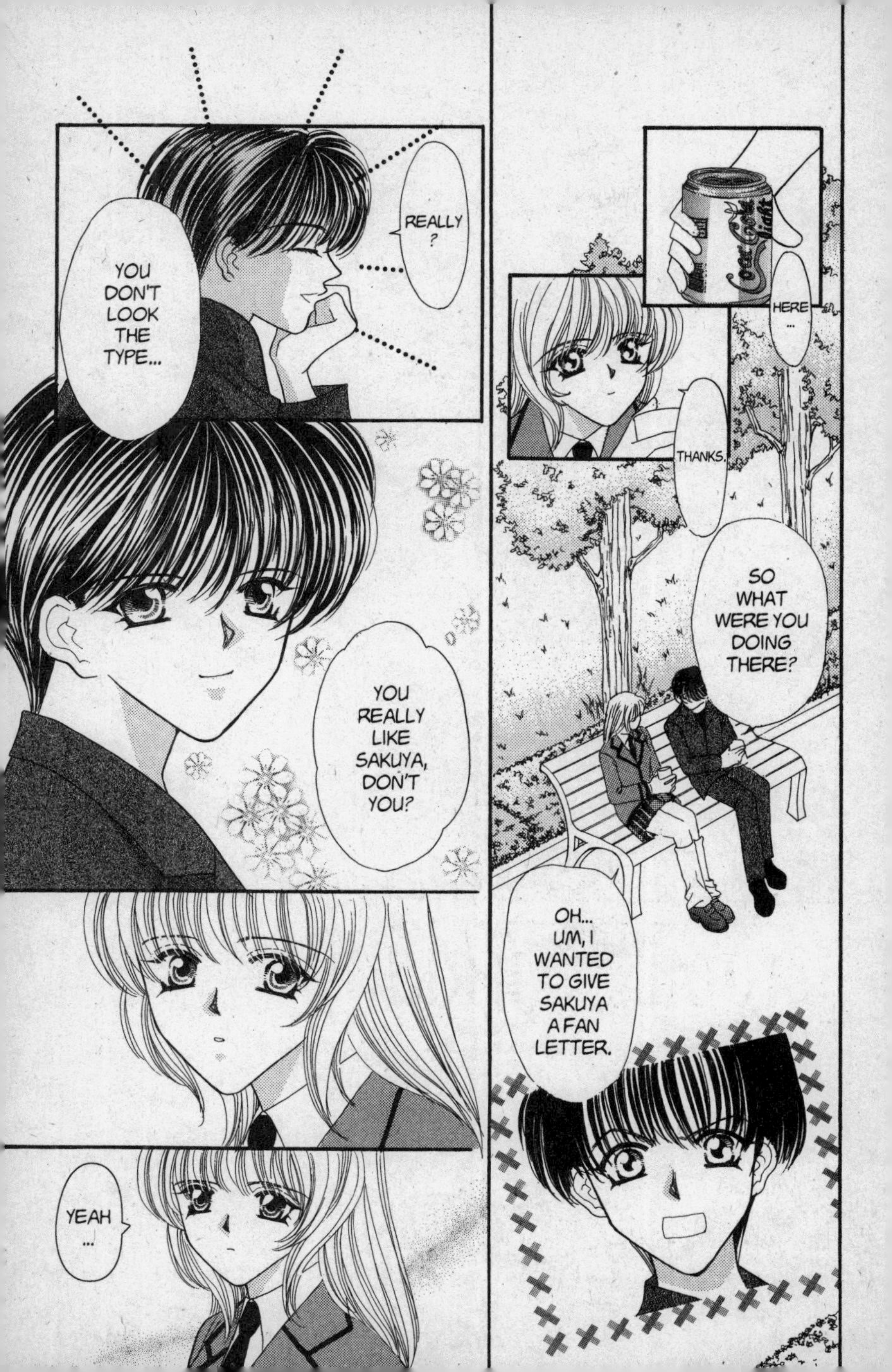
HERE...
THANKS.
SO WHAT WERE YOU DOING THERE?
OH... UM, I WANTED TO GIVE SAKUYA A FAN LETTER.
REALLY?
YOU DON'T LOOK THE TYPE...
YOU REALLY LIKE SAKUYA, DON'T YOU?
YEAH...

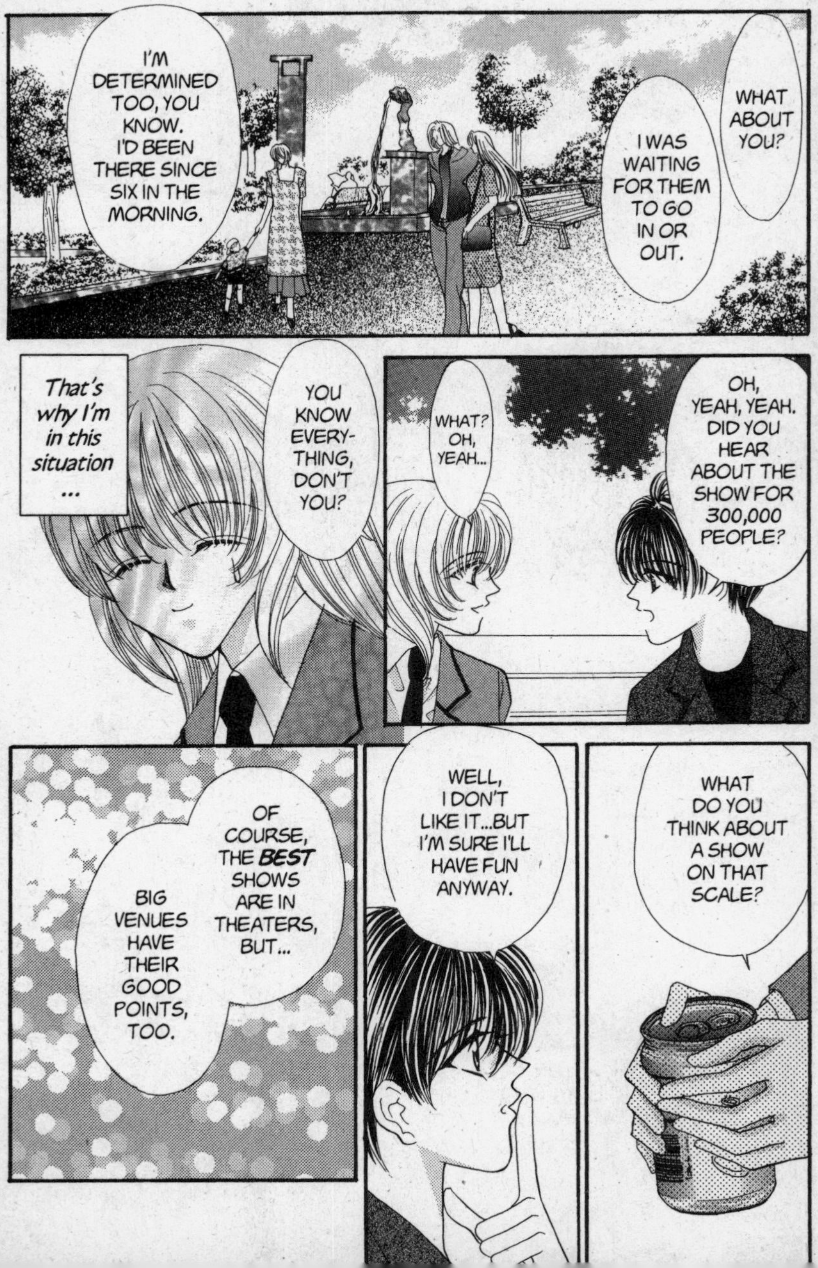
WHAT ABOUT YOU?
I WAS WAITING FOR THEM TO GO IN OR OUT.
I'M DETERMINED TOO, YOU KNOW. I'D BEEN THERE SINCE SIX IN THE MORNING.
OH, YEAH, YEAH. DID YOU HEAR ABOUT THE SHOW FOR 300,000 PEOPLE?
WHAT? OH, YEAH...
YOU KNOW EVERY-THING, DON'T YOU?
That's why I'm in this situation ...
WHAT DO YOU THINK ABOUT A SHOW ON THAT SCALE?
WELL, I DON'T LIKE IT...BUT I'M SURE I'LL HAVE FUN ANYWAY.
OF COURSE, THE **BEST** SHOWS ARE IN THEATERS, BUT...
BIG VENUES HAVE THEIR GOOD POINTS, TOO.

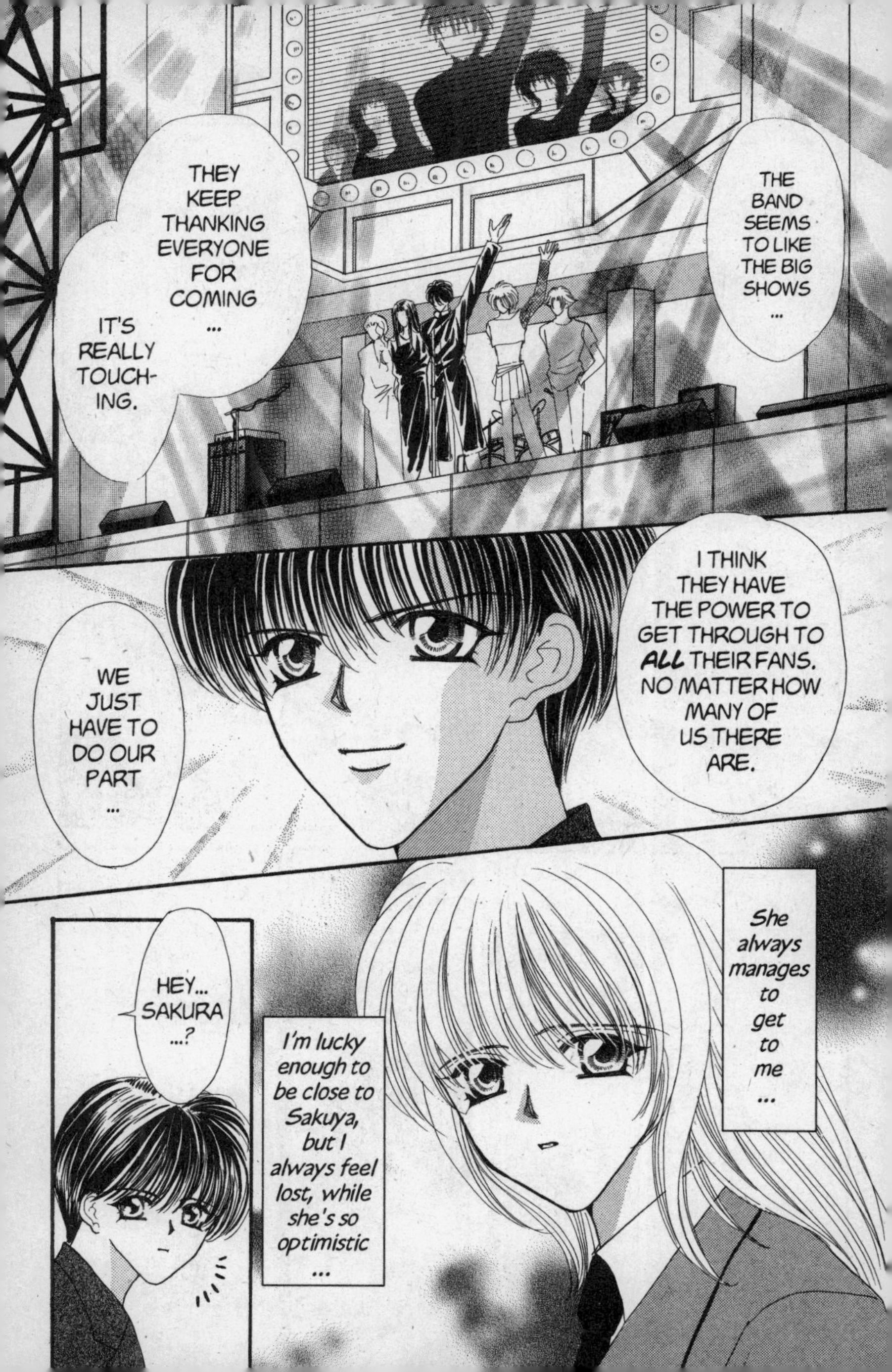
THE BAND SEEMS TO LIKE THE BIG SHOWS ...
THEY KEEP THANKING EVERYONE FOR COMING ... IT'S REALLY TOUCHING.
I THINK THEY HAVE THE POWER TO GET THROUGH TO **ALL** THEIR FANS. NO MATTER HOW MANY OF US THERE ARE.
WE JUST HAVE TO DO OUR PART ...
She always manages to get to me ...
I'm lucky enough to be close to Sakuya, but I always feel lost, while she's so optimistic ...
HEY... SAKURA ...?

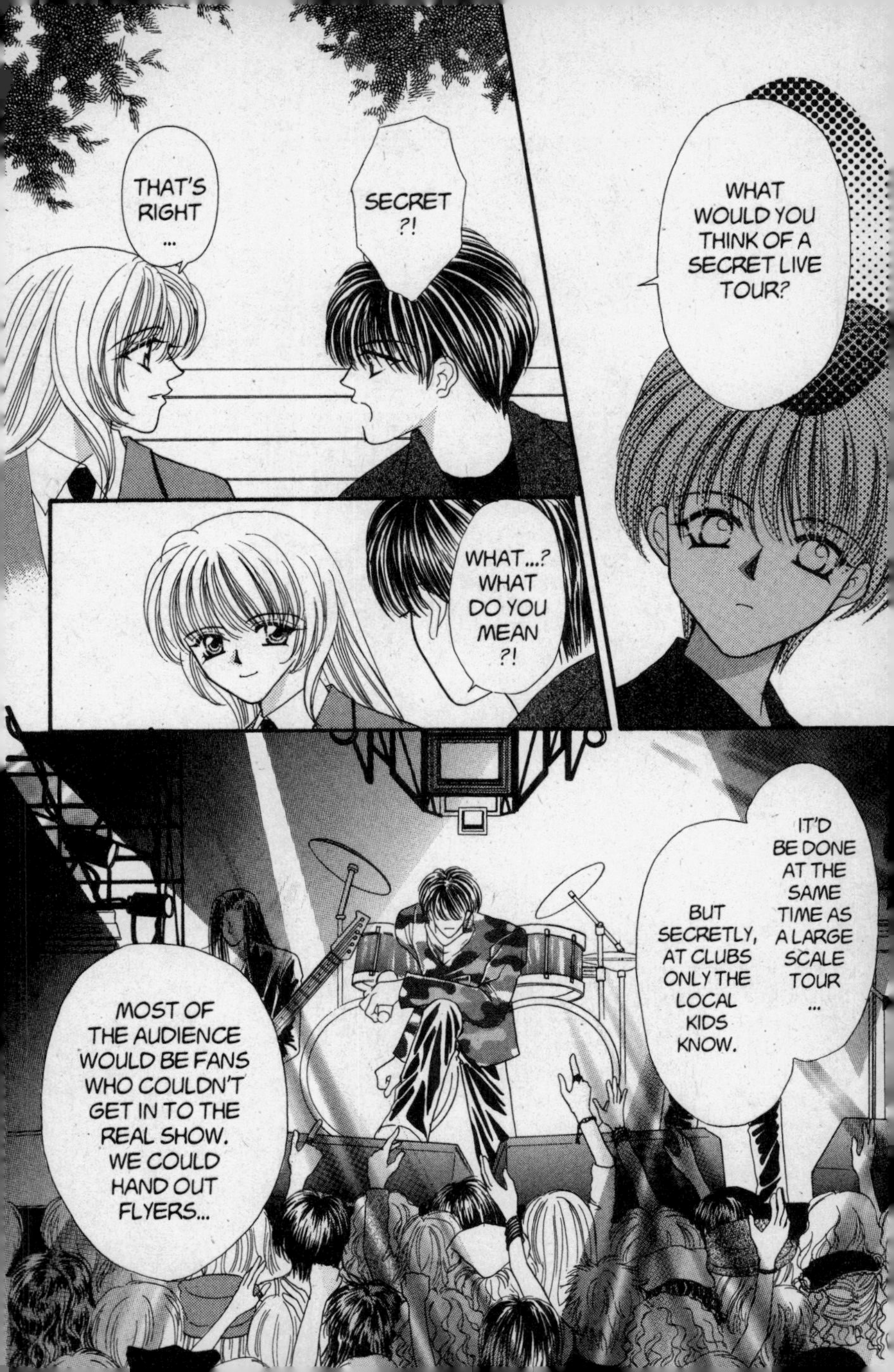
WHAT WOULD YOU THINK OF A SECRET LIVE TOUR?
SECRET?!
THAT'S RIGHT ...
WHAT...? WHAT DO YOU MEAN?!
IT'D BE DONE AT THE SAME TIME AS A LARGE SCALE TOUR ...
BUT SECRETLY, AT CLUBS ONLY THE LOCAL KIDS KNOW.
MOST OF THE AUDIENCE WOULD BE FANS WHO COULDN'T GET IN TO THE REAL SHOW. WE COULD HAND OUT FLYERS...

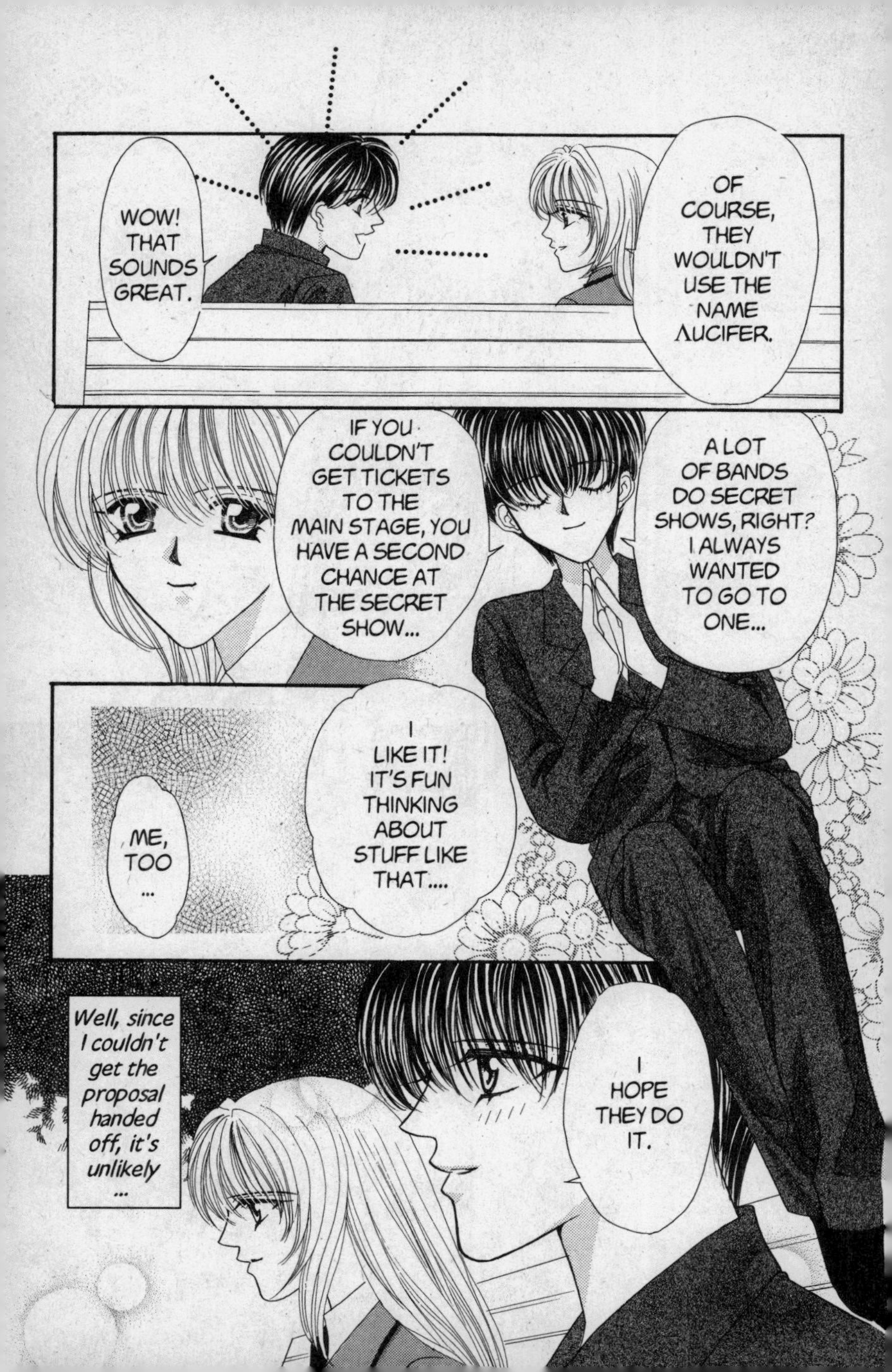
OF COURSE, THEY WOULDN'T USE THE NAME ΛUCIFER.
WOW! THAT SOUNDS GREAT.
A LOT OF BANDS DO SECRET SHOWS, RIGHT? I ALWAYS WANTED TO GO TO ONE...
IF YOU COULDN'T GET TICKETS TO THE MAIN STAGE, YOU HAVE A SECOND CHANCE AT THE SECRET SHOW...
I LIKE IT! IT'S FUN THINKING ABOUT STUFF LIKE THAT....
ME, TOO ...
I HOPE THEY DO IT.
Well, since I couldn't get the proposal handed off, it's unlikely ...

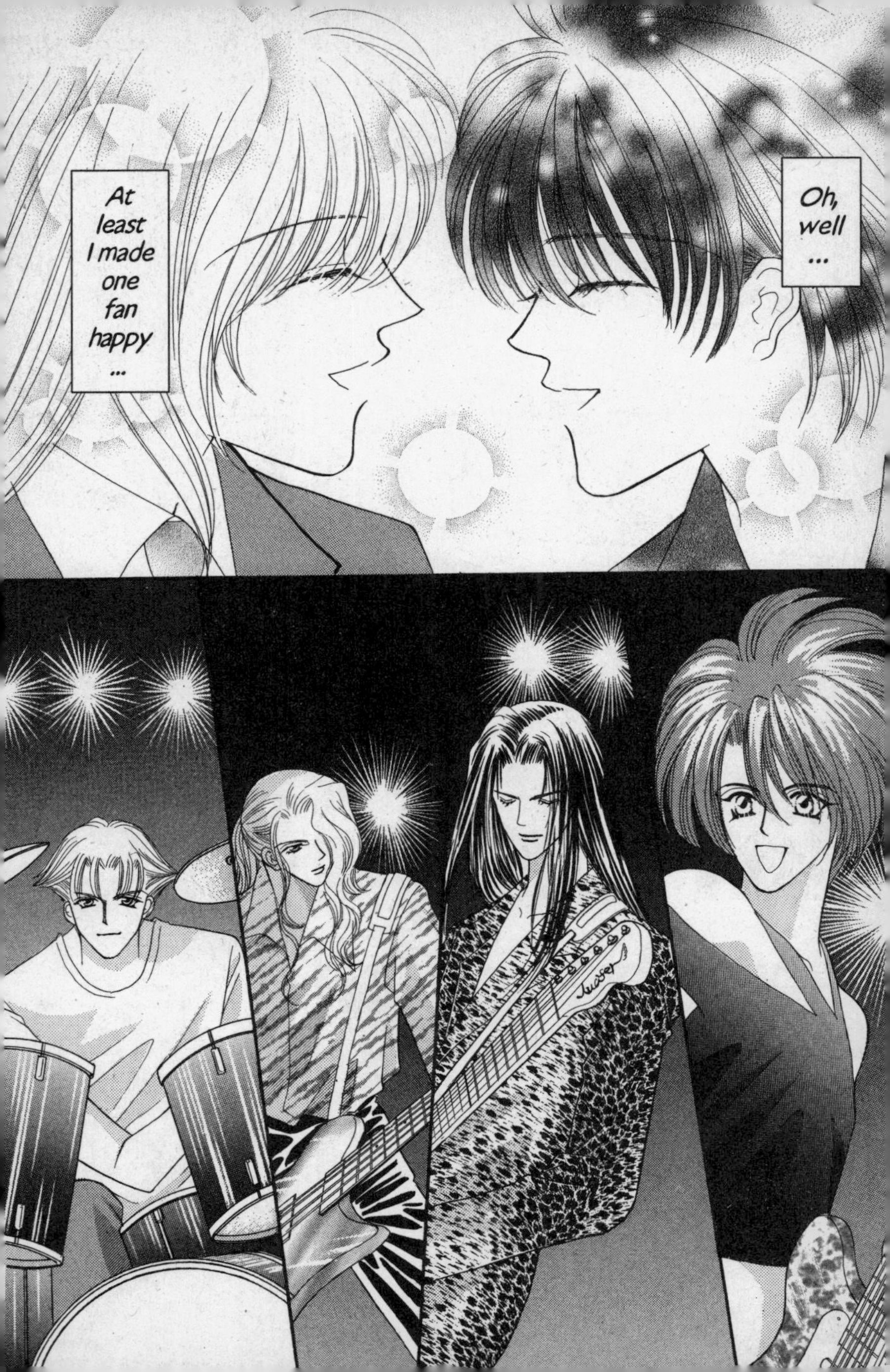
Oh, well ...
At least I made one fan happy ...

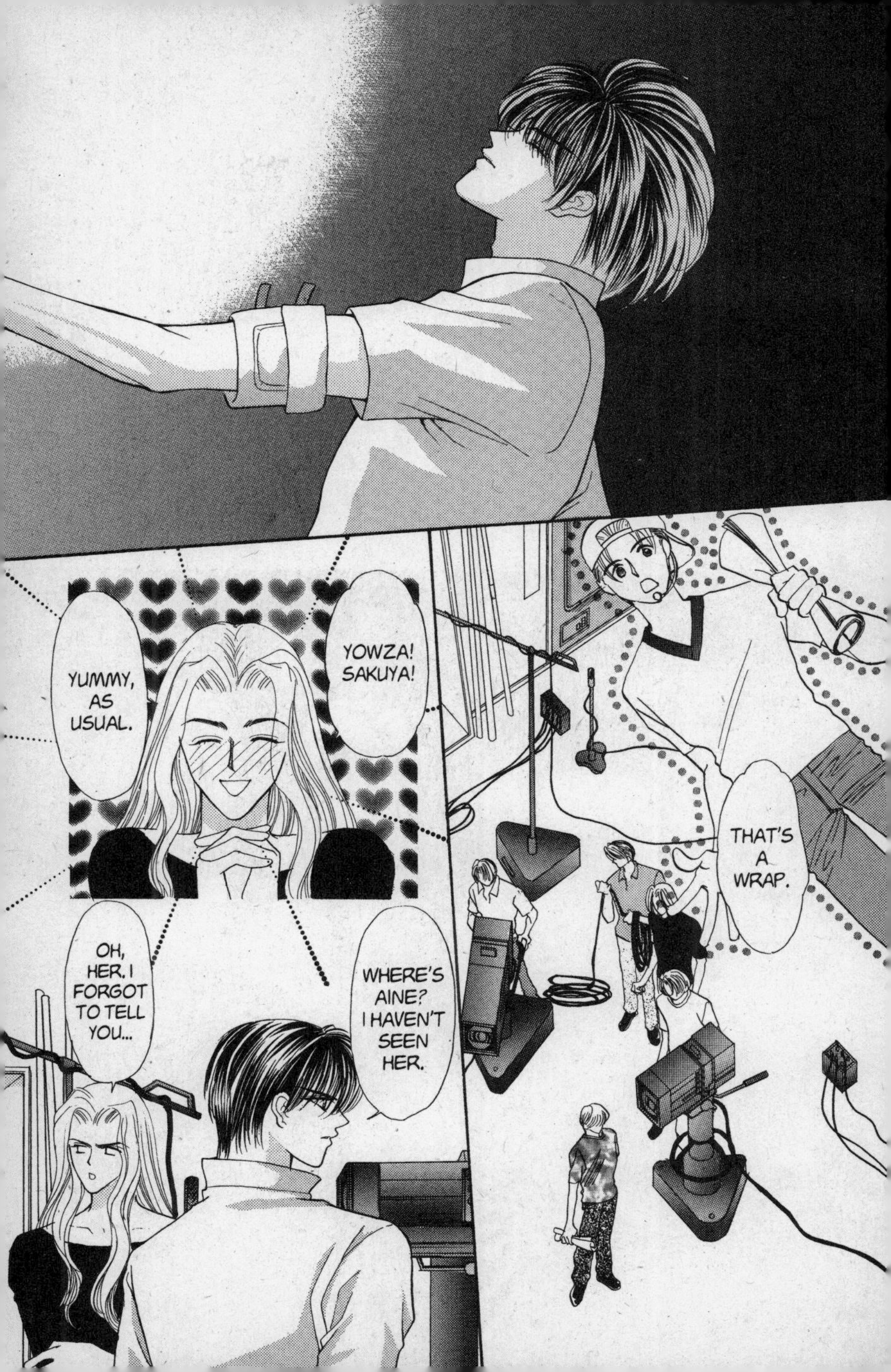
THAT'S A WRAP.
YOWZA! SAKUYA!
YUMMY, AS USUAL.
WHERE'S AINE? I HAVEN'T SEEN HER.
OH, HER. I FORGOT TO TELL YOU...

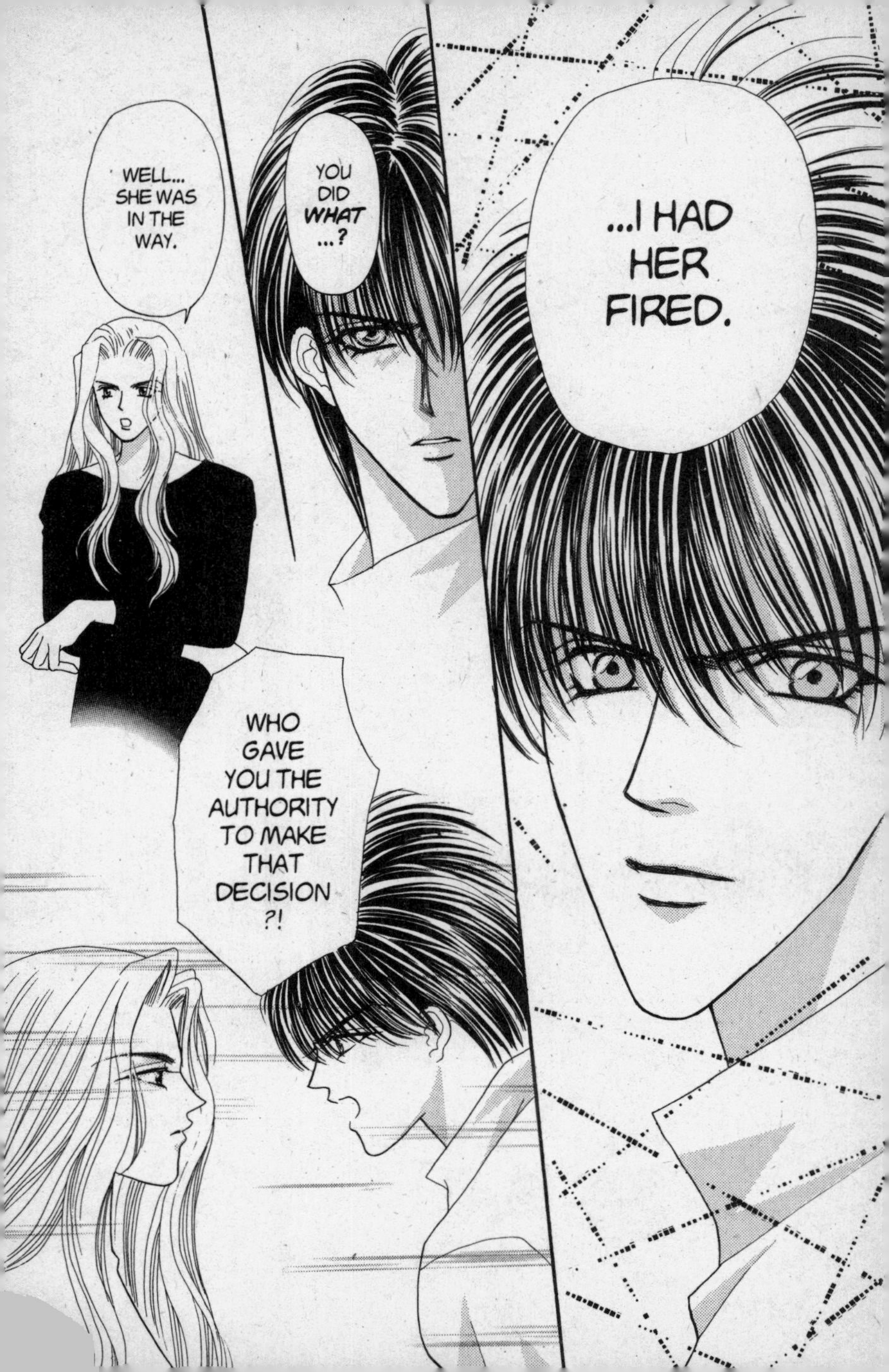
...I HAD HER FIRED.
YOU DID WHAT ...?
WELL... SHE WAS IN THE WAY.
WHO GAVE YOU THE AUTHORITY TO MAKE THAT DECISION ?!

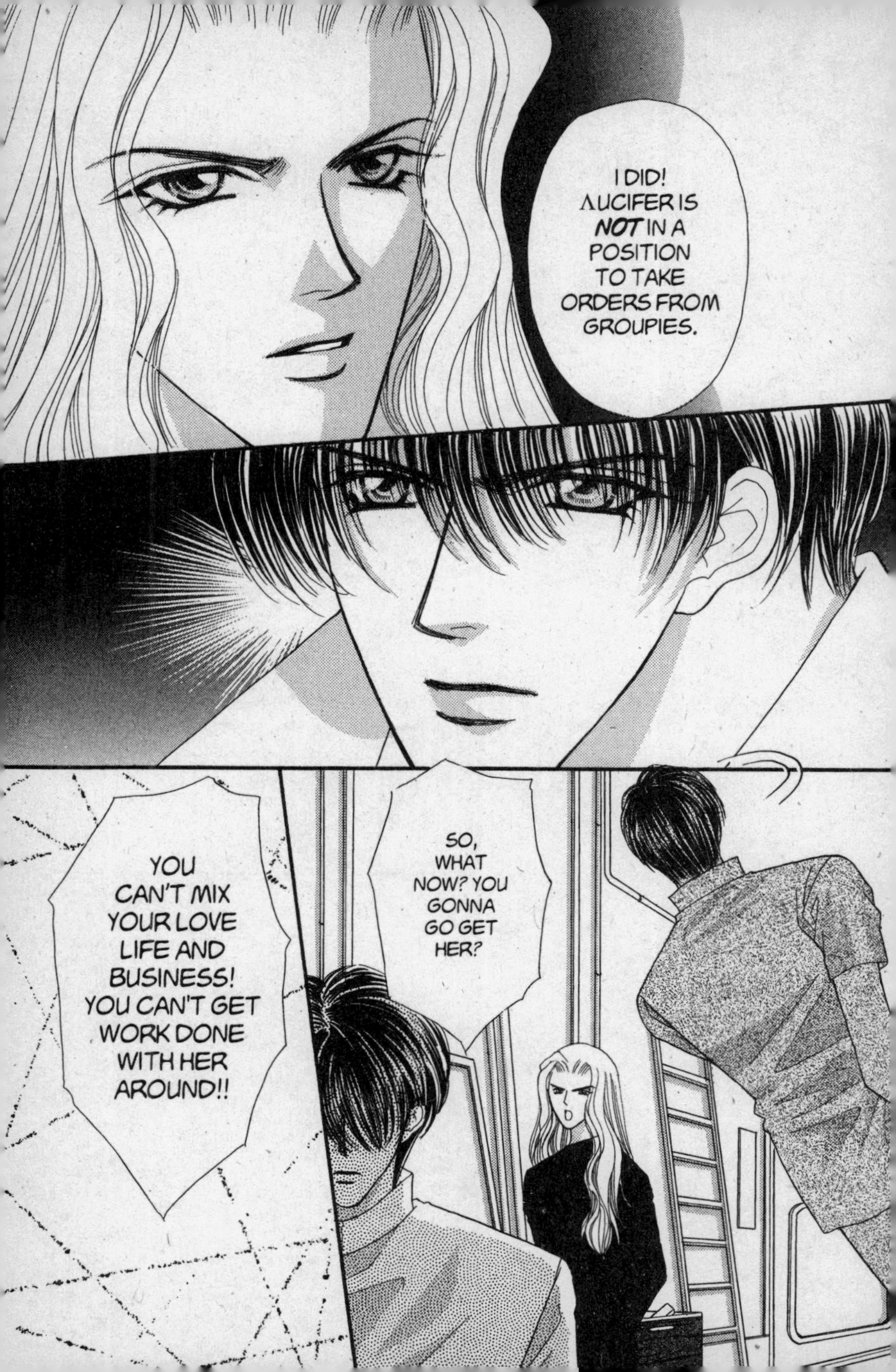
I DID! ΛUCIFER IS **NOT** IN A POSITION TO TAKE ORDERS FROM GROUPIES.
SO, WHAT NOW? YOU GONNA GO GET HER?
YOU CAN'T MIX YOUR LOVE LIFE AND BUSINESS! YOU CAN'T GET WORK DONE WITH HER AROUND!!

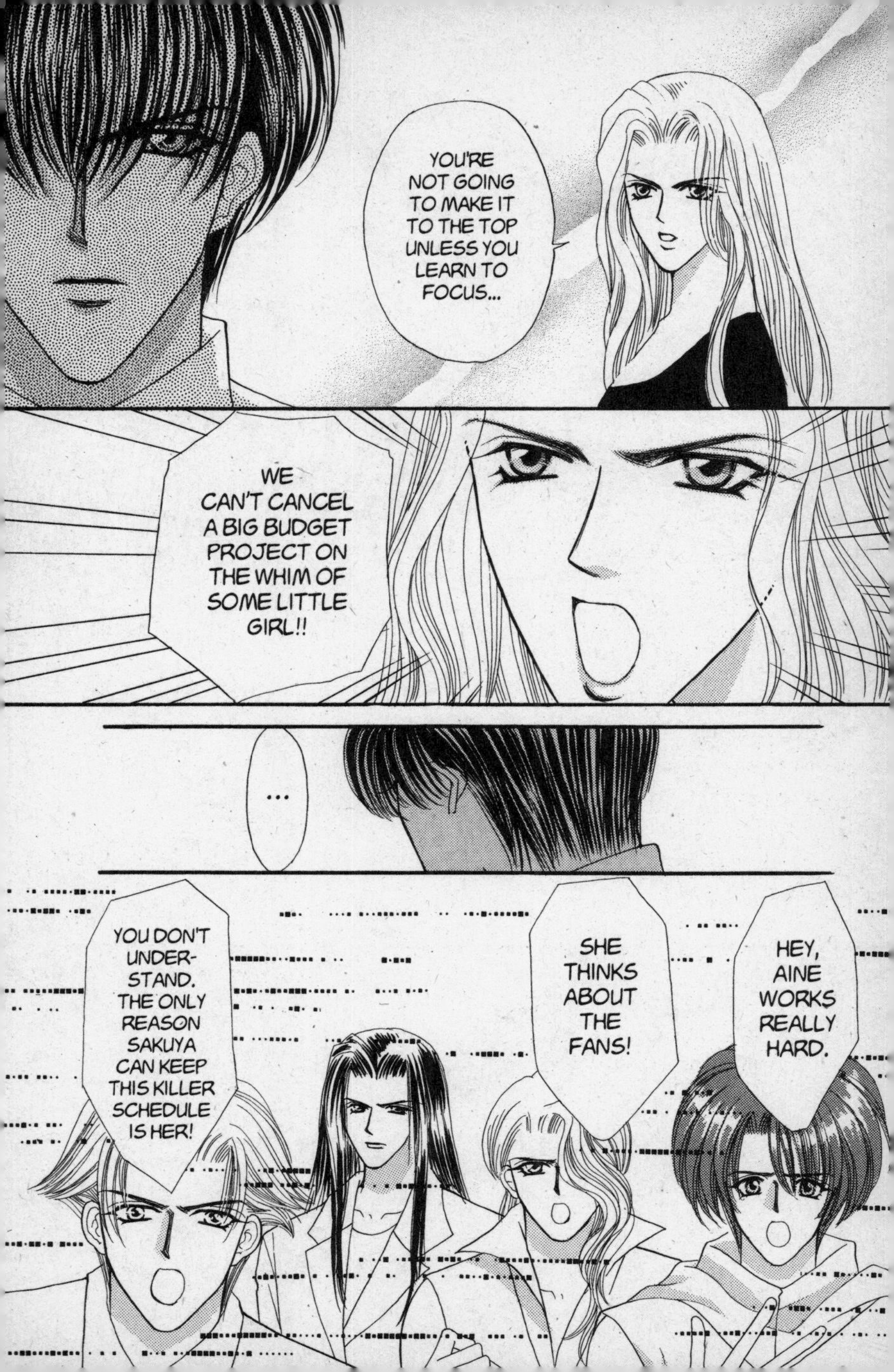
YOU'RE NOT GOING TO MAKE IT TO THE TOP UNLESS YOU LEARN TO FOCUS...
WE CAN'T CANCEL A BIG BUDGET PROJECT ON THE WHIM OF SOME LITTLE GIRL!!
...
HEY, AINE WORKS REALLY HARD.
SHE THINKS ABOUT THE FANS!
YOU DON'T UNDER-STAND. THE ONLY REASON SAKUYA CAN KEEP THIS KILLER SCHEDULE IS HER!

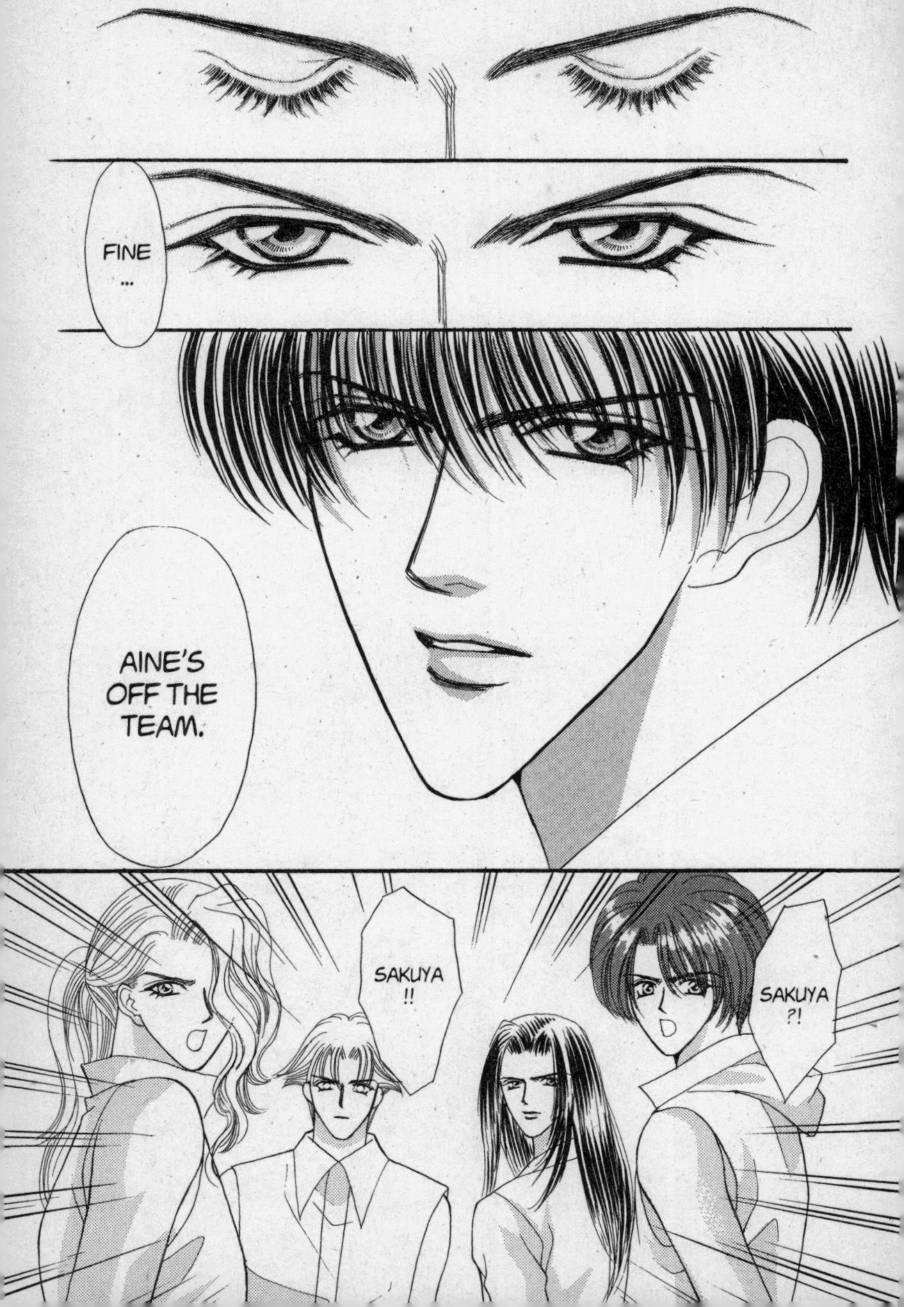
FINE ...
AINE'S OFF THE TEAM.
SAKUYA ?!
SAKUYA !!

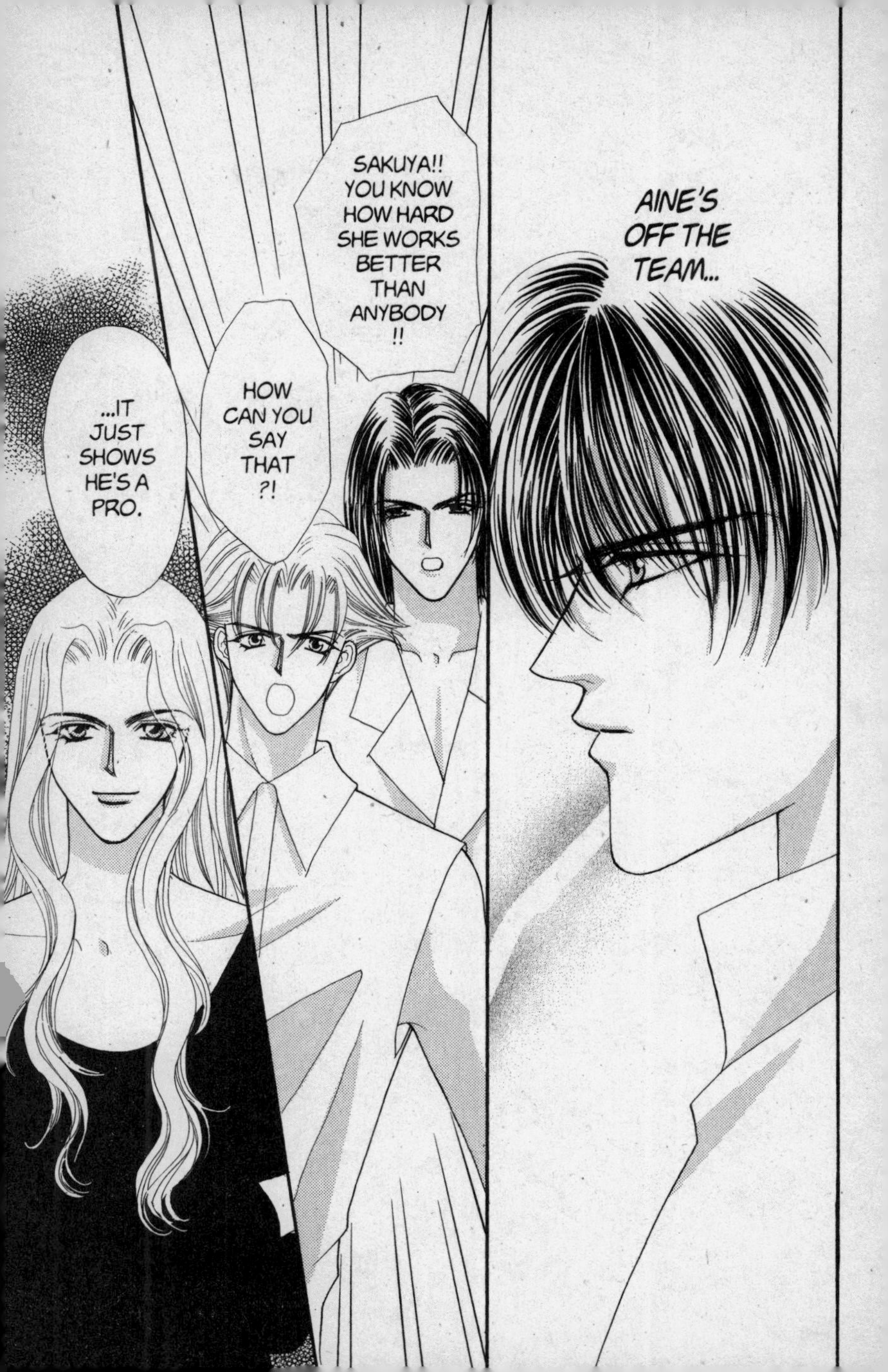
AINE'S OFF THE TEAM...
SAKUYA!! YOU KNOW HOW HARD SHE WORKS BETTER THAN ANYBODY !!
HOW CAN YOU SAY THAT ?!
...IT JUST SHOWS HE'S A PRO.

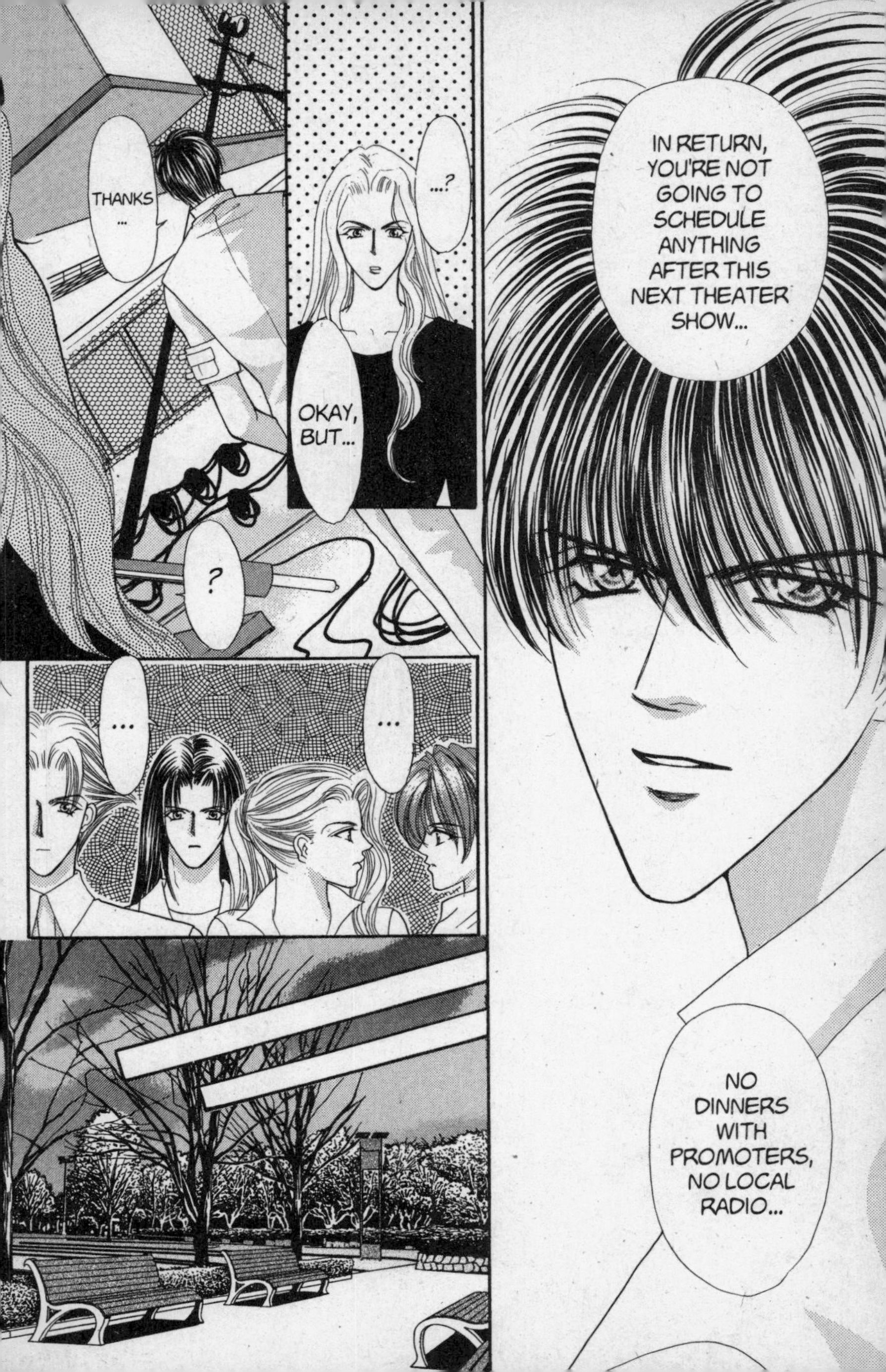
IN RETURN, YOU'RE NOT GOING TO SCHEDULE ANYTHING AFTER THIS NEXT THEATER SHOW...
NO DINNERS WITH PROMOTERS, NO LOCAL RADIO...
...?
OKAY, BUT...
THANKS ...
?
...
...

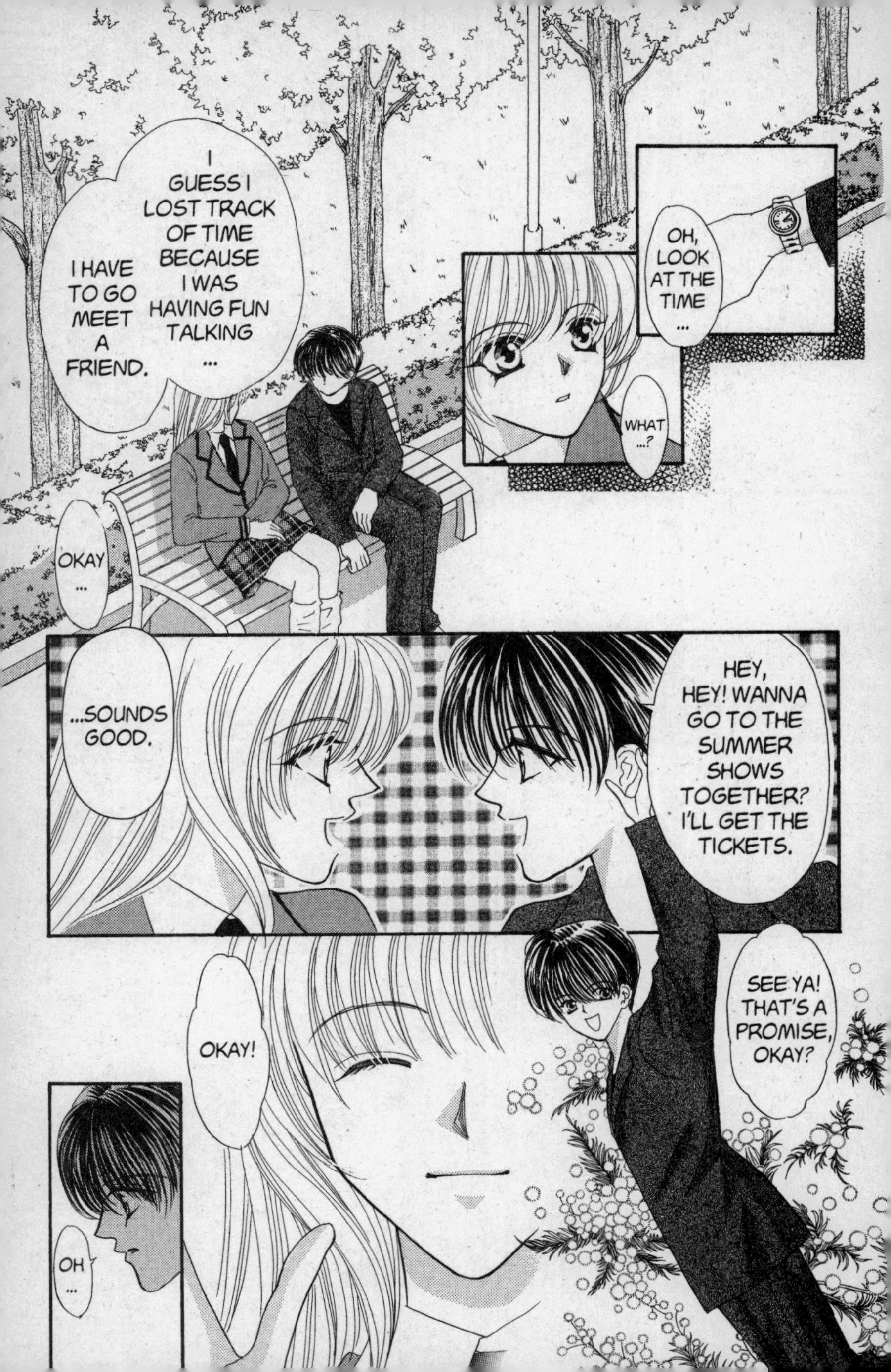
OH, LOOK AT THE TIME ...
WHAT ...?
I GUESS I LOST TRACK OF TIME BECAUSE I WAS HAVING FUN TALKING ...
I HAVE TO GO MEET A FRIEND.
OKAY ...
HEY, HEY! WANNA GO TO THE SUMMER SHOWS TOGETHER? I'LL GET THE TICKETS.
...SOUNDS GOOD.
SEE YA! THAT'S A PROMISE, OKAY?
OKAY!
OH ...

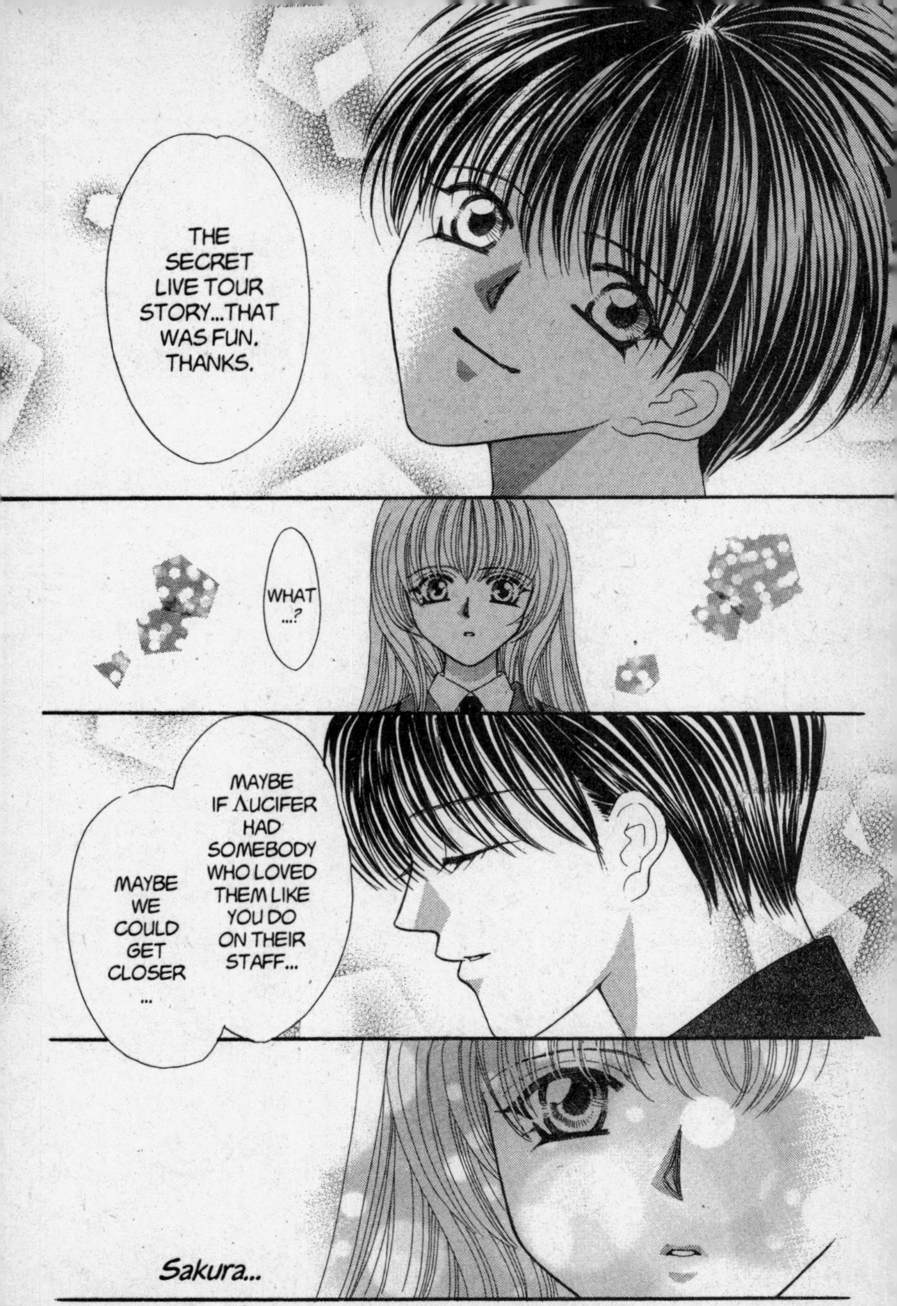
THE SECRET LIVE TOUR STORY...THAT WAS FUN. THANKS.
WHAT ...?
MAYBE IF ΛUCIFER HAD SOMEBODY WHO LOVED THEM LIKE YOU DO ON THEIR STAFF...
MAYBE WE COULD GET CLOSER ...
Sakura...

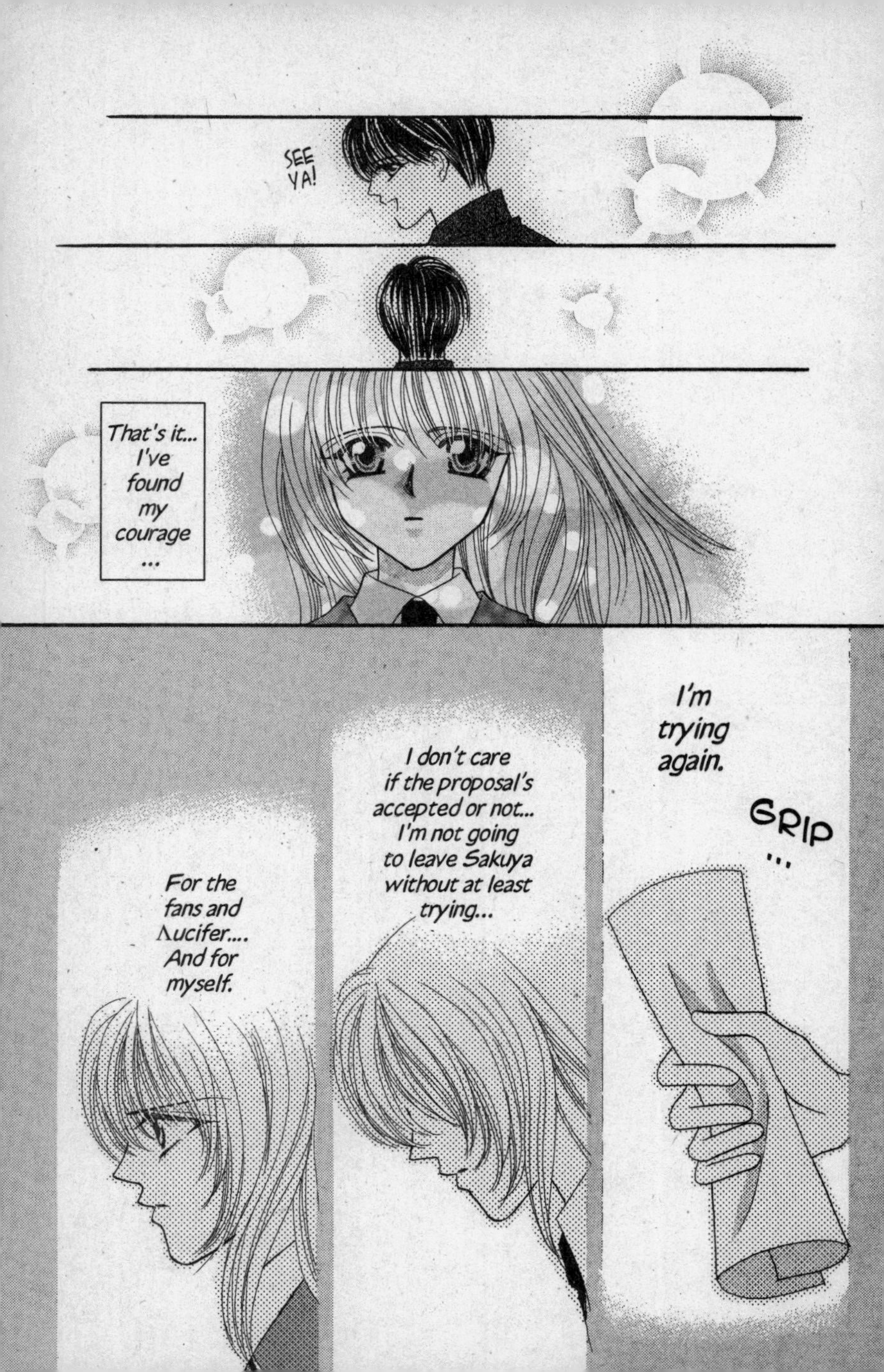
SEE YA!
That's it... I've found my courage...
I'm trying again.
GRIP...
I don't care if the proposal's accepted or not... I'm not going to leave Sakuya without at least trying...
For the fans and Lucifer.... And for myself.

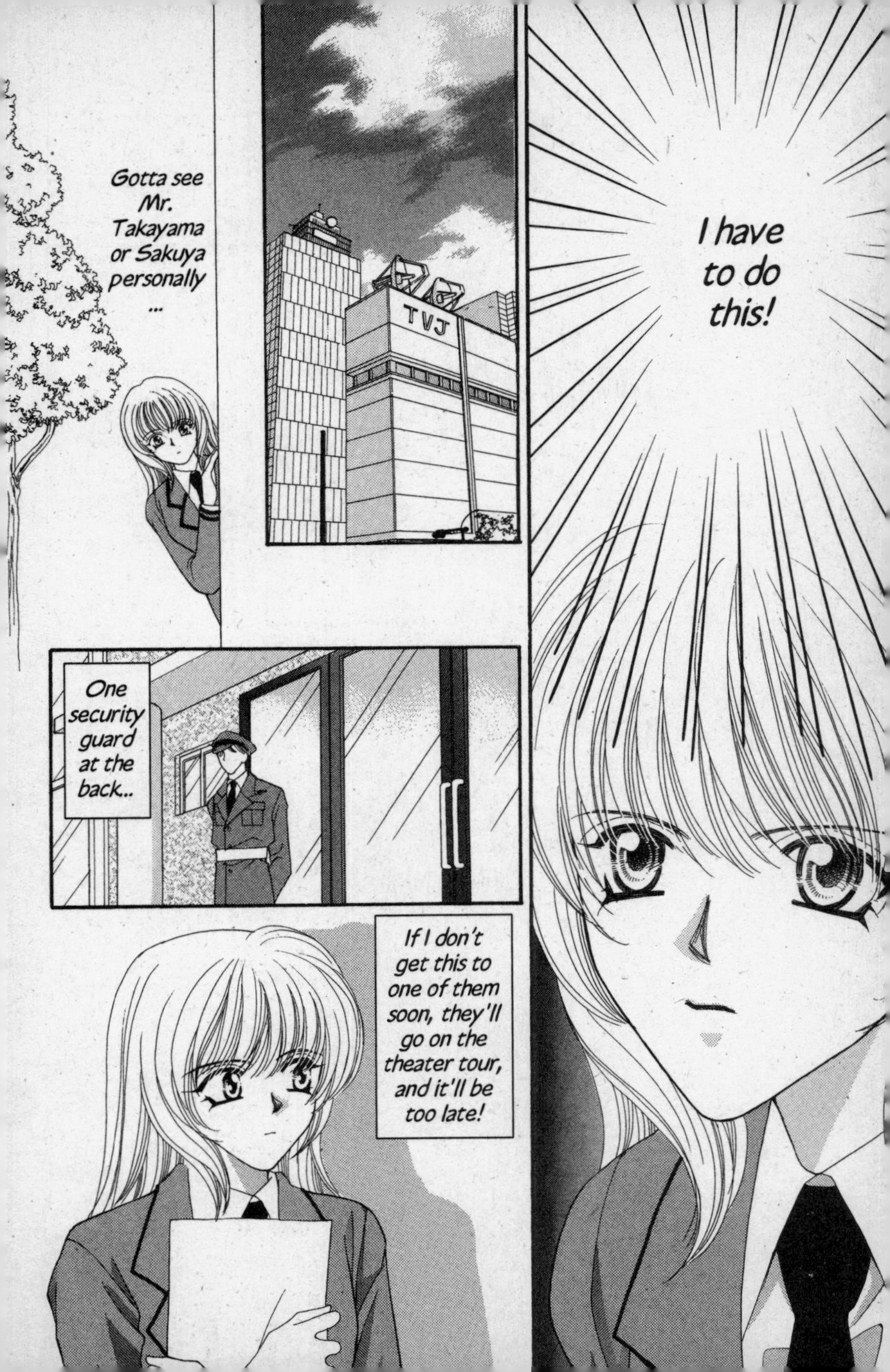

I have to do this!
Gotta see Mr. Takayama or Sakuya personally ...
One security guard at the back..
If I don't get this to one of them soon, they'll go on the theater tour, and it'll be too late!

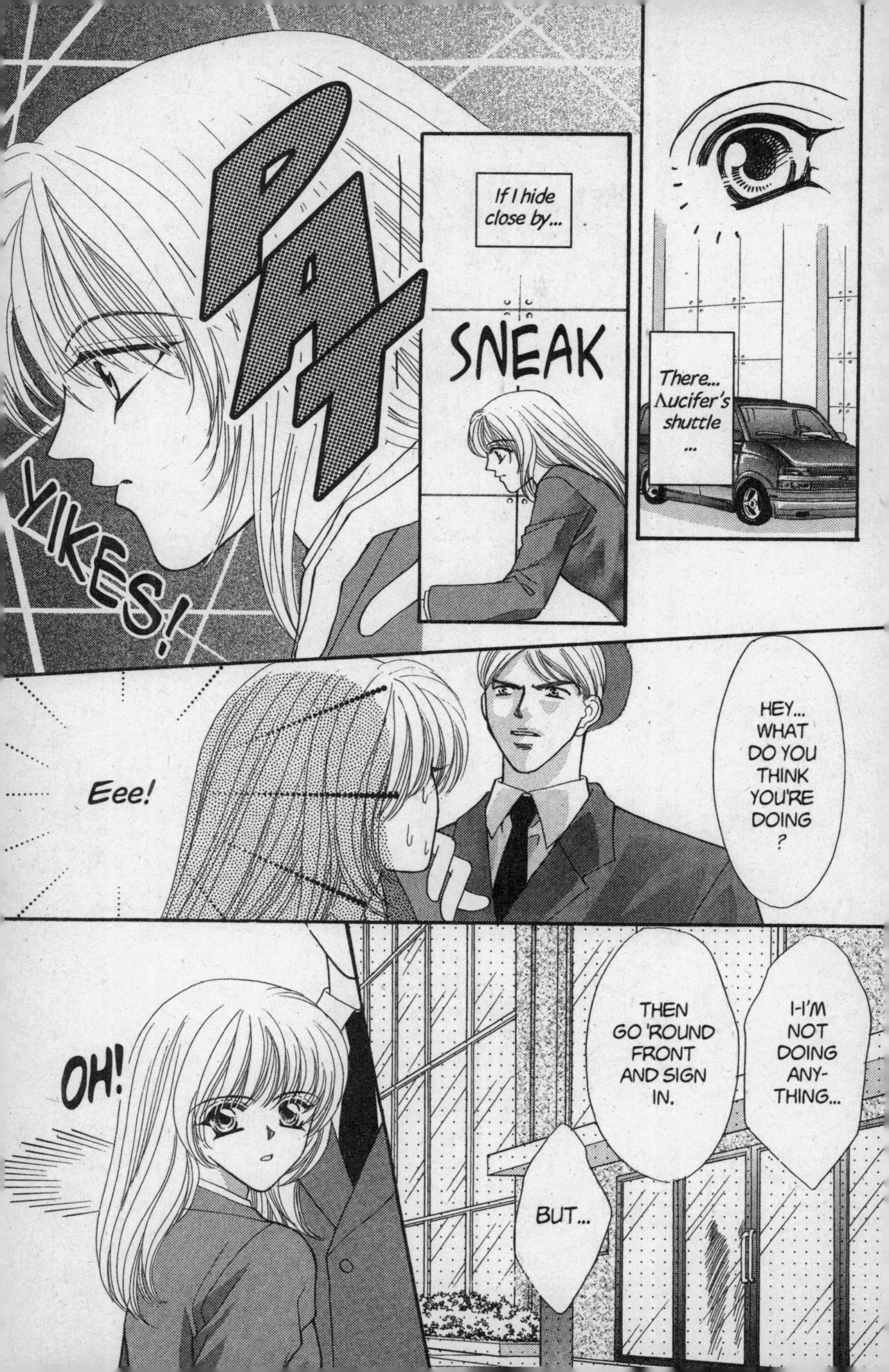
There... Lucifer's shuttle ...
If I hide close by...
SNEAK
PAT
YIKES!
HEY... WHAT DO YOU THINK YOU'RE DOING ?
Eee!
I-I'M NOT DOING ANY-THING...
THEN GO 'ROUND FRONT AND SIGN IN.
BUT...
OH!

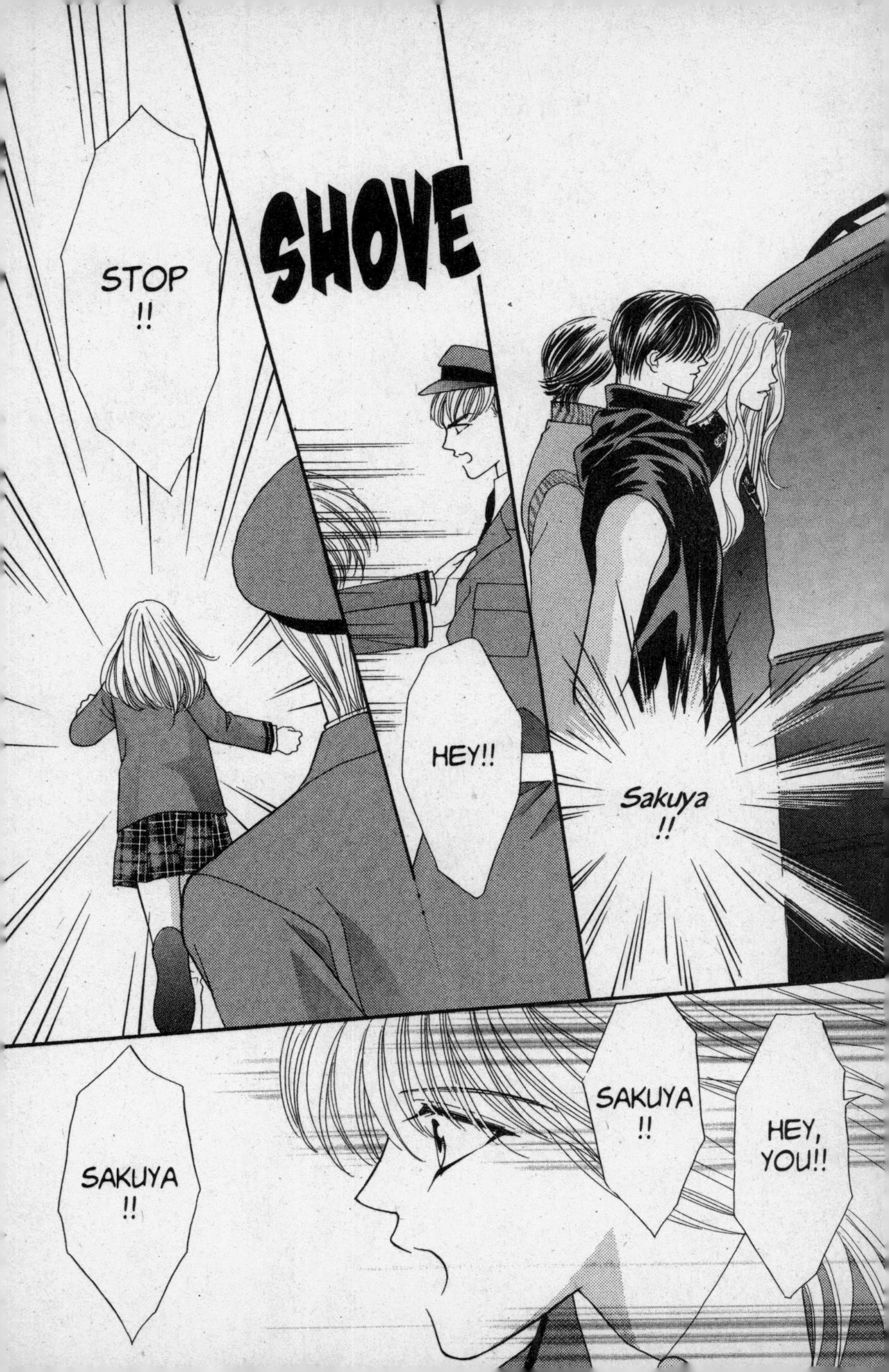
Sakuya !!
SHOVE
HEY!!
STOP !!
HEY, YOU!!
SAKUYA !!
SAKUYA !!

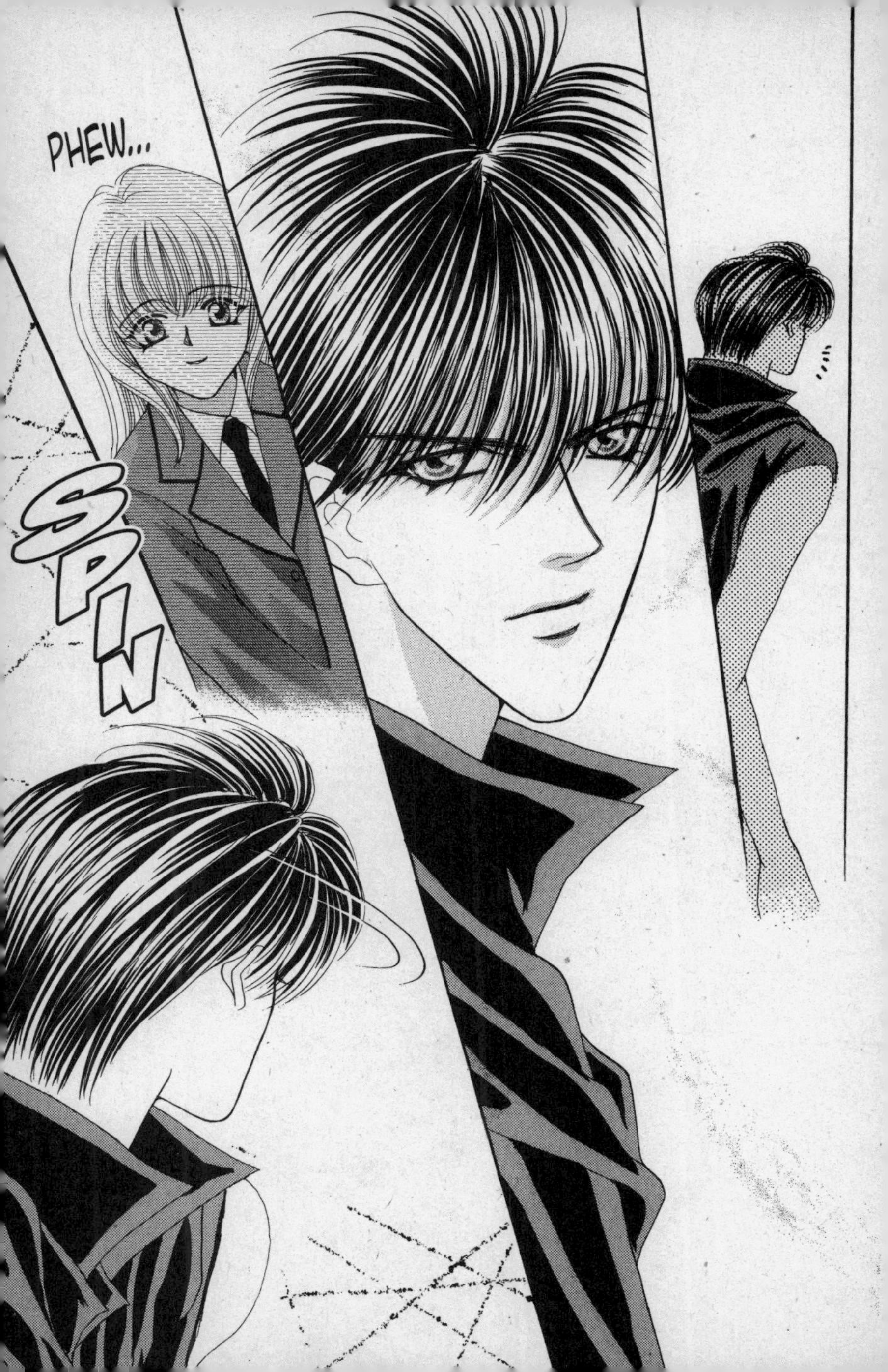
PHEW...
SPIN

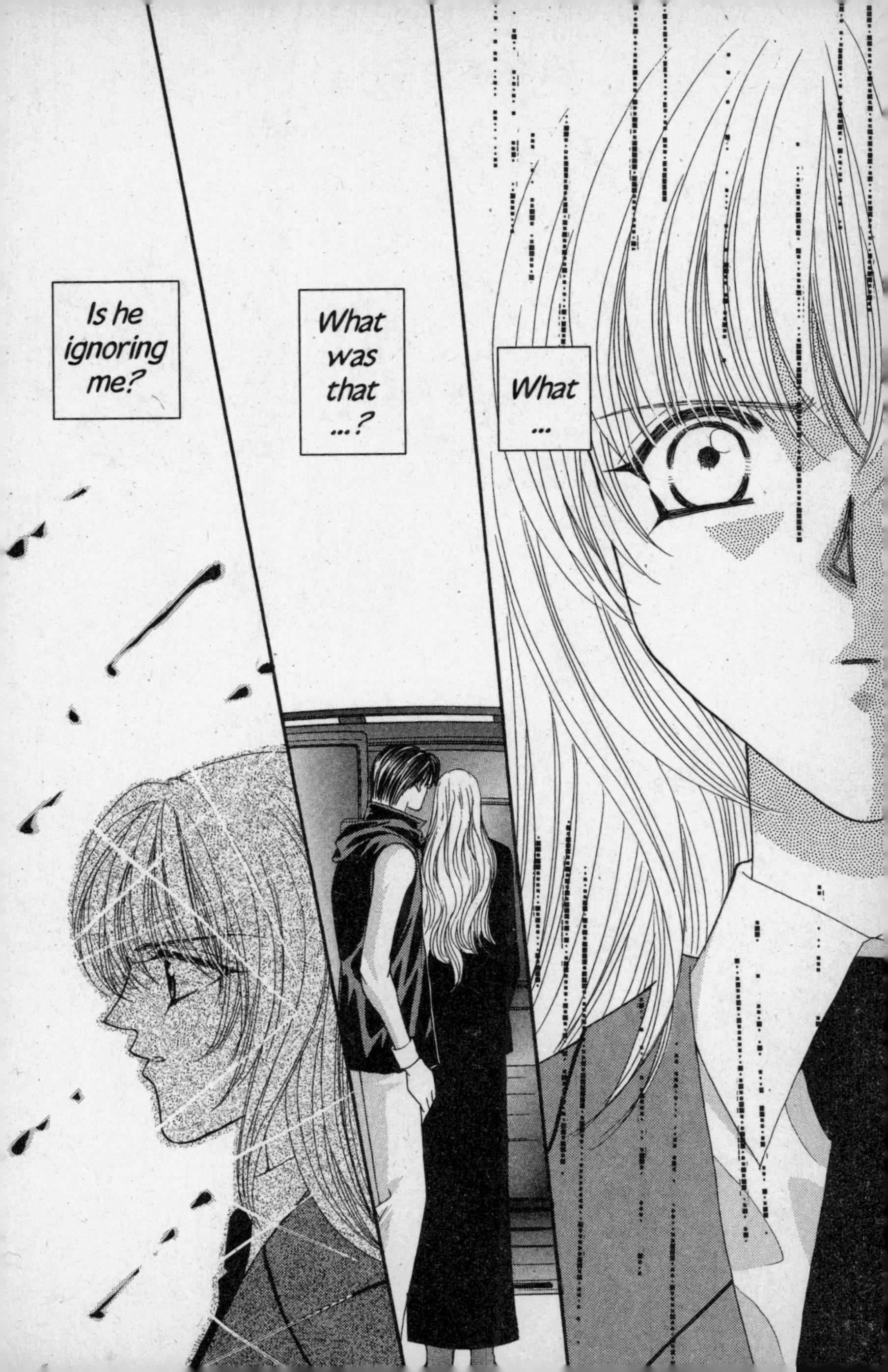
What ...
What was that ...?
Is he ignoring me?

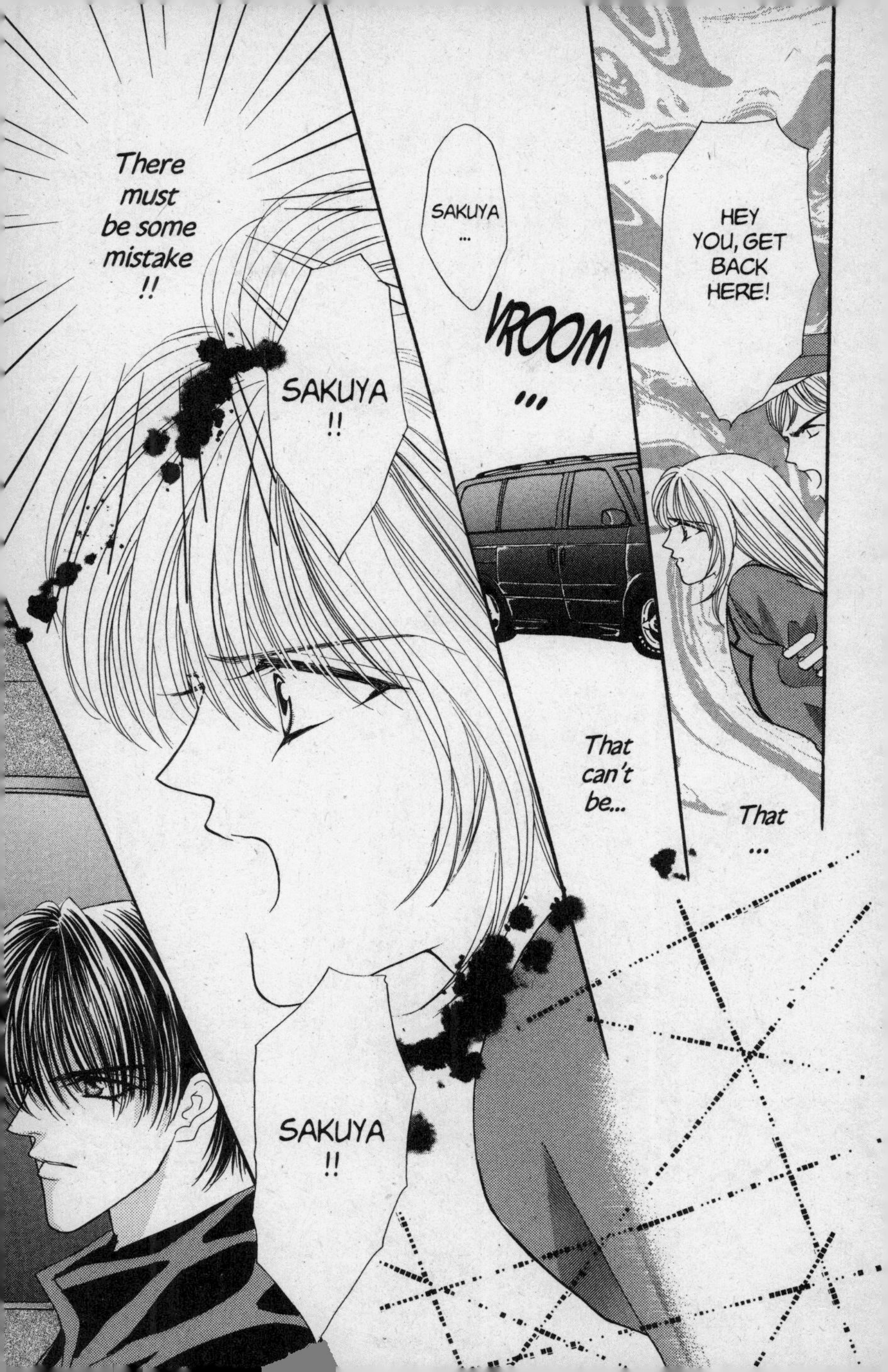
HEY YOU, GET BACK HERE!
SAKUYA ...
VROOM ...
That ...
That can't be...
There must be some mistake !!
SAKUYA !!
SAKUYA !!

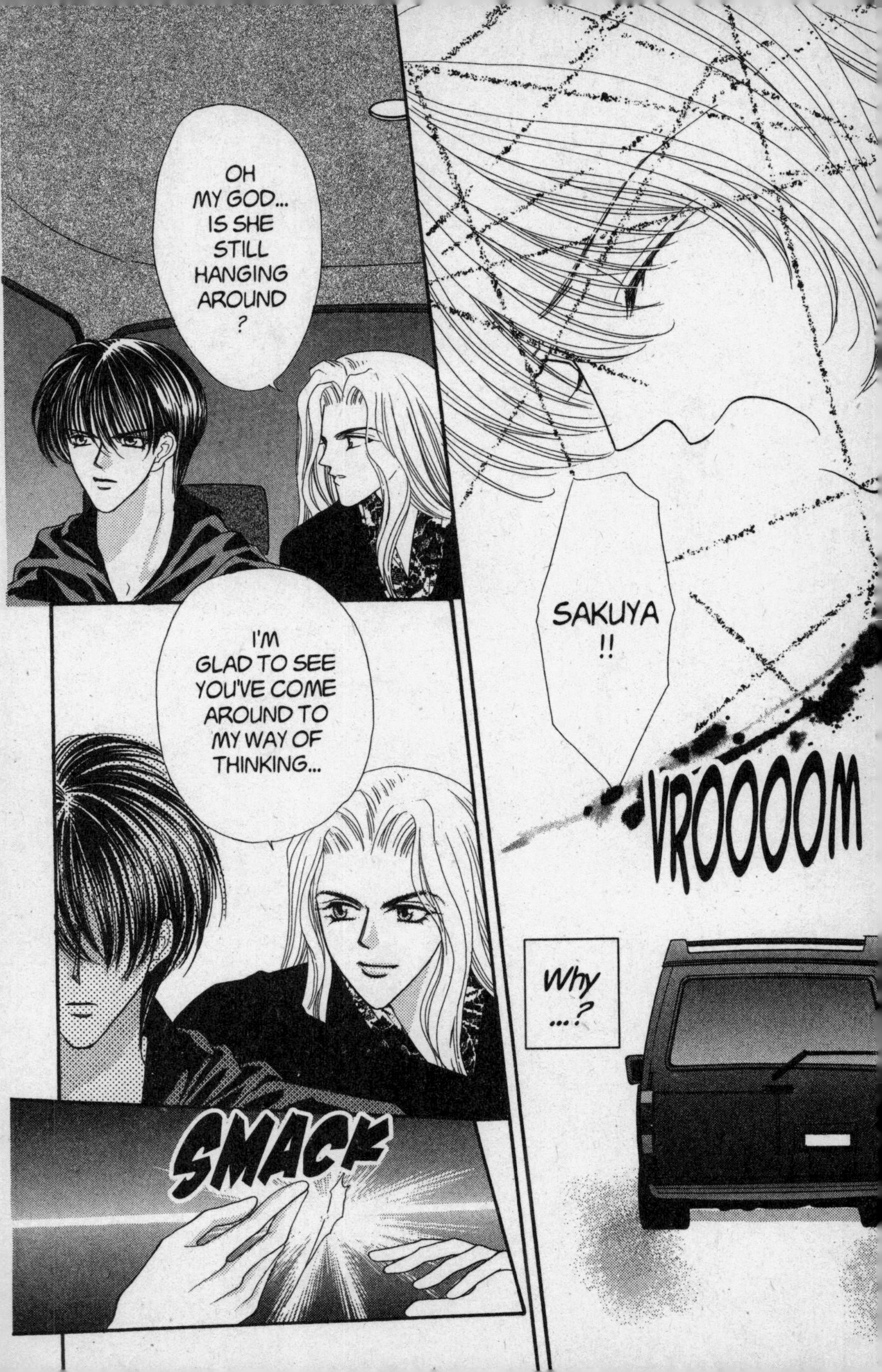
SAKUYA !!
VROOOOM
Why ...?
OH MY GOD... IS SHE STILL HANGING AROUND ?
I'M GLAD TO SEE YOU'VE COME AROUND TO MY WAY OF THINKING...
SMACK

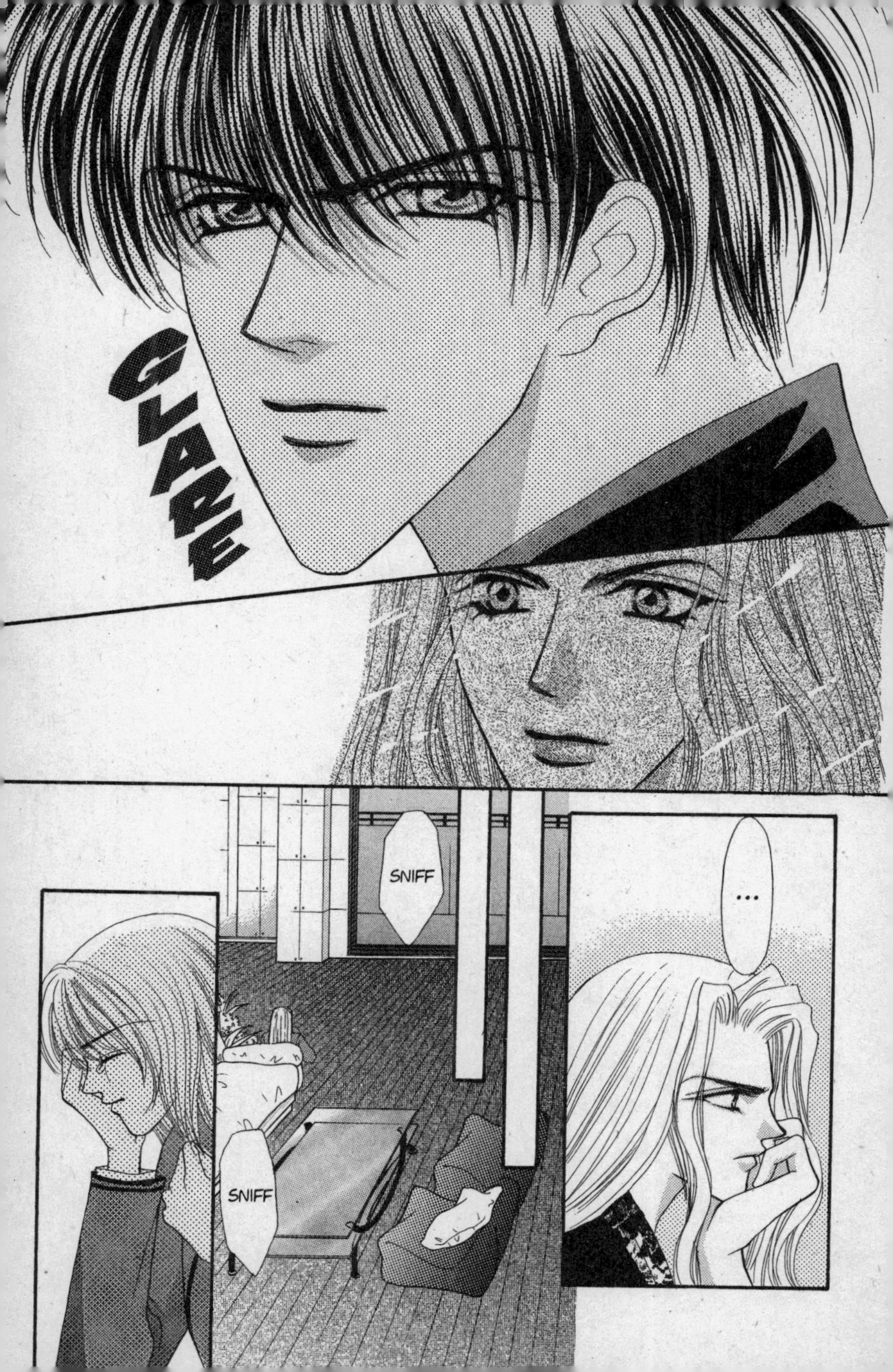
GLARE
...
SNIFF
SNIFF

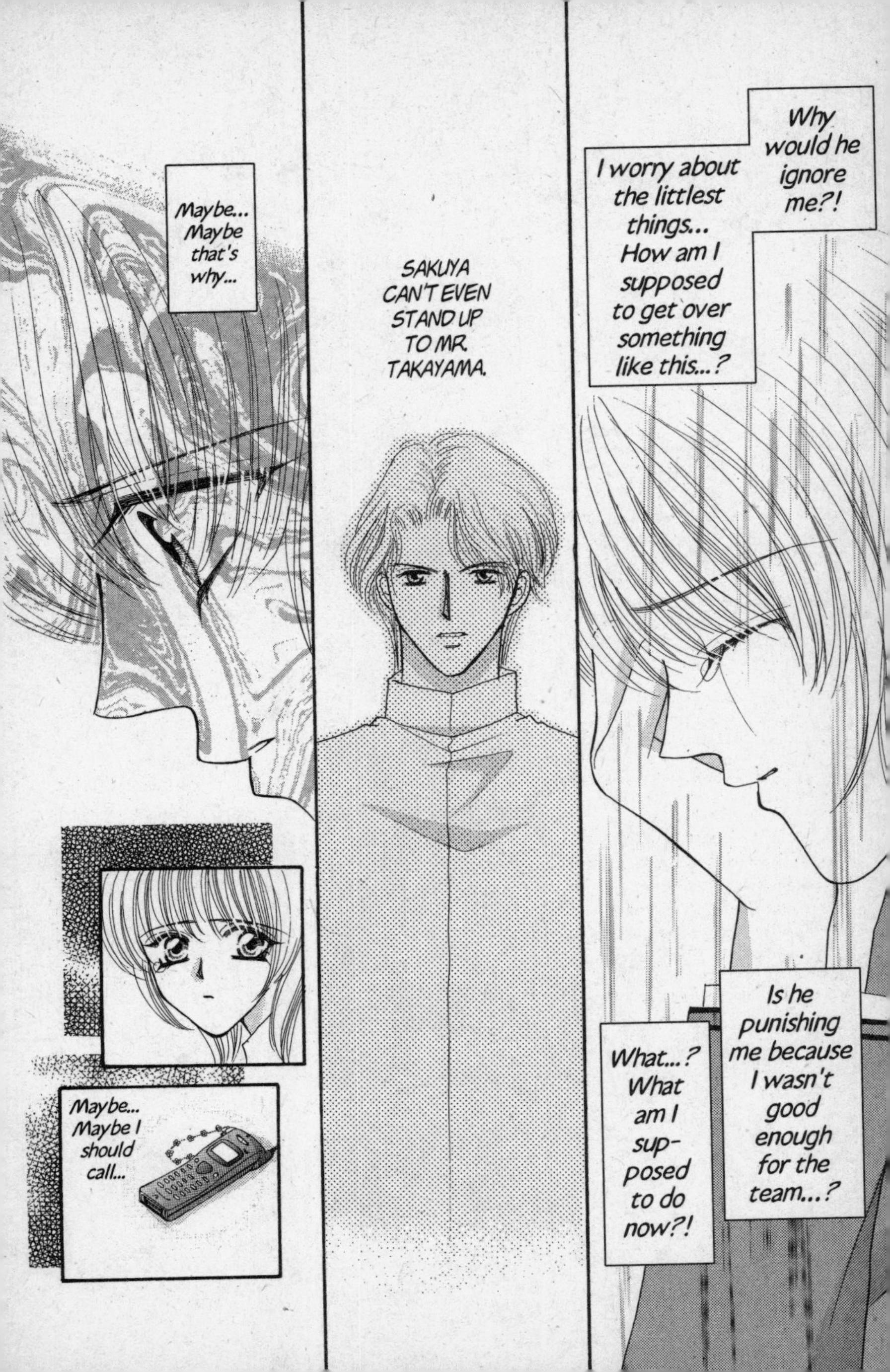
Why would he ignore me?!
I worry about the littlest things... How am I supposed to get over something like this...?
Is he punishing me because I wasn't good enough for the team...?
What...? What am I sup-posed to do now?!
SAKUYA CAN'T EVEN STAND UP TO MR. TAKAYAMA.
Maybe... Maybe that's why...
Maybe... Maybe I should call...

Λucifer Live Report!!
I was there!! Λucifer's debut shows: 8/25 in Osaka and 8/31 in Tokyo. The Tokyo show sold out in one hour! Wow... I was shocked!

I wasn't sure what kind of show it was gonna be, so I thought I'd watch from the stands—that was a big mistake! I was completely overwhelmed. The fans were going crazy from the very first moment of the very first song. They were screaming the names of the band members at the top of their lungs!! Then there was the screaming for an encore! In Tokyo, Chisato (of the band Penicillin) appeared as a special guest!! He wrote the second single, you know, so he came and played "Plas Magic" with Λucifer. (O-Jiro and Gisho showed up to watch the show, too.)

Makato was so! cool! Unbelievable. How can I even explain it? It made me feel very blessed. Is that corny?

They showed scenes from the latest Sensual Phrase anime episode—where Aine makes her first appearance. The second Aine appeared on the screen, there was a huge cheer. I was surprised at how popular she is. They played Λucifer's "Fallen Angel Blue" video after that, it was all so very cool. I love that video.

It is such a dream come true to see a band that I created come to life. There were kids outside holding signs saying "need tickets." I was touched by that, too.

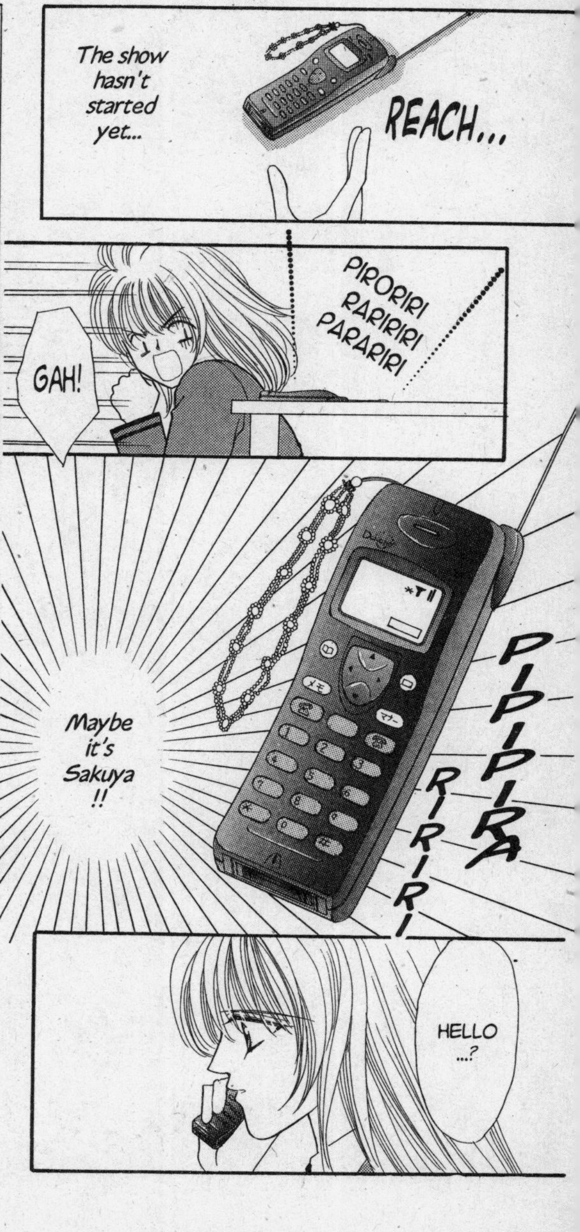
REACH...
The show hasn't started yet...
PIRORIRI RARIRIRI PARARIRI
GAH!
PIPIPIRA
RIRIRIRI
Maybe it's Sakuya!!
HELLO ...?

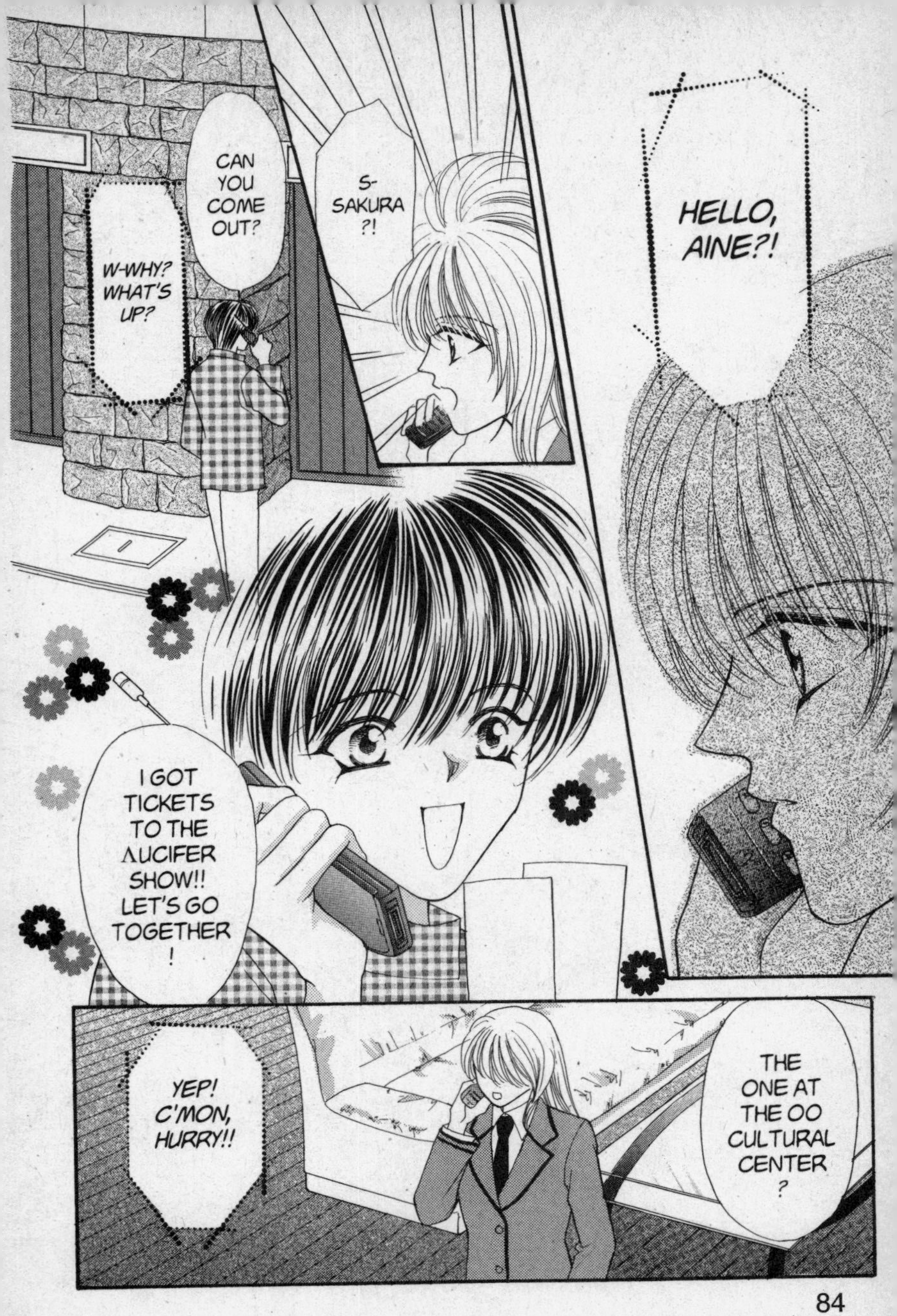
HELLO, AINE?!
S-SAKURA?!
CAN YOU COME OUT?
W-WHY? WHAT'S UP?
I GOT TICKETS TO THE ΛUCIFER SHOW!! LET'S GO TOGETHER!
THE ONE AT THE OO CULTURAL CENTER?
YEP! C'MON, HURRY!!

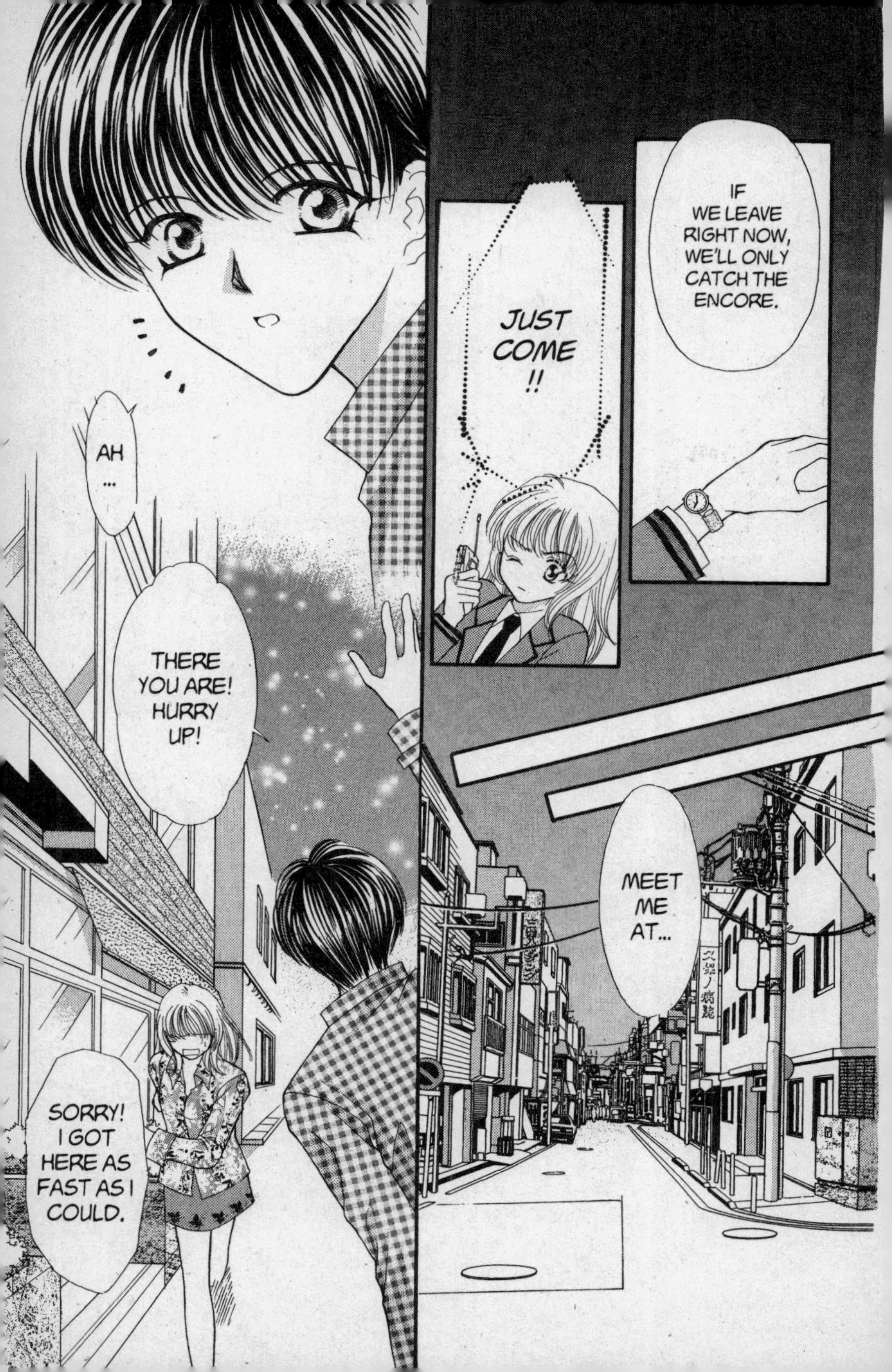
IF WE LEAVE RIGHT NOW, WE'LL ONLY CATCH THE ENCORE.
JUST COME !!
MEET ME AT...
AH ...
THERE YOU ARE! HURRY UP!
SORRY! I GOT HERE AS FAST AS I COULD.

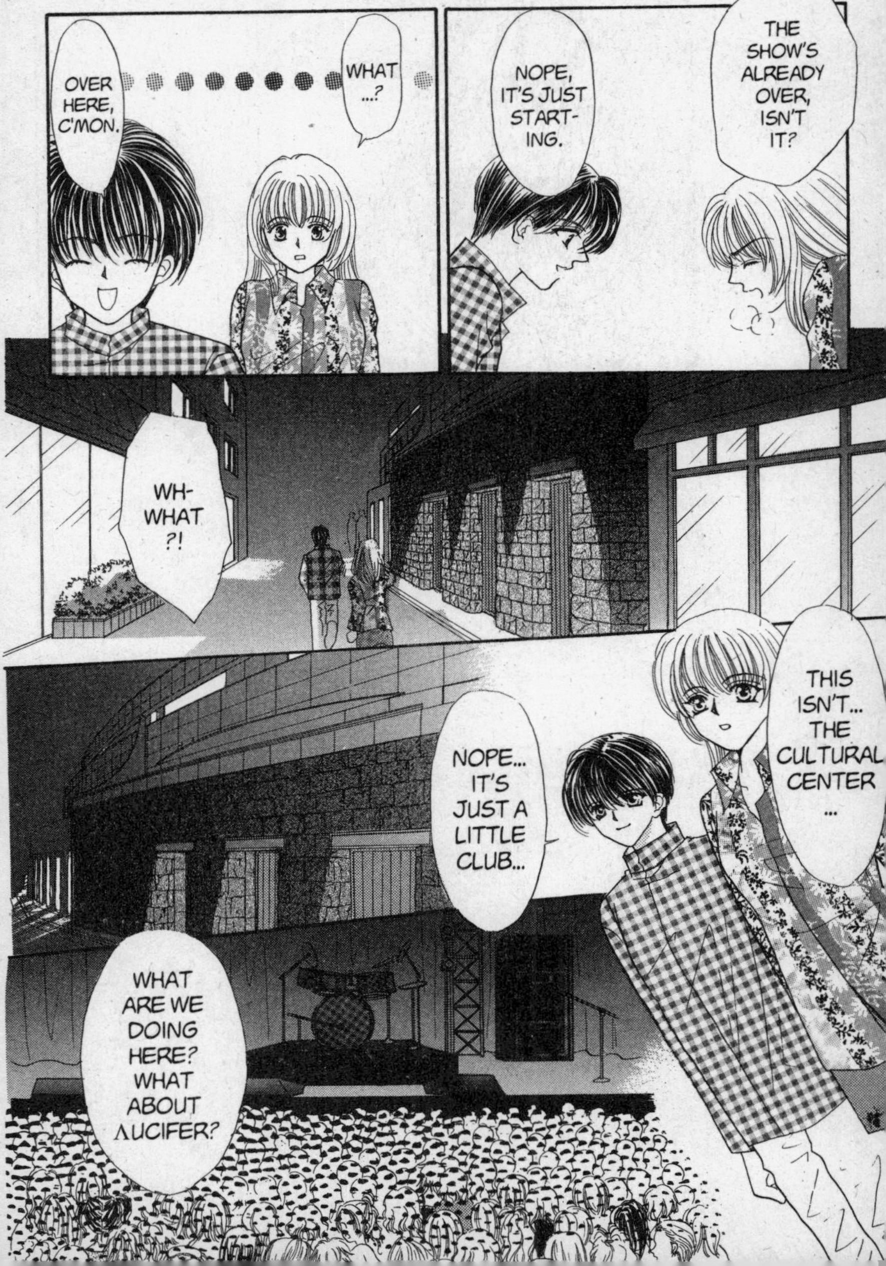
THE SHOW'S ALREADY OVER, ISN'T IT?
NOPE, IT'S JUST START-ING.
WHAT ...?
OVER HERE, C'MON.
WH-WHAT ?!
THIS ISN'T... THE CULTURAL CENTER ...
NOPE... IT'S JUST A LITTLE CLUB...
WHAT ARE WE DOING HERE? WHAT ABOUT ΛUCIFER?

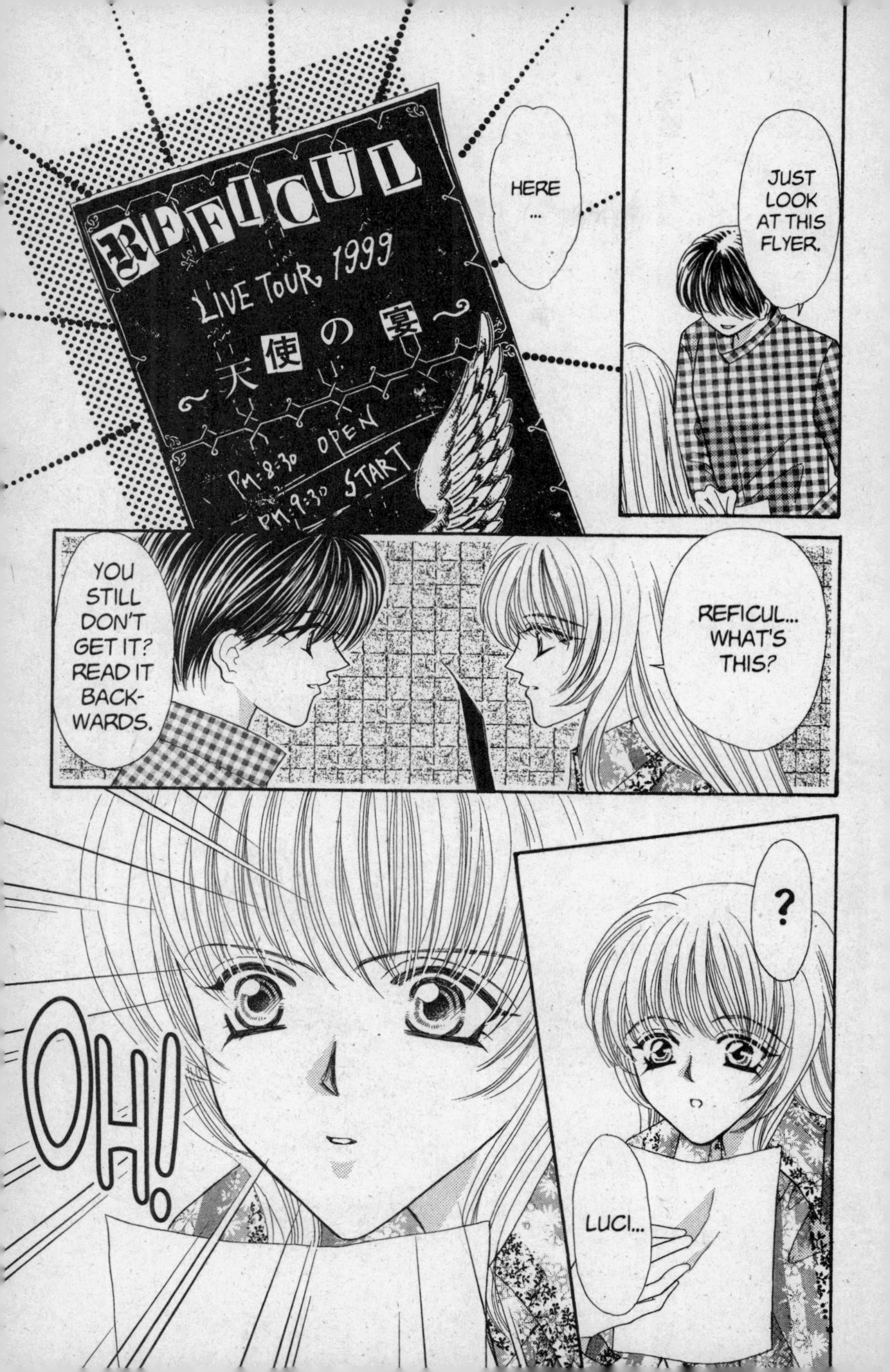
JUST LOOK AT THIS FLYER.
HERE ...
REFICUL
LIVE TOUR 1999
~天使の宴~
PM 8:30 OPEN
PM 9:30 START
REFICUL... WHAT'S THIS?
YOU STILL DON'T GET IT? READ IT BACKWARDS.
?
LUCI...
OH!

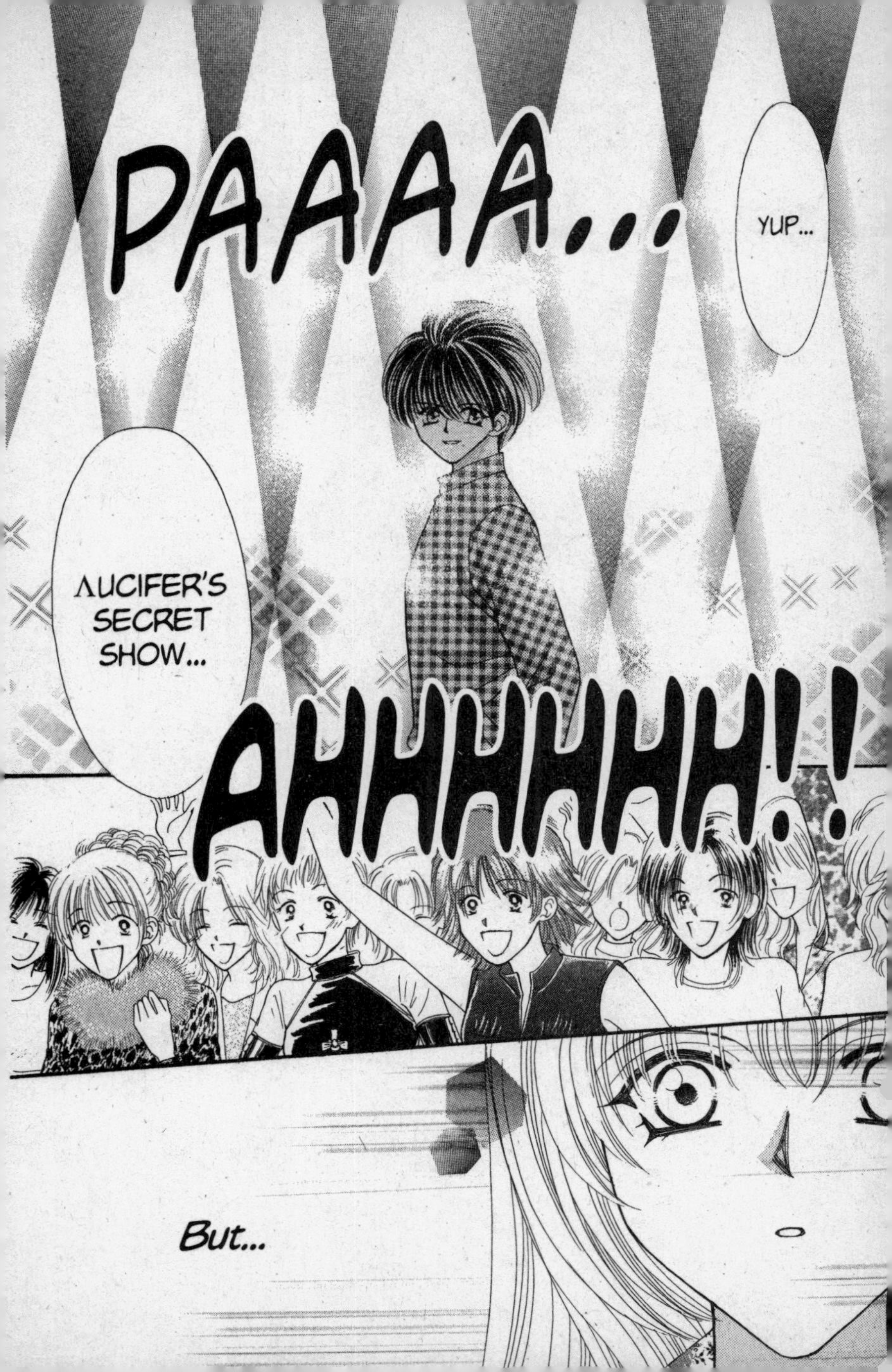
PAAAA...
YUP...
ΛUCIFER'S SECRET SHOW...
AHHHHHH!!
But...

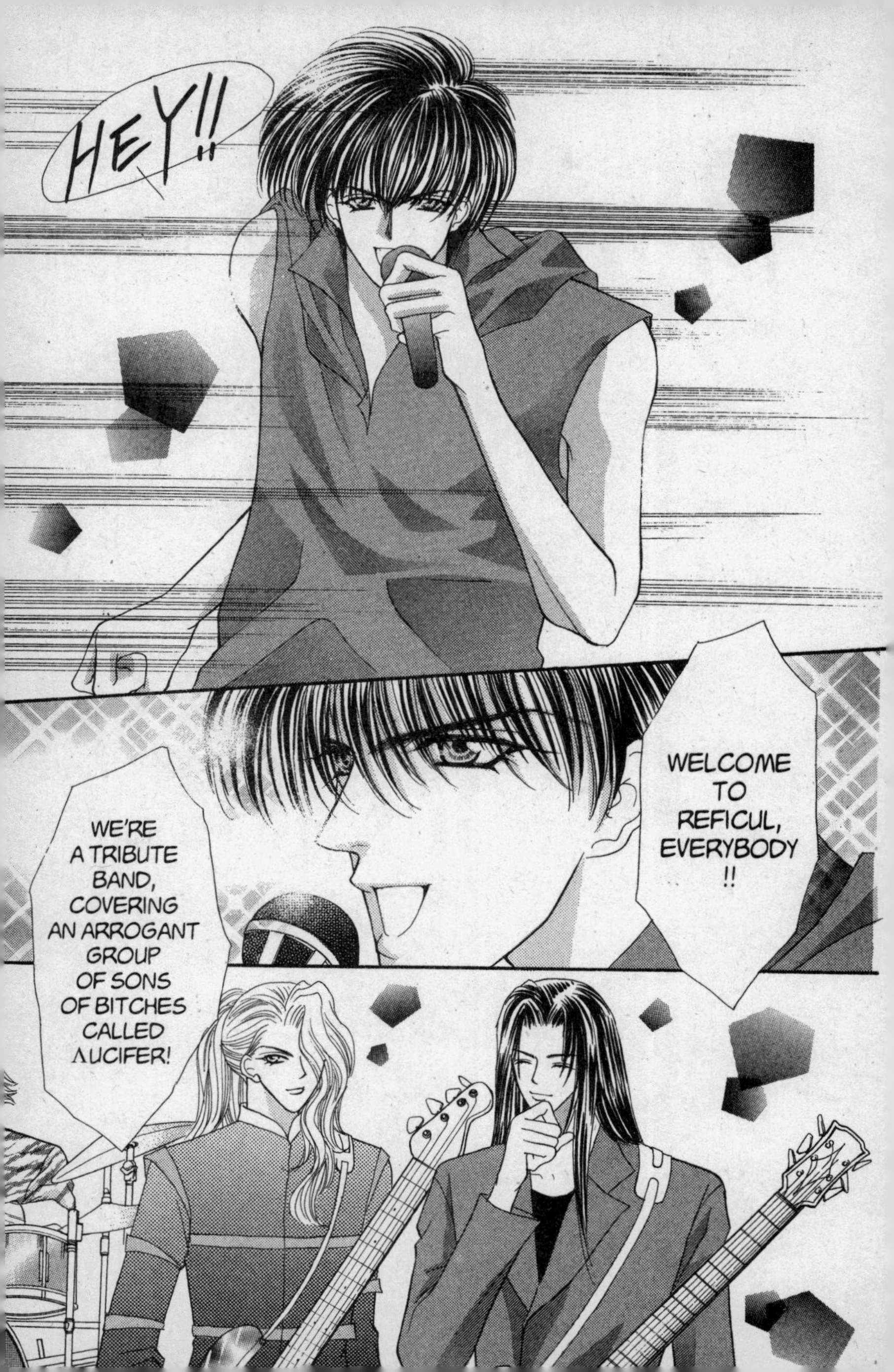
HEY!!
WELCOME TO REFICUL, EVERYBODY !!
WE'RE A TRIBUTE BAND, COVERING AN ARROGANT GROUP OF SONS OF BITCHES CALLED ΛUCIFER!

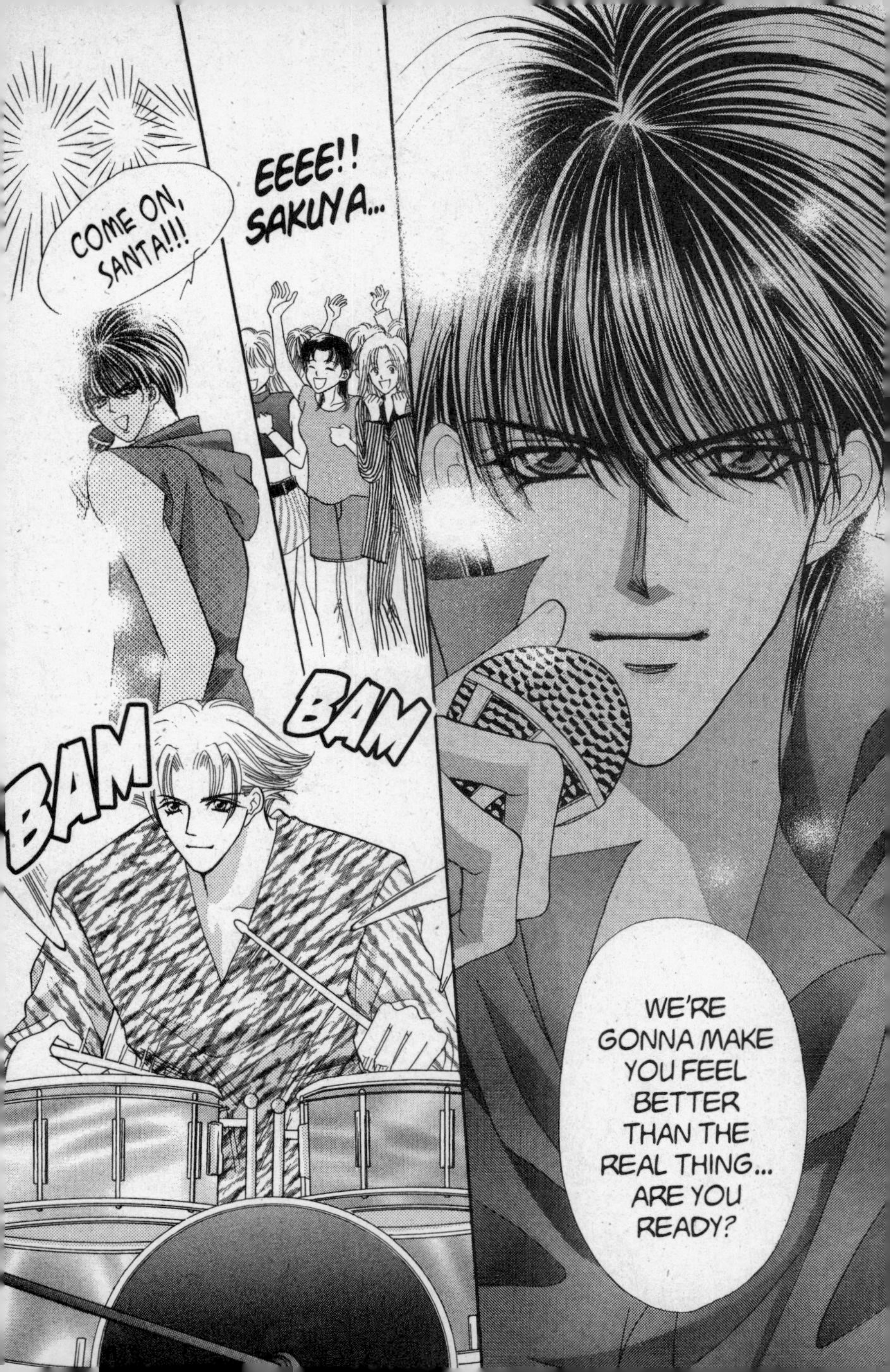
WE'RE GONNA MAKE YOU FEEL BETTER THAN THE REAL THING... ARE YOU READY?
EEEE!! SAKUYA...
COME ON, SANTA!!!
BAM
BAM

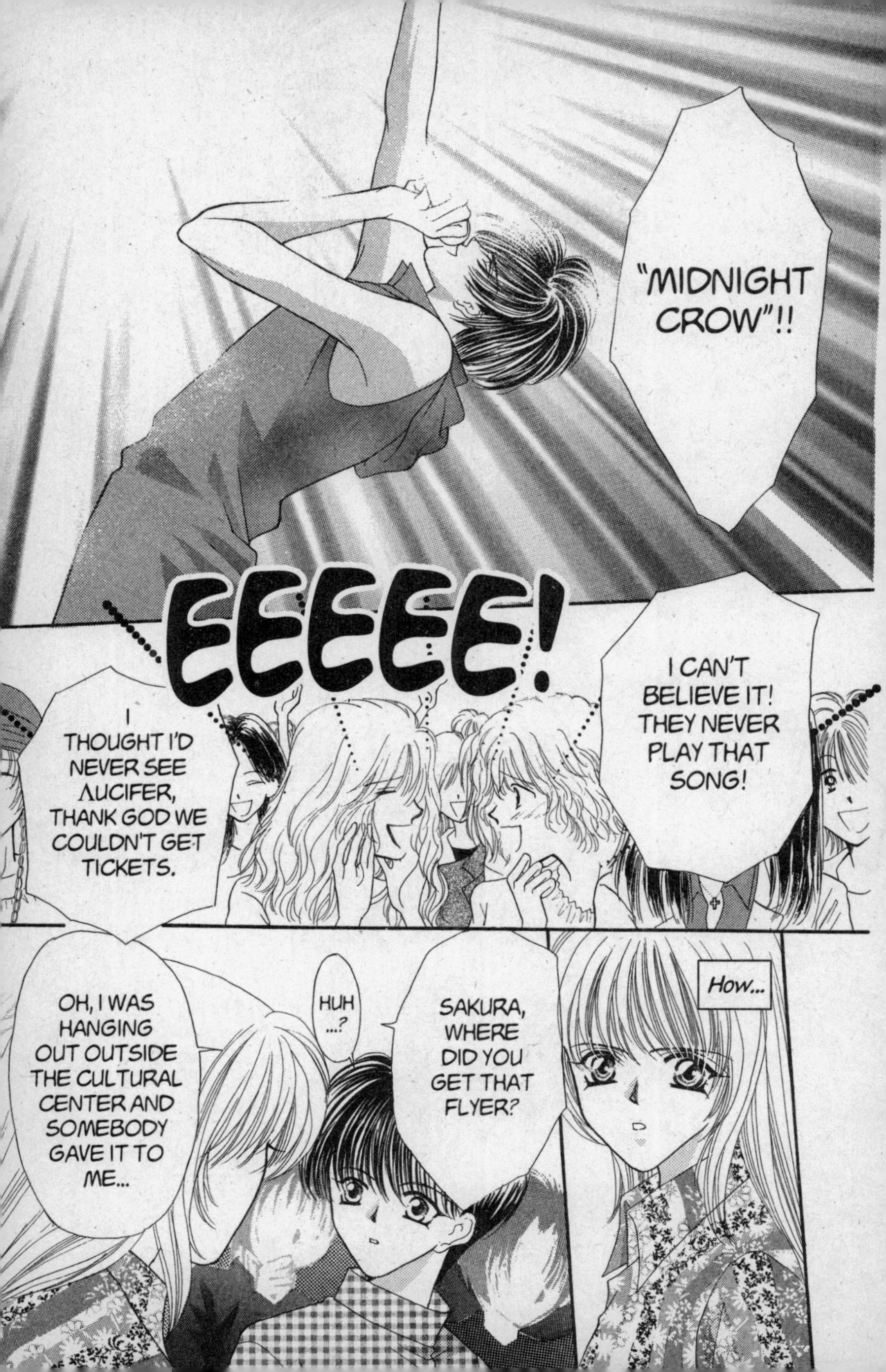
"MIDNIGHT CROW"!!
EEEEE!
I CAN'T BELIEVE IT! THEY NEVER PLAY THAT SONG!
I THOUGHT I'D NEVER SEE ΛUCIFER, THANK GOD WE COULDN'T GET TICKETS.
How...
SAKURA, WHERE DID YOU GET THAT FLYER?
HUH ...?
OH, I WAS HANGING OUT OUTSIDE THE CULTURAL CENTER AND SOMEBODY GAVE IT TO ME...

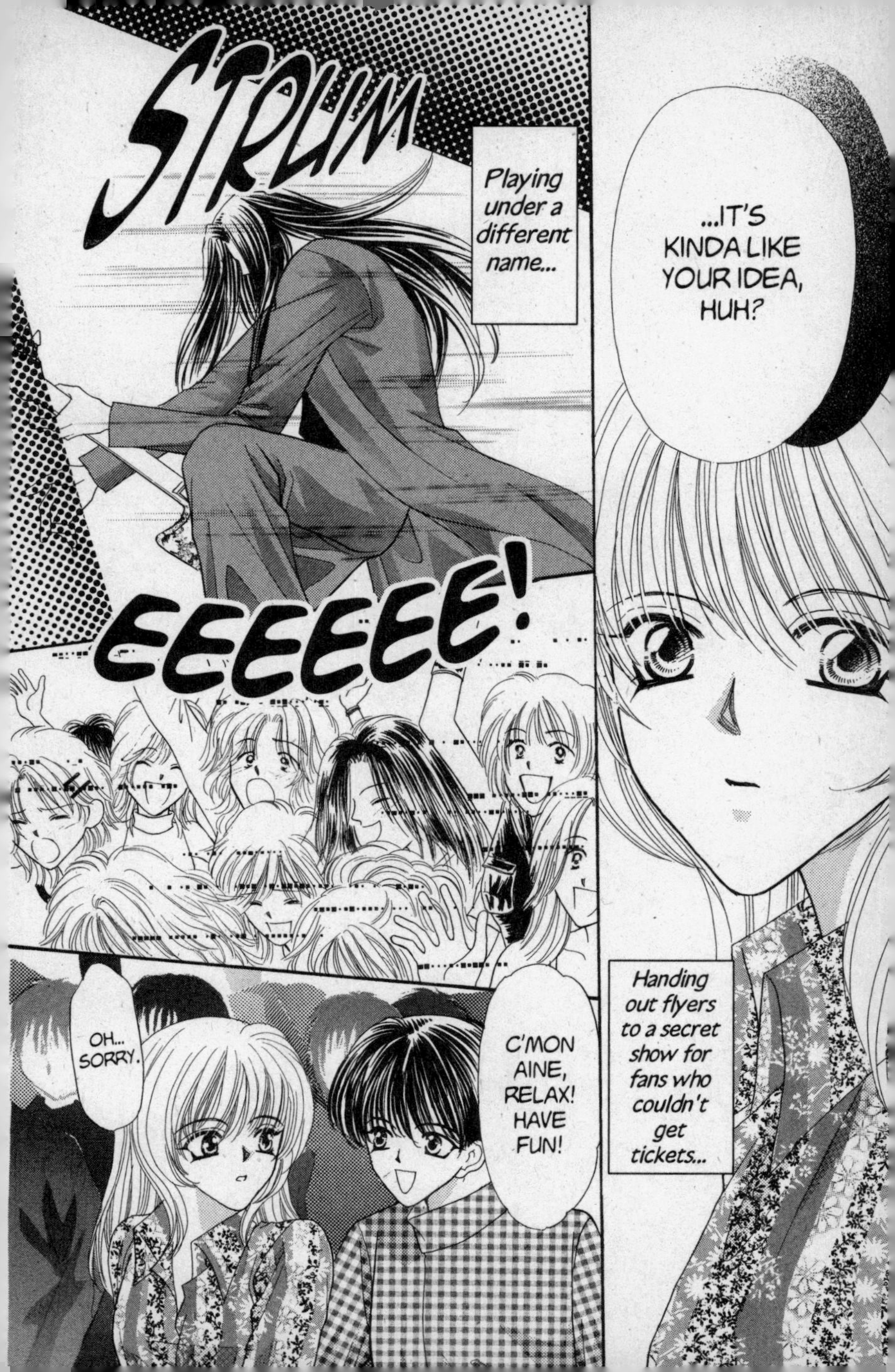
...IT'S KINDA LIKE YOUR IDEA, HUH?
Handing out flyers to a secret show for fans who couldn't get tickets...
STRUM
Playing under a different name...
EEEEEE!
C'MON AINE, RELAX! HAVE FUN!
OH... SORRY.

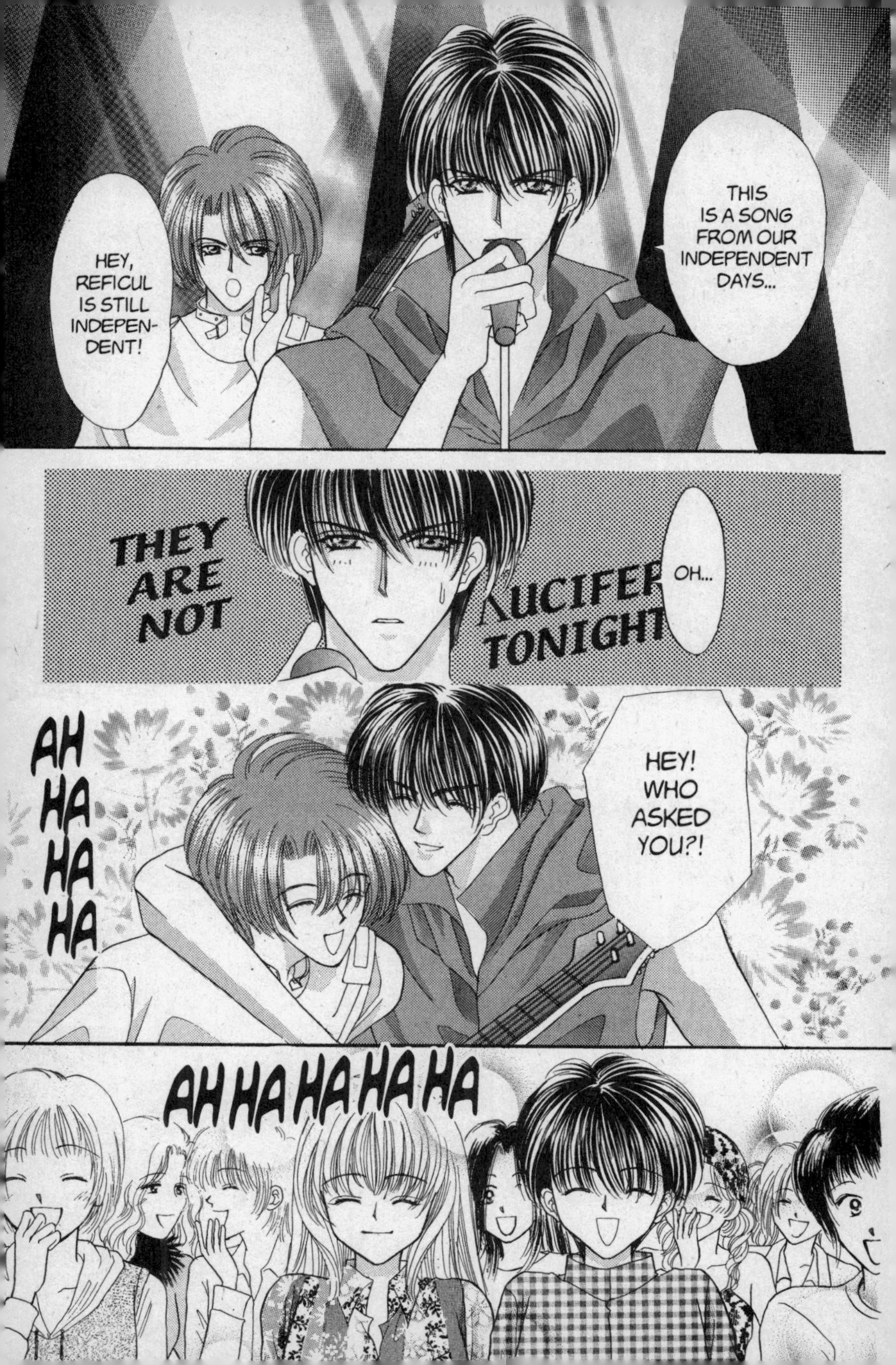
THIS IS A SONG FROM OUR INDEPENDENT DAYS...
HEY, REFICUL IS STILL INDEPEN- DENT!
OH...
THEY ARE NOT LUCIFER TONIGHT
HEY! WHO ASKED YOU?!
AH HA HA HA HA
AH HA HA HA HA HA

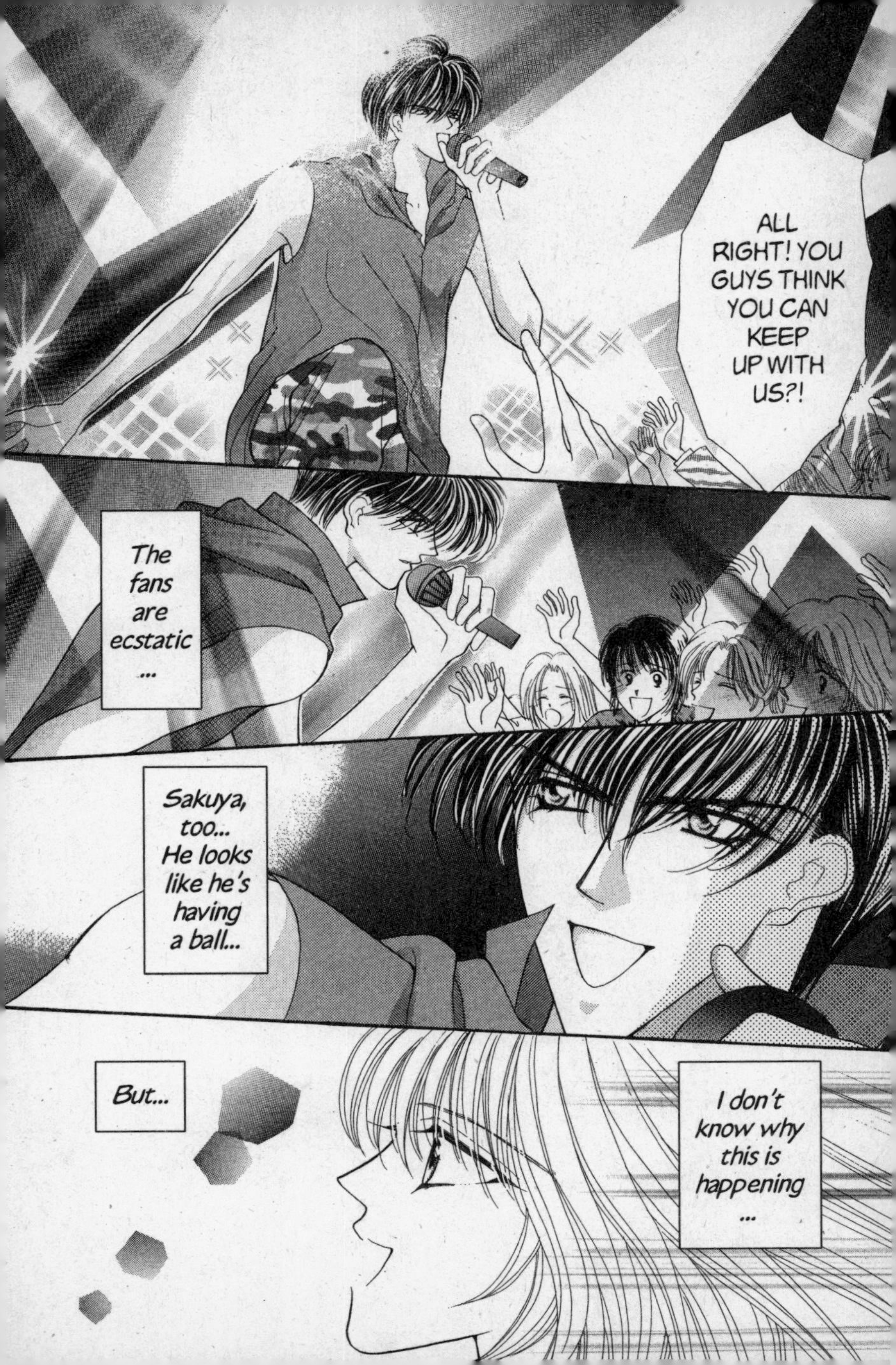
ALL RIGHT! YOU GUYS THINK YOU CAN KEEP UP WITH US?!
The fans are ecstatic ...
Sakuya, too... He looks like he's having a ball...
I don't know why this is happening ...
But...

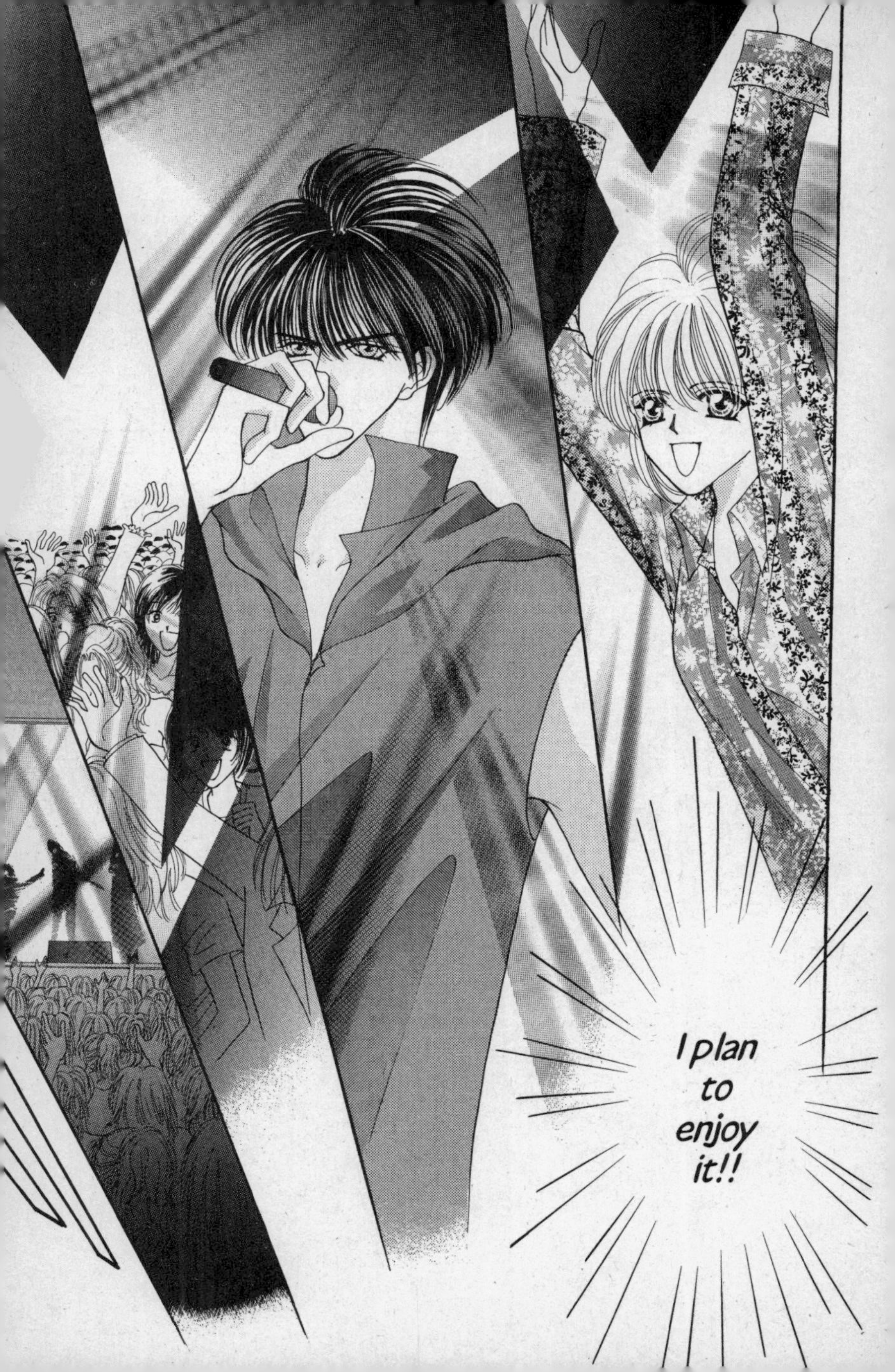
I plan to enjoy it!!

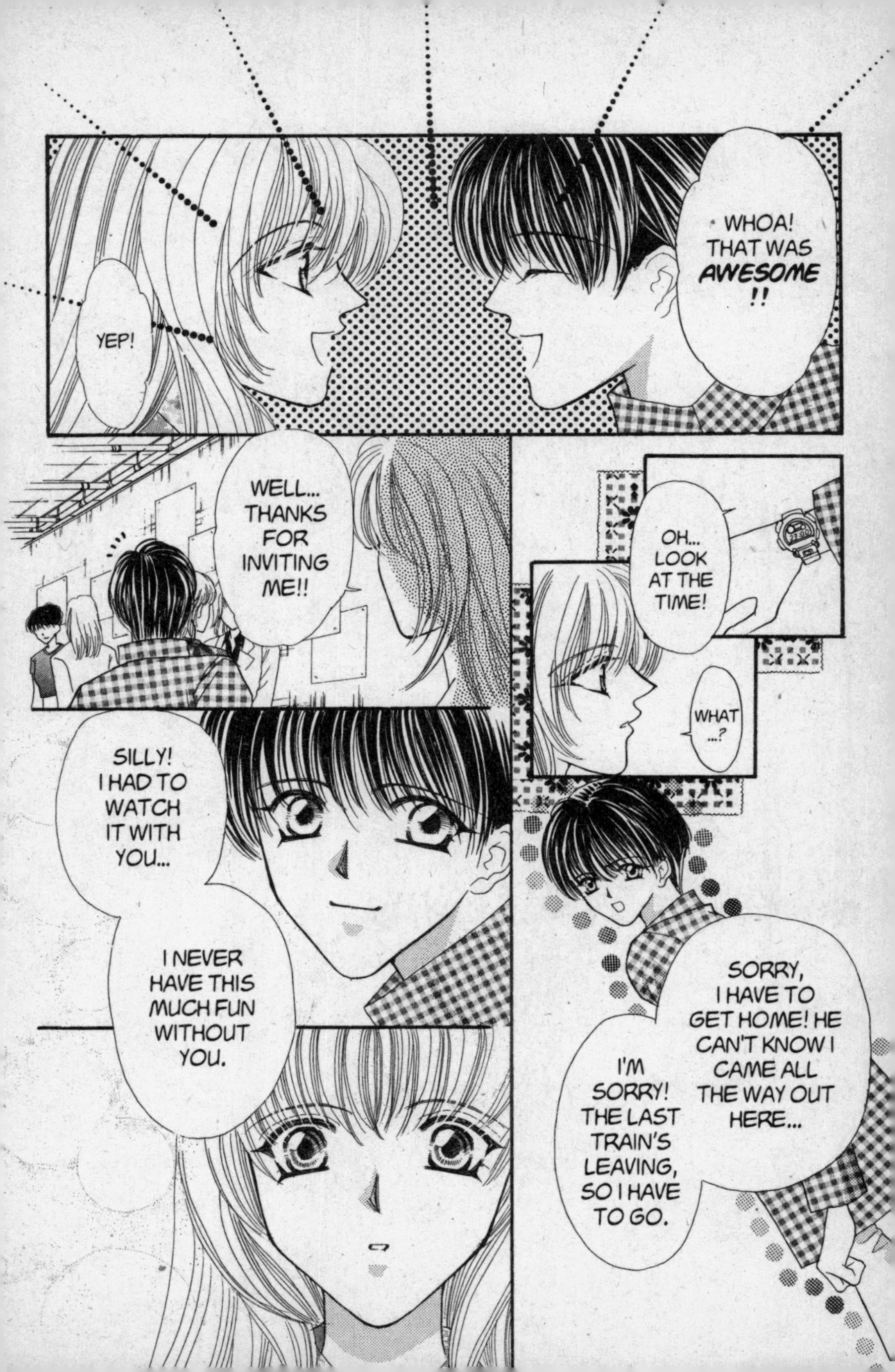
WHOA! THAT WAS **AWESOME** !!
YEP!
OH... LOOK AT THE TIME!
WHAT ...?
SORRY, I HAVE TO GET HOME! HE CAN'T KNOW I CAME ALL THE WAY OUT HERE...
I'M SORRY! THE LAST TRAIN'S LEAVING, SO I HAVE TO GO.
WELL... THANKS FOR INVITING ME!!
SILLY! I HAD TO WATCH IT WITH YOU...
I NEVER HAVE THIS MUCH FUN WITHOUT YOU.

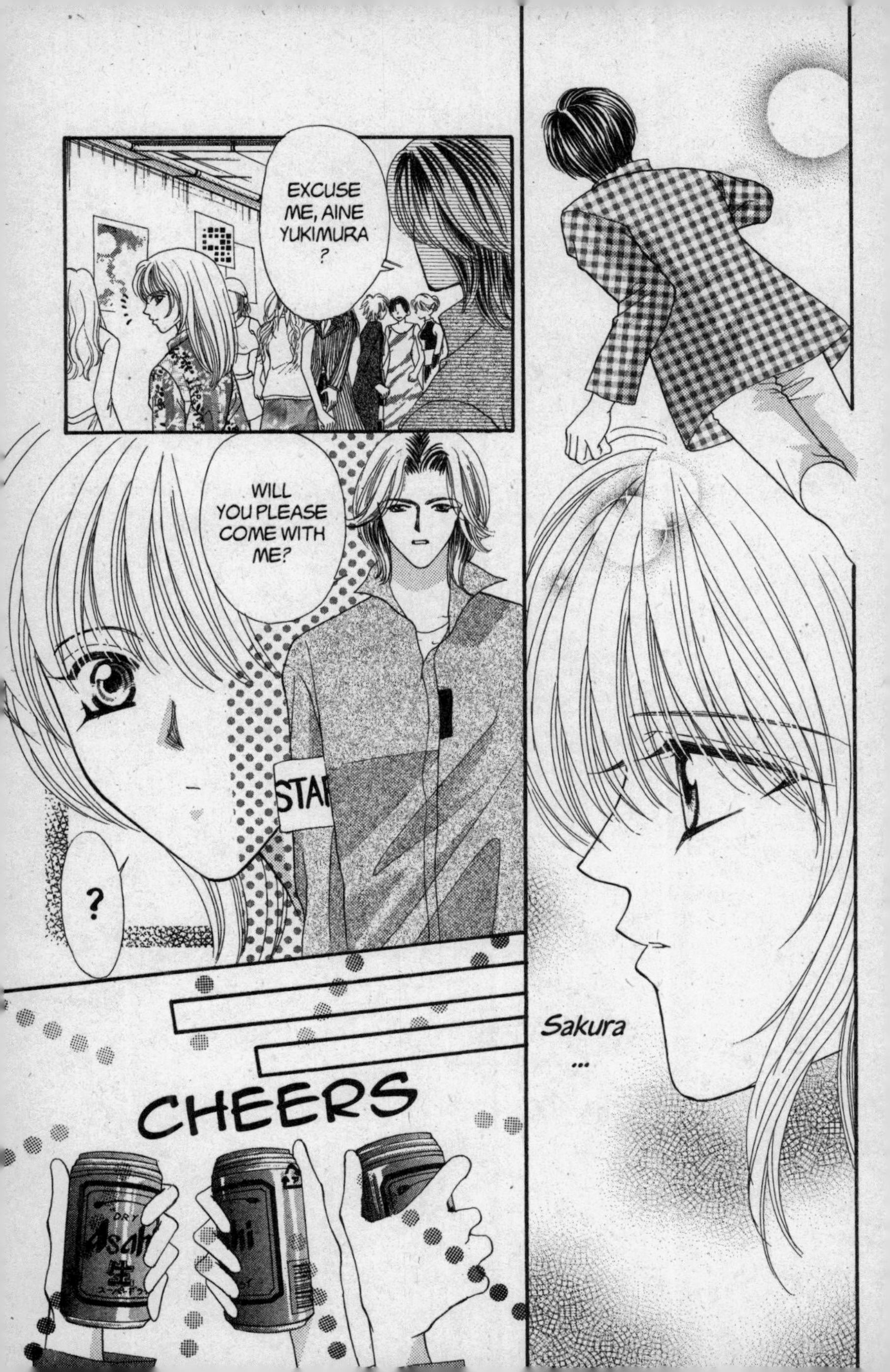
Sakura ...
EXCUSE ME, AINE YUKIMURA ?
WILL YOU PLEASE COME WITH ME?
?
CHEERS

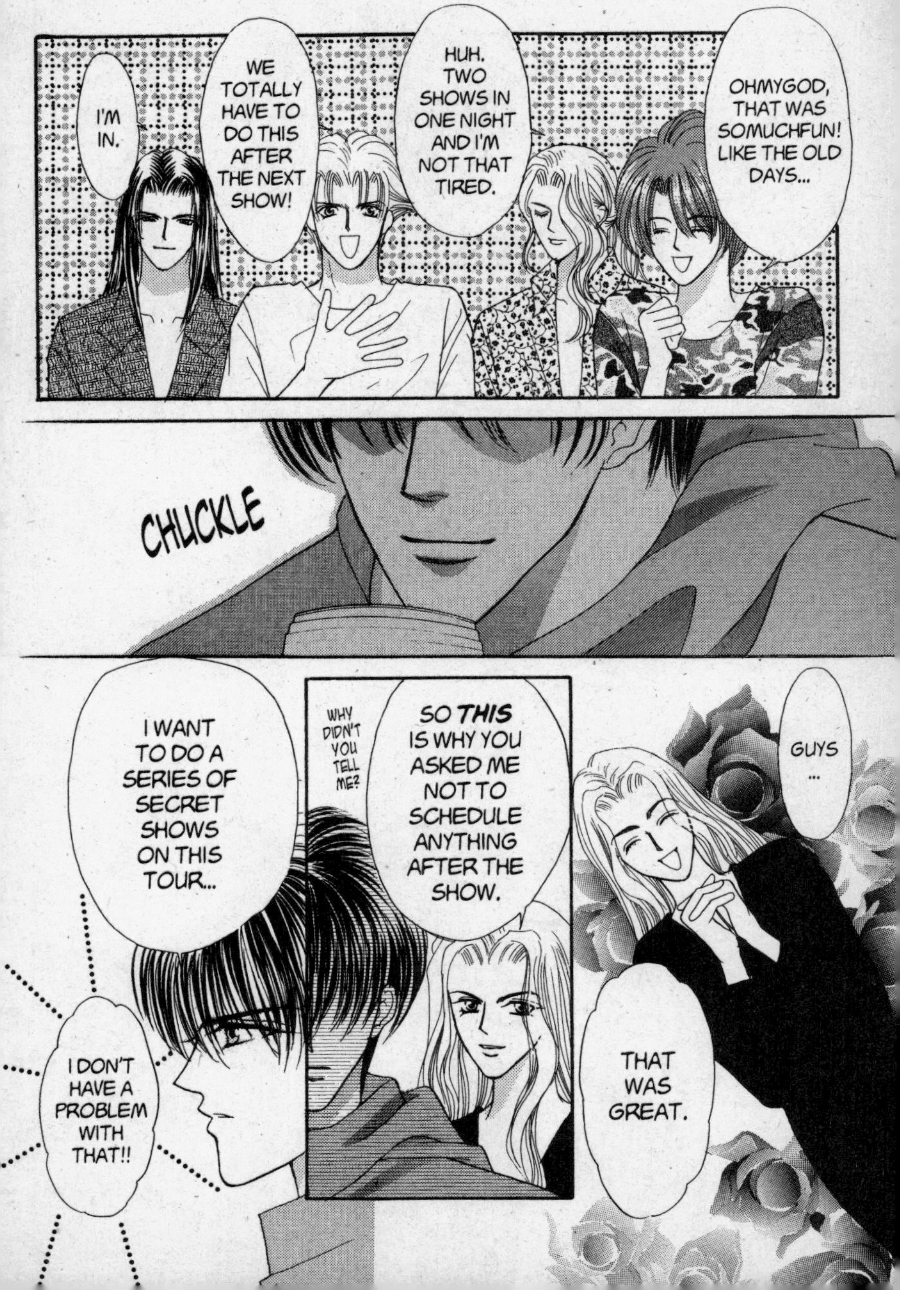
OHMYGOD, THAT WAS SOMUCHFUN! LIKE THE OLD DAYS...
HUH. TWO SHOWS IN ONE NIGHT AND I'M NOT THAT TIRED.
WE TOTALLY HAVE TO DO THIS AFTER THE NEXT SHOW!
I'M IN.
CHUCKLE
GUYS ...
THAT WAS GREAT.
SO **THIS** IS WHY YOU ASKED ME NOT TO SCHEDULE ANYTHING AFTER THE SHOW.
WHY DIDN'T YOU TELL ME?
I WANT TO DO A SERIES OF SECRET SHOWS ON THIS TOUR...
I DON'T HAVE A PROBLEM WITH THAT!!

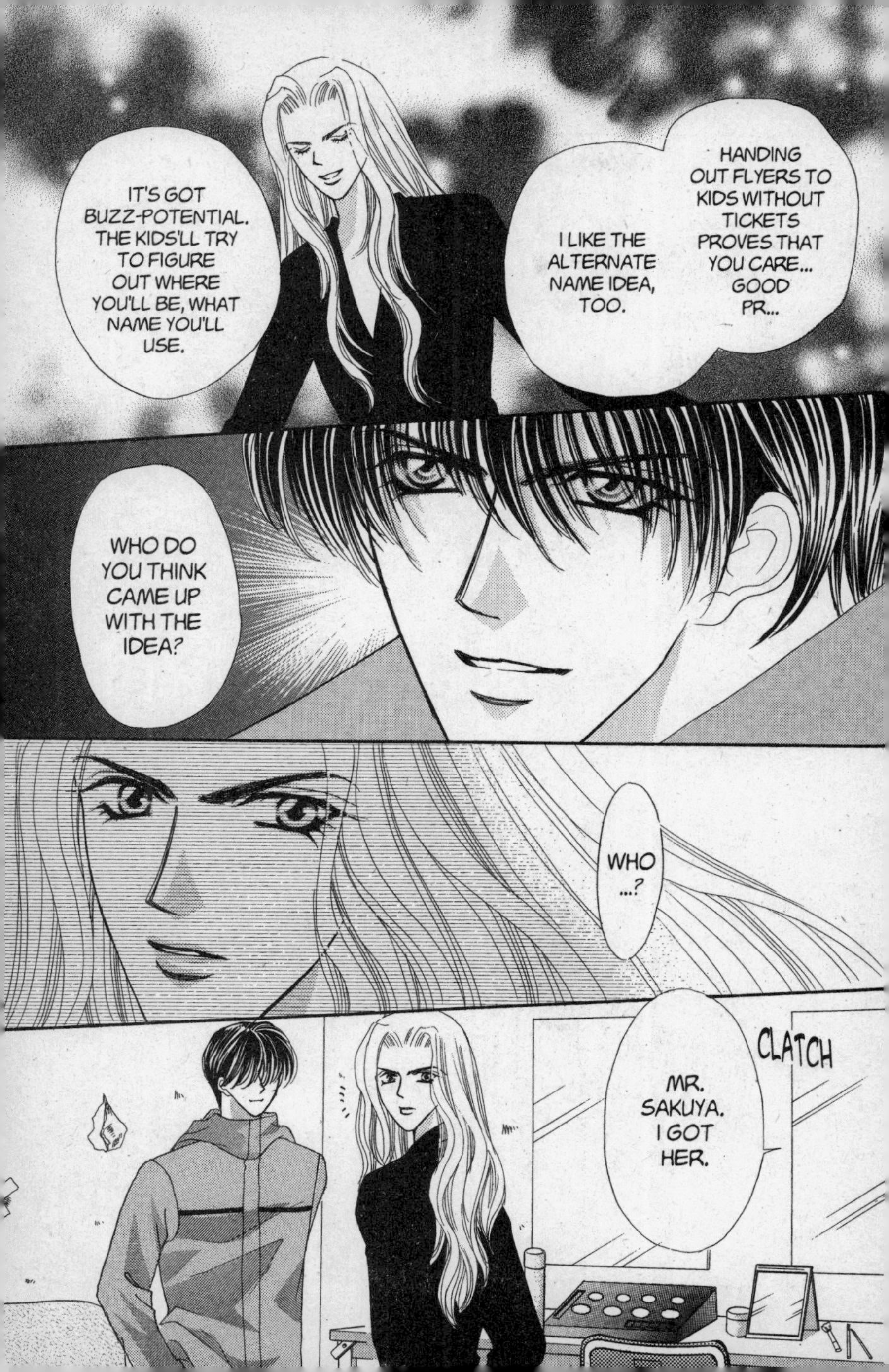
HANDING OUT FLYERS TO KIDS WITHOUT TICKETS PROVES THAT YOU CARE... GOOD PR...
I LIKE THE ALTERNATE NAME IDEA, TOO.
IT'S GOT BUZZ-POTENTIAL. THE KIDS'LL TRY TO FIGURE OUT WHERE YOU'LL BE, WHAT NAME YOU'LL USE.
WHO DO YOU THINK CAME UP WITH THE IDEA?
WHO ...?
CLATCH
MR. SAKUYA. I GOT HER.

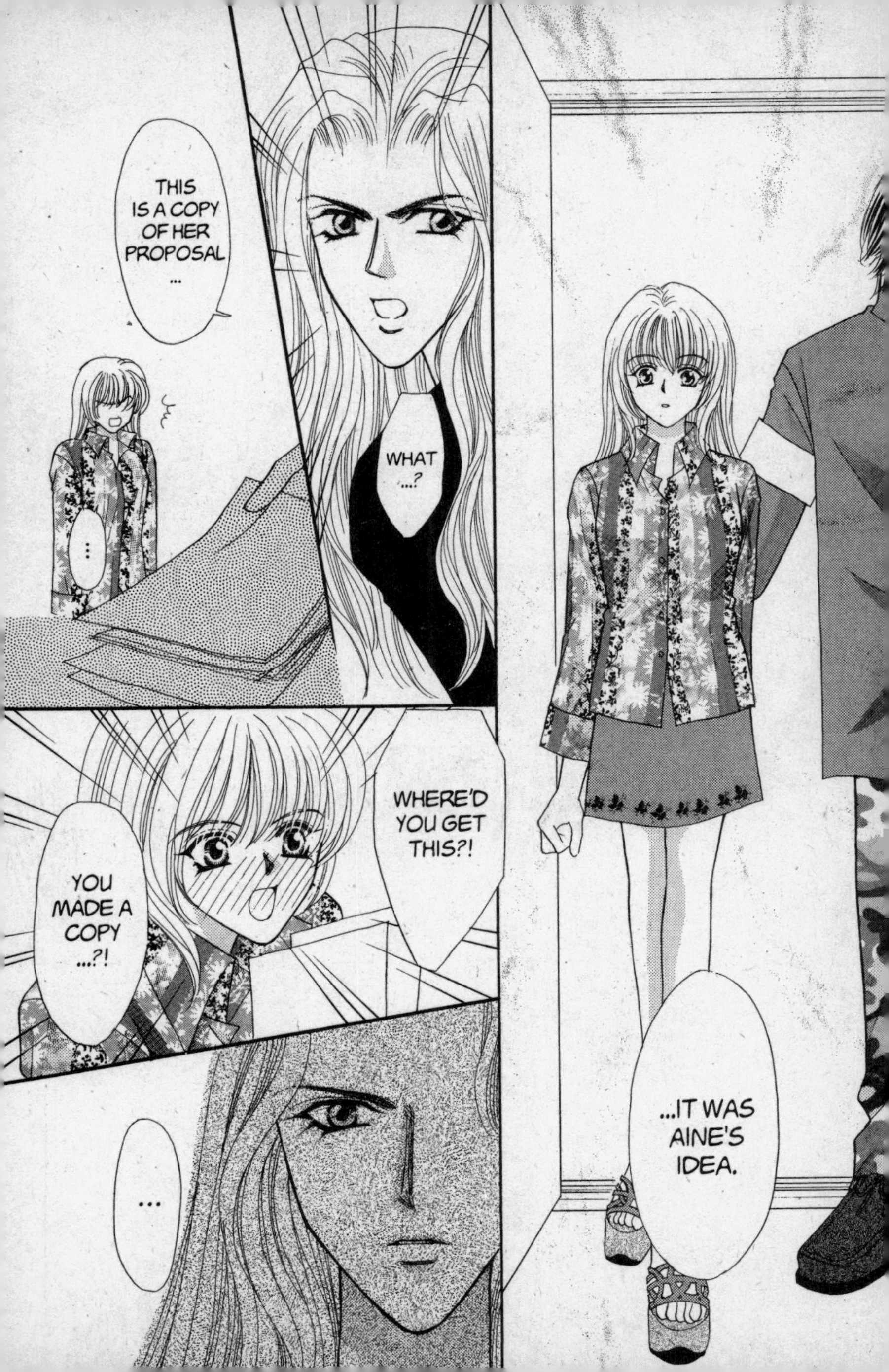
...IT WAS AINE'S IDEA.
WHAT ...?
THIS IS A COPY OF HER PROPOSAL ...
...
WHERE'D YOU GET THIS?!
YOU MADE A COPY ...?!
...

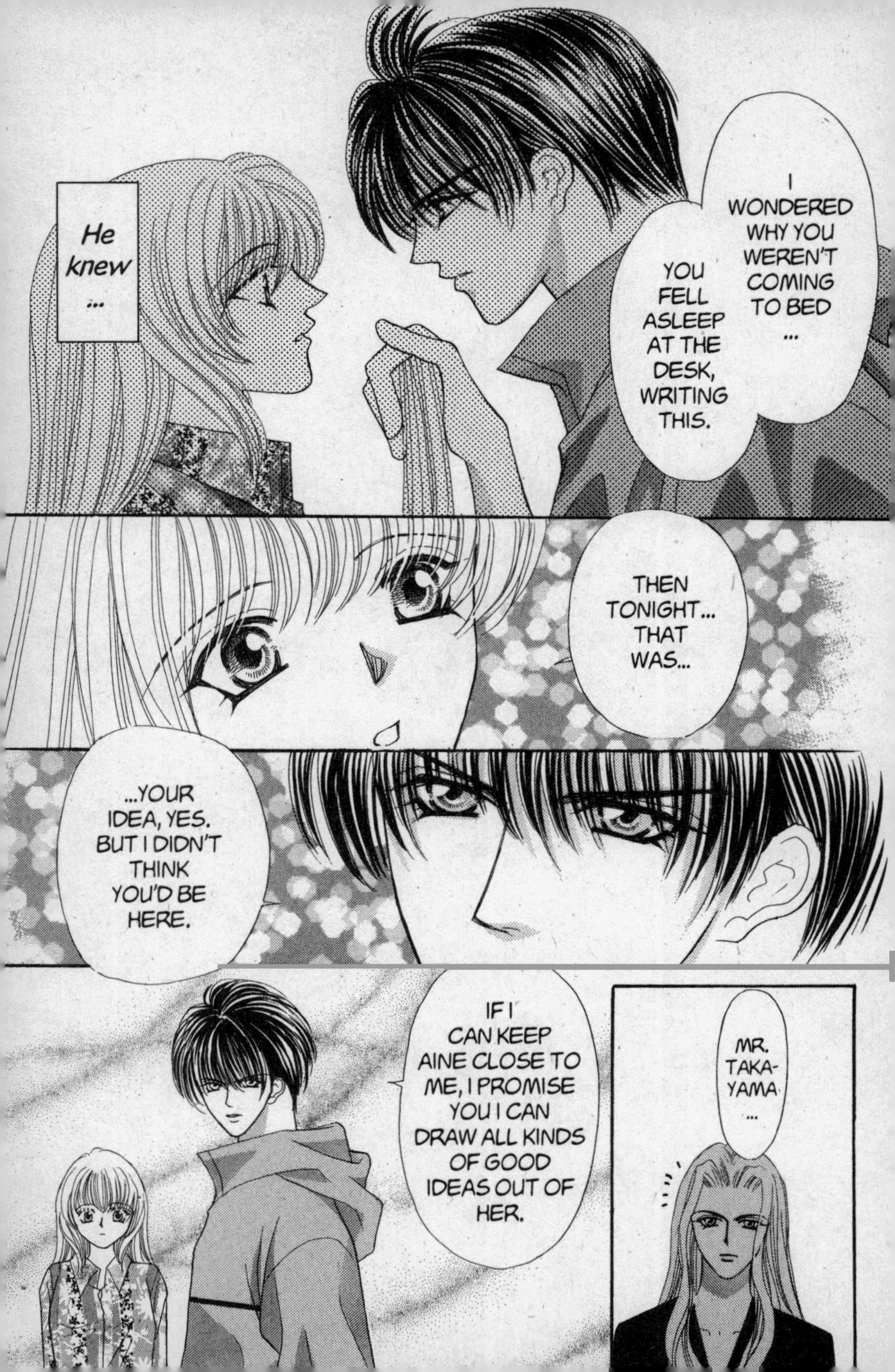
I WONDERED WHY YOU WEREN'T COMING TO BED ...
YOU FELL ASLEEP AT THE DESK, WRITING THIS.
He knew ...
THEN TONIGHT... THAT WAS...
...YOUR IDEA, YES. BUT I DIDN'T THINK YOU'D BE HERE.
MR. TAKA-YAMA ...
IF I CAN KEEP AINE CLOSE TO ME, I PROMISE YOU I CAN DRAW ALL KINDS OF GOOD IDEAS OUT OF HER.

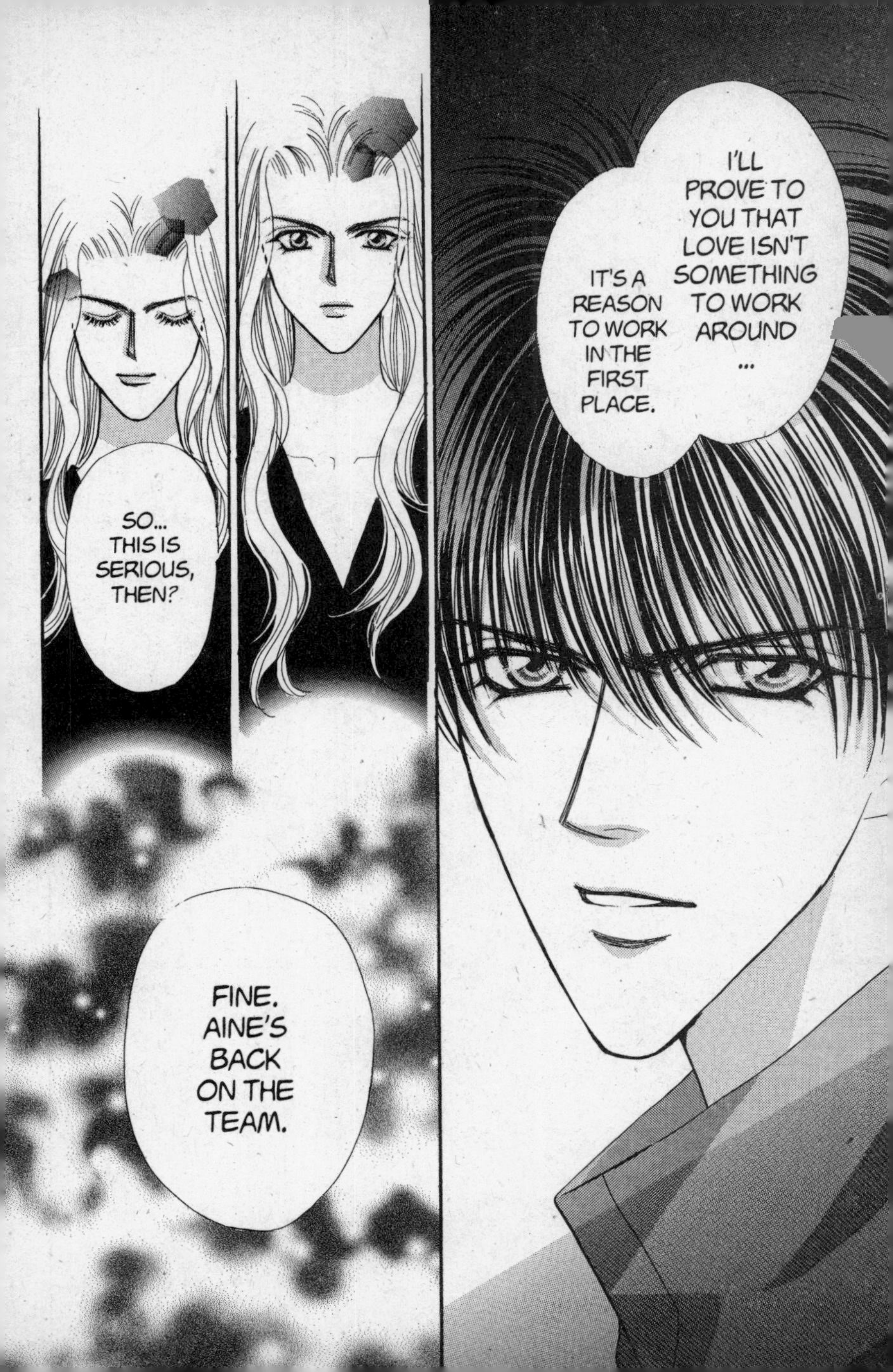
I'LL PROVE TO YOU THAT LOVE ISN'T SOMETHING TO WORK AROUND ...
IT'S A REASON TO WORK IN THE FIRST PLACE.
SO... THIS IS SERIOUS, THEN?
FINE. AINE'S BACK ON THE TEAM.

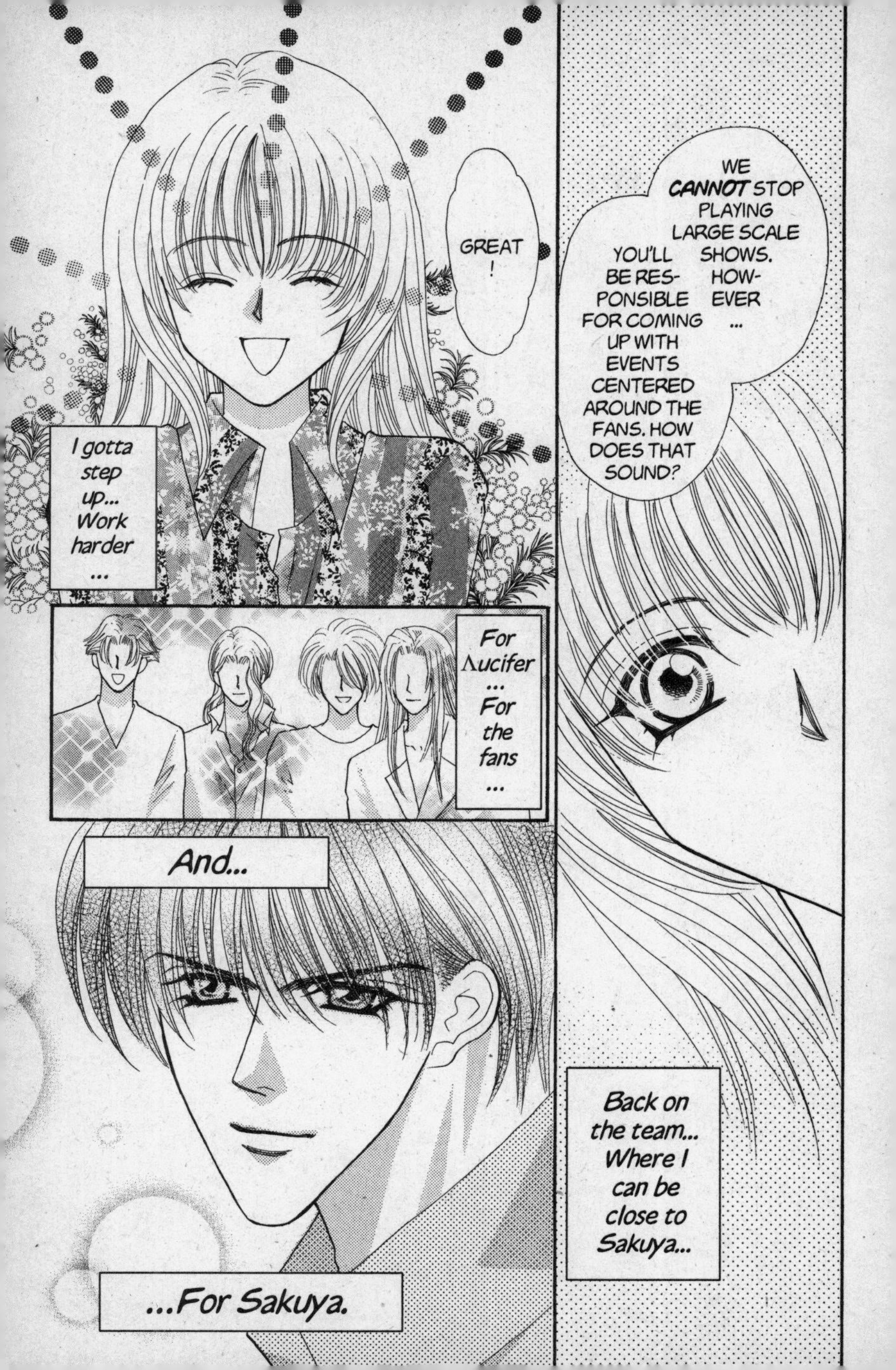
WE CANNOT STOP PLAYING LARGE SCALE SHOWS. HOWEVER...
YOU'LL BE RESPONSIBLE FOR COMING UP WITH EVENTS CENTERED AROUND THE FANS. HOW DOES THAT SOUND?
Back on the team... Where I can be close to Sakuya...
GREAT!
I gotta step up... Work harder...
For Λucifer... For the fans...
And...
...For Sakuya.

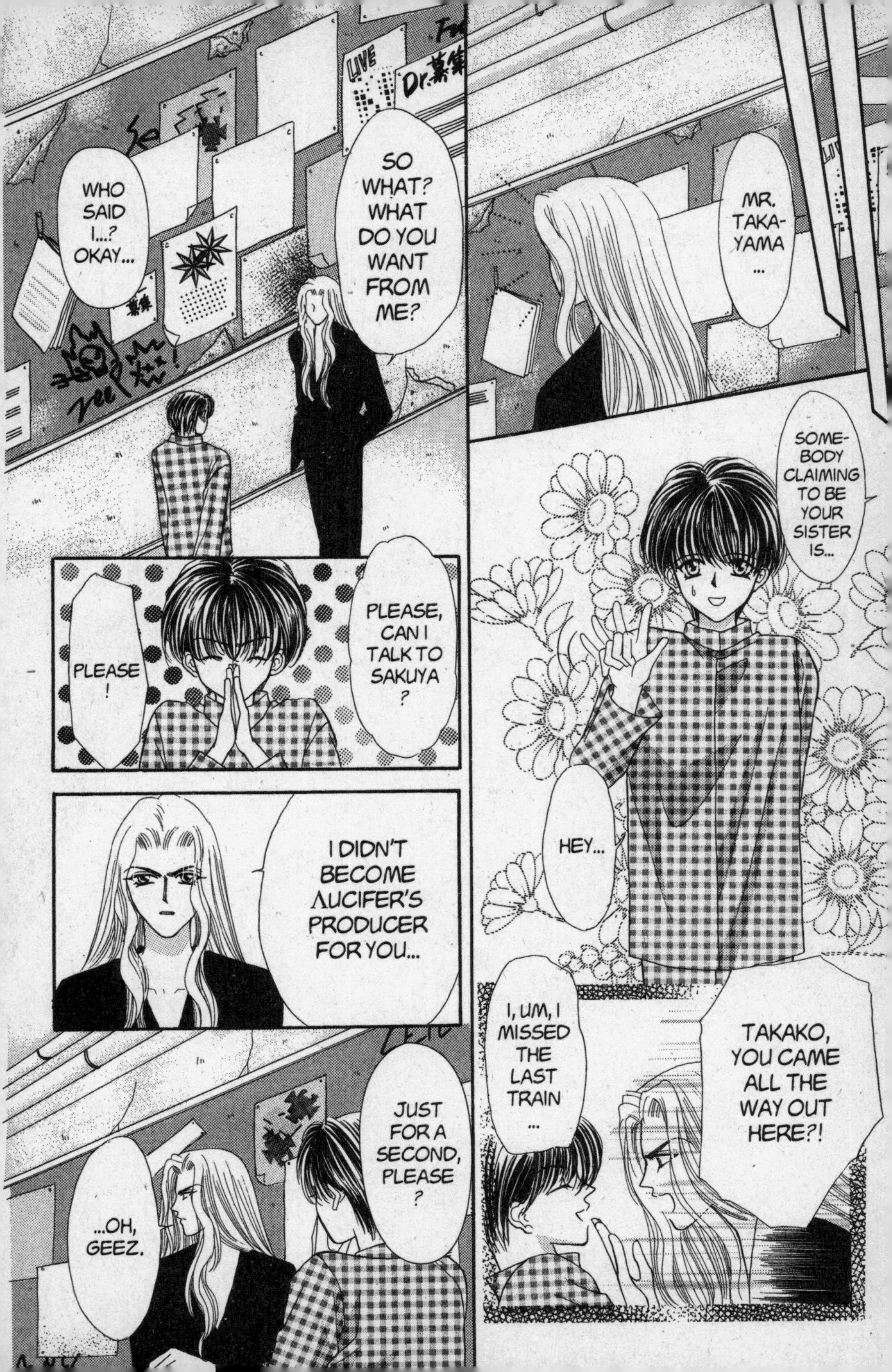

MR. TAKAYAMA...
SOMEBODY CLAIMING TO BE YOUR SISTER IS...
HEY...
TAKAKO, YOU CAME ALL THE WAY OUT HERE?!
I, UM, I MISSED THE LAST TRAIN...
SO WHAT? WHAT DO YOU WANT FROM ME?
WHO SAID I...? OKAY...
PLEASE, CAN I TALK TO SAKUYA?
PLEASE!
I DIDN'T BECOME ΛUCIFER'S PRODUCER FOR YOU...
JUST FOR A SECOND, PLEASE?
...OH, GEEZ.

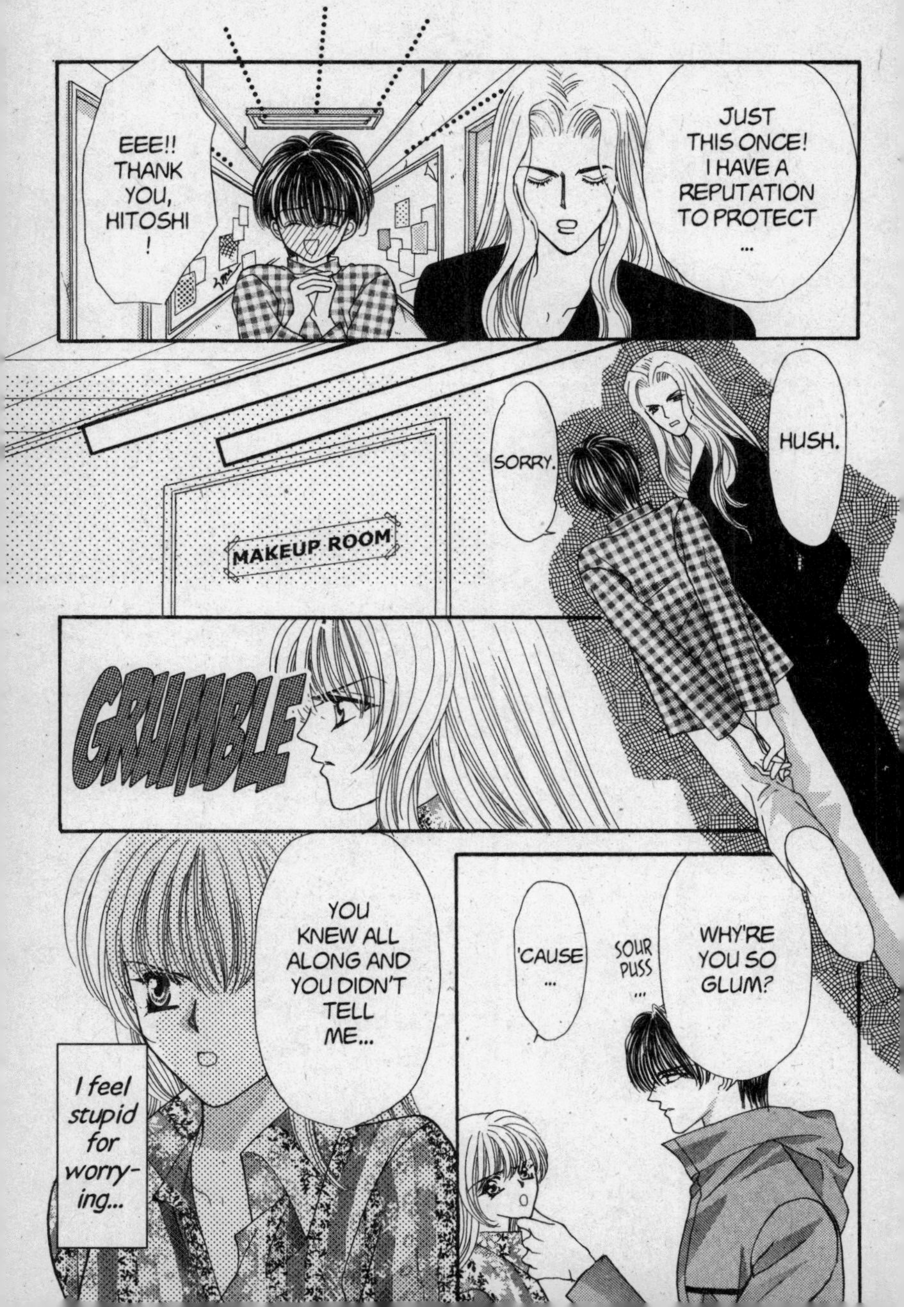
JUST THIS ONCE! I HAVE A REPUTATION TO PROTECT ...
EEE!! THANK YOU, HITOSHI !
HUSH.
SORRY.
MAKEUP ROOM
GRUMBLE
WHY'RE YOU SO GLUM?
SOUR PUSS ...
'CAUSE ...
YOU KNEW ALL ALONG AND YOU DIDN'T TELL ME...
I feel stupid for worrying...

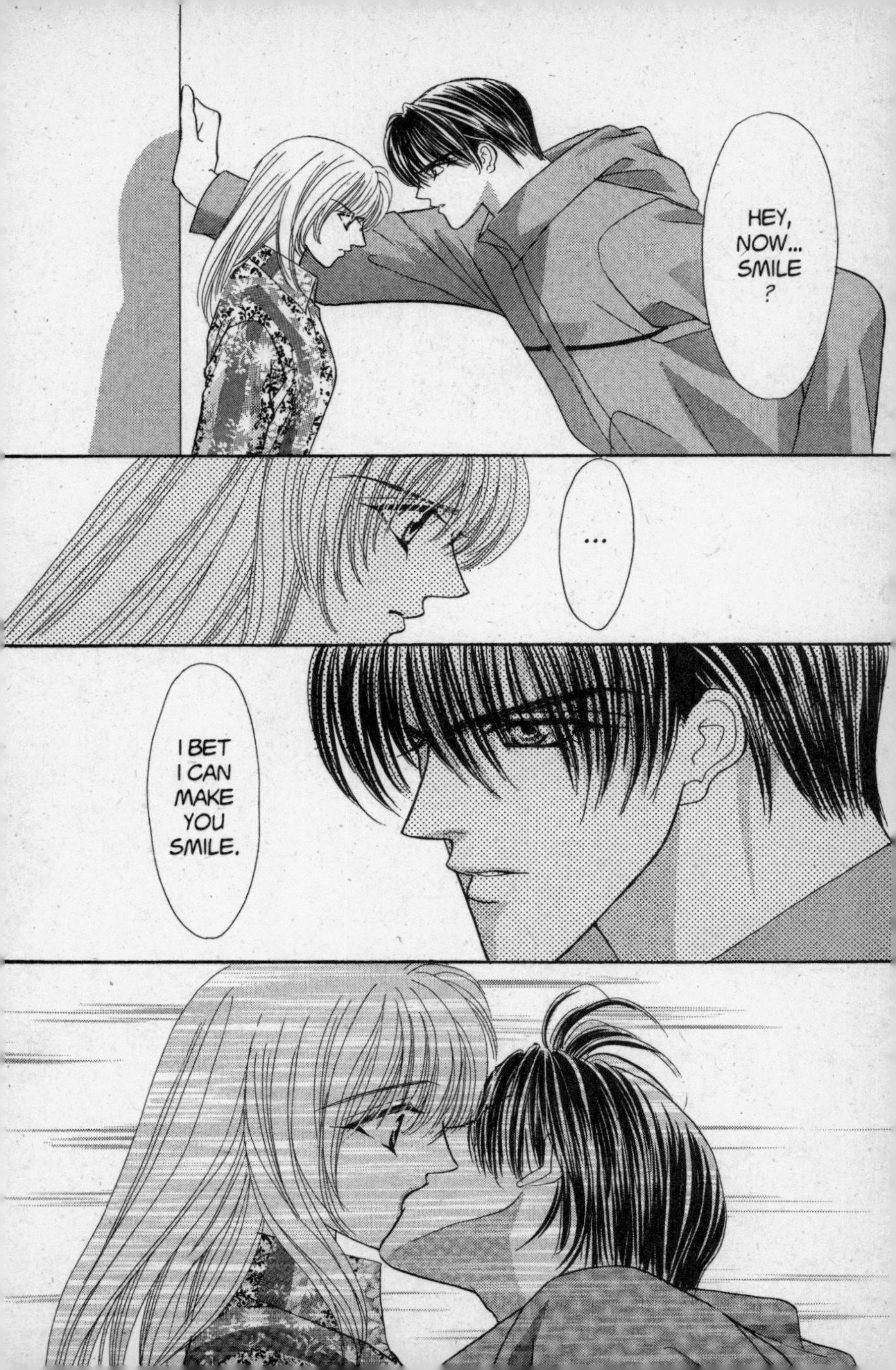
HEY, NOW... SMILE ?
...
I BET I CAN MAKE YOU SMILE.

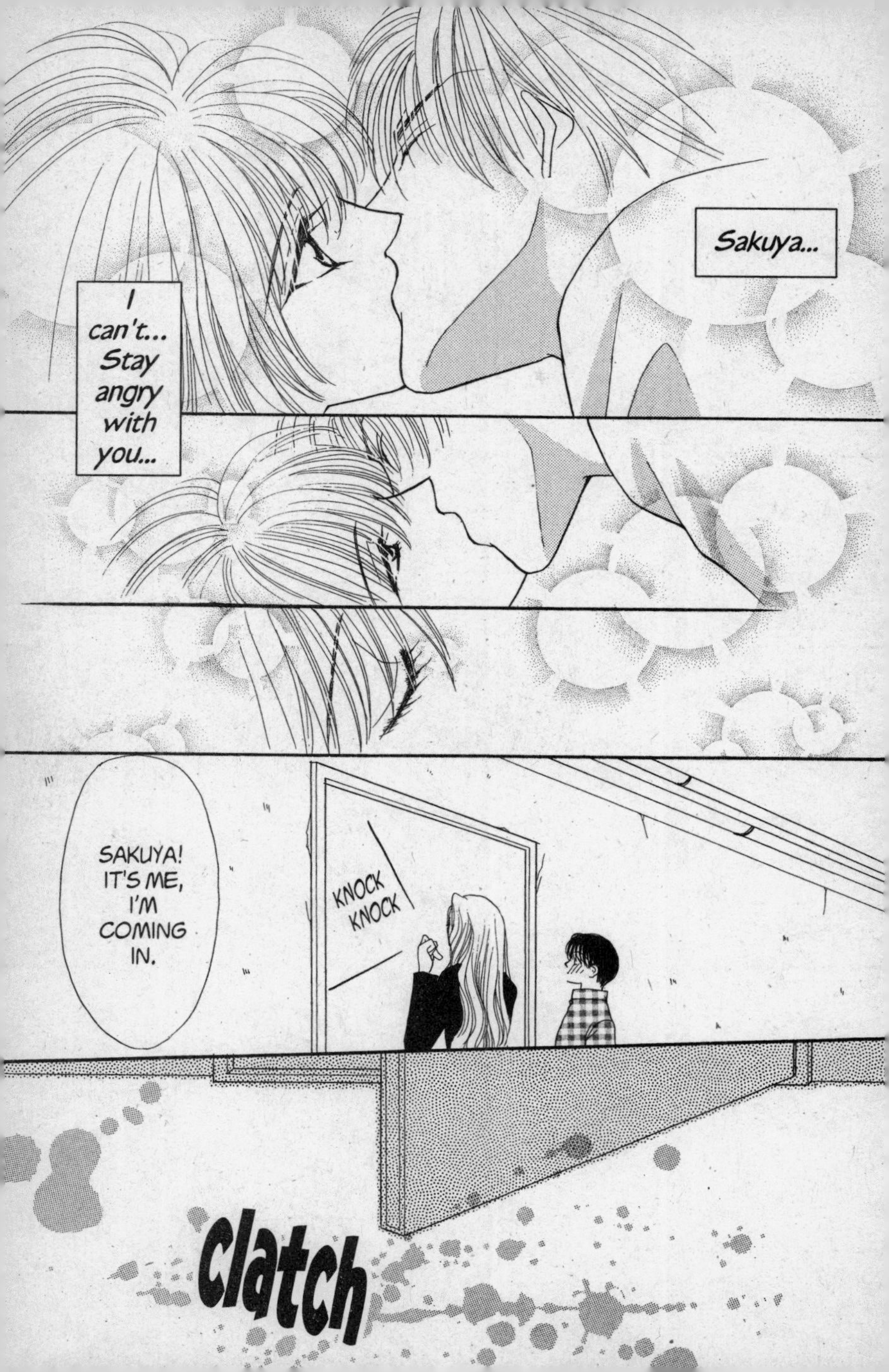
Sakuya...
I can't... Stay angry with you...
KNOCK KNOCK
SAKUYA! IT'S ME, I'M COMING IN.
clatch

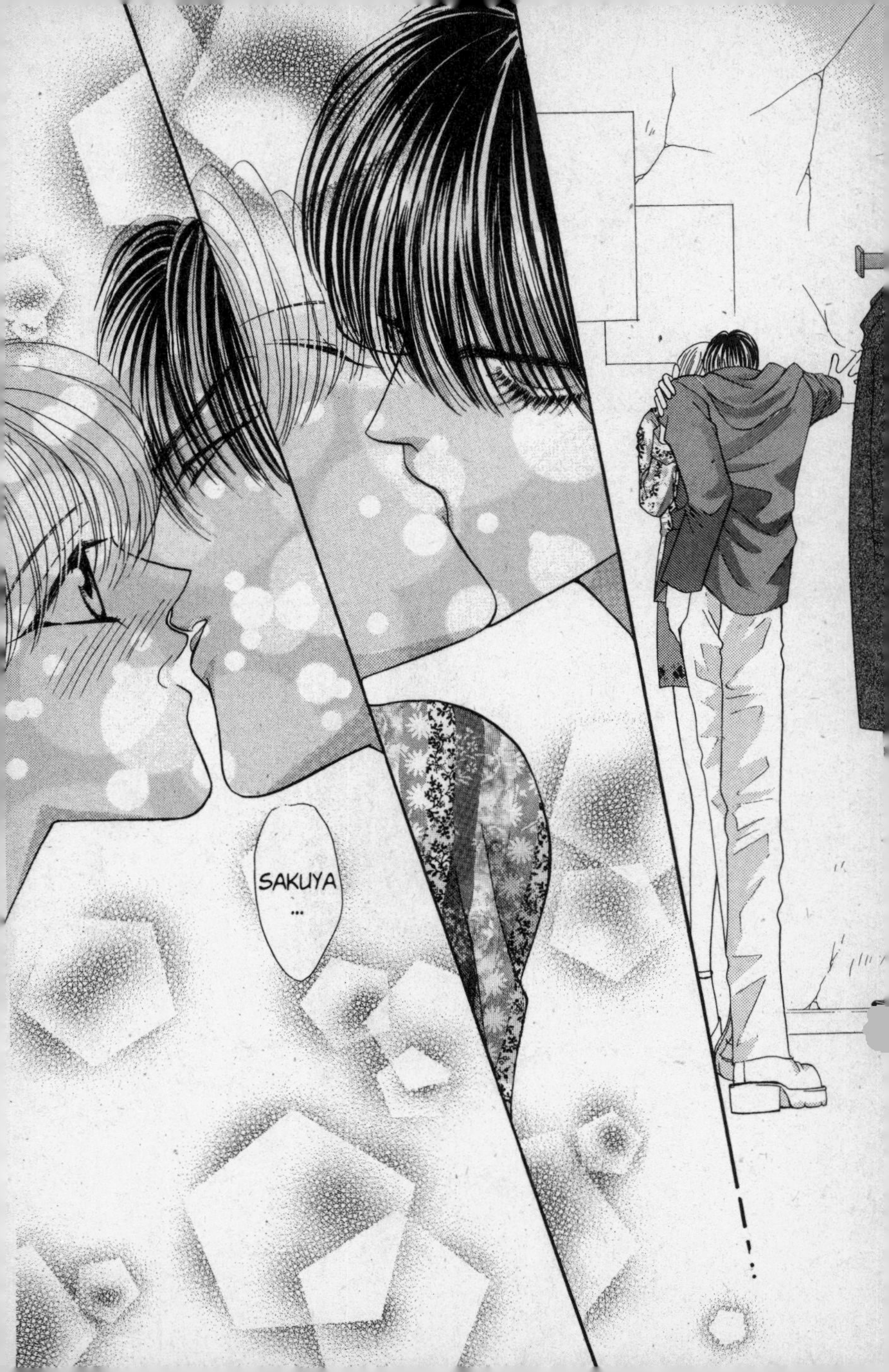
SAKUYA ...

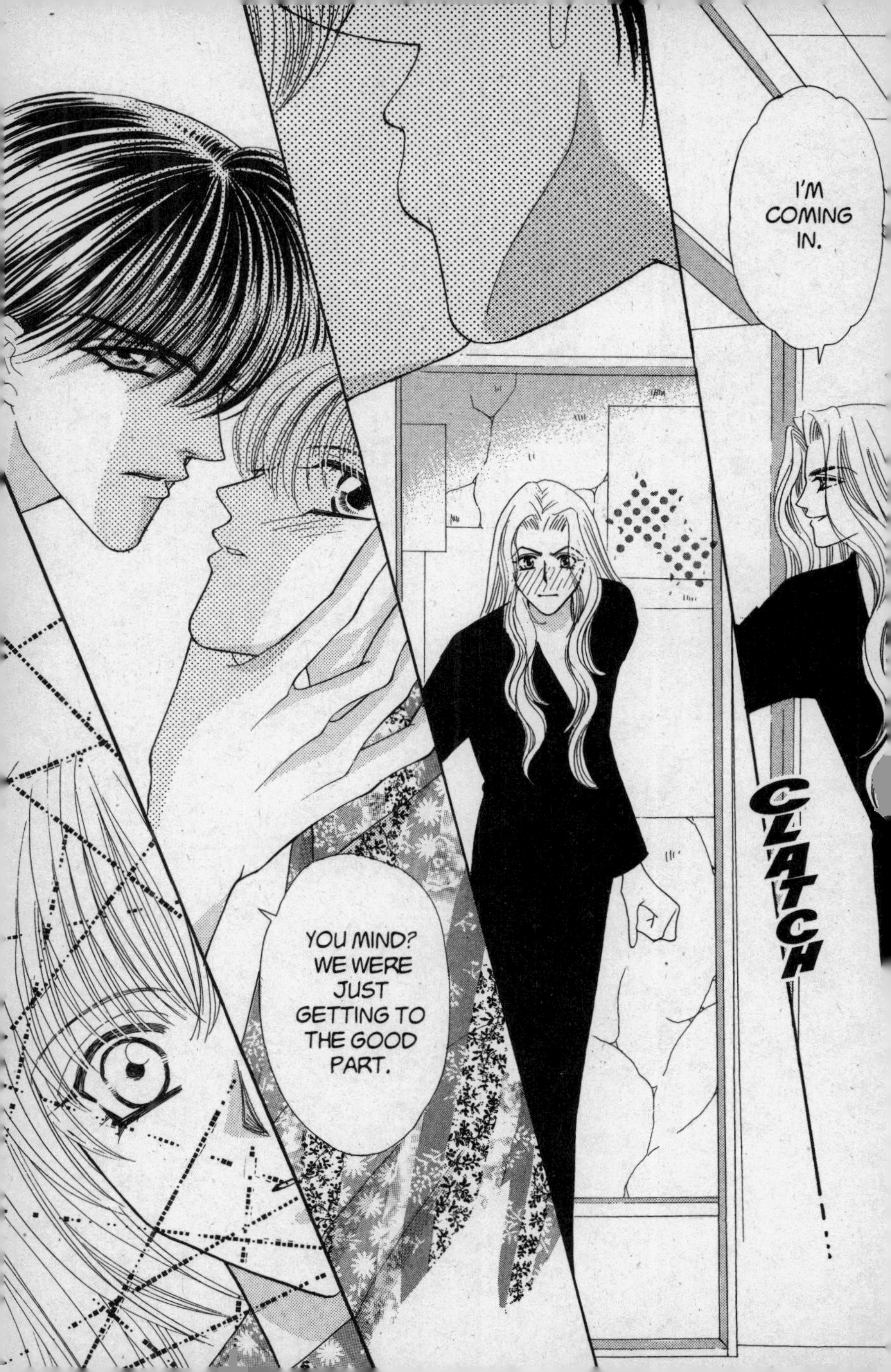
I'M COMING IN.
CLATCH
YOU MIND? WE WERE JUST GETTING TO THE GOOD PART.

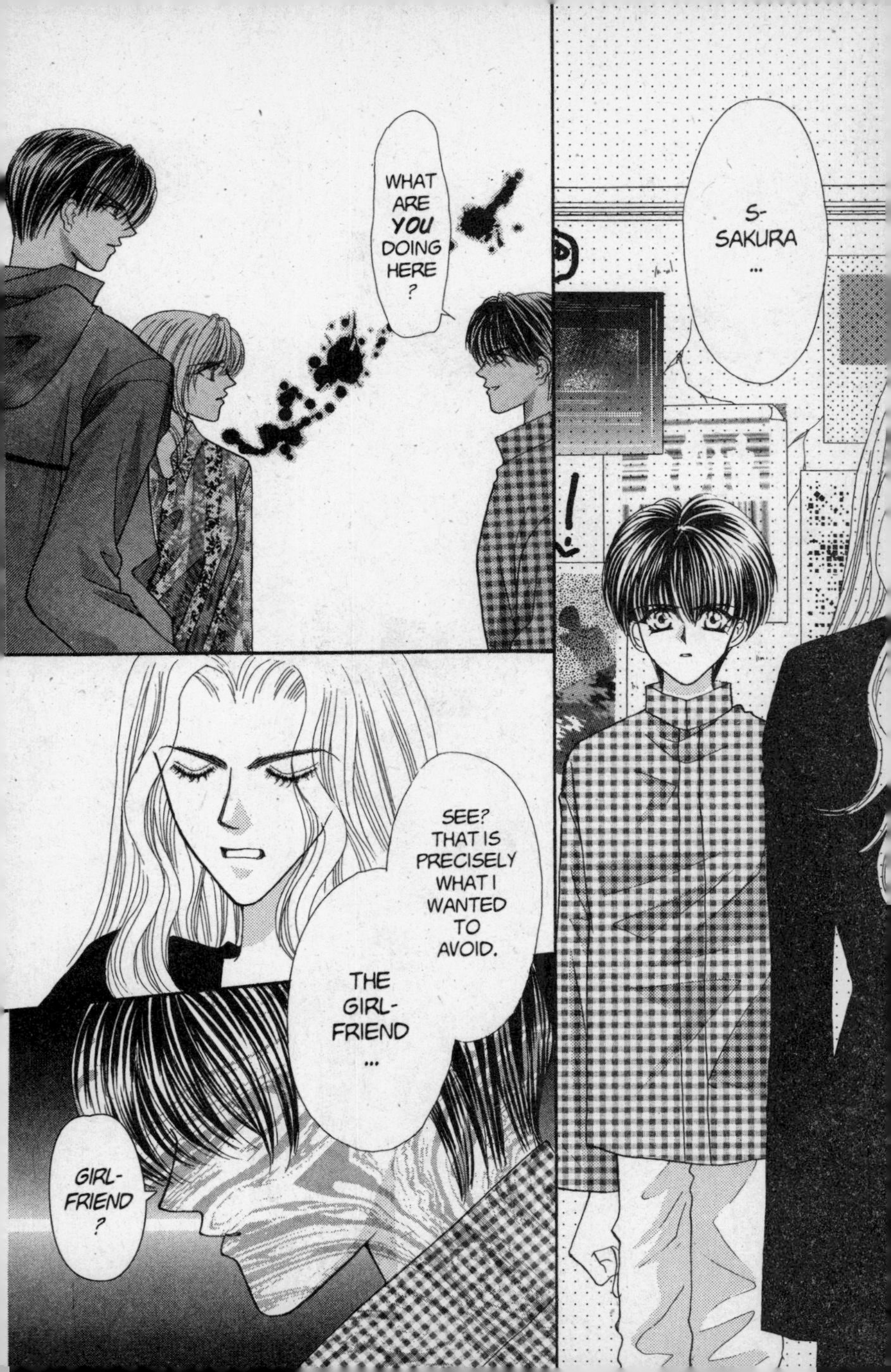
S-SAKURA ...
!
WHAT ARE YOU DOING HERE?
SEE? THAT IS PRECISELY WHAT I WANTED TO AVOID.
THE GIRL-FRIEND ...
GIRL-FRIEND?

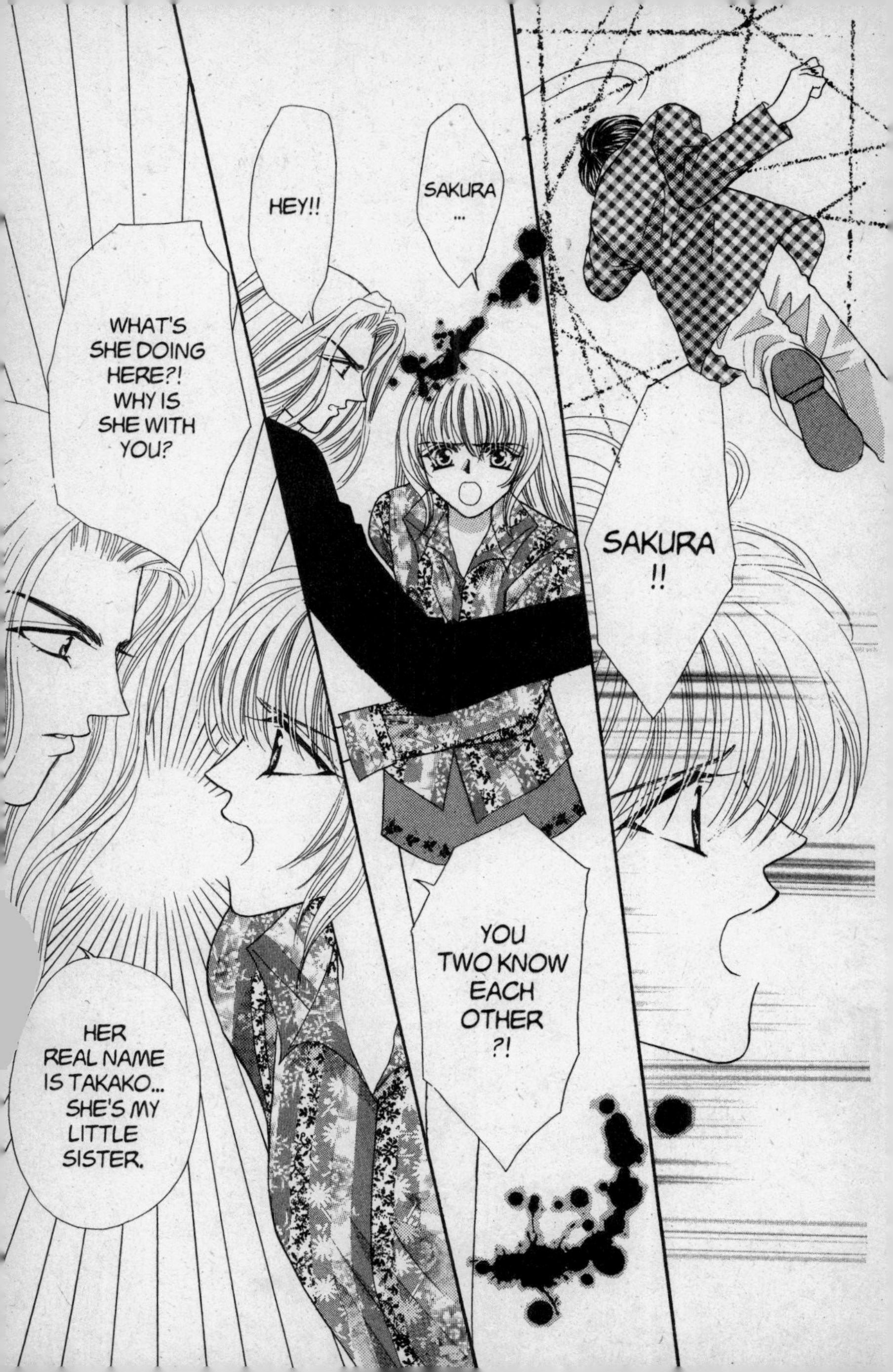
SAKURA !!
SAKURA ...
HEY!!
YOU TWO KNOW EACH OTHER ?!
WHAT'S SHE DOING HERE?! WHY IS SHE WITH YOU?
HER REAL NAME IS TAKAKO... SHE'S MY LITTLE SISTER.

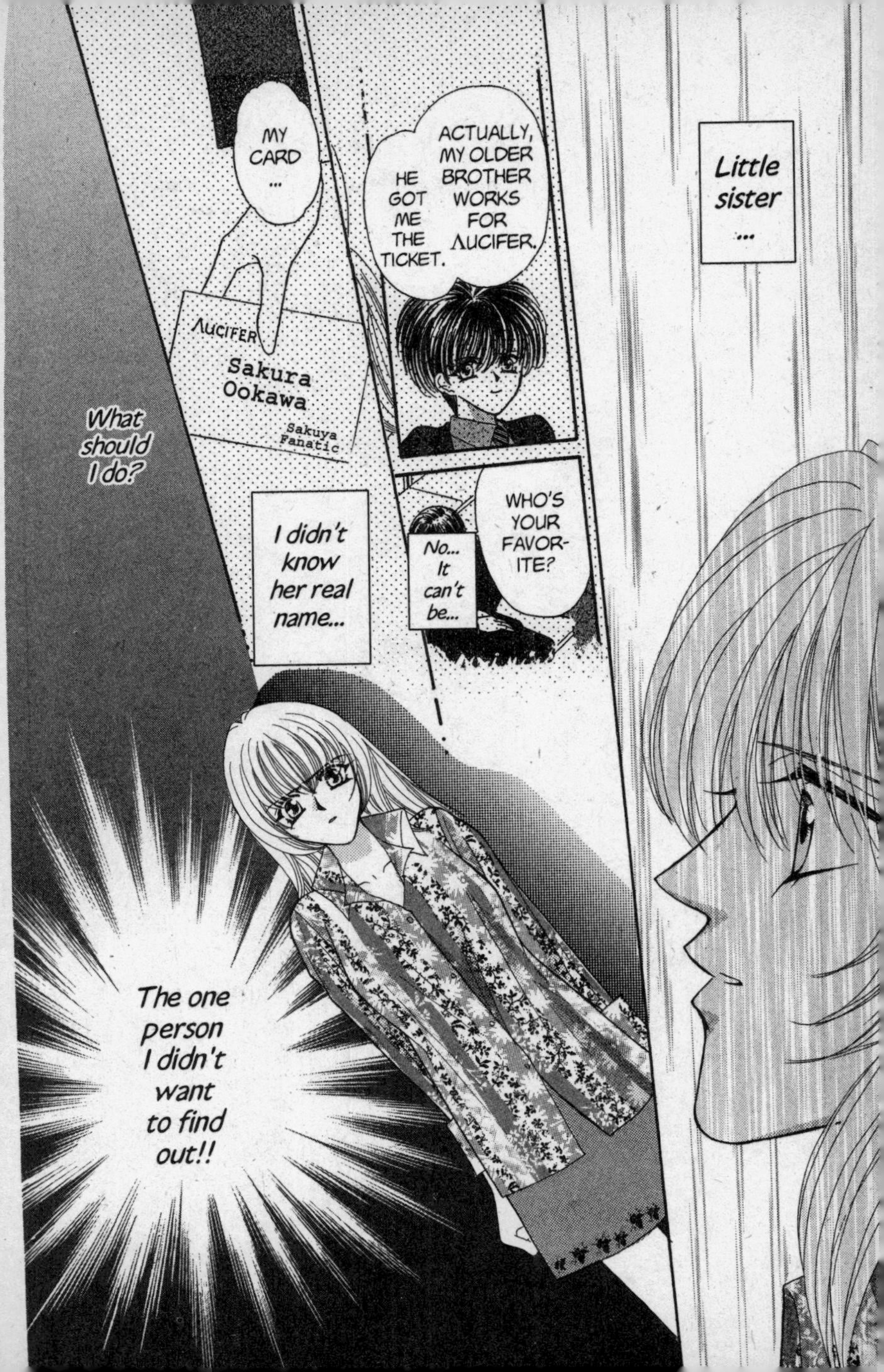

Little sister ...
ACTUALLY, MY OLDER BROTHER WORKS FOR ΛUCIFER.
HE GOT ME THE TICKET.
MY CARD ...
ΛUCIFER
Sakura Ookawa
Sakuya Fanatic
WHO'S YOUR FAVOR-ITE?
No... It can't be...
I didn't know her real name...
What should I do?
The one person I didn't want to find out!!

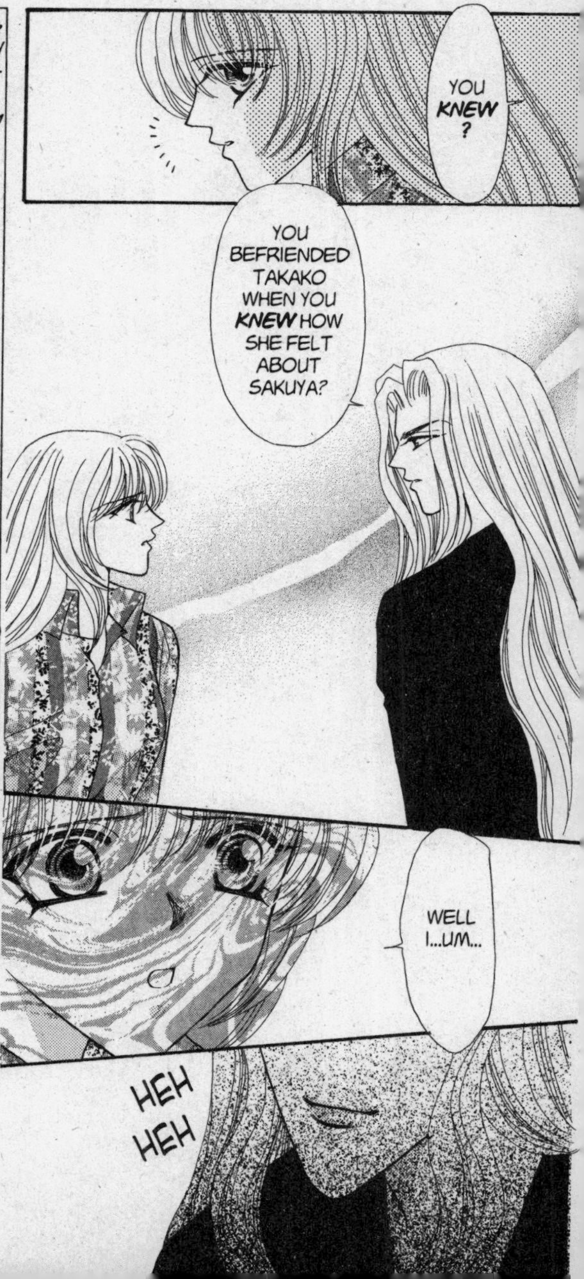
YOU KNEW?
YOU BEFRIENDED TAKAKO WHEN YOU KNEW HOW SHE FELT ABOUT SAKUYA?
WELL I...UM...
HEH HEH

I've had so much media exposure recently that I've actually started getting recognized out in public—just like a proper celebrity! It happened at the Λucifer show in Osaka and at the one in Tokyo. Next time, I think I'm going to have to sneak in! Eee! Think I'll get caught? If you see me, go ahead and tell your friends, but do me a favor and whisper, okay? (Ha ha!)

Okay, last time I recommended Transtic Nerve. Did you guys listen to them? I'm even more into them now. Great music for driving. (The other day, I was blaring TN in my car and I guess I wasn't paying attention because I accidentally made an illegal U-turn and got pulled over. To make matters worse, I didn't realize I was being pulled over at first and it looked like I was trying to flee the scene! Oops.)

Anyway, my recommendation for this volume is...

...Oblivion Dust!! They're so cool I can't believe they're Japanese! The sound of the guitar is the deciding factor in whether or not I like a band. Oblivion Dust totally gets that. Give them a listen and let me know what you think!

Most of the bands I've been listening to lately are already on major labels—that's because I've been so busy I haven't had time to hit the clubs and check out independent bands. (Wah!)

I need a break! I must discover new artists!!

...If I hear anything good, I'll let you know.

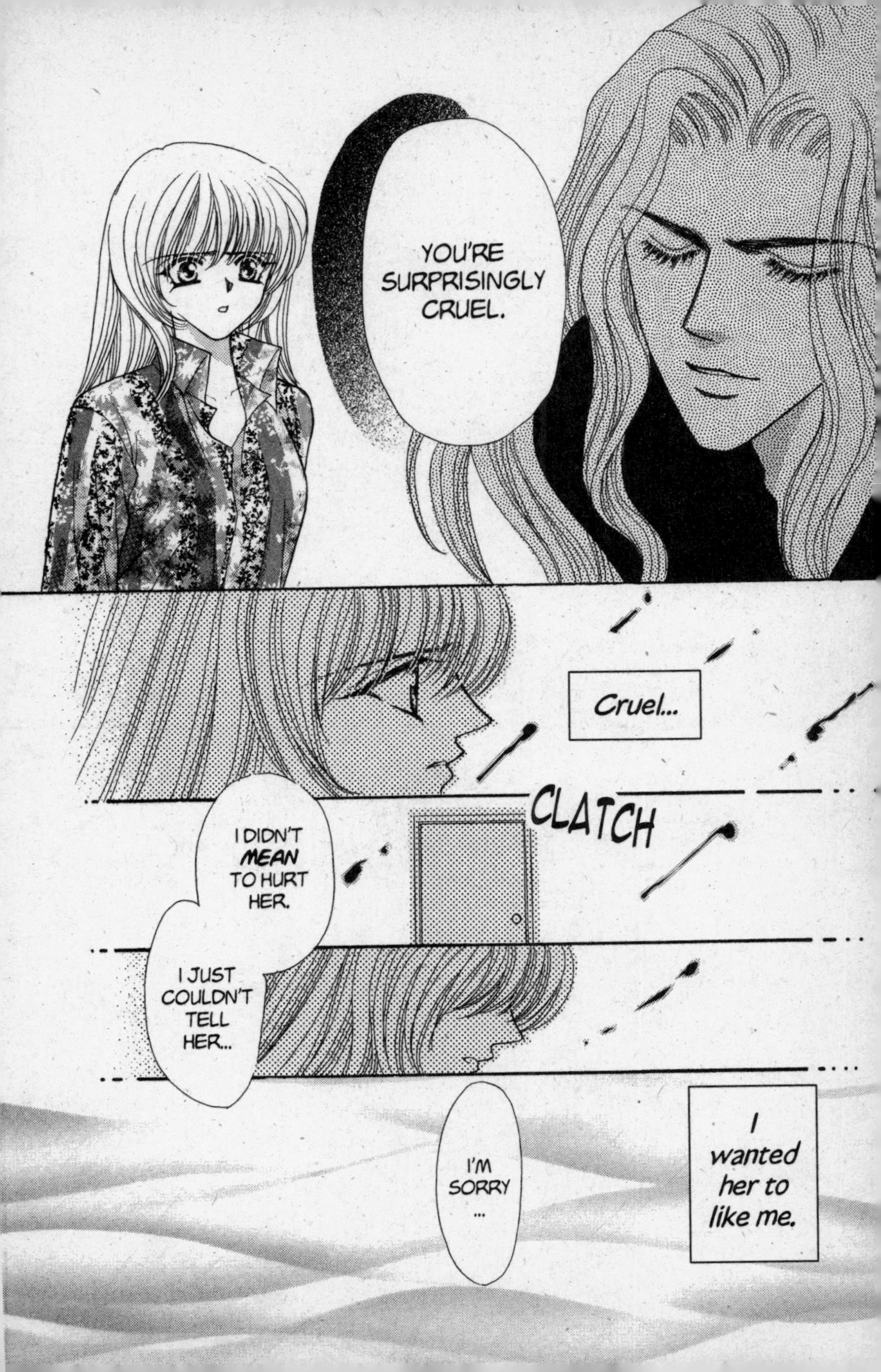
YOU'RE SURPRISINGLY CRUEL.
Cruel...
CLATCH
I DIDN'T MEAN TO HURT HER.
I JUST COULDN'T TELL HER...
I wanted her to like me.
I'M SORRY ...

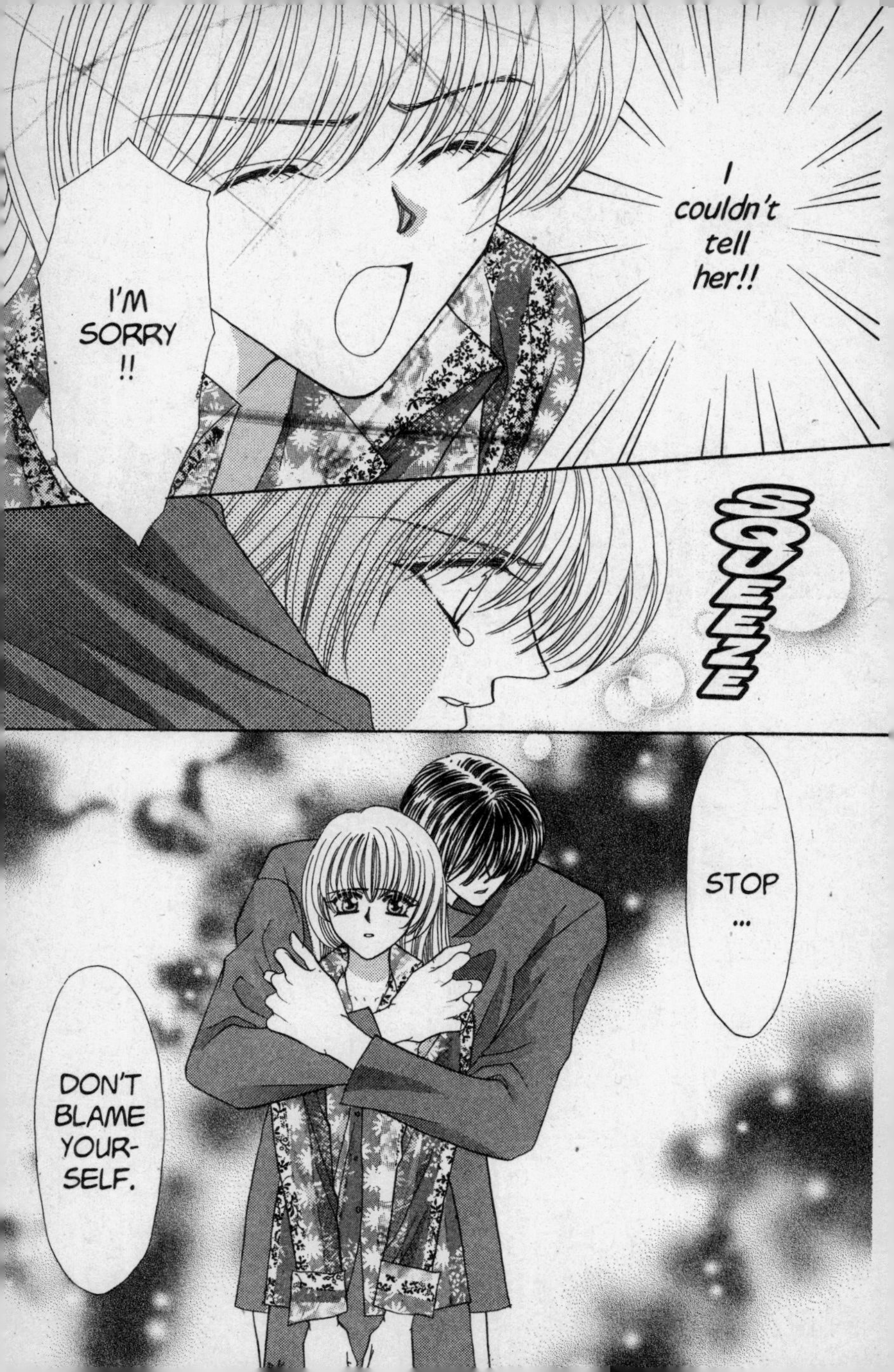
I couldn't tell her!!
I'M SORRY !!
SQUEEZE
STOP ...
DON'T BLAME YOUR-SELF.

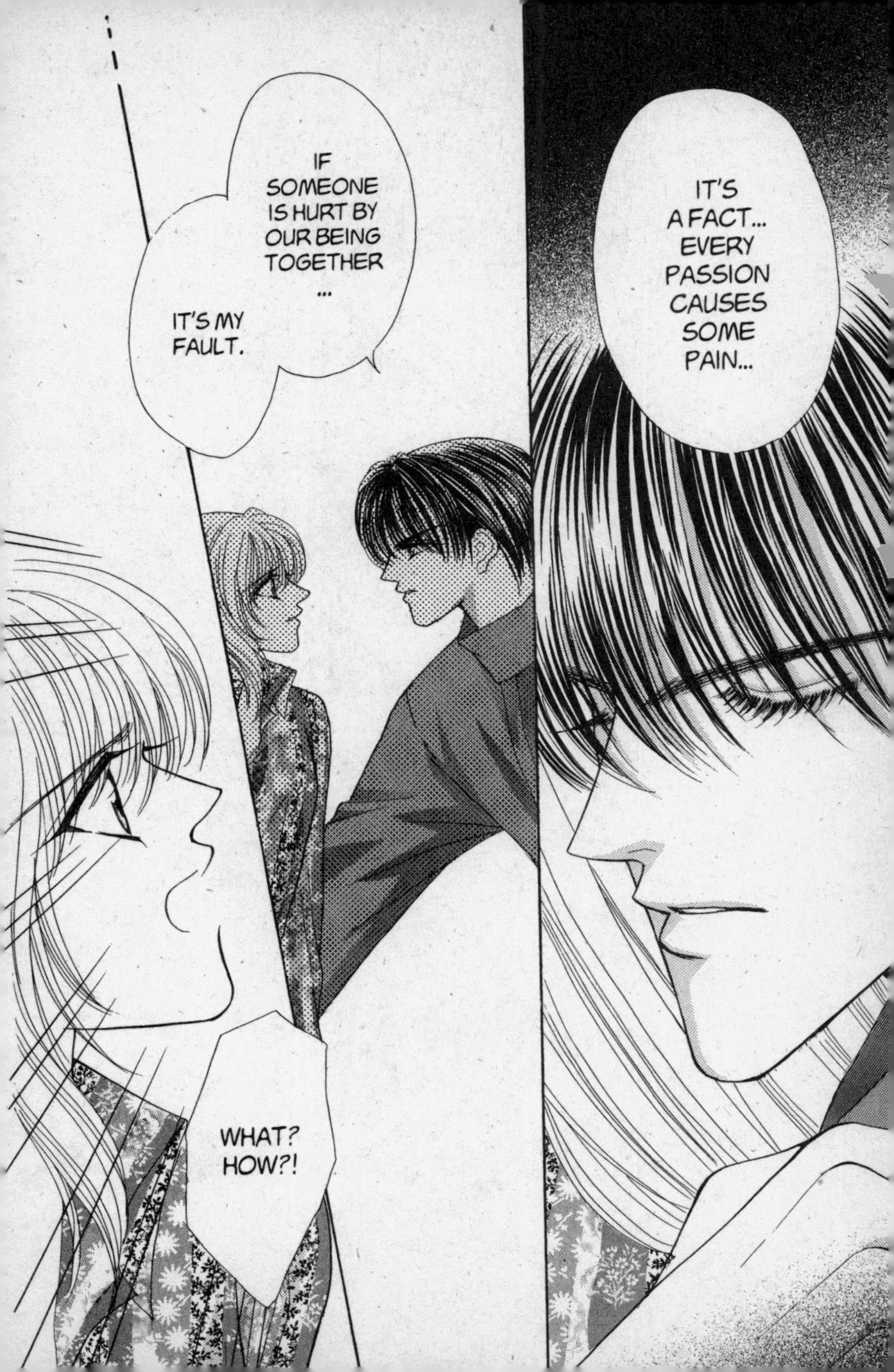
IT'S A FACT... EVERY PASSION CAUSES SOME PAIN...
IF SOMEONE IS HURT BY OUR BEING TOGETHER ...
IT'S MY FAULT.
WHAT? HOW?!

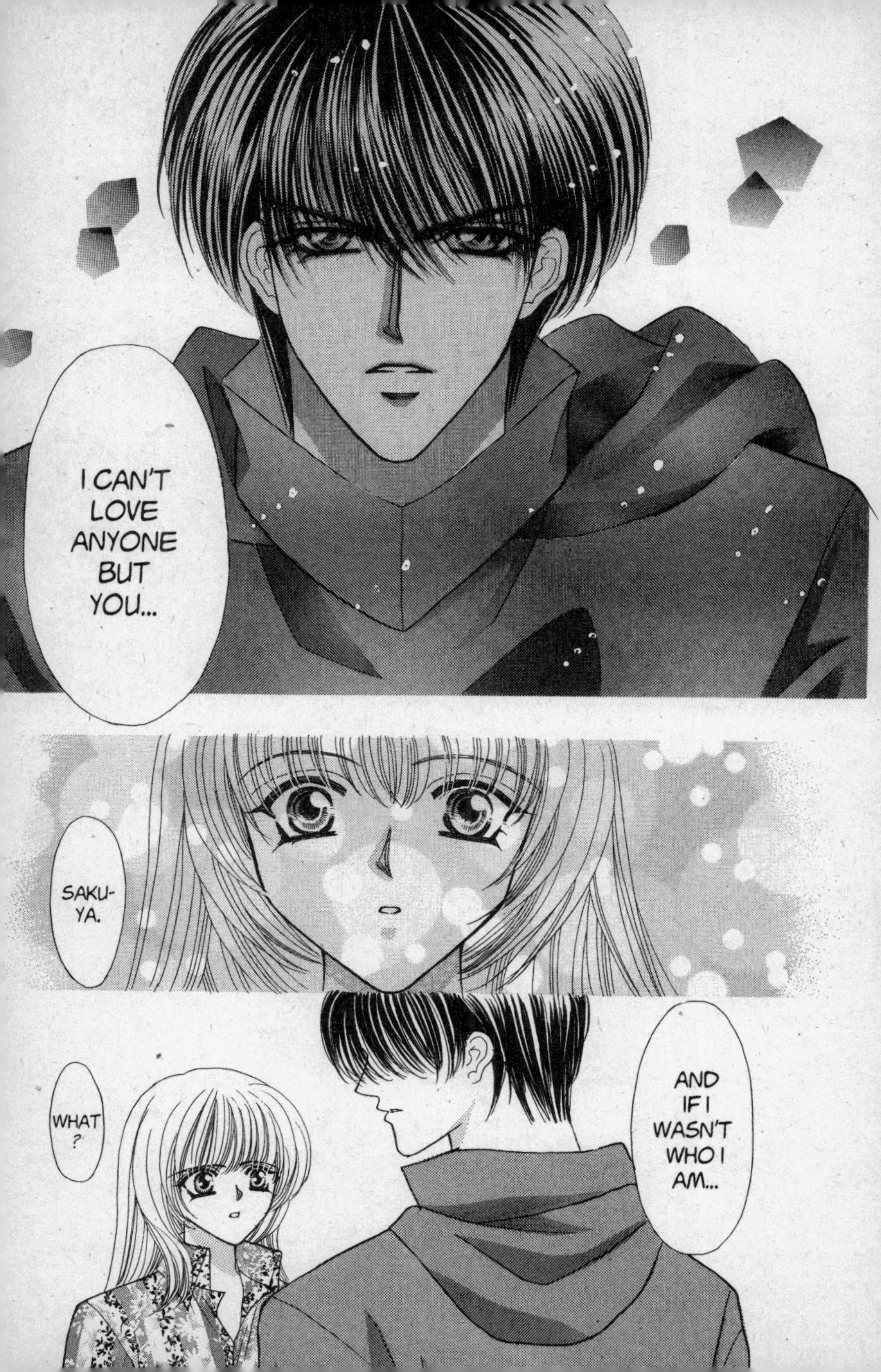
I CAN'T LOVE ANYONE BUT YOU...
SAKU-YA.
AND IF I WASN'T WHO I AM...
WHAT?

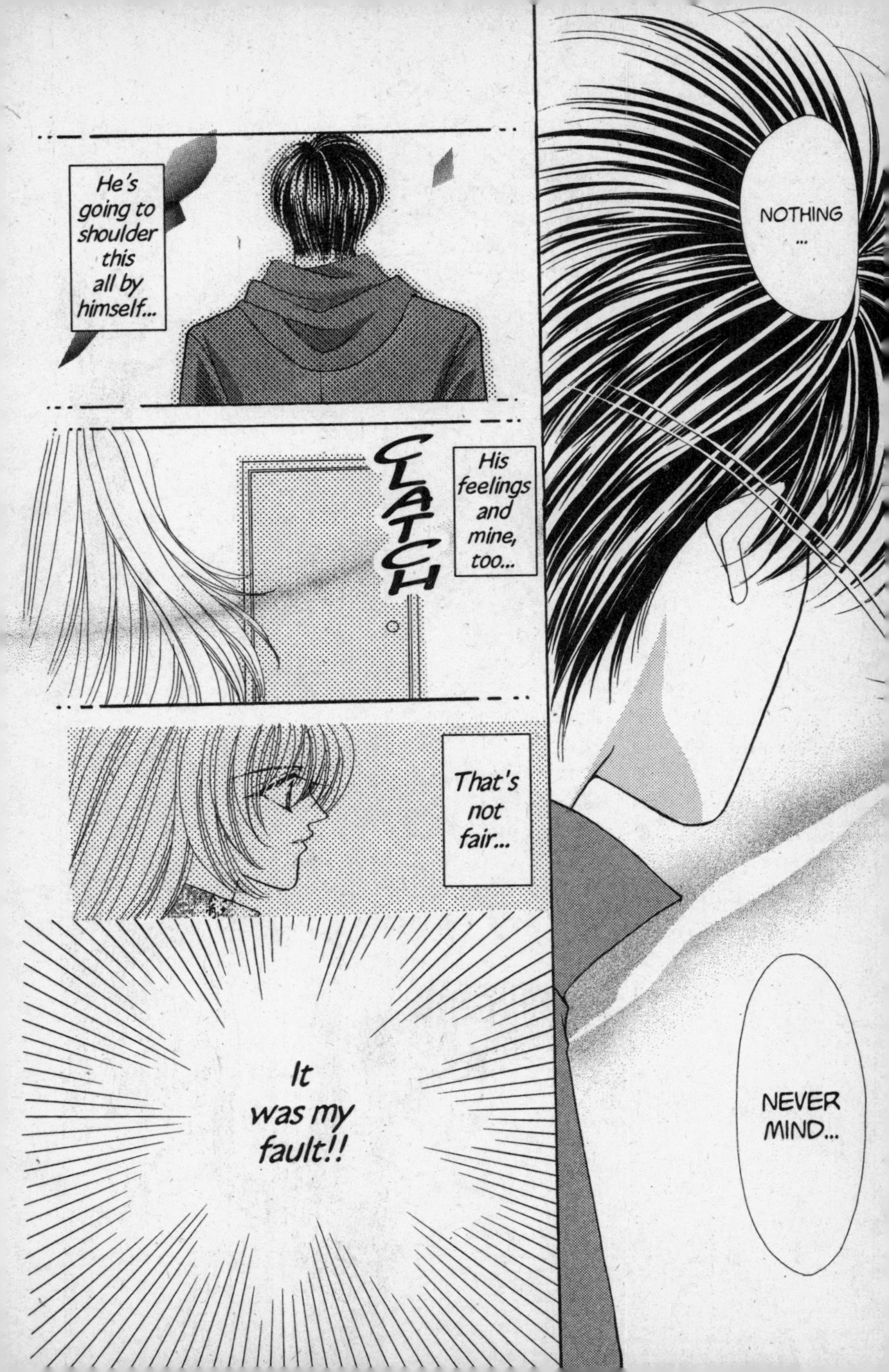
NOTHING ...
NEVER MIND...
He's going to shoulder this all by himself...
His feelings and mine, too...
CLATCH
That's not fair...
It was my fault!!

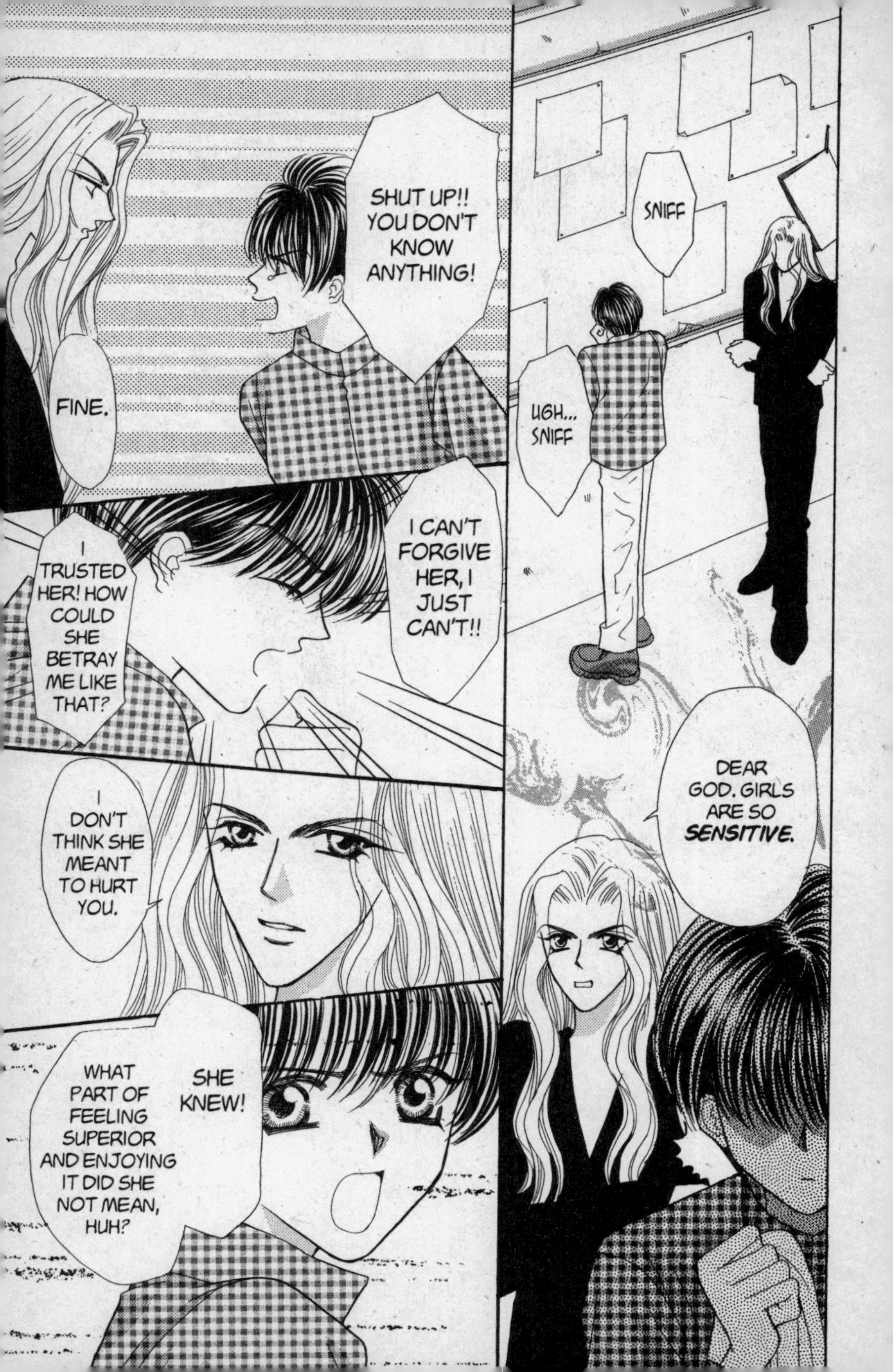
SNIFF
UGH... SNIFF
DEAR GOD. GIRLS ARE SO ***SENSITIVE.***
SHUT UP!! YOU DON'T KNOW ANYTHING!
FINE.
I CAN'T FORGIVE HER, I JUST CAN'T!!
I TRUSTED HER! HOW COULD SHE BETRAY ME LIKE THAT?
I DON'T THINK SHE MEANT TO HURT YOU.
SHE KNEW!
WHAT PART OF FEELING SUPERIOR AND ENJOYING IT DID SHE NOT MEAN, HUH?

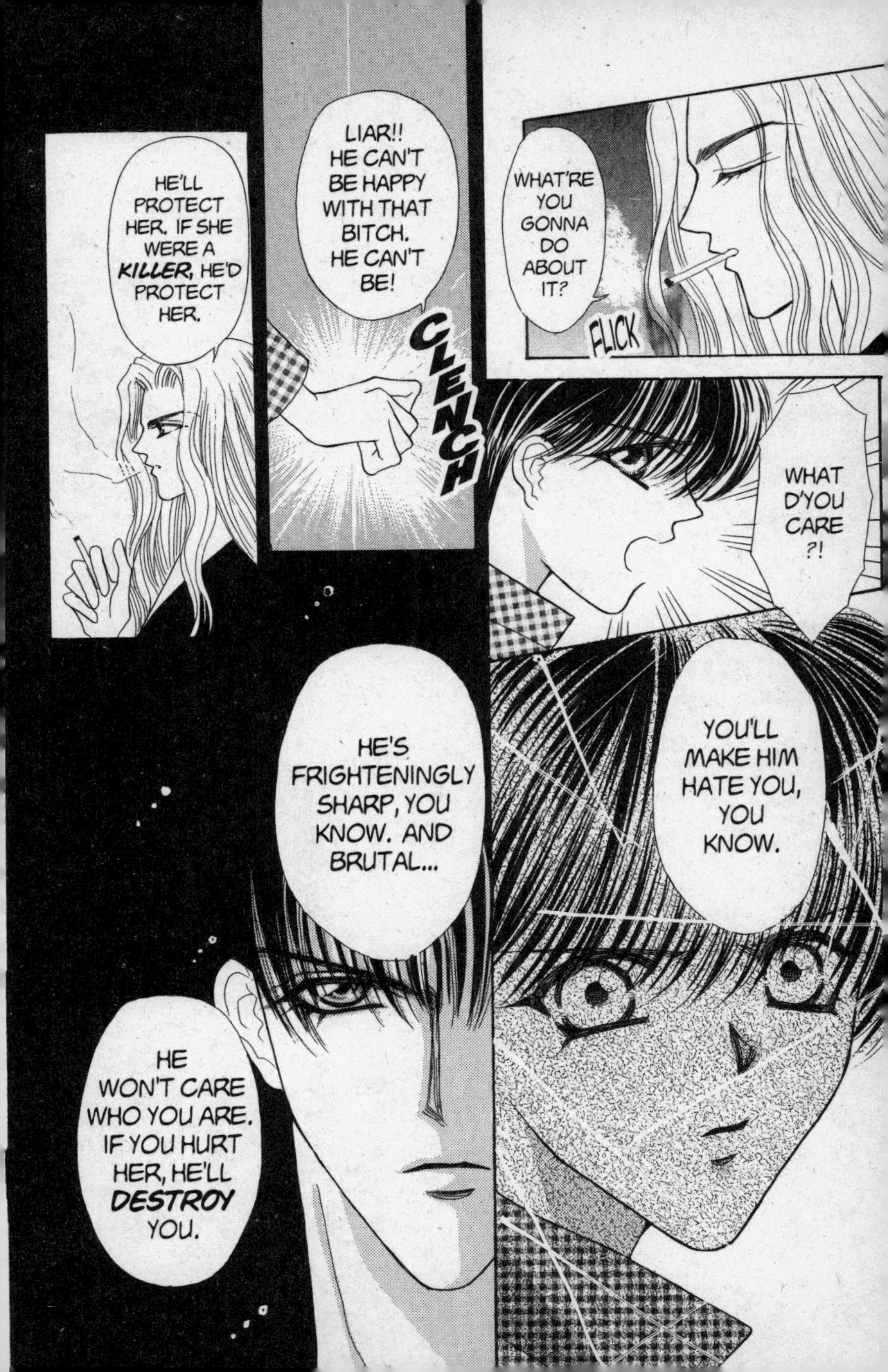
WHAT'RE YOU GONNA DO ABOUT IT?
FLICK
LIAR!! HE CAN'T BE HAPPY WITH THAT BITCH. HE CAN'T BE!
CLENCH
HE'LL PROTECT HER. IF SHE WERE A **KILLER**, HE'D PROTECT HER.
WHAT D'YOU CARE ?!
YOU'LL MAKE HIM HATE YOU, YOU KNOW.
HE'S FRIGHTENINGLY SHARP, YOU KNOW. AND BRUTAL...
HE WON'T CARE WHO YOU ARE. IF YOU HURT HER, HE'LL **DESTROY** YOU.

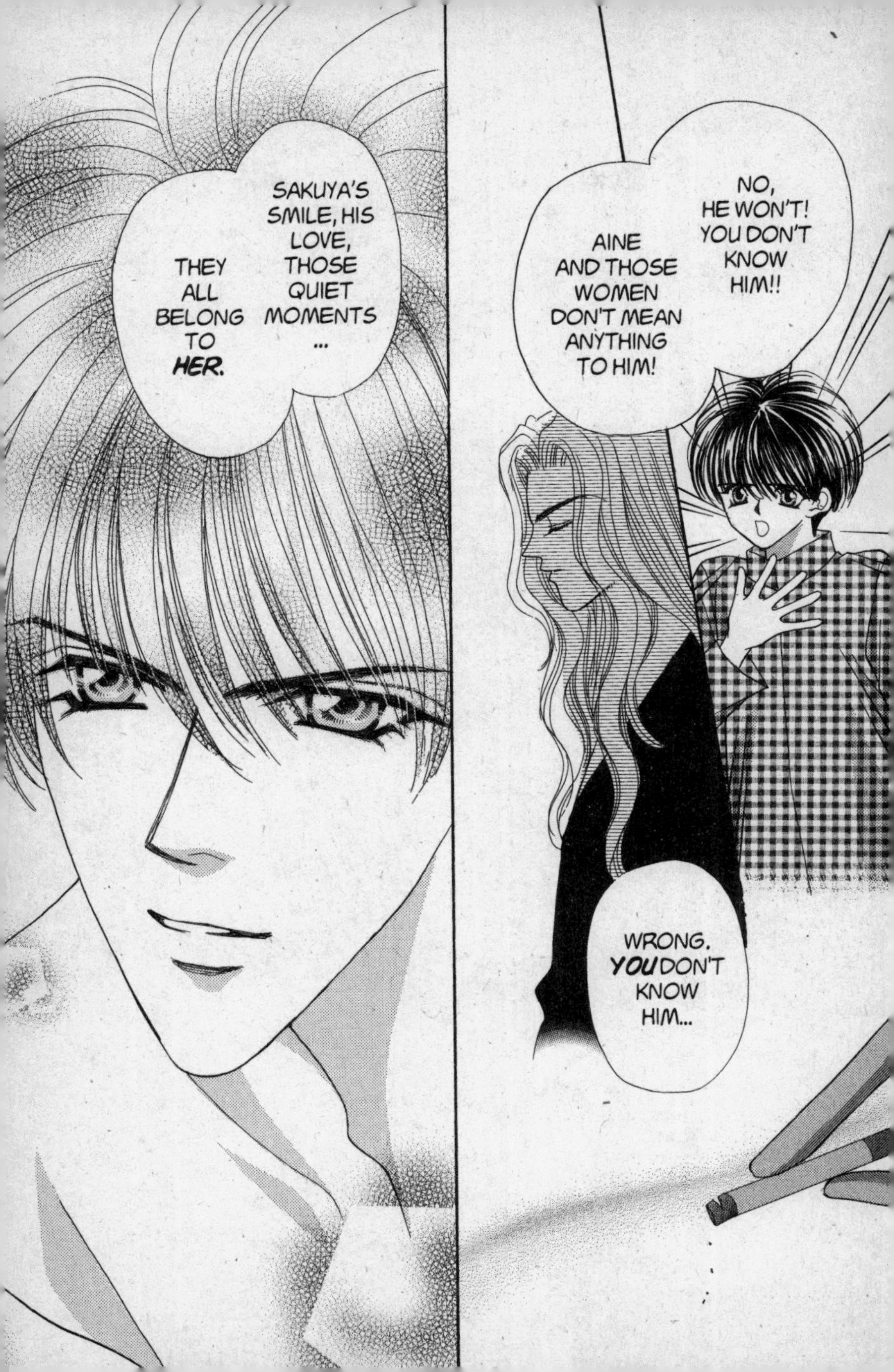
NO, HE WON'T! YOU DON'T KNOW HIM!!
AINE AND THOSE WOMEN DON'T MEAN ANYTHING TO HIM!
WRONG. YOU DON'T KNOW HIM...
SAKUYA'S SMILE, HIS LOVE, THOSE QUIET MOMENTS ...
THEY ALL BELONG TO HER.

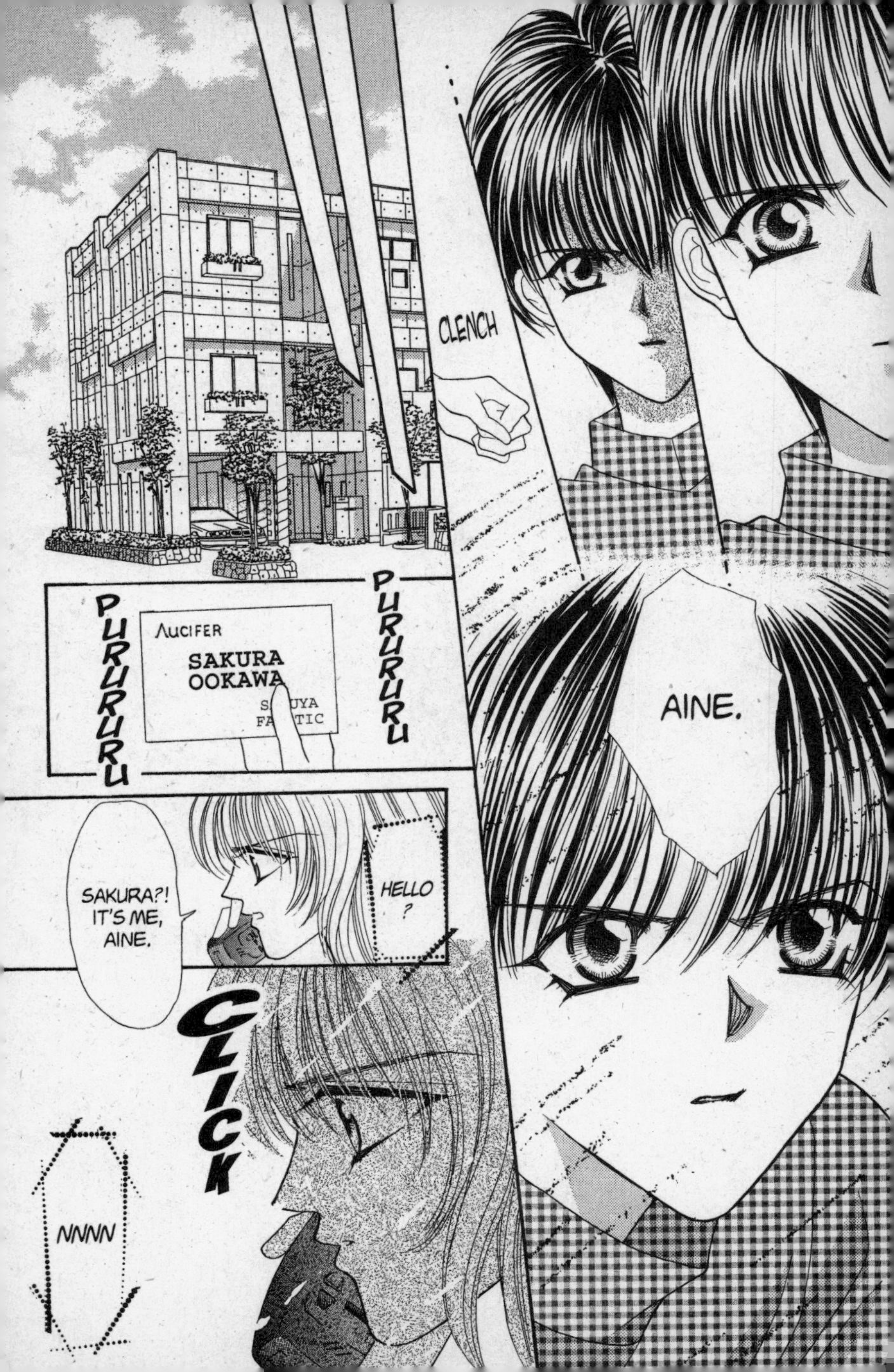
CLENCH
AINE.
PURURURU
PURURURU
SAKURA OOKAWA
HELLO?
SAKURA?! IT'S ME, AINE.
CLICK
NNNN

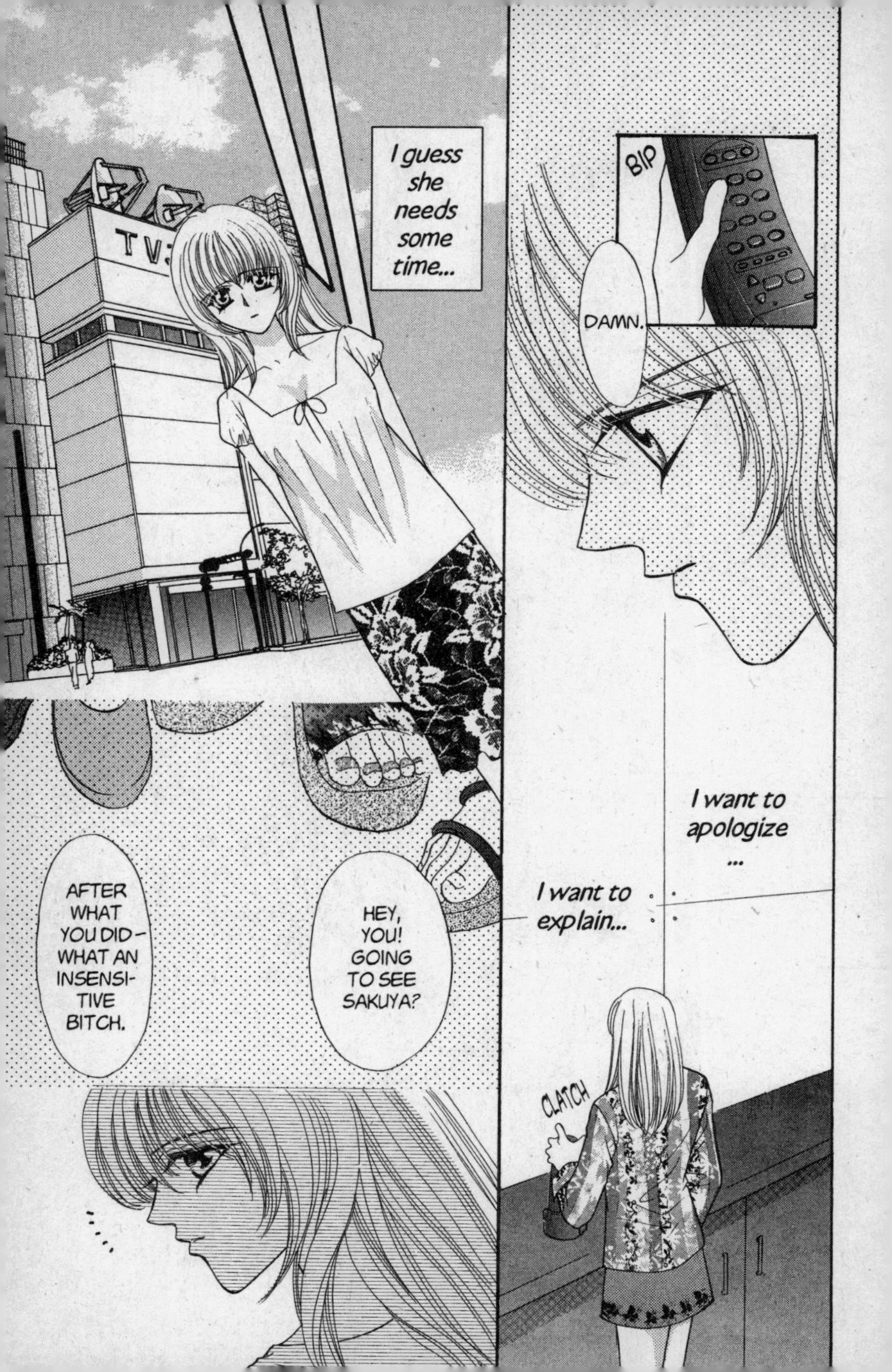
BIP
DAMN.
I want to apologize ...
I want to explain...
CLATCH
I guess she needs some time...
HEY, YOU! GOING TO SEE SAKUYA?
AFTER WHAT YOU DID-WHAT AN INSENSI-TIVE BITCH.
...

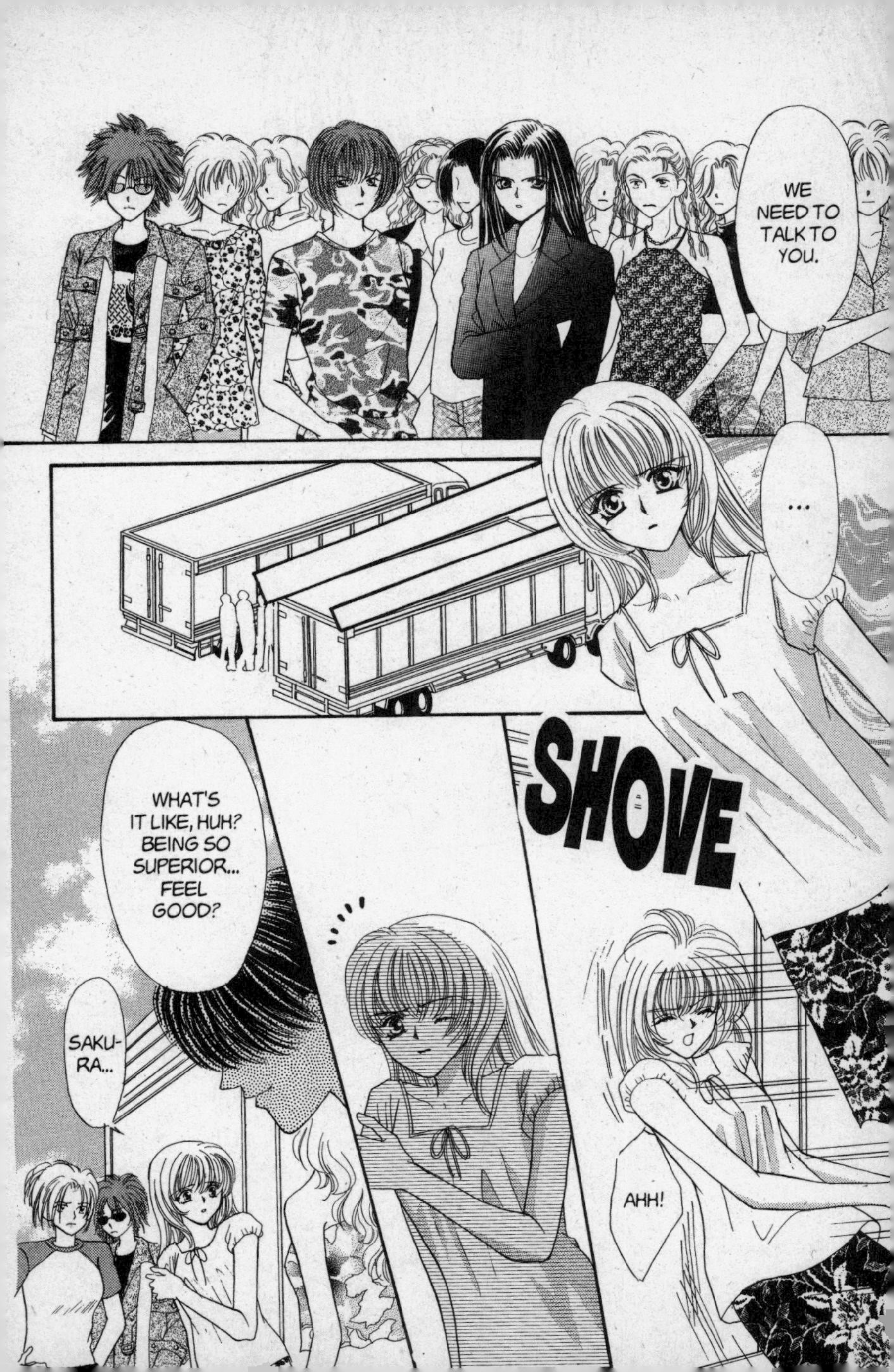
WE NEED TO TALK TO YOU.
...
SHOVE
AHH!
WHAT'S IT LIKE, HUH? BEING SO SUPERIOR... FEEL GOOD?
SAKU-RA...

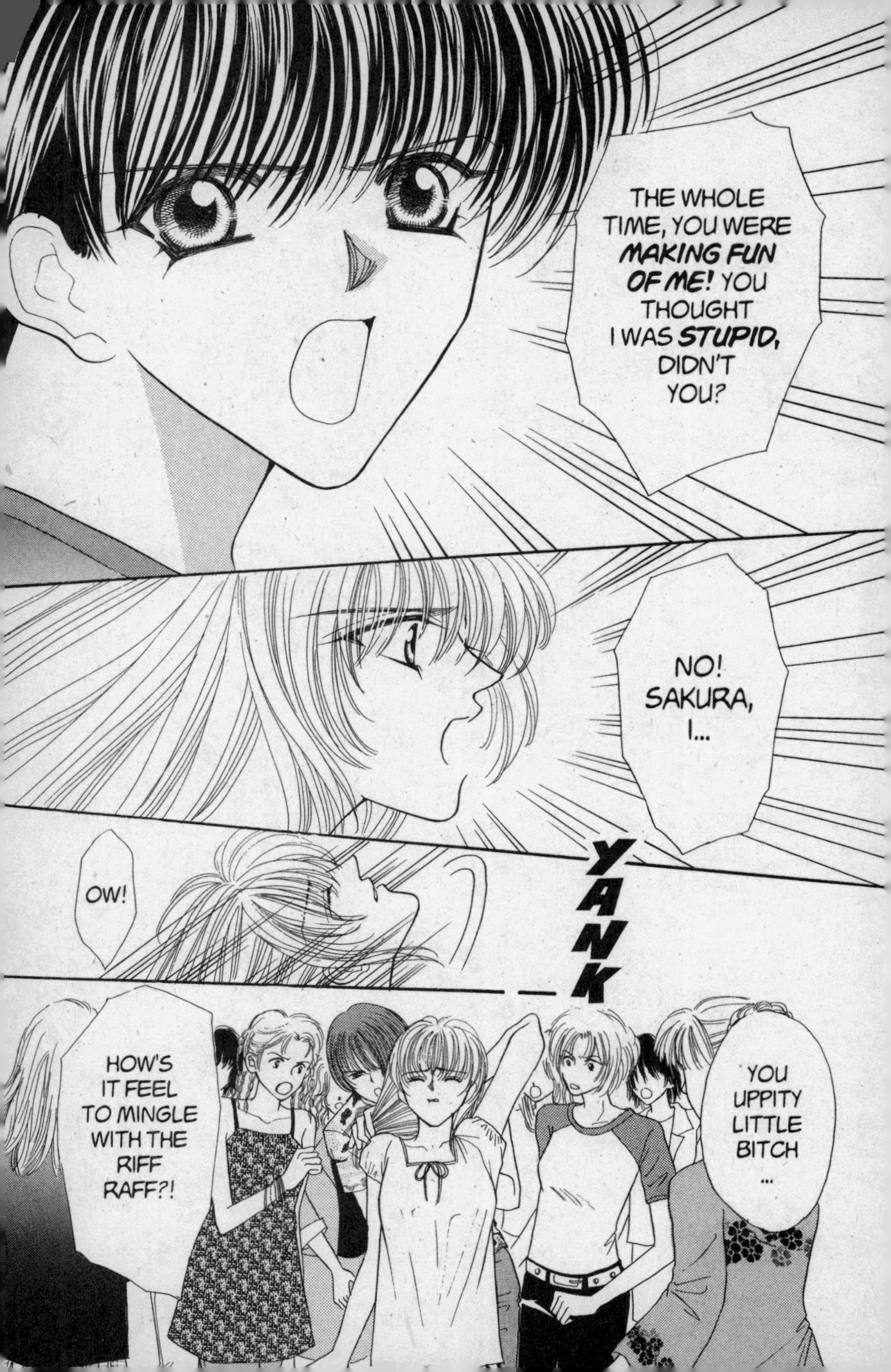

THE WHOLE TIME, YOU WERE MAKING FUN OF ME! YOU THOUGHT I WAS STUPID, DIDN'T YOU?
NO! SAKURA, I...
YANK
OW!
YOU UPPITY LITTLE BITCH ...
HOW'S IT FEEL TO MINGLE WITH THE RIFF RAFF?!

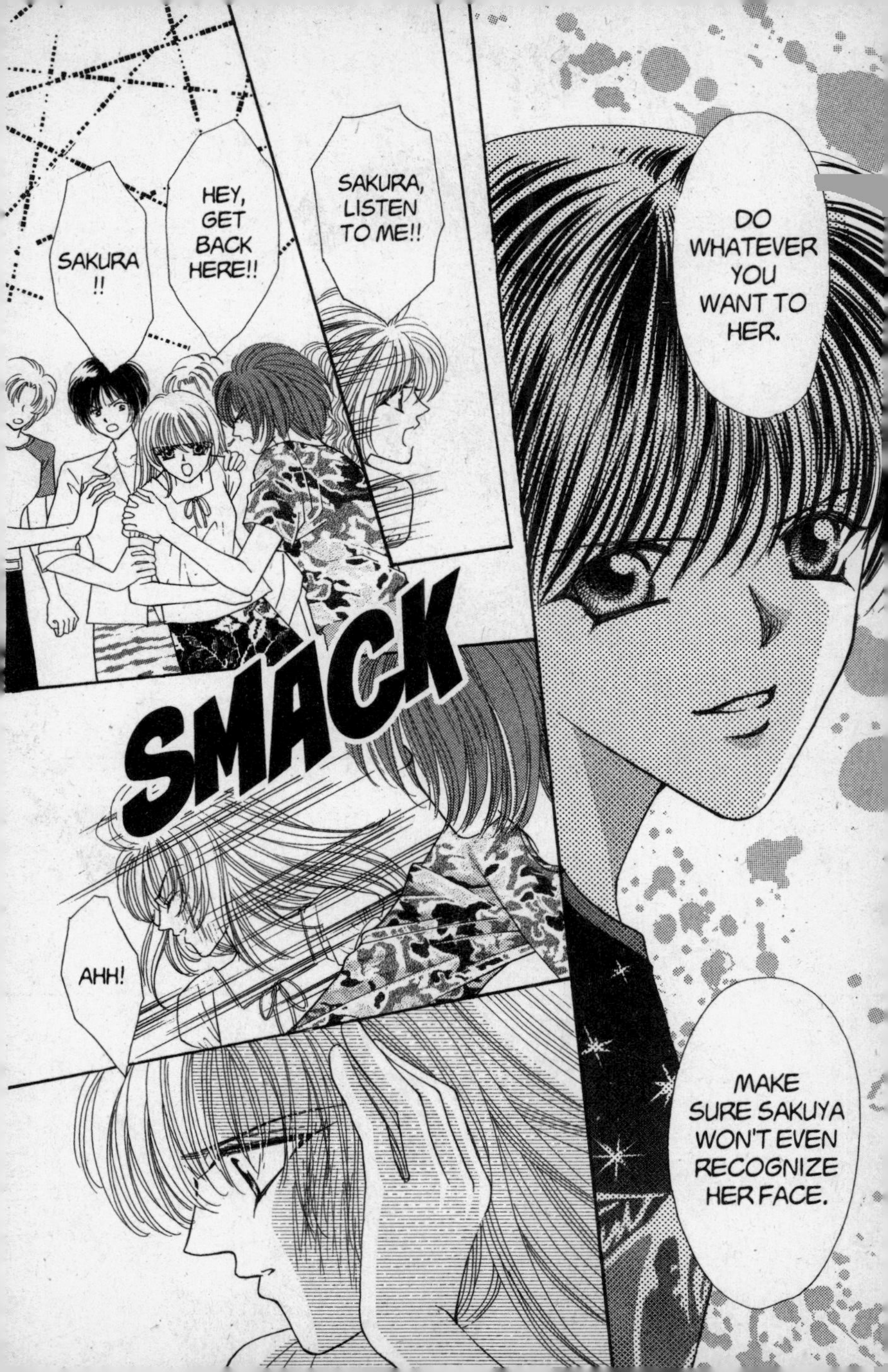
DO WHATEVER YOU WANT TO HER.
MAKE SURE SAKUYA WON'T EVEN RECOGNIZE HER FACE.
SAKURA, LISTEN TO ME!!
HEY, GET BACK HERE!!
SAKURA !!
SMACK
AHH!

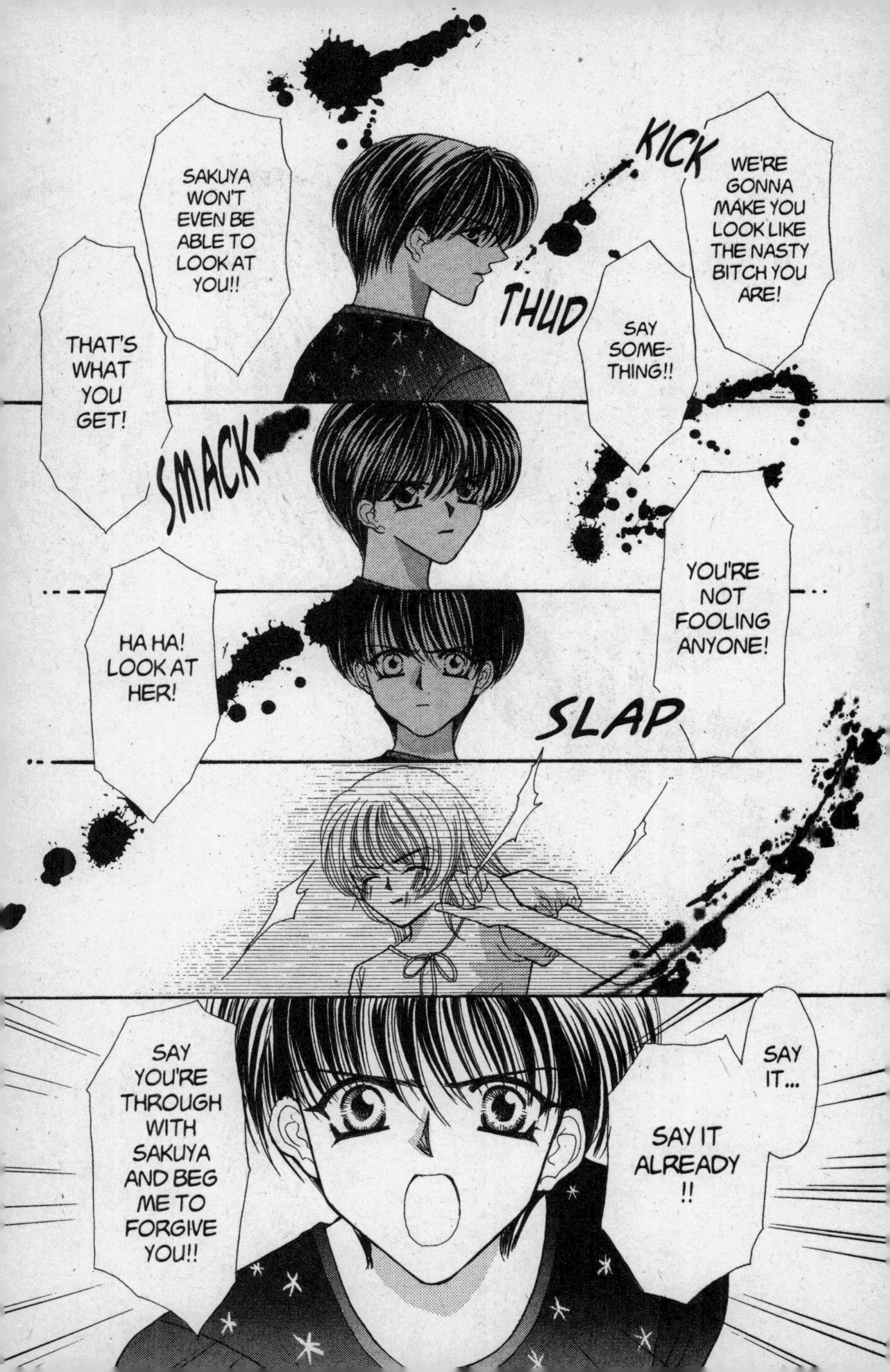
KICK
WE'RE GONNA MAKE YOU LOOK LIKE THE NASTY BITCH YOU ARE!
THUD
SAY SOME-THING!!
SAKUYA WON'T EVEN BE ABLE TO LOOK AT YOU!!
SMACK
THAT'S WHAT YOU GET!
YOU'RE NOT FOOLING ANYONE!
HA HA! LOOK AT HER!
SLAP
SAY IT...
SAY IT ALREADY !!
SAY YOU'RE THROUGH WITH SAKUYA AND BEG ME TO FORGIVE YOU!!

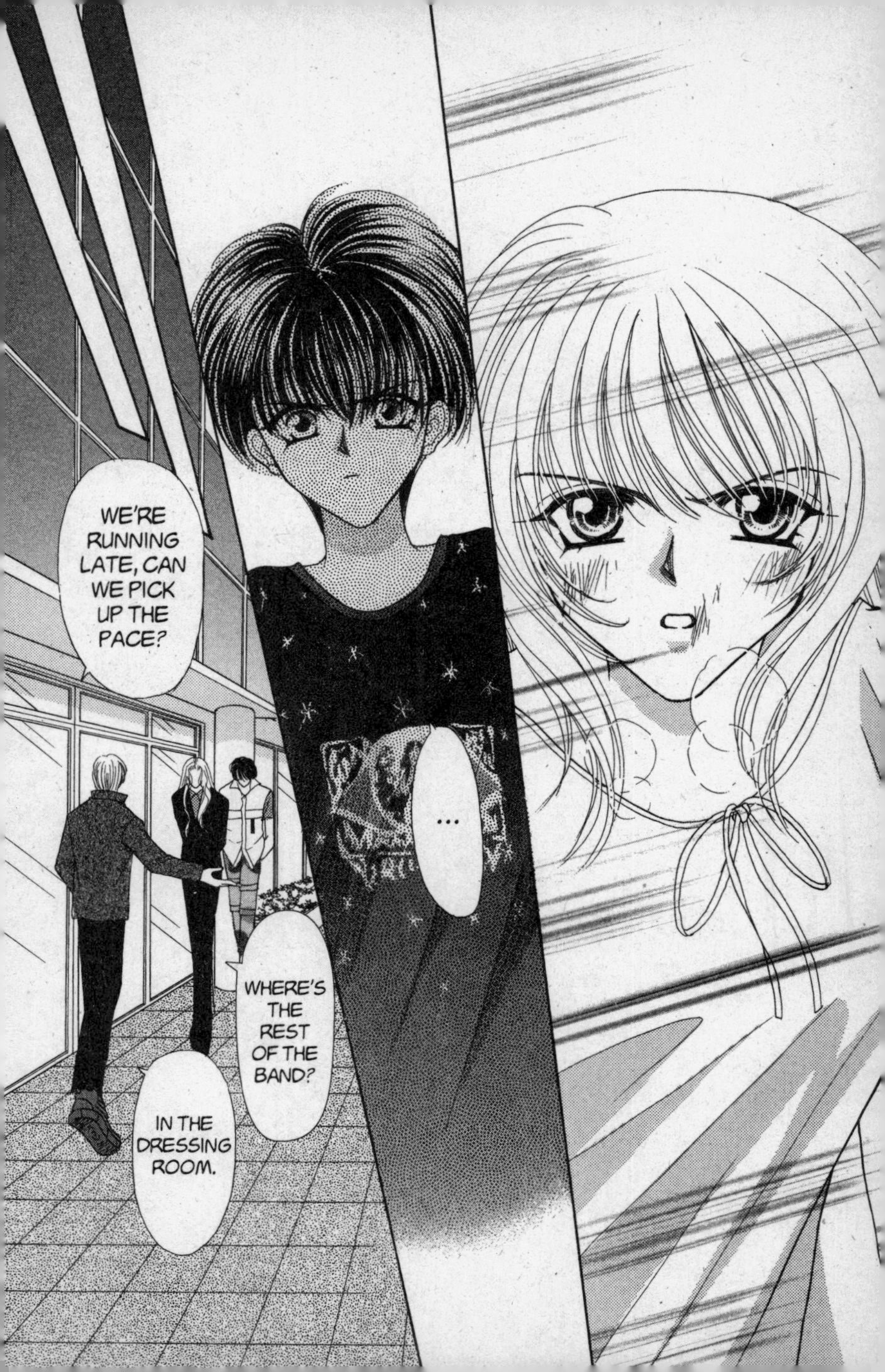
WE'RE RUNNING LATE, CAN WE PICK UP THE PACE?
...
WHERE'S THE REST OF THE BAND?
IN THE DRESSING ROOM.

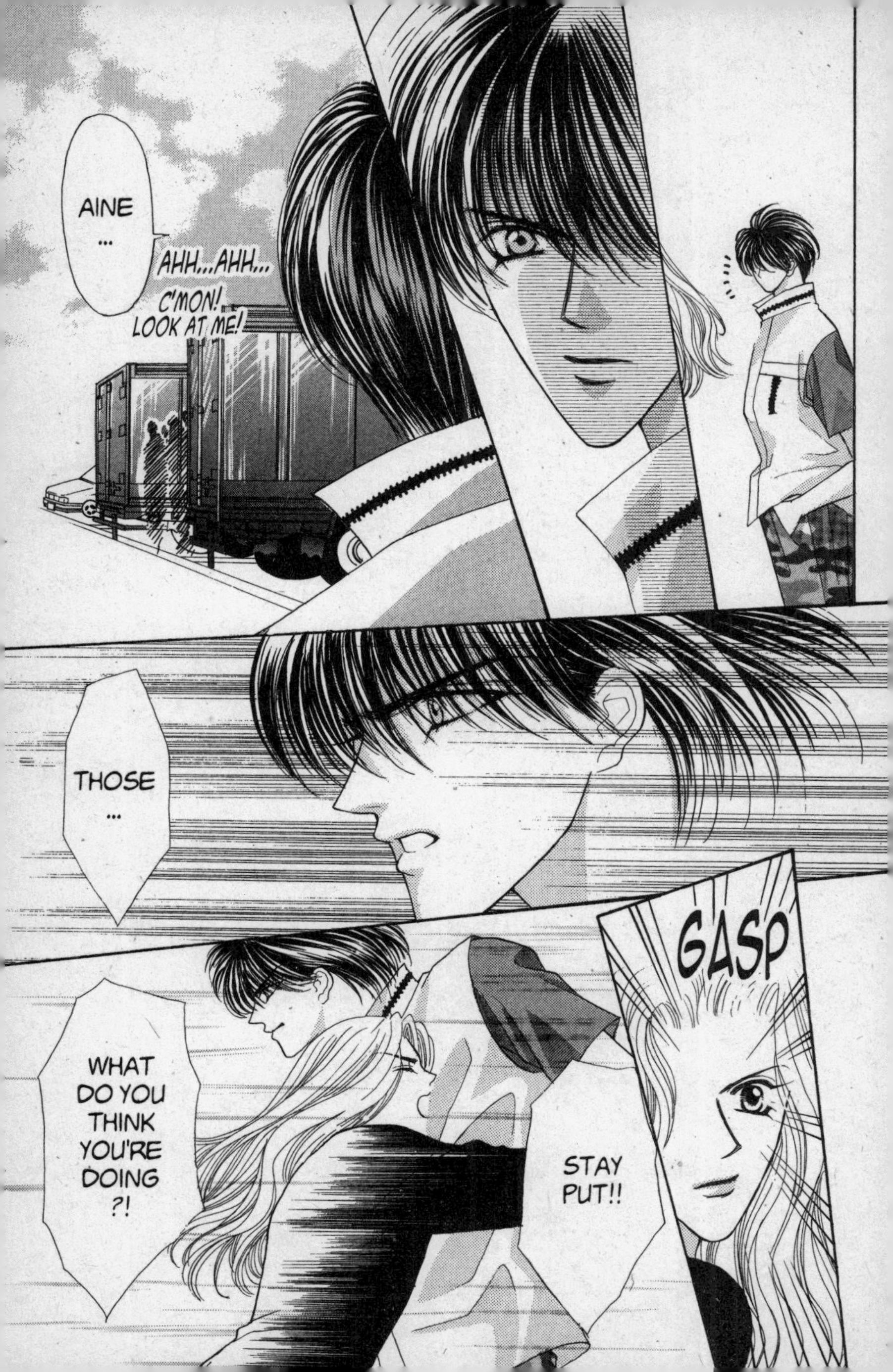
AINE ...
AHH...AHH... C'MON! LOOK AT ME!
THOSE ...
GASP
STAY PUT!!
WHAT DO YOU THINK YOU'RE DOING ?!

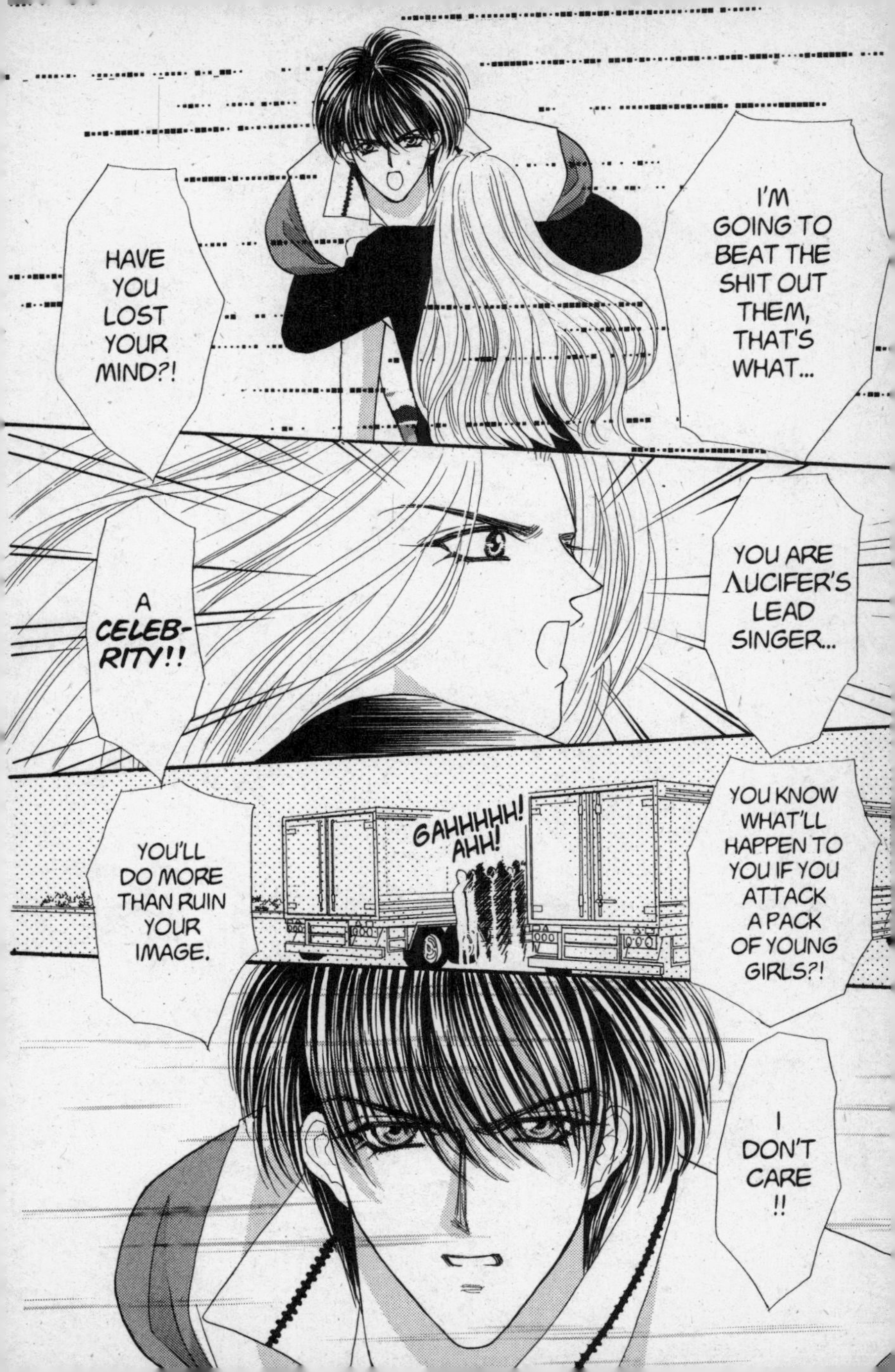
I'M GOING TO BEAT THE SHIT OUT THEM, THAT'S WHAT...
HAVE YOU LOST YOUR MIND?!
YOU ARE ΛUCIFER'S LEAD SINGER...
A CELEBRITY!!
YOU KNOW WHAT'LL HAPPEN TO YOU IF YOU ATTACK A PACK OF YOUNG GIRLS?!
GAHHHHH! AHH!
YOU'LL DO MORE THAN RUIN YOUR IMAGE.
I DON'T CARE !!

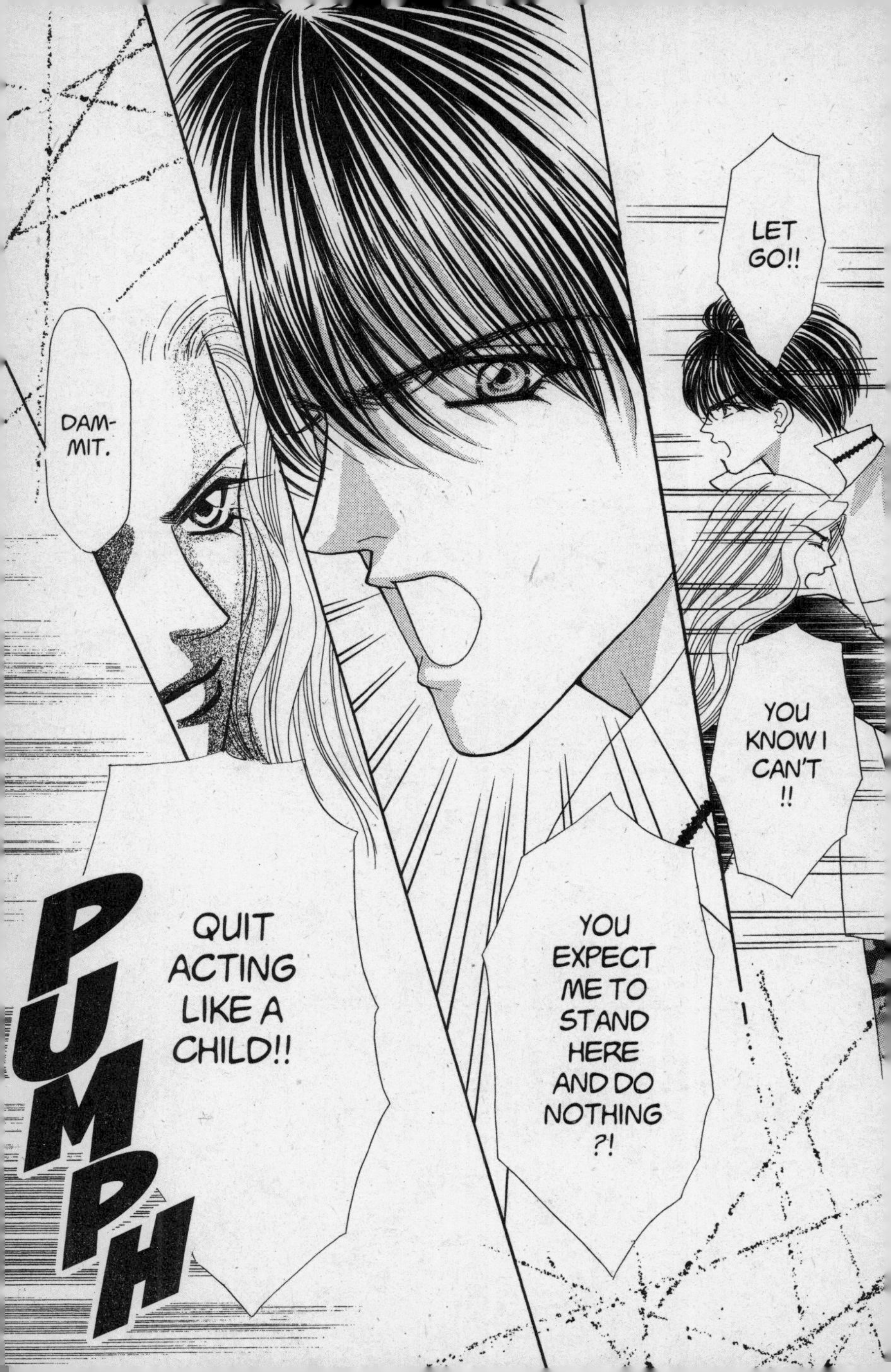
LET GO!!
YOU KNOW I CAN'T !!
YOU EXPECT ME TO STAND HERE AND DO NOTHING ?!
DAM-MIT.
QUIT ACTING LIKE A CHILD!!
PUMPH

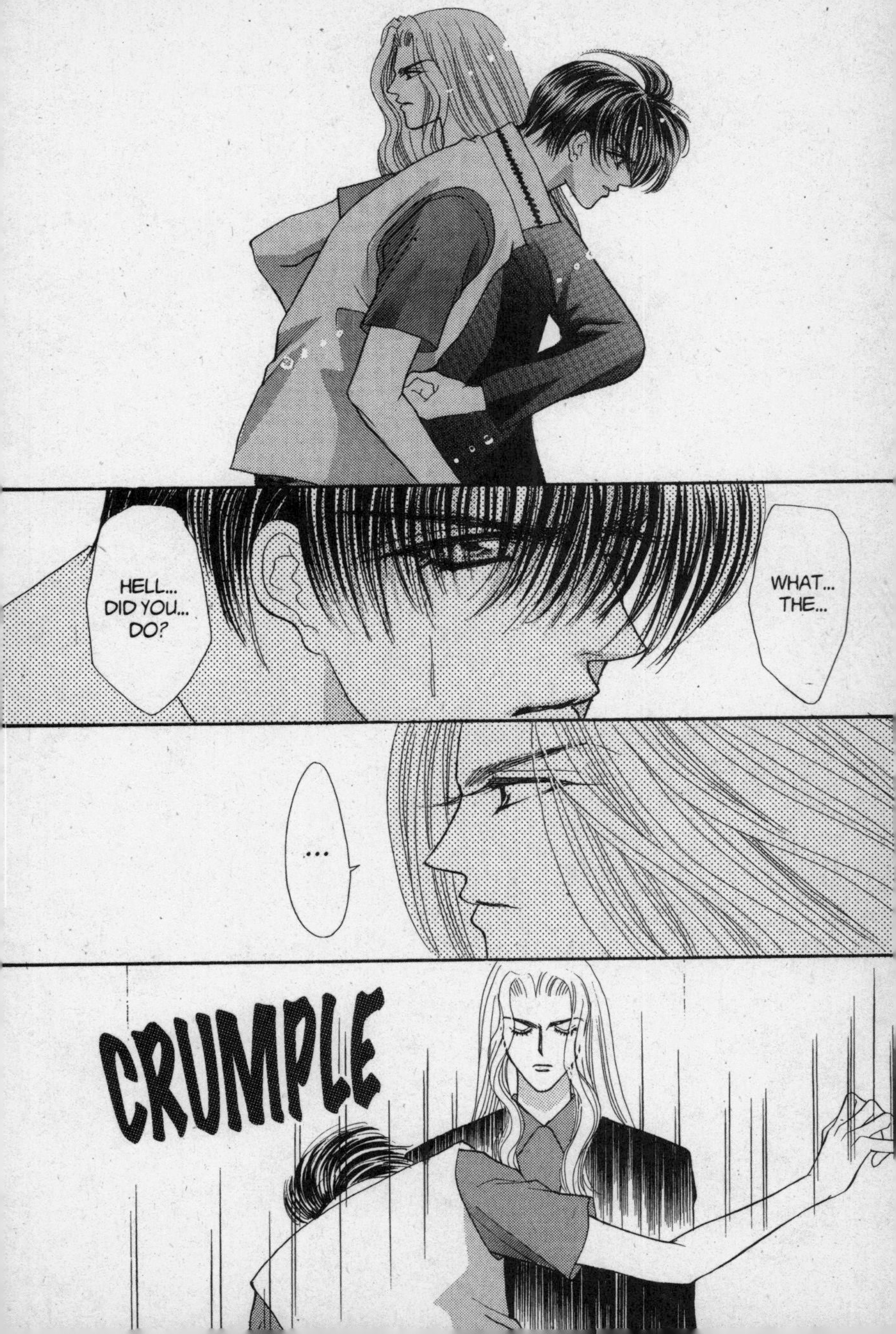
WHAT... THE...
HELL... DID YOU... DO?
...
CRUMPLE

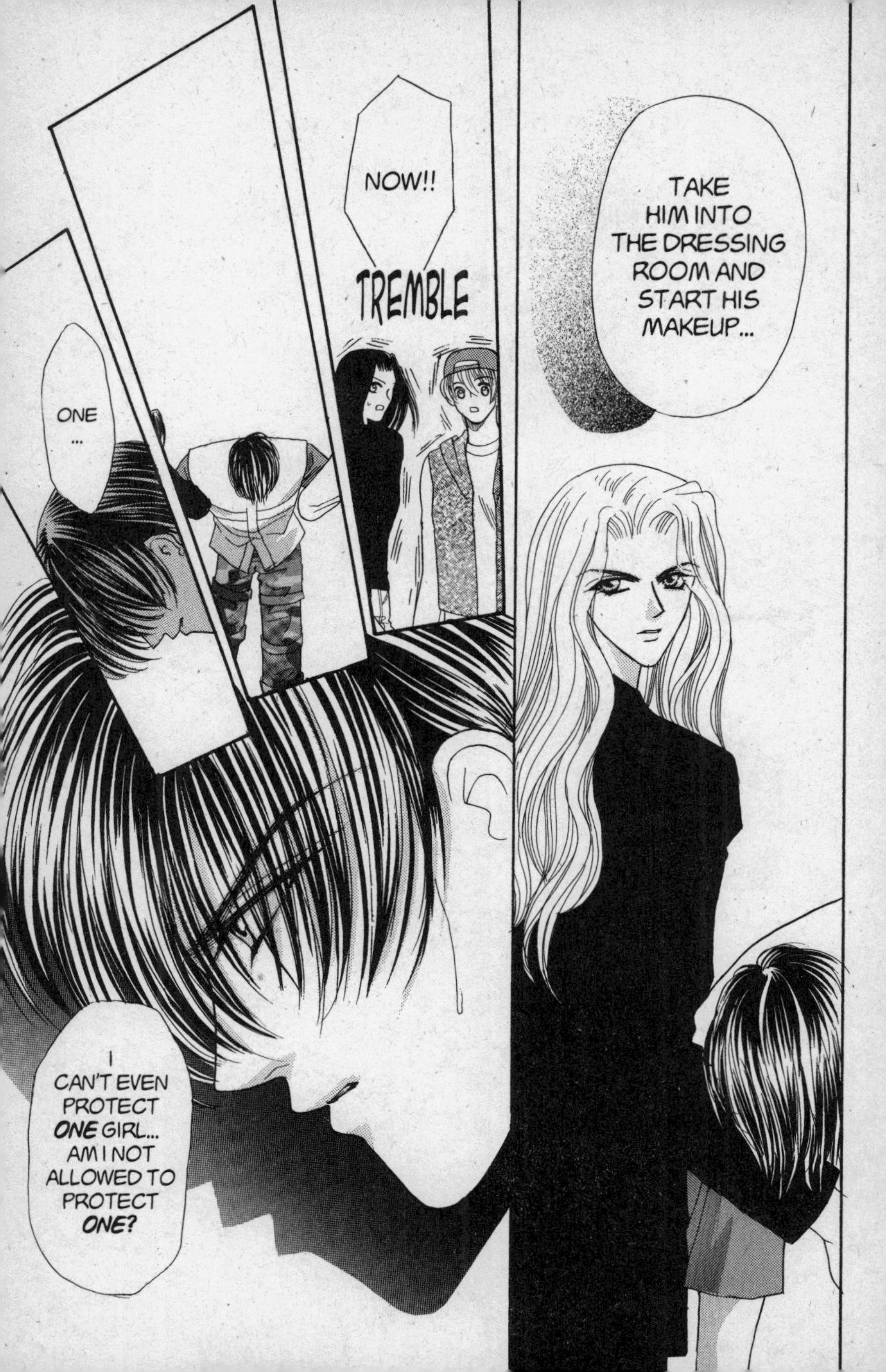
TAKE HIM INTO THE DRESSING ROOM AND START HIS MAKEUP...
NOW!!
TREMBLE
ONE ...
I CAN'T EVEN PROTECT ONE GIRL... AM I NOT ALLOWED TO PROTECT ONE?

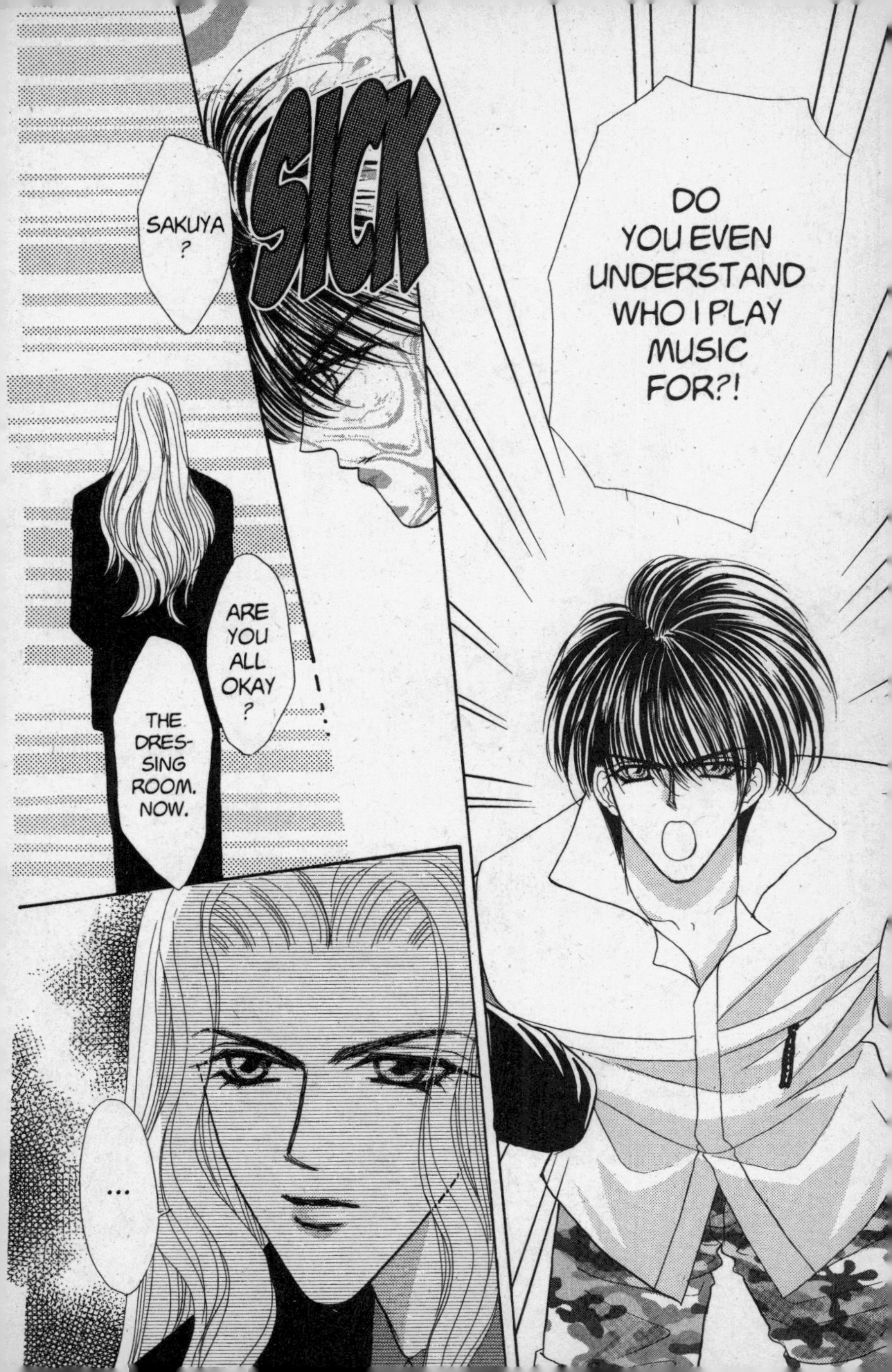
DO YOU EVEN UNDERSTAND WHO I PLAY MUSIC FOR?!
SICK
SAKUYA?
...
ARE YOU ALL OKAY?
THE DRES-SING ROOM. NOW.
...

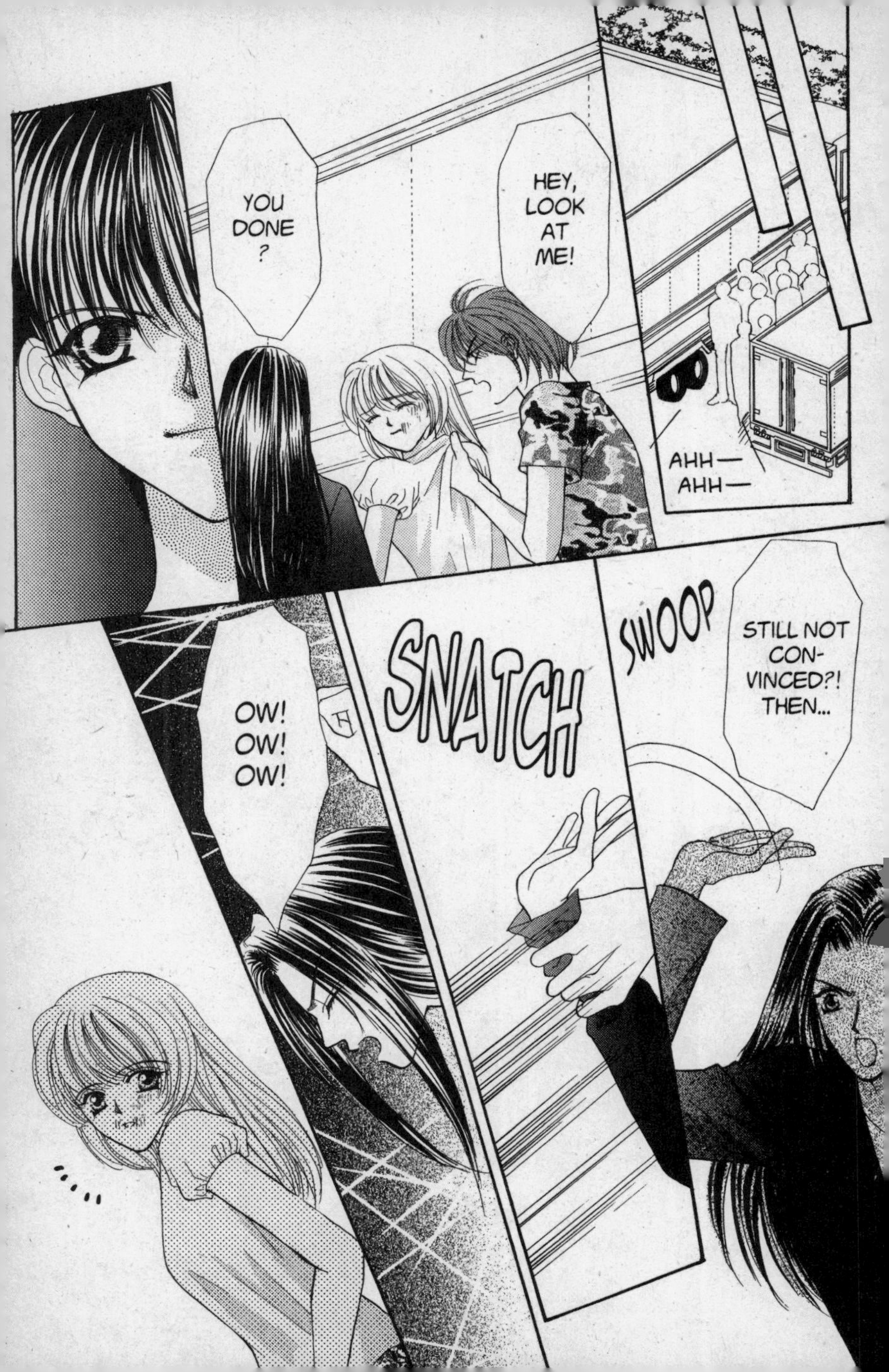
AHH— AHH—
HEY, LOOK AT ME!
YOU DONE?
SWOOP
STILL NOT CON-VINCED?! THEN...
SNATCH
OW! OW! OW!

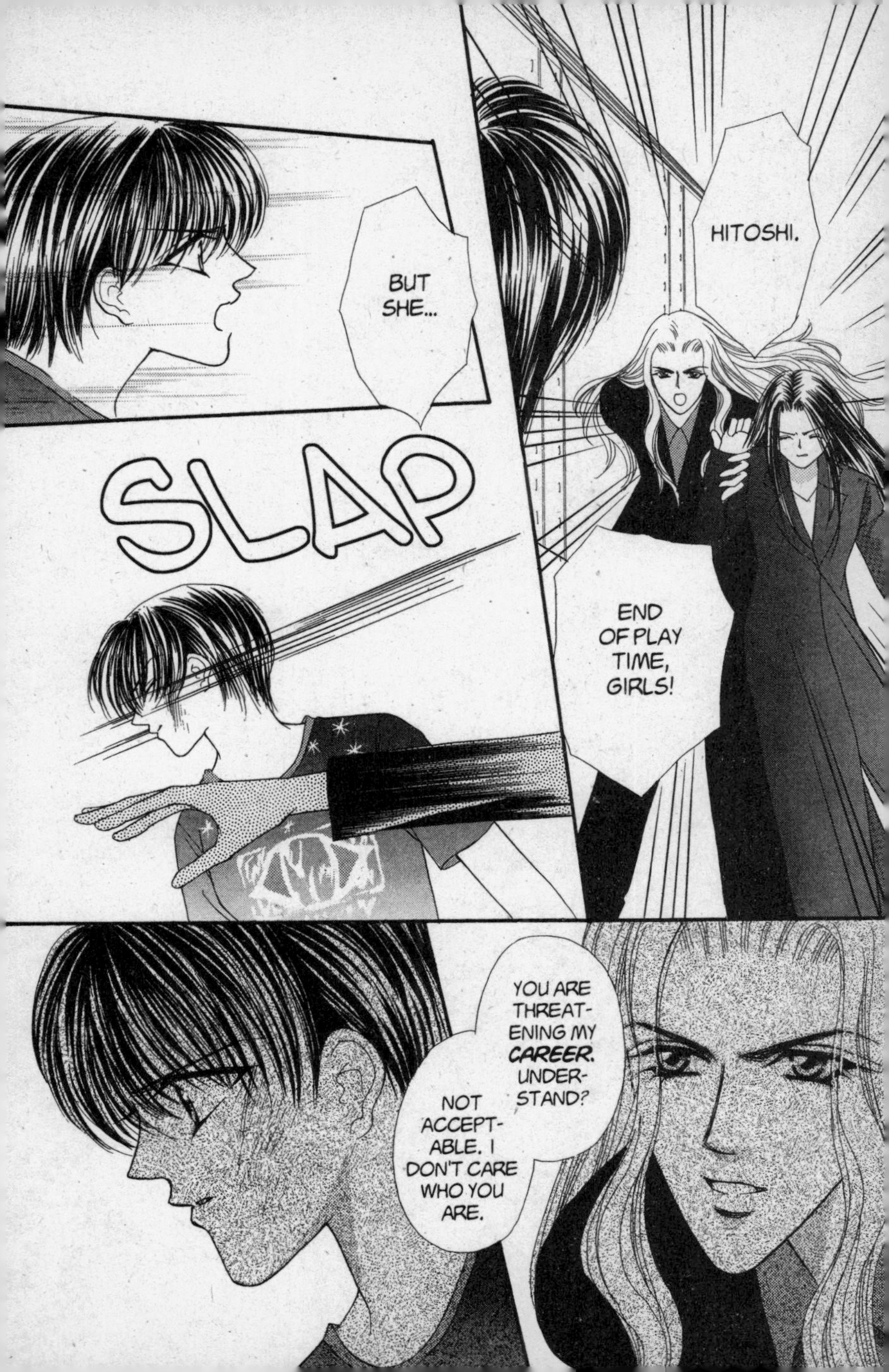
HITOSHI.
END OF PLAY TIME, GIRLS!
BUT SHE...
SLAP
YOU ARE THREAT-ENING MY **CAREER.** UNDER-STAND?
NOT ACCEPT-ABLE. I DON'T CARE WHO YOU ARE.

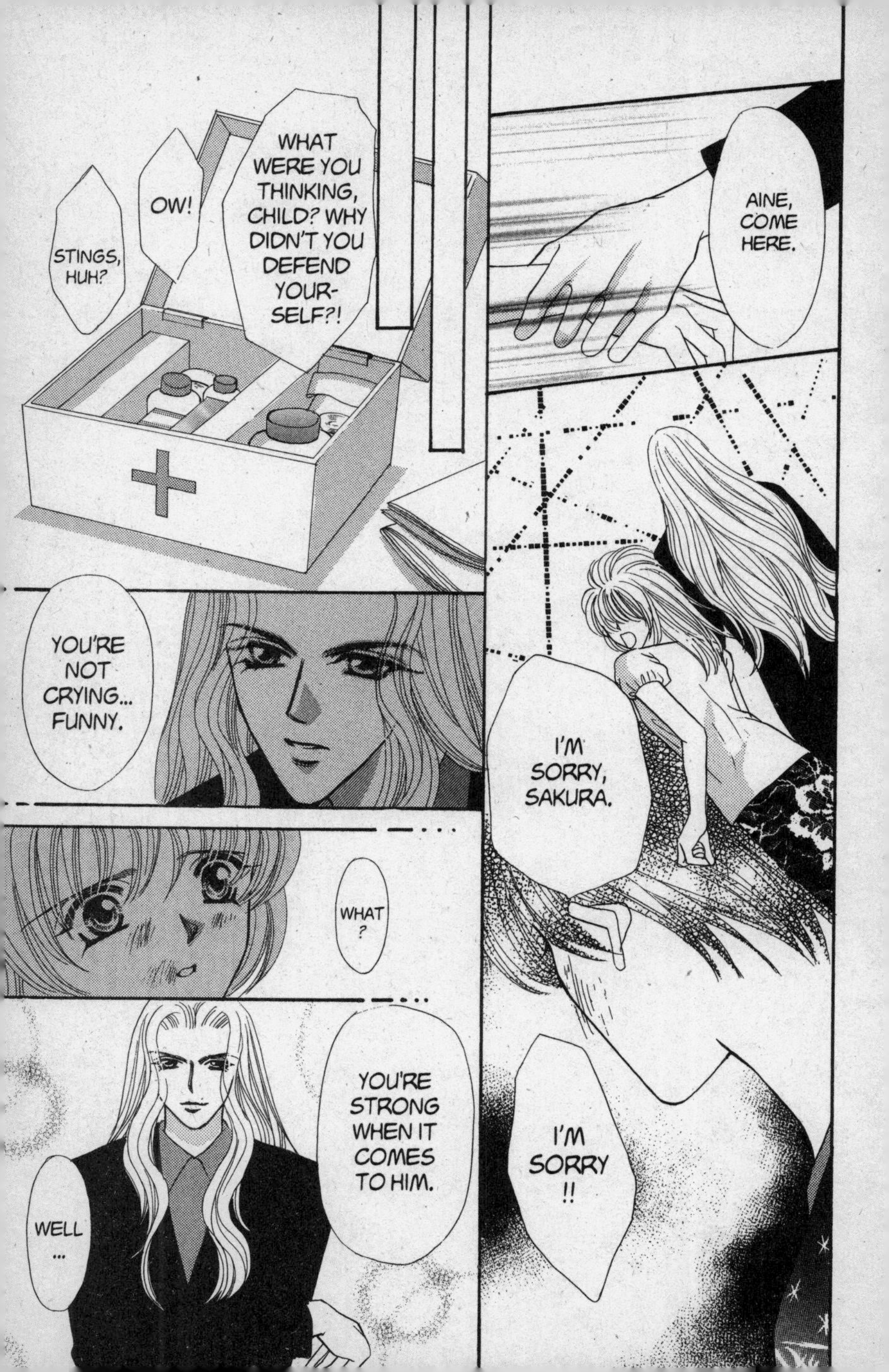
AINE, COME HERE.
I'M SORRY, SAKURA.
I'M SORRY !!
WHAT WERE YOU THINKING, CHILD? WHY DIDN'T YOU DEFEND YOUR-SELF?!
OW!
STINGS, HUH?
YOU'RE NOT CRYING... FUNNY.
WHAT ?
YOU'RE STRONG WHEN IT COMES TO HIM.
WELL ...

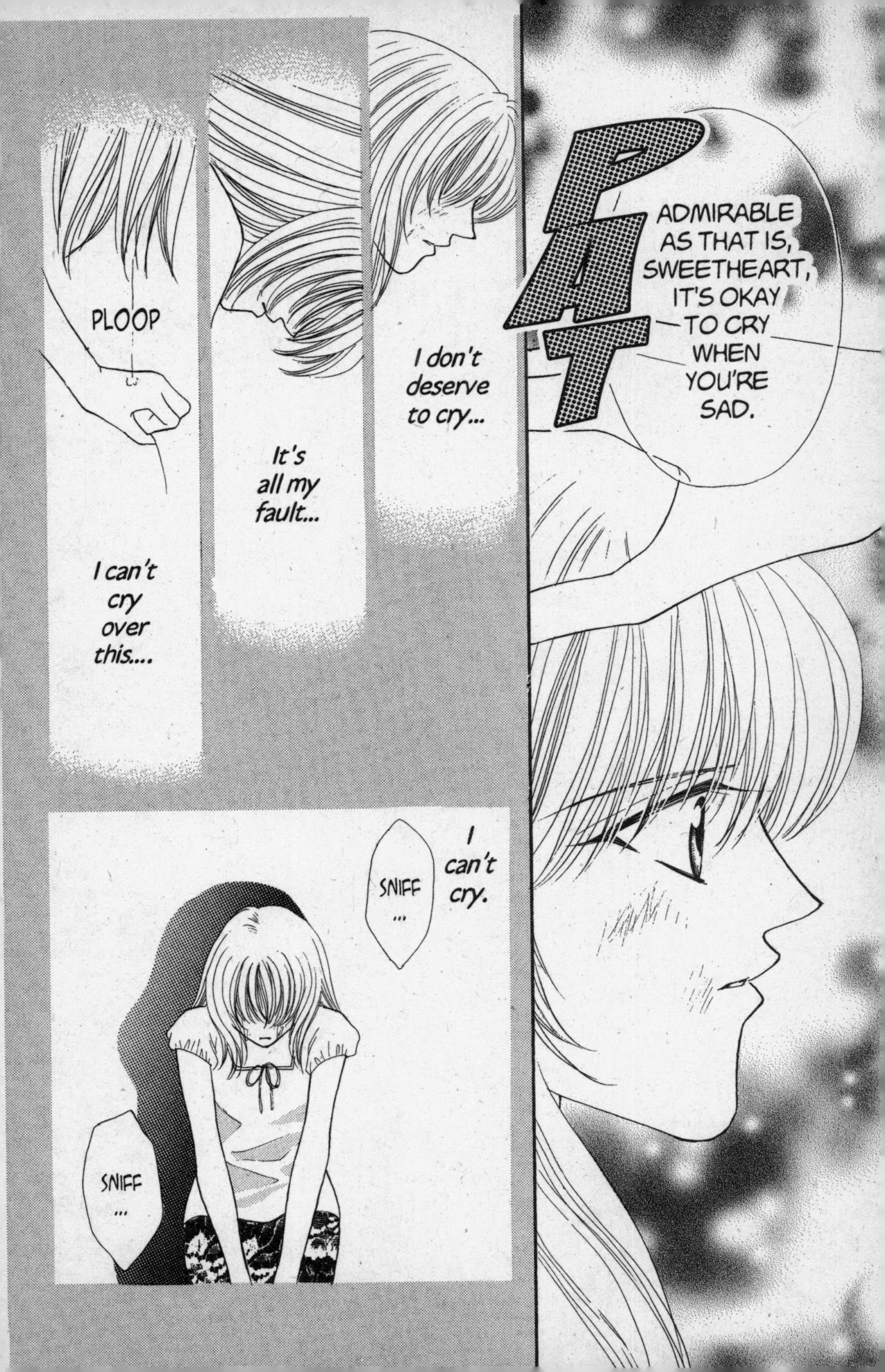
PAT
ADMIRABLE AS THAT IS, SWEETHEART, IT'S OKAY TO CRY WHEN YOU'RE SAD.
I don't deserve to cry...
It's all my fault...
PLOOP
I can't cry over this....
I can't cry.
SNIFF ...
SNIFF ...

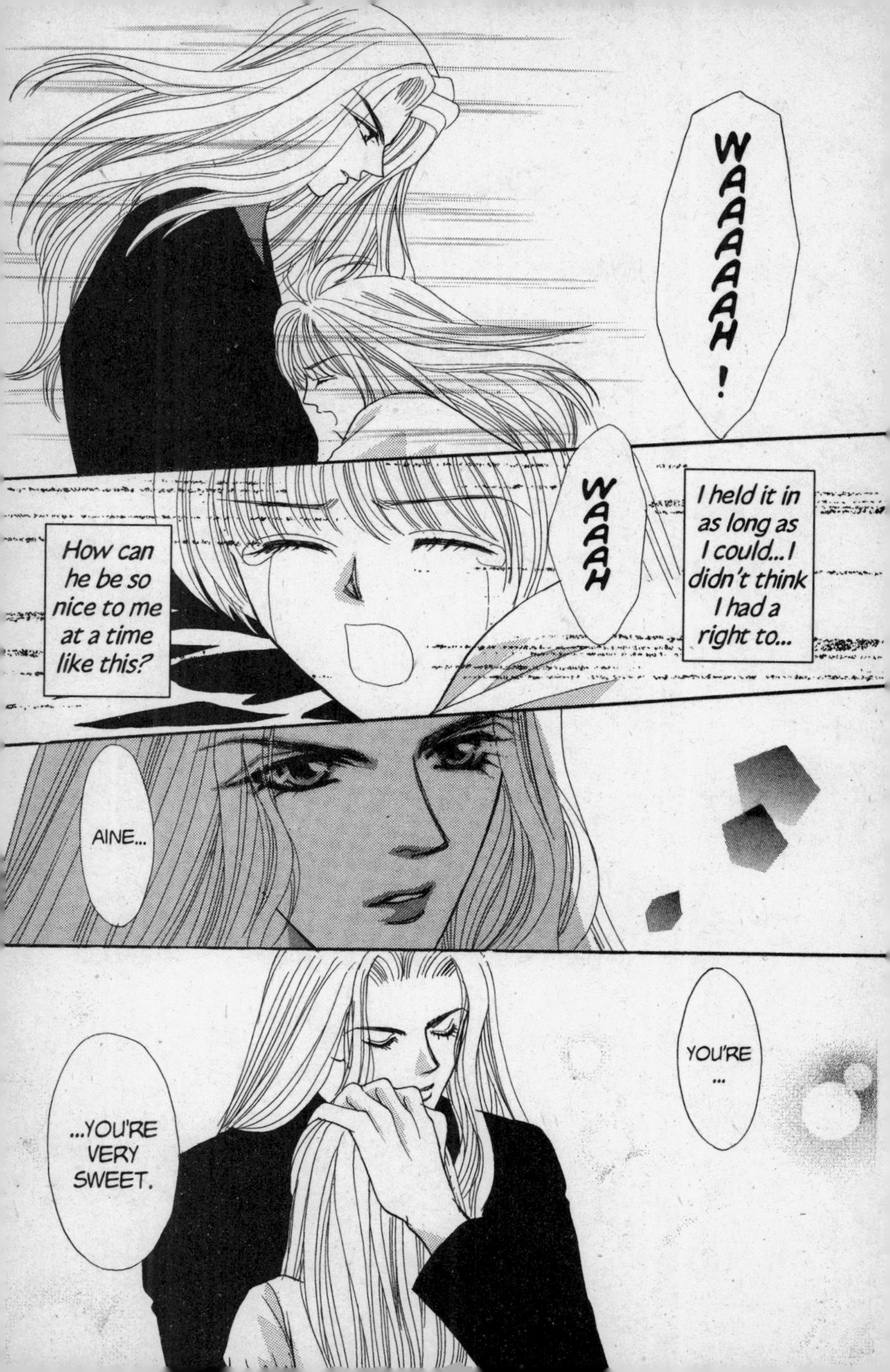
WAAAAAH!
I held it in as long as I could...I didn't think I had a right to...
WAAAH
How can he be so nice to me at a time like this?
AINE...
YOU'RE ...
...YOU'RE VERY SWEET.

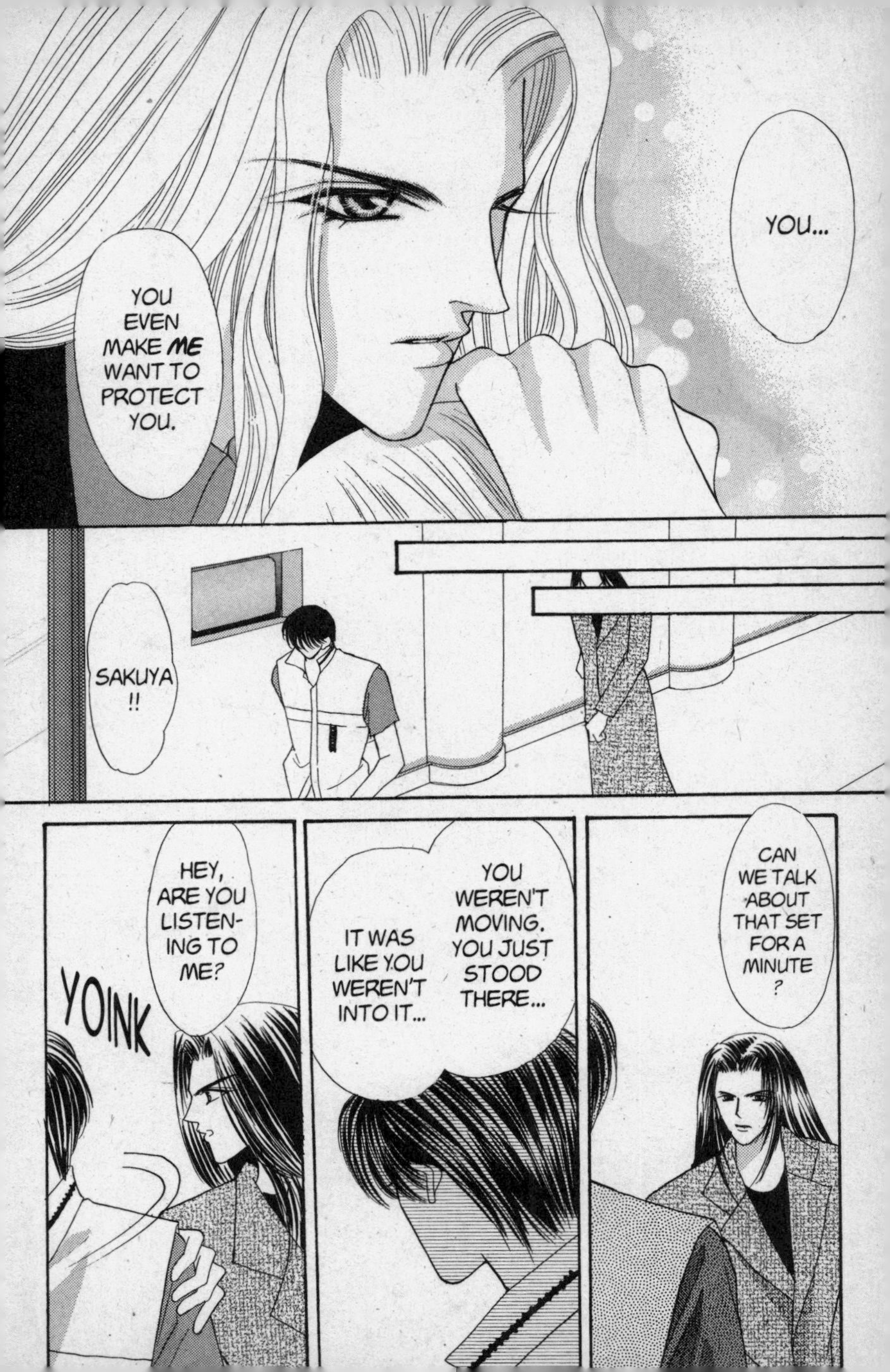
YOU...
YOU EVEN MAKE *ME* WANT TO PROTECT YOU.
SAKUYA !!
CAN WE TALK ABOUT THAT SET FOR A MINUTE ?
YOU WEREN'T MOVING. YOU JUST STOOD THERE...
IT WAS LIKE YOU WEREN'T INTO IT...
HEY, ARE YOU LISTEN-ING TO ME?
YOINK

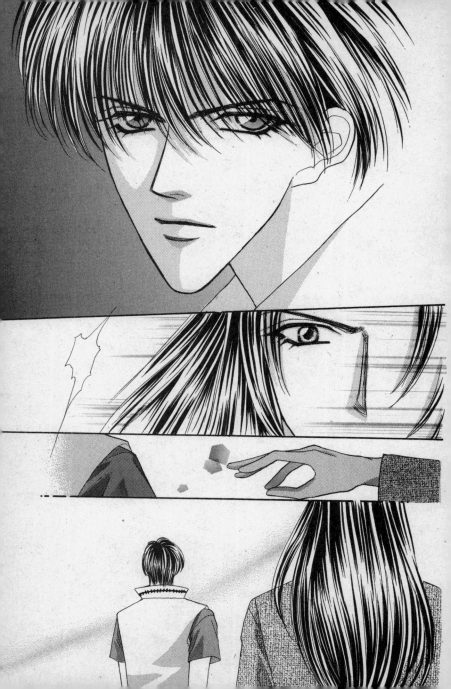

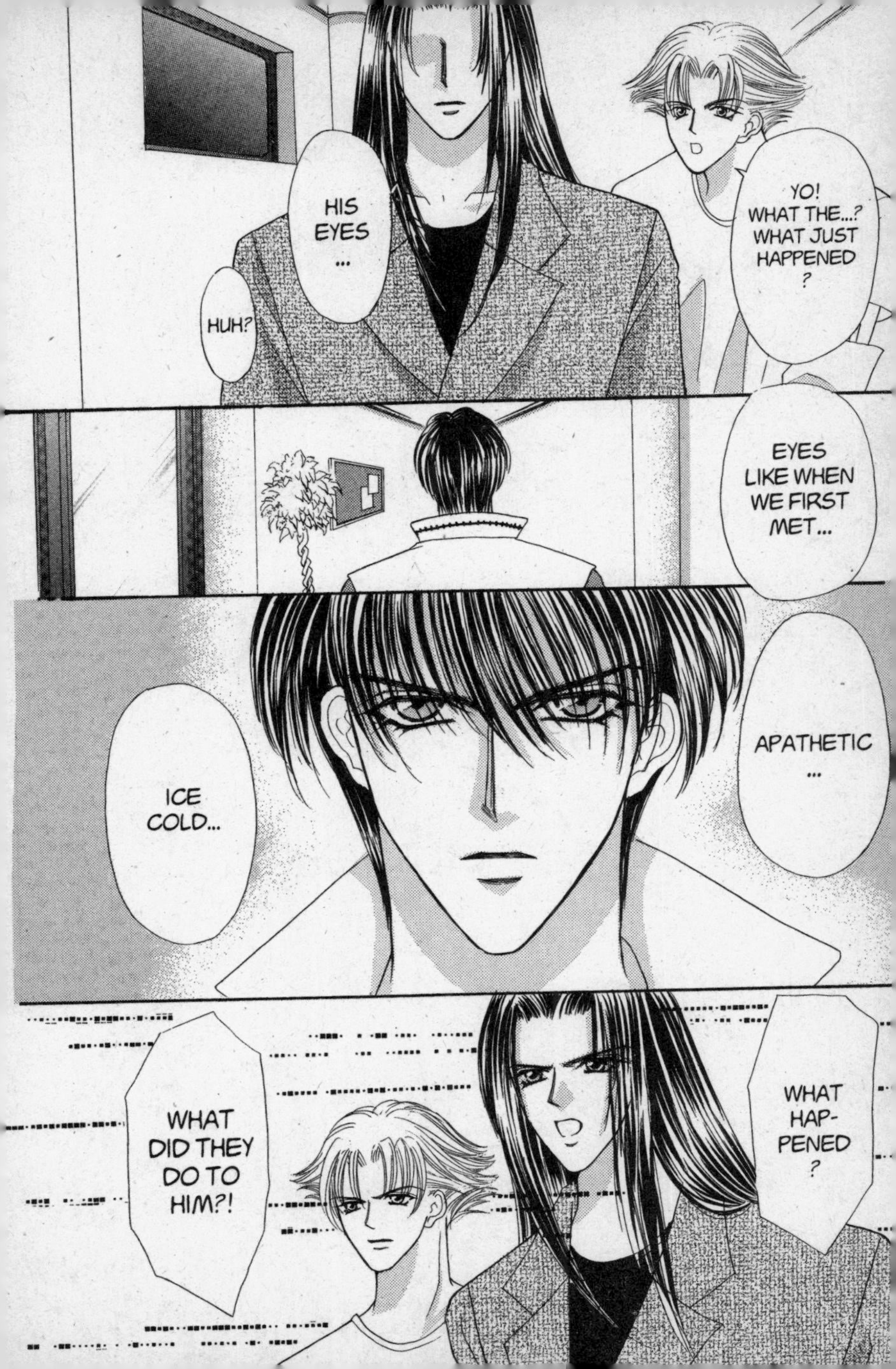
YO! WHAT THE...? WHAT JUST HAPPENED?
HIS EYES...
HUH?
EYES LIKE WHEN WE FIRST MET...
APATHETIC...
ICE COLD...
WHAT HAP-PENED?
WHAT DID THEY DO TO HIM?!

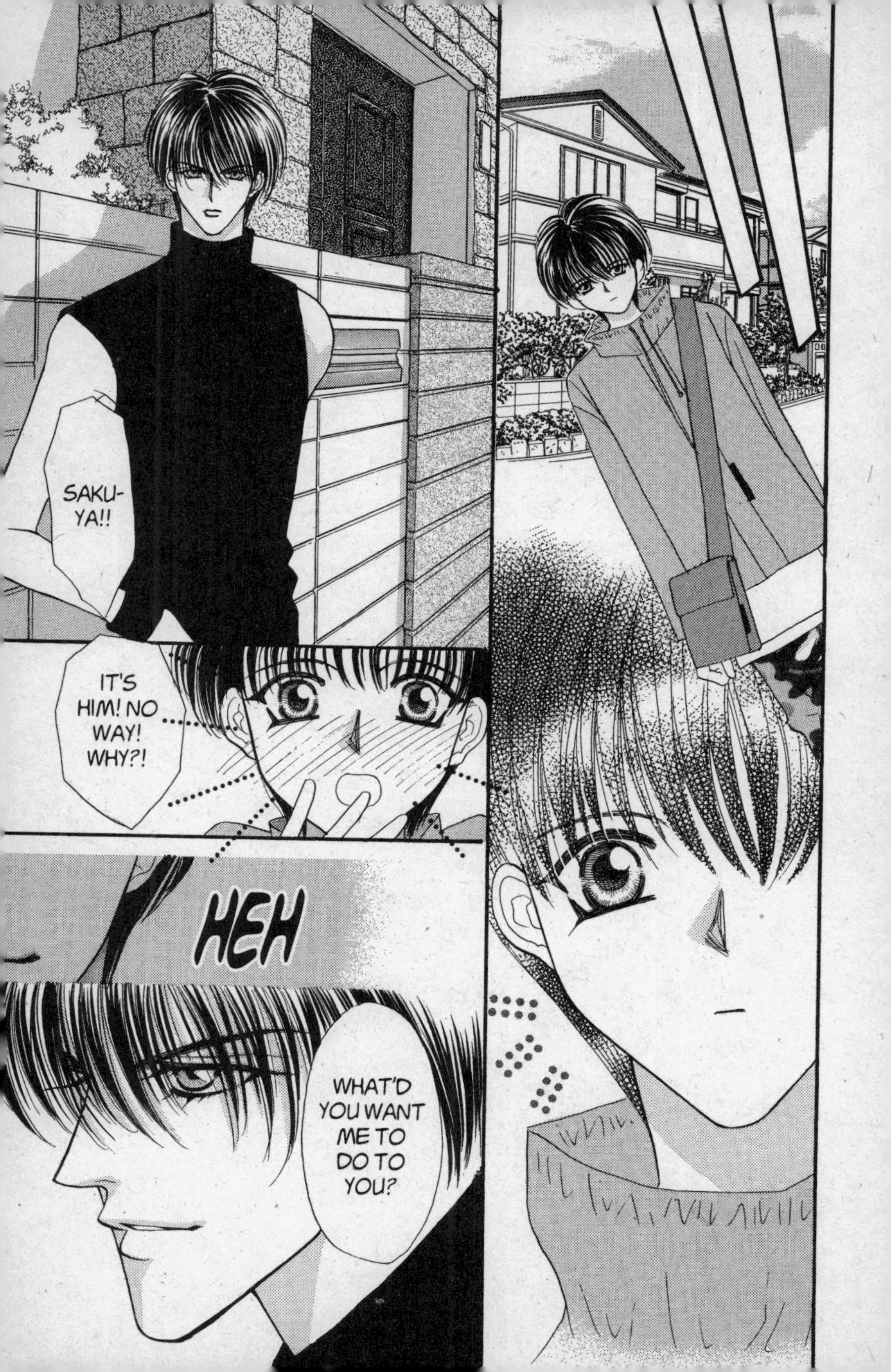
SAKU-YA!!
IT'S HIM! NO WAY! WHY?!
HEH
WHAT'D YOU WANT ME TO DO TO YOU?

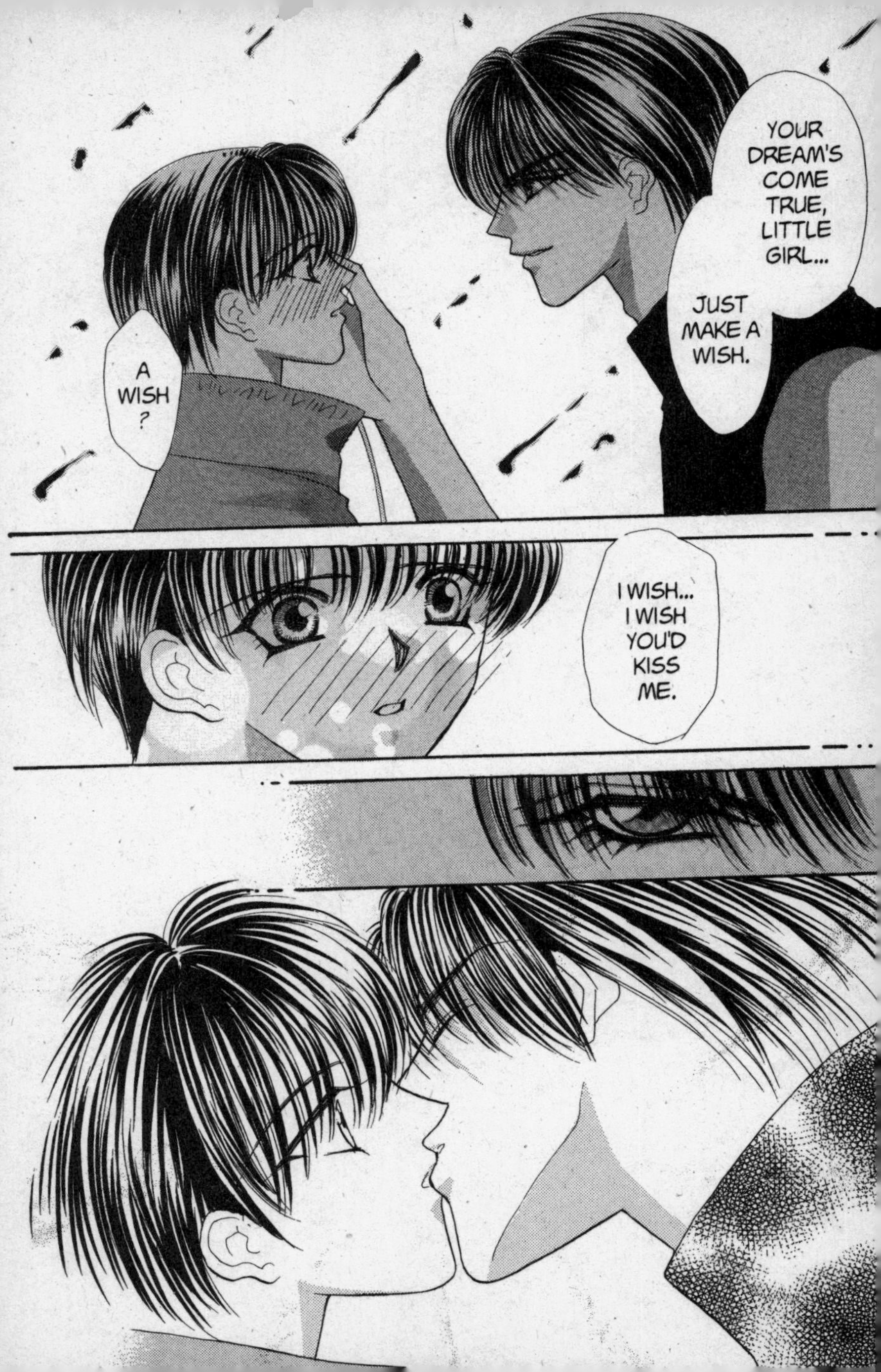
YOUR DREAM'S COME TRUE, LITTLE GIRL...
JUST MAKE A WISH.
A WISH?
I WISH... I WISH YOU'D KISS ME.

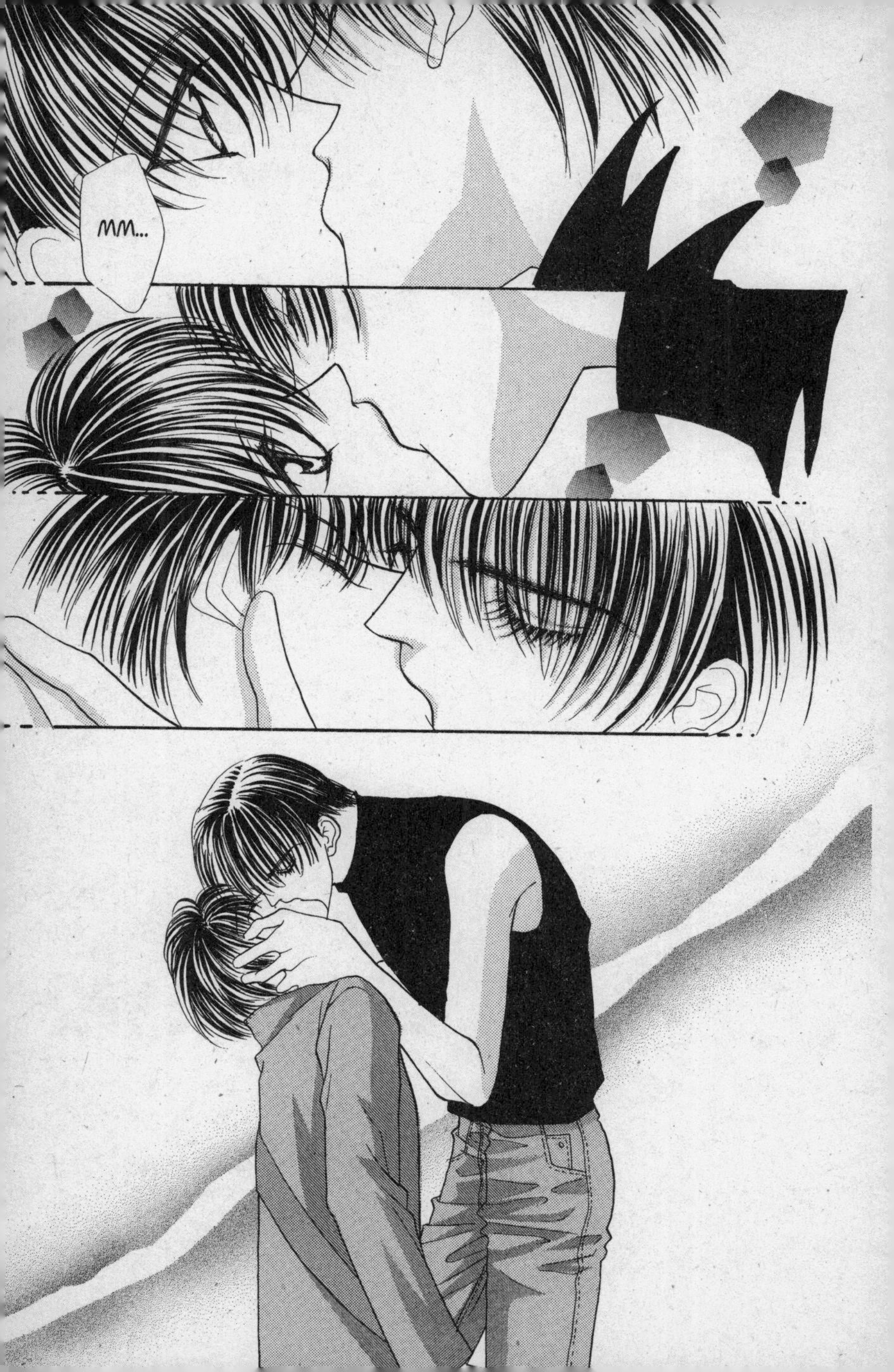
MM...

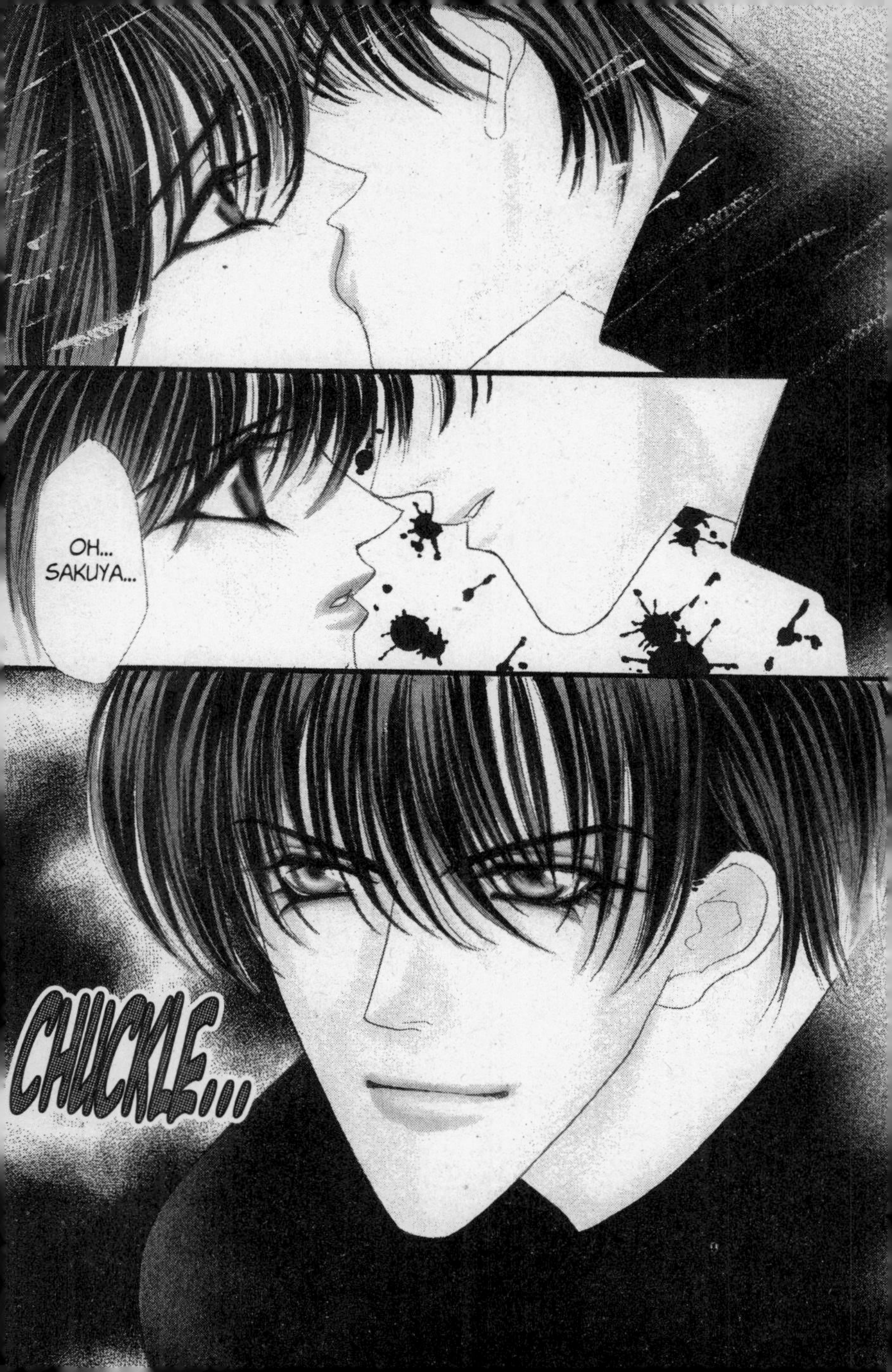
OH... SAKUYA...
CHUCKLE...

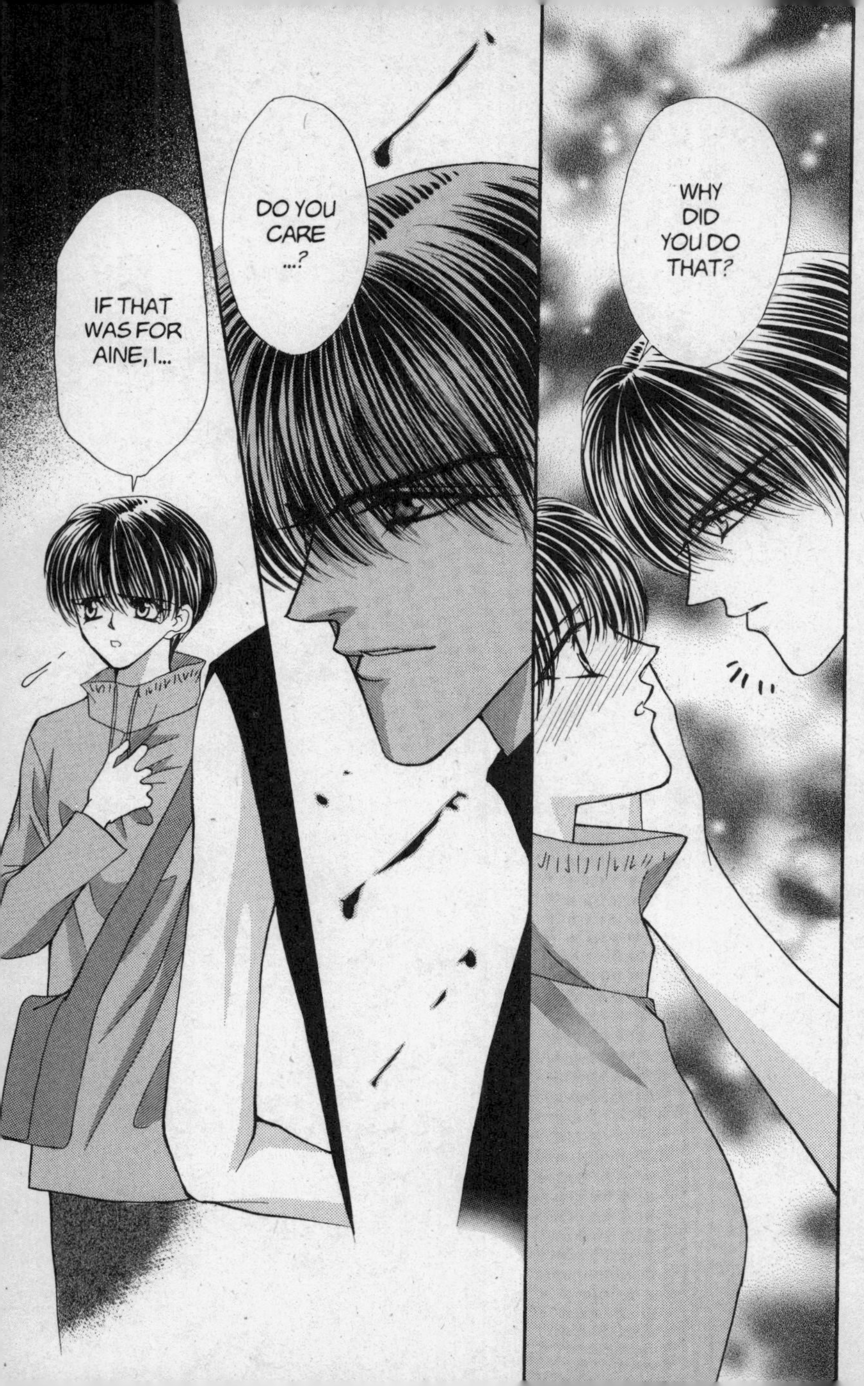
WHY DID YOU DO THAT?
DO YOU CARE ...?
IF THAT WAS FOR AINE, I...

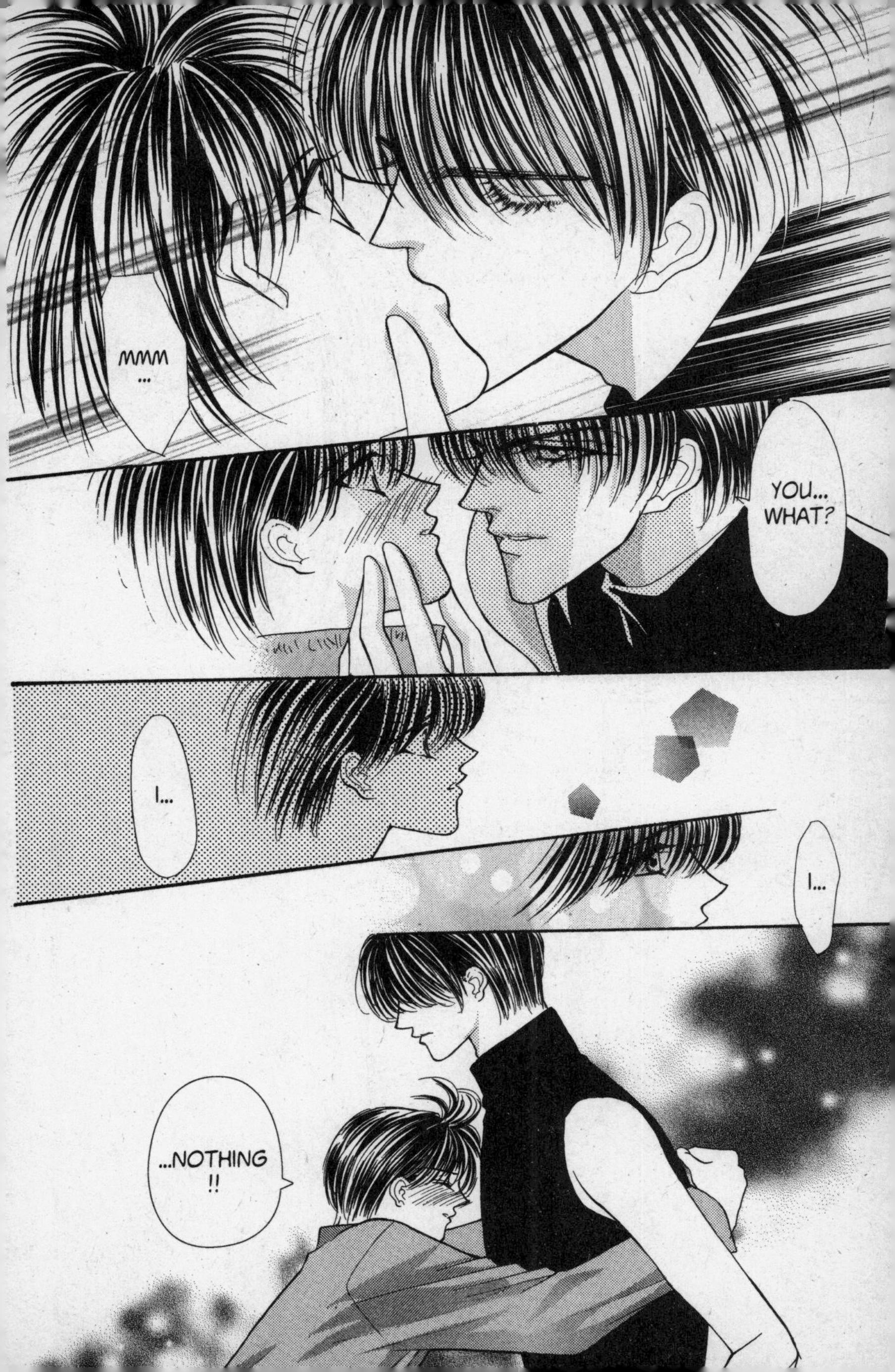
MMM...
YOU... WHAT?
I...
I...
...NOTHING !!

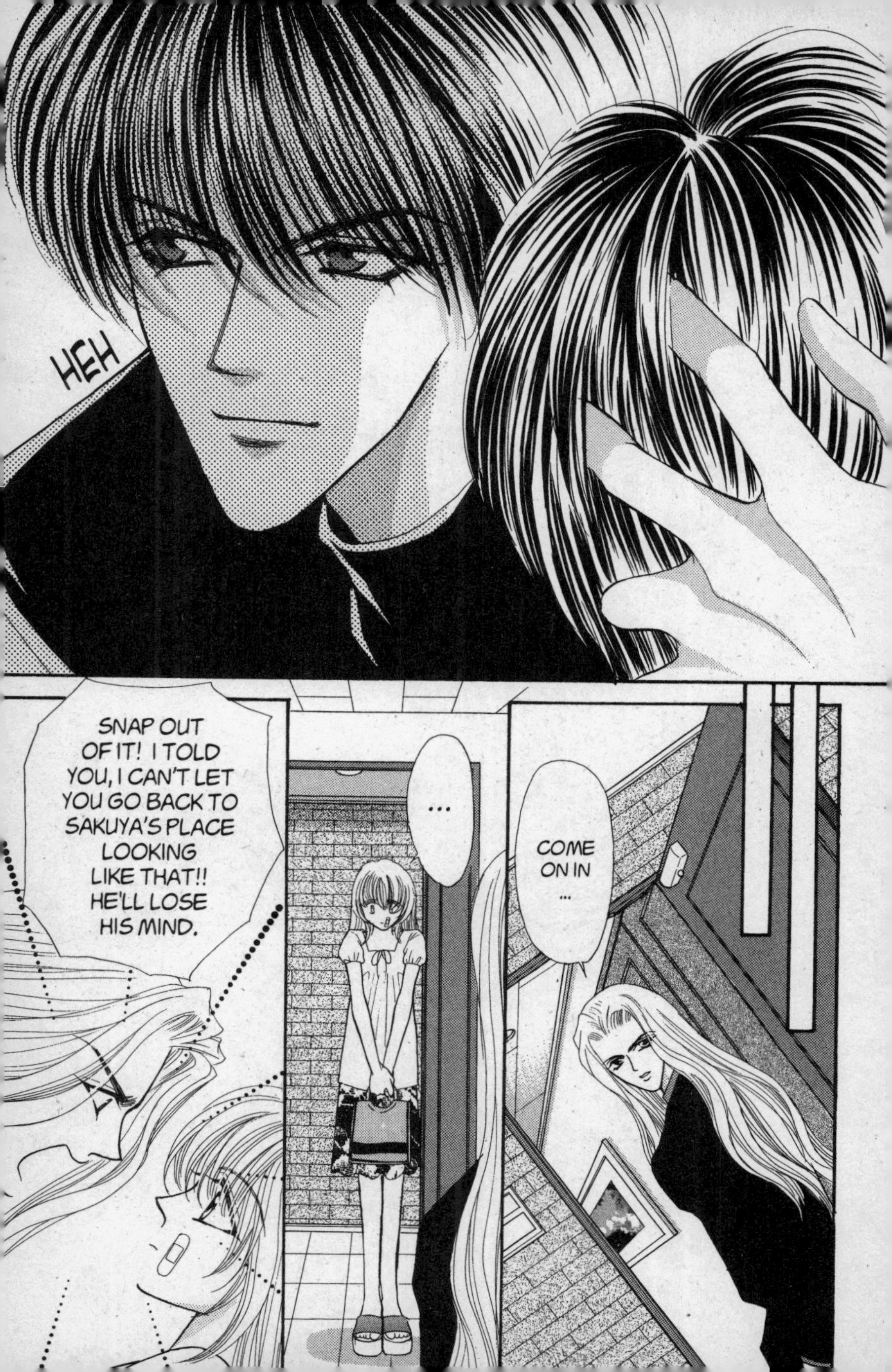
HEH
COME ON IN ...
...
SNAP OUT OF IT! I TOLD YOU, I CAN'T LET YOU GO BACK TO SAKUYA'S PLACE LOOKING LIKE THAT!! HE'LL LOSE HIS MIND.

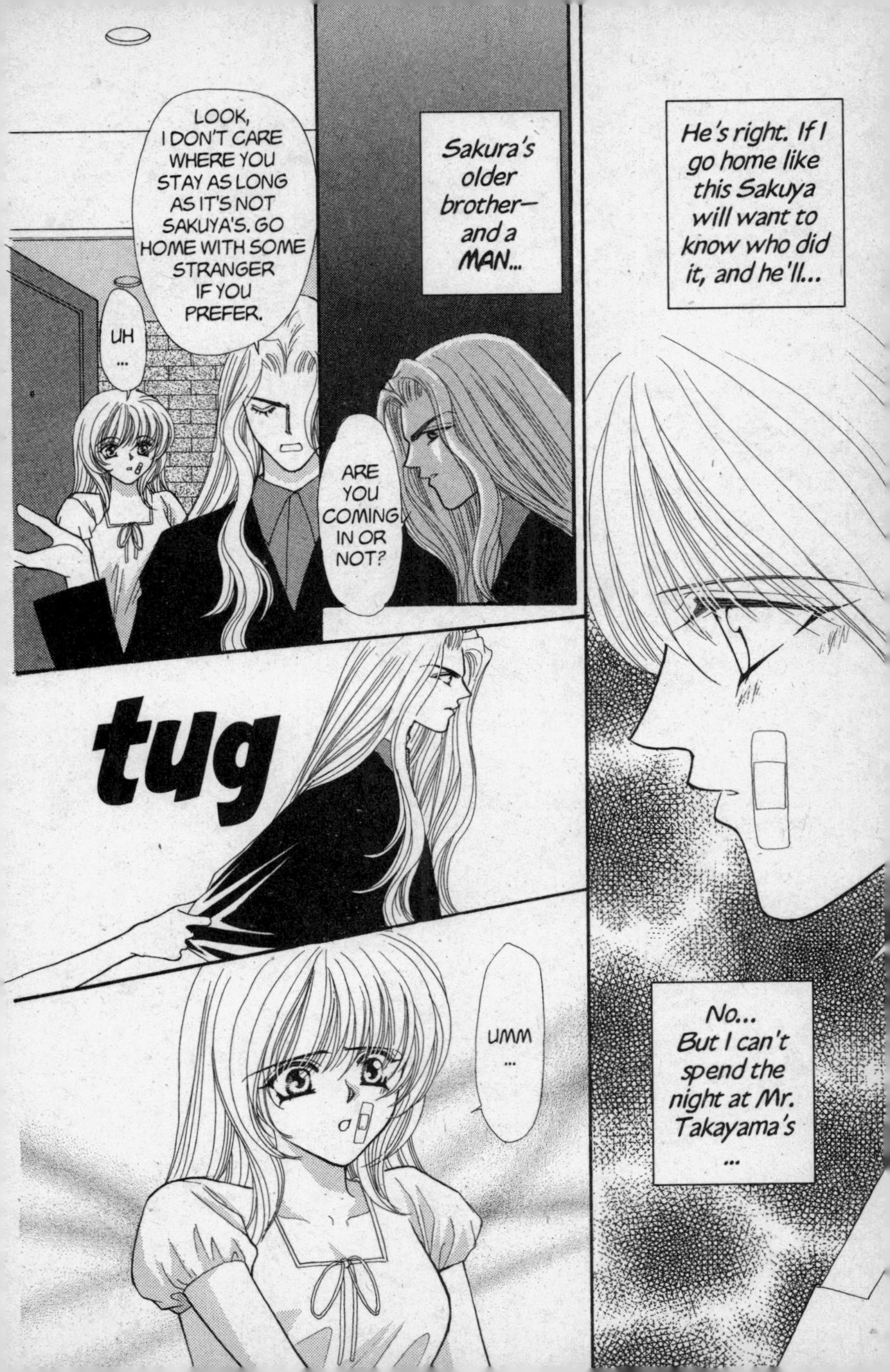
He's right. If I go home like this Sakuya will want to know who did it, and he'll...
No... But I can't spend the night at Mr. Takayama's ...
Sakura's older brother— and a MAN...
ARE YOU COMING IN OR NOT?
LOOK, I DON'T CARE WHERE YOU STAY AS LONG AS IT'S NOT SAKUYA'S. GO HOME WITH SOME STRANGER IF YOU PREFER.
UH ...
tug
UMM ...

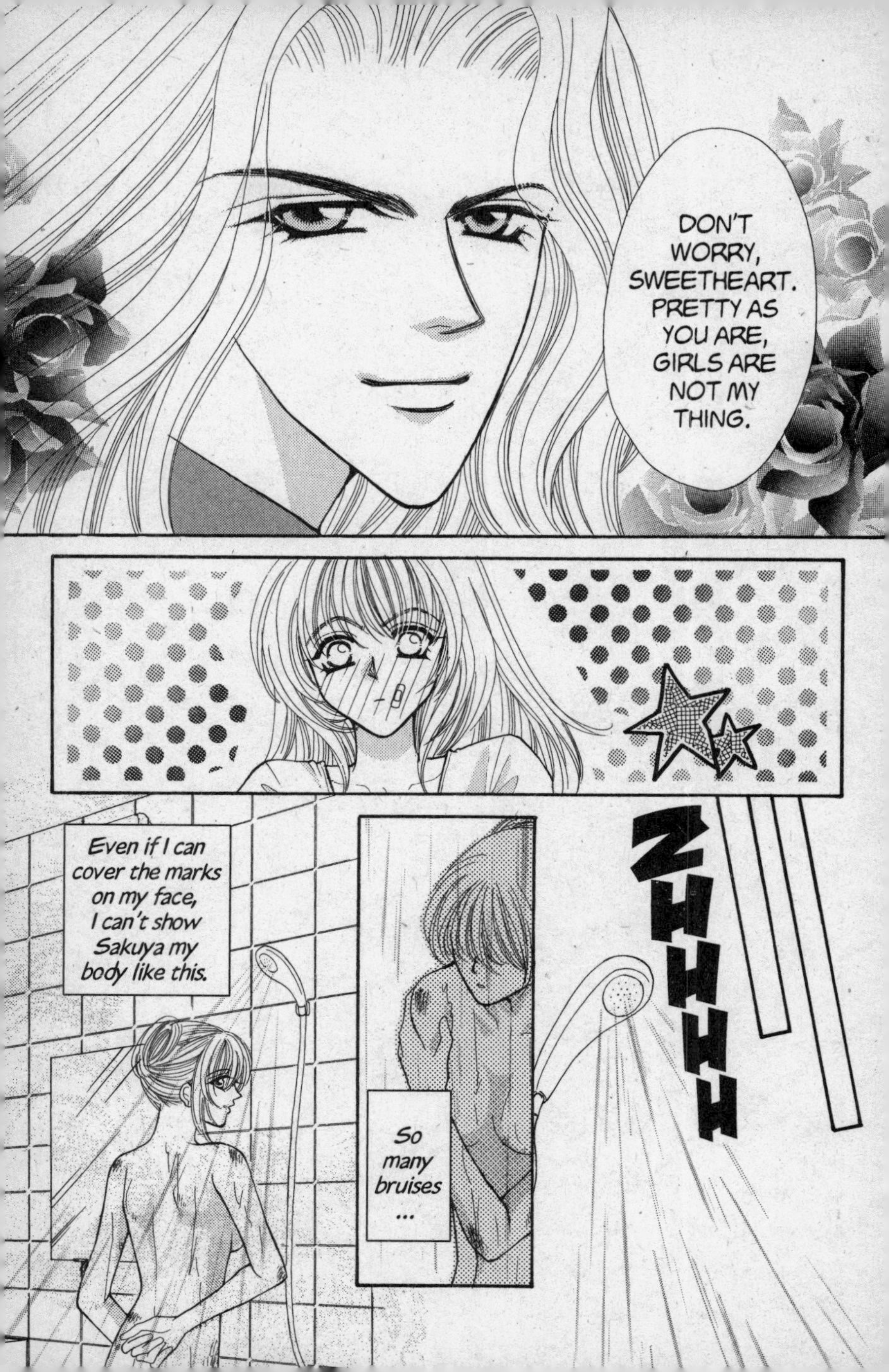
DON'T WORRY, SWEETHEART. PRETTY AS YOU ARE, GIRLS ARE NOT MY THING.
ZHHHH
Even if I can cover the marks on my face, I can't show Sakuya my body like this.
So many bruises ...

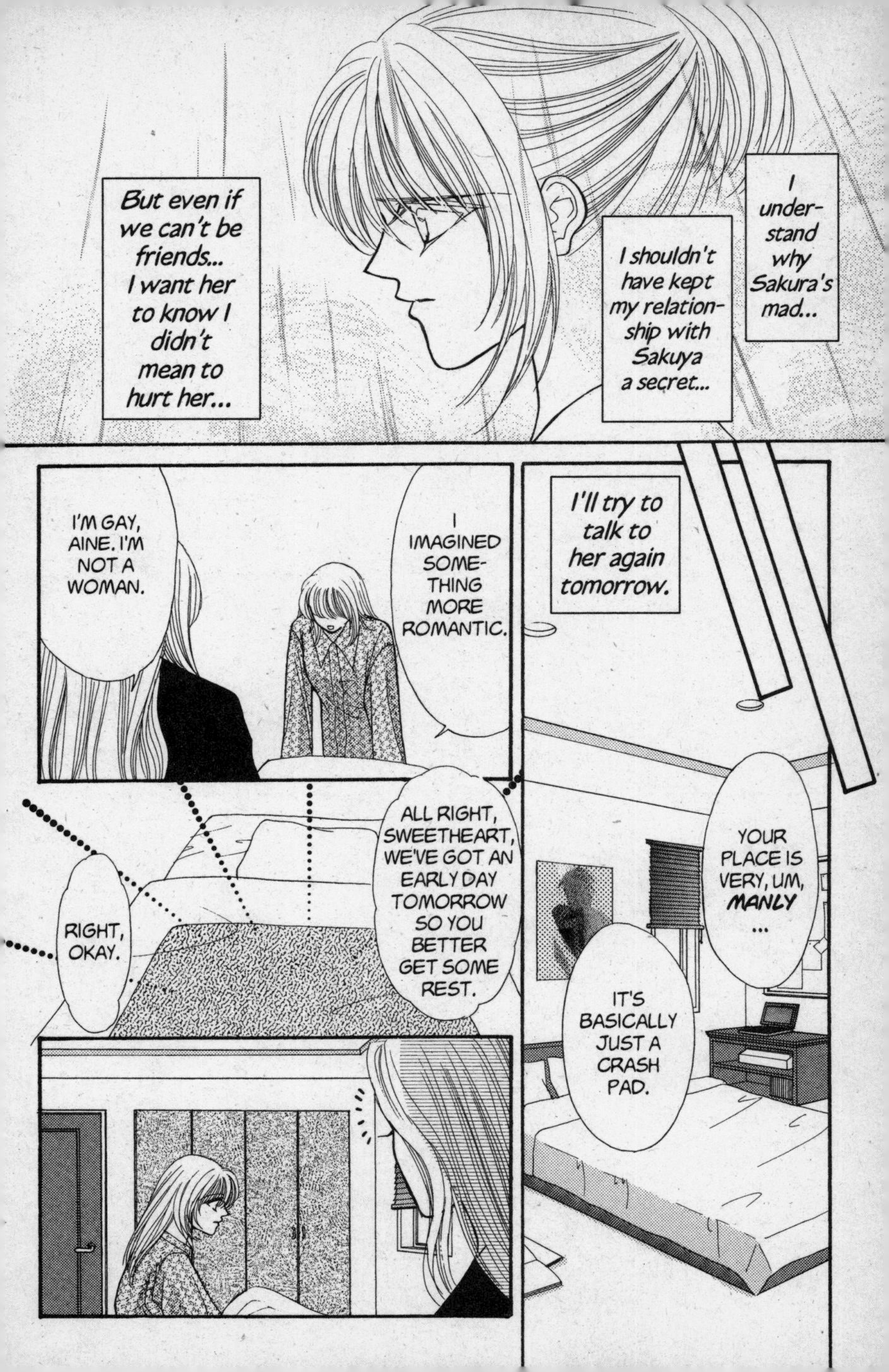
I understand why Sakura's mad...
I shouldn't have kept my relationship with Sakuya a secret...
But even if we can't be friends... I want her to know I didn't mean to hurt her...
I'll try to talk to her again tomorrow.
YOUR PLACE IS VERY, UM, MANLY ...
IT'S BASICALLY JUST A CRASH PAD.
I IMAGINED SOMETHING MORE ROMANTIC.
I'M GAY, AINE. I'M NOT A WOMAN.
ALL RIGHT, SWEETHEART, WE'VE GOT AN EARLY DAY TOMORROW SO YOU BETTER GET SOME REST.
RIGHT, OKAY.

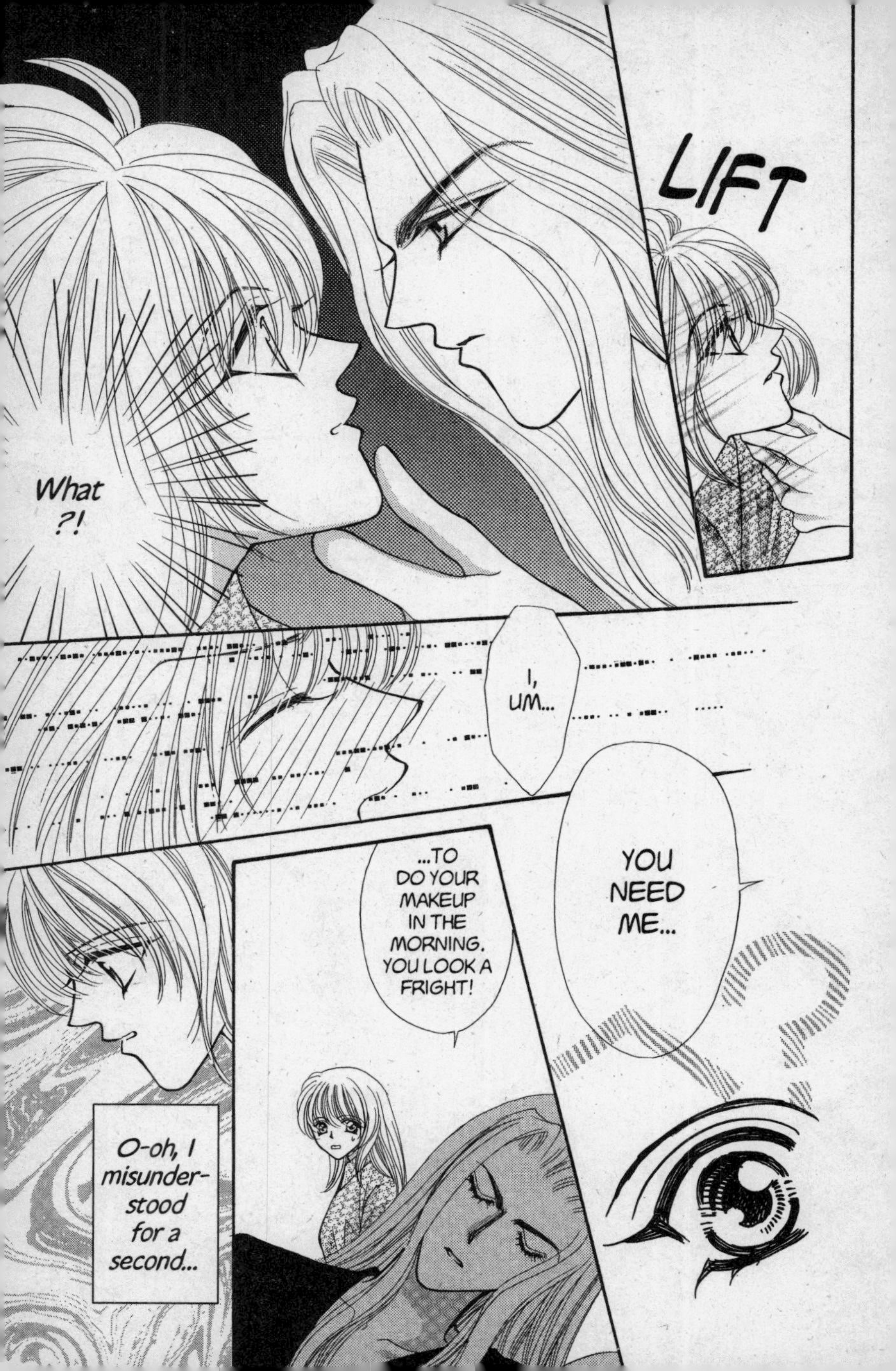
LIFT
What ?!
I, UM...
YOU NEED ME...
...TO DO YOUR MAKEUP IN THE MORNING. YOU LOOK A FRIGHT!
O-oh, I misunder-stood for a second...

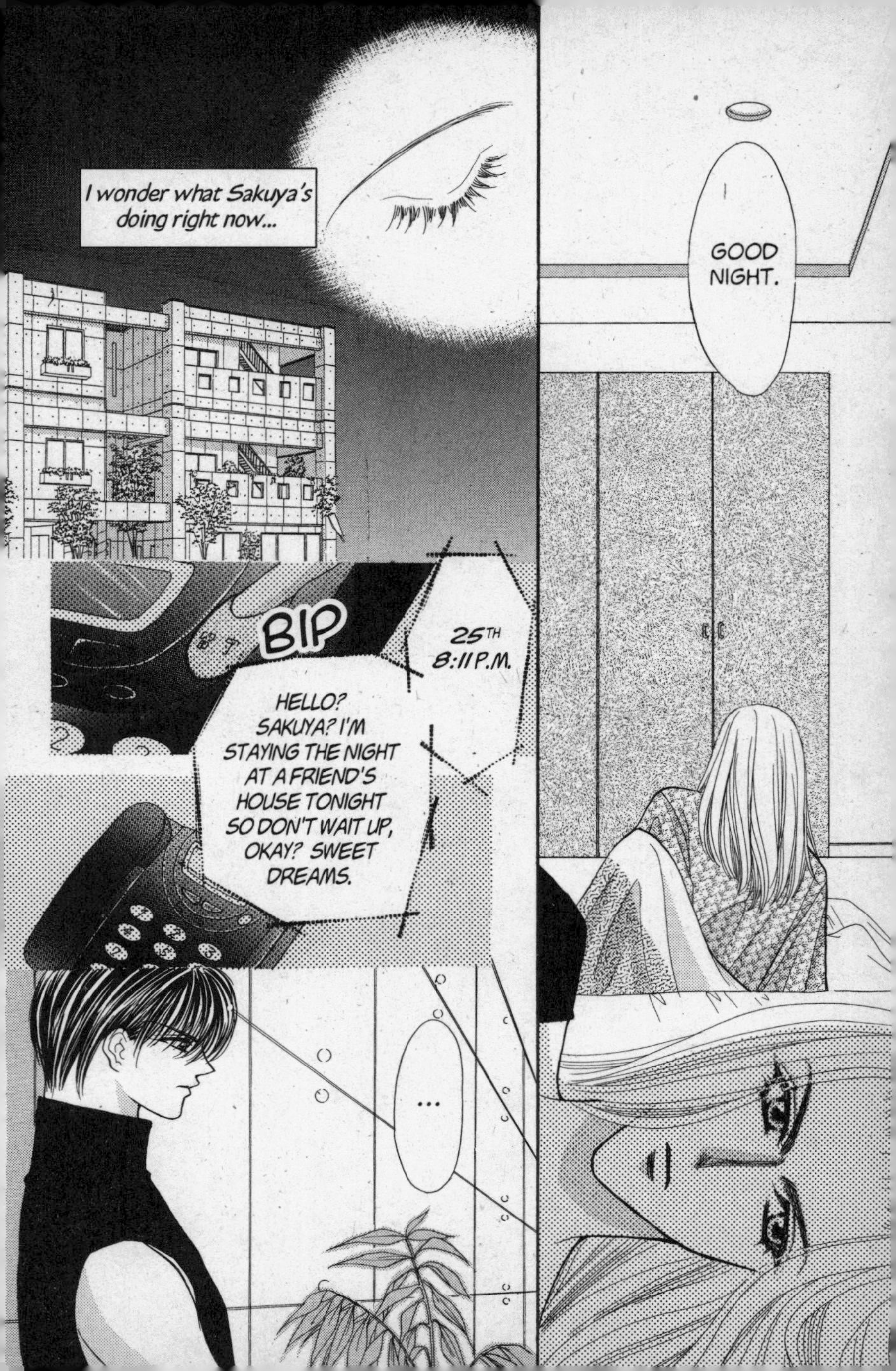
GOOD NIGHT.
I wonder what Sakuya's doing right now...
25TH 8:11 P.M.
BIP
HELLO? SAKUYA? I'M STAYING THE NIGHT AT A FRIEND'S HOUSE TONIGHT SO DON'T WAIT UP, OKAY? SWEET DREAMS.
...

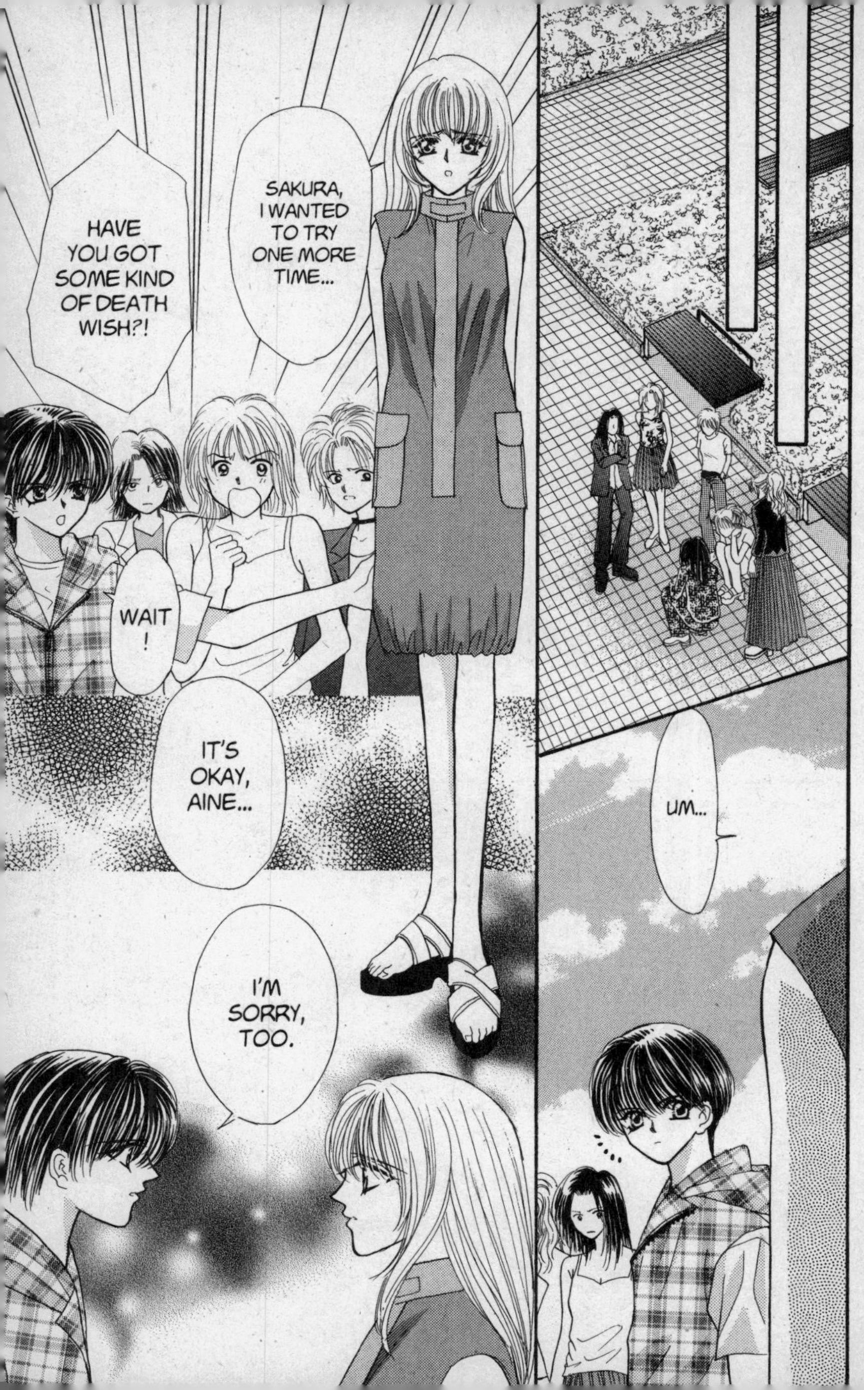
UM...
SAKURA, I WANTED TO TRY ONE MORE TIME...
HAVE YOU GOT SOME KIND OF DEATH WISH?!
WAIT!
IT'S OKAY, AINE...
I'M SORRY, TOO.

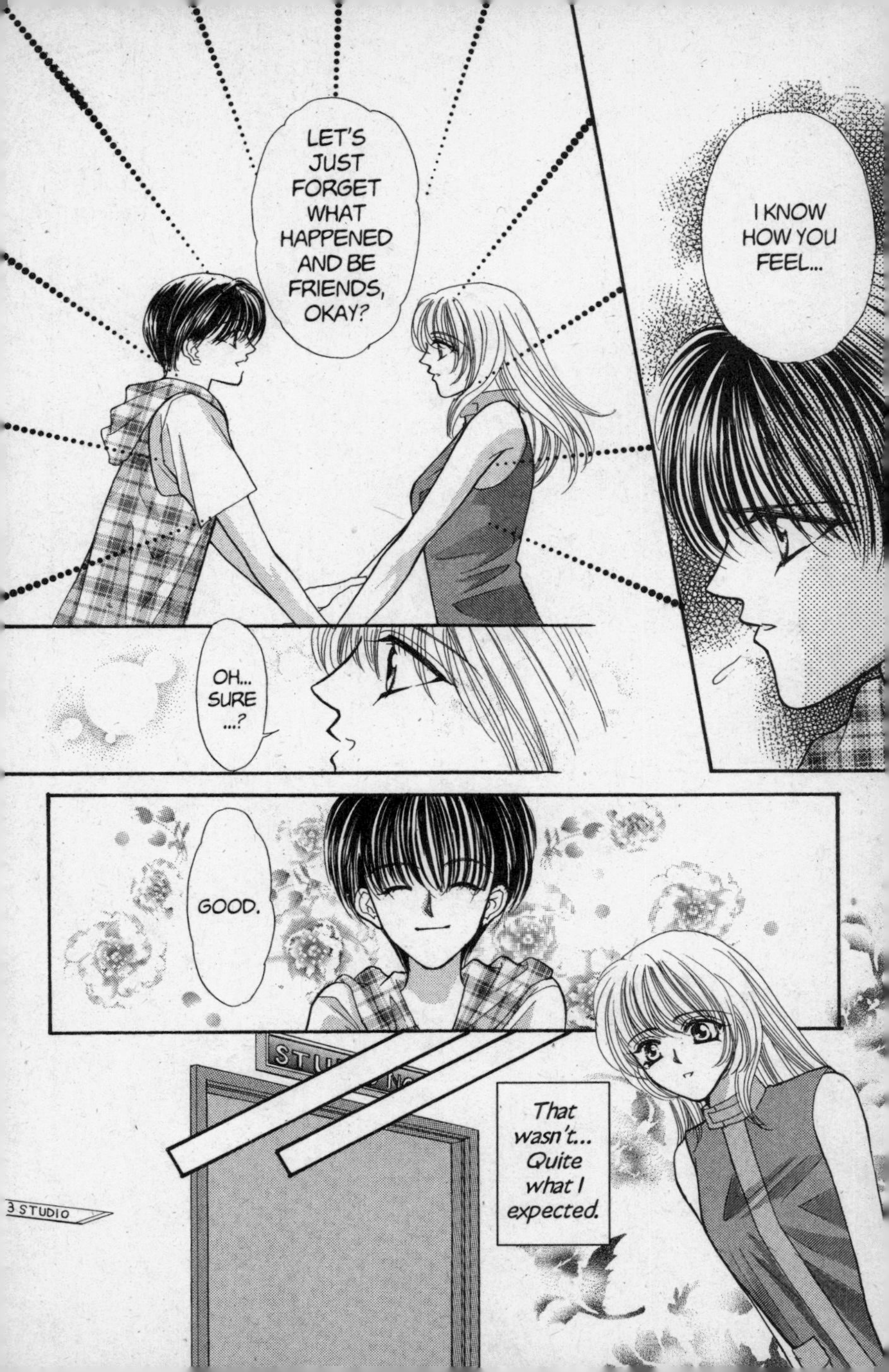
I KNOW HOW YOU FEEL...
LET'S JUST FORGET WHAT HAPPENED AND BE FRIENDS, OKAY?
OH... SURE ...?
GOOD.
That wasn't... Quite what I expected.
3 STUDIO

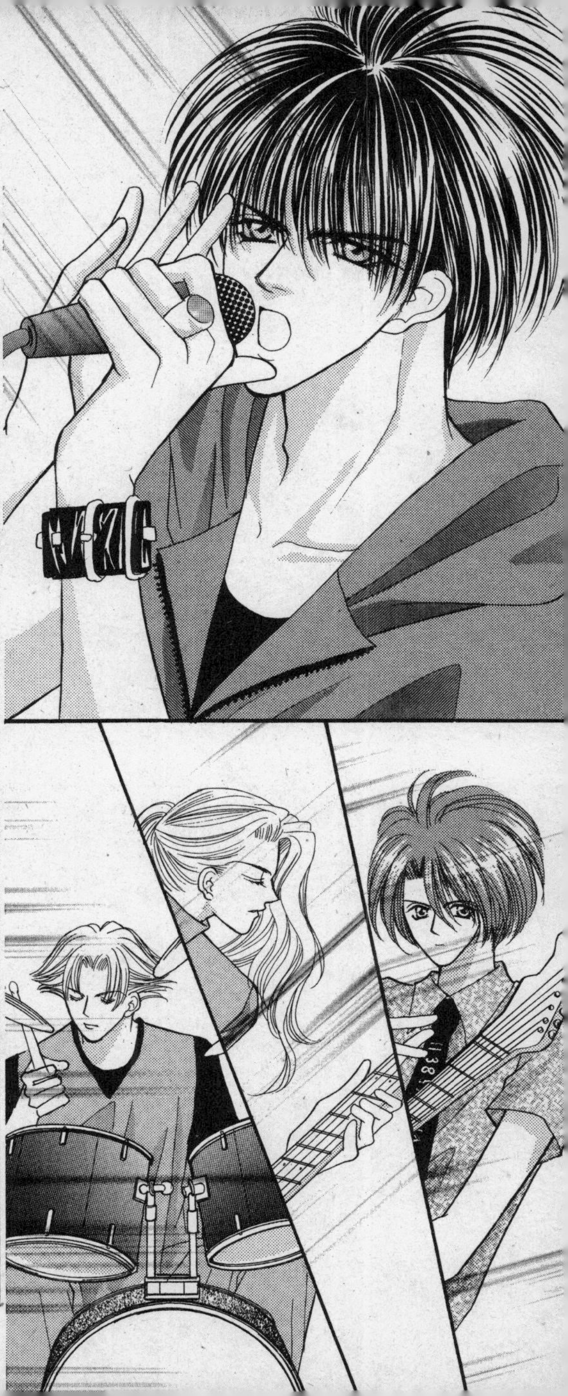

The final 1/3 already!

Let's see, I might have some big Λucifer news soon, so my heart's pounding. Don't forget—their second single comes out shortly! Everybody go buy it!

If you haven't seen them live yet, you have to go check them out. They're amazing!

I still need to write about the voice over actors, huh? I'll get to it, I promise. Oh, and I'm putting out a calendar too, so stay tuned. (I almost forgot to shill for myself! Ha ha!)

Okay then, take care until I see you in Volume 12!

Special Thanks:
Mashin Osakabe
Migiwa Nakahara
Satomi Naruke
Ikuko Abe

...Thank you for always being people I can count on.

Unlimited Records
Pony Canyon
Shogakukan Production
Studio Suzume

...Thank you for taking care of me and for your continued support.

Send cards and letters to:

Mayu Shinjo/Sensual Phrase
c/o Viz Media
P.O. BOX 77010
San Francisco, CA 94107

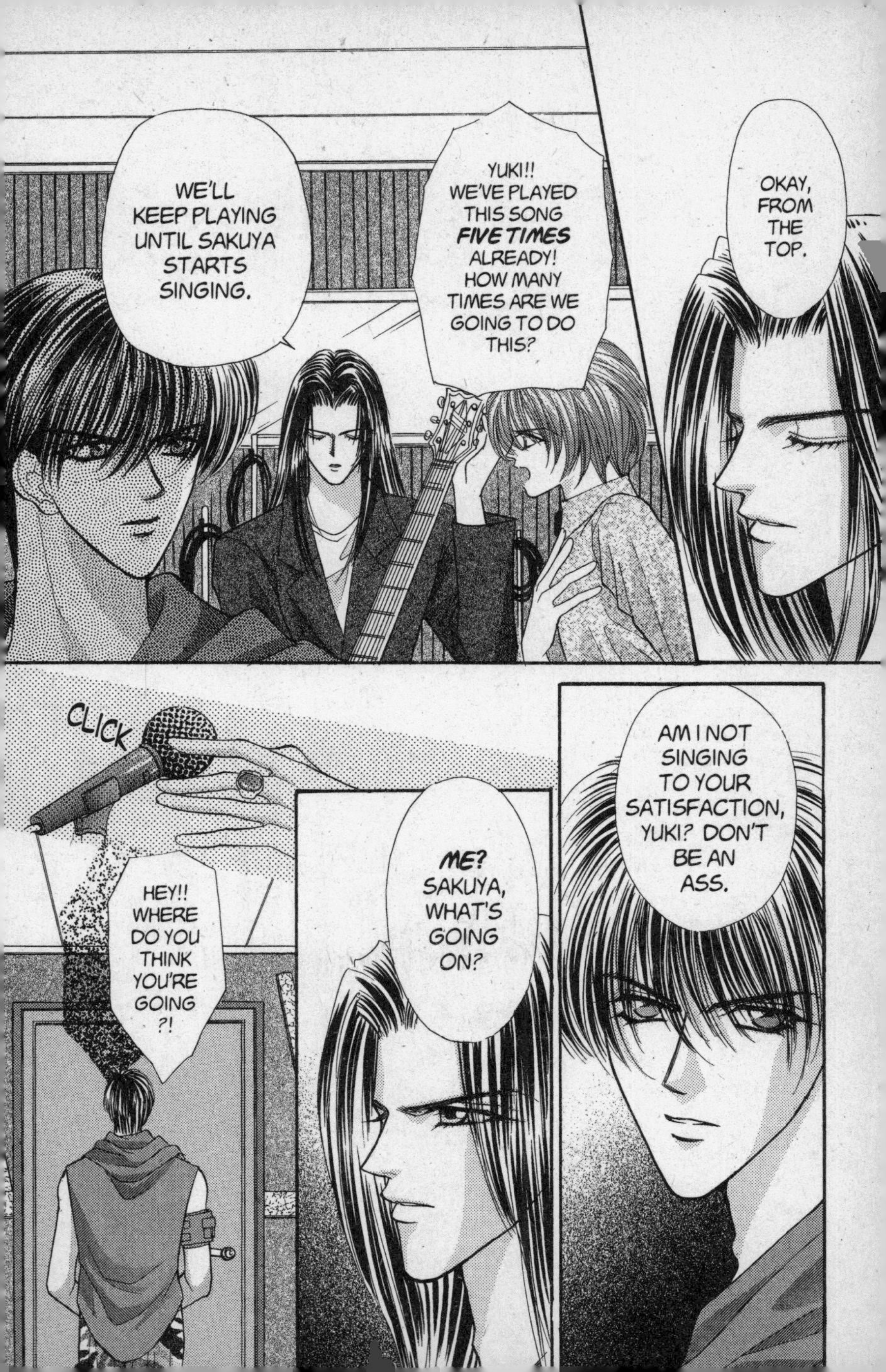
OKAY, FROM THE TOP.
YUKI!! WE'VE PLAYED THIS SONG **FIVE TIMES** ALREADY! HOW MANY TIMES ARE WE GOING TO DO THIS?
WE'LL KEEP PLAYING UNTIL SAKUYA STARTS SINGING.
AM I NOT SINGING TO YOUR SATISFACTION, YUKI? DON'T BE AN ASS.
ME? SAKUYA, WHAT'S GOING ON?
CLICK
HEY!! WHERE DO YOU THINK YOU'RE GOING ?!

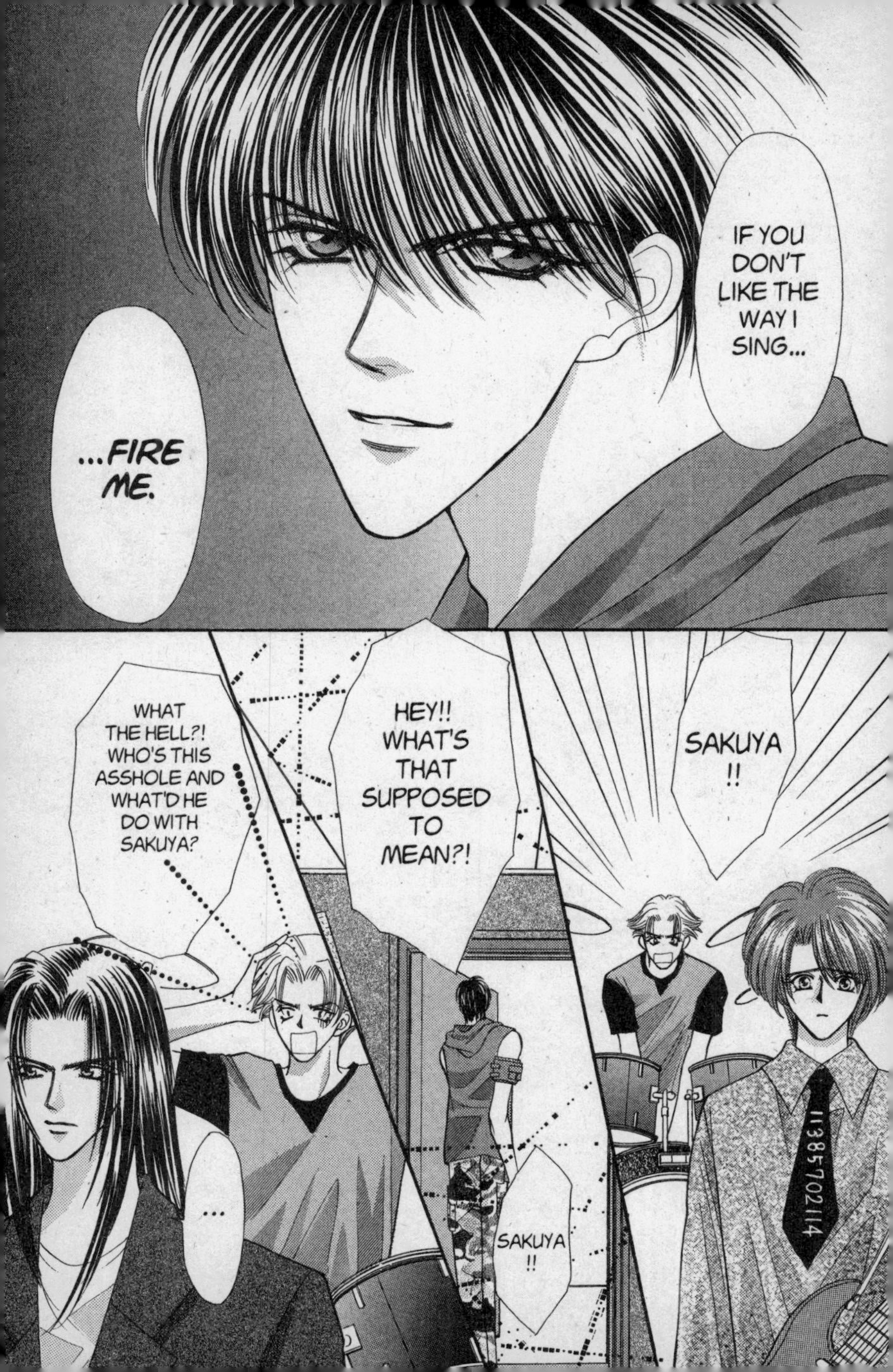
IF YOU DON'T LIKE THE WAY I SING...
...FIRE ME.
SAKUYA !!
HEY!! WHAT'S THAT SUPPOSED TO MEAN?!
SAKUYA !!
WHAT THE HELL?! WHO'S THIS ASSHOLE AND WHAT'D HE DO WITH SAKUYA?
...

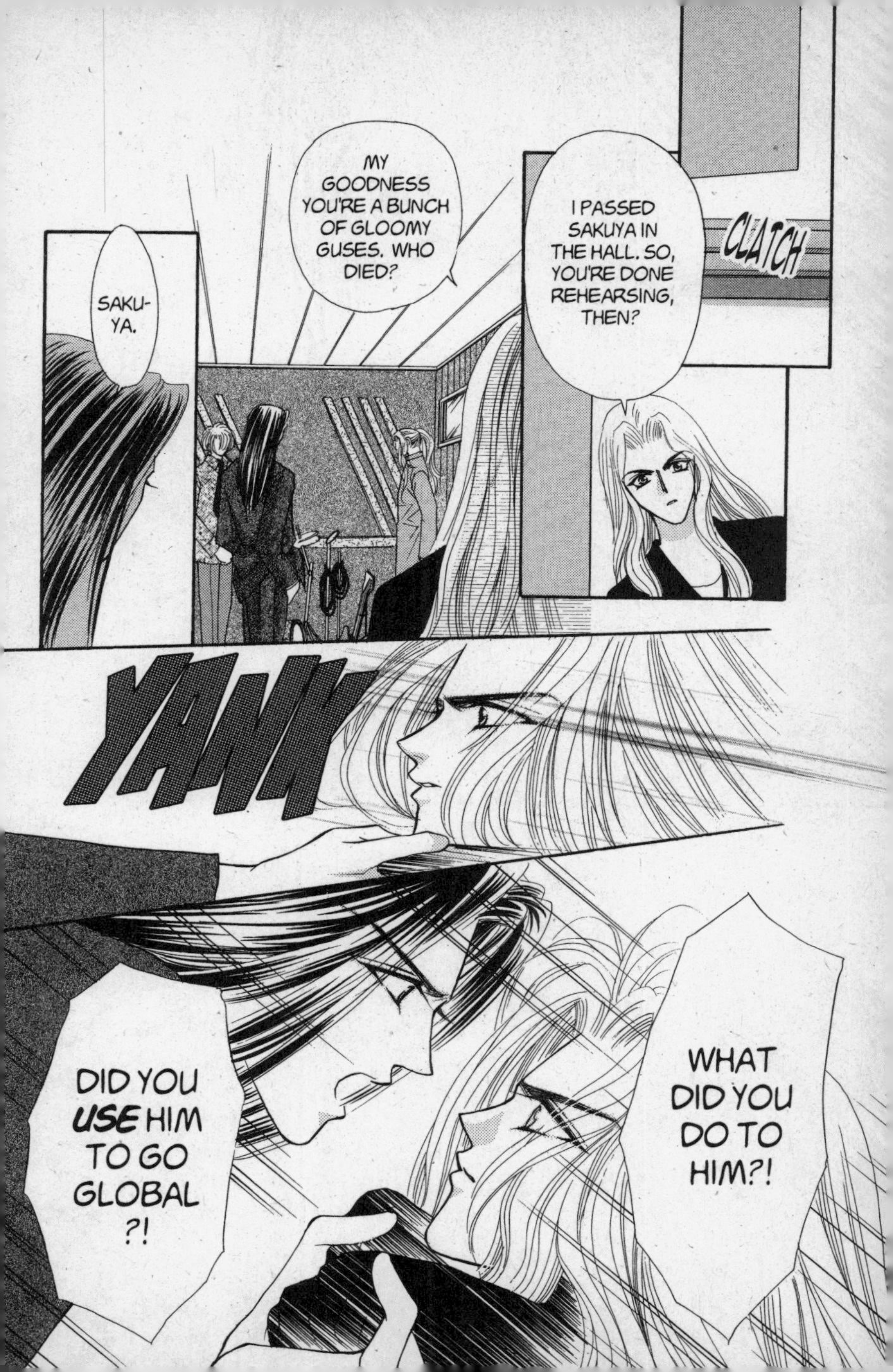
CLATCH
I PASSED SAKUYA IN THE HALL. SO, YOU'RE DONE REHEARSING, THEN?
MY GOODNESS YOU'RE A BUNCH OF GLOOMY GUSES. WHO DIED?
SAKU-YA.
YANK
WHAT DID YOU DO TO HIM?!
DID YOU USE HIM TO GO GLOBAL ?!

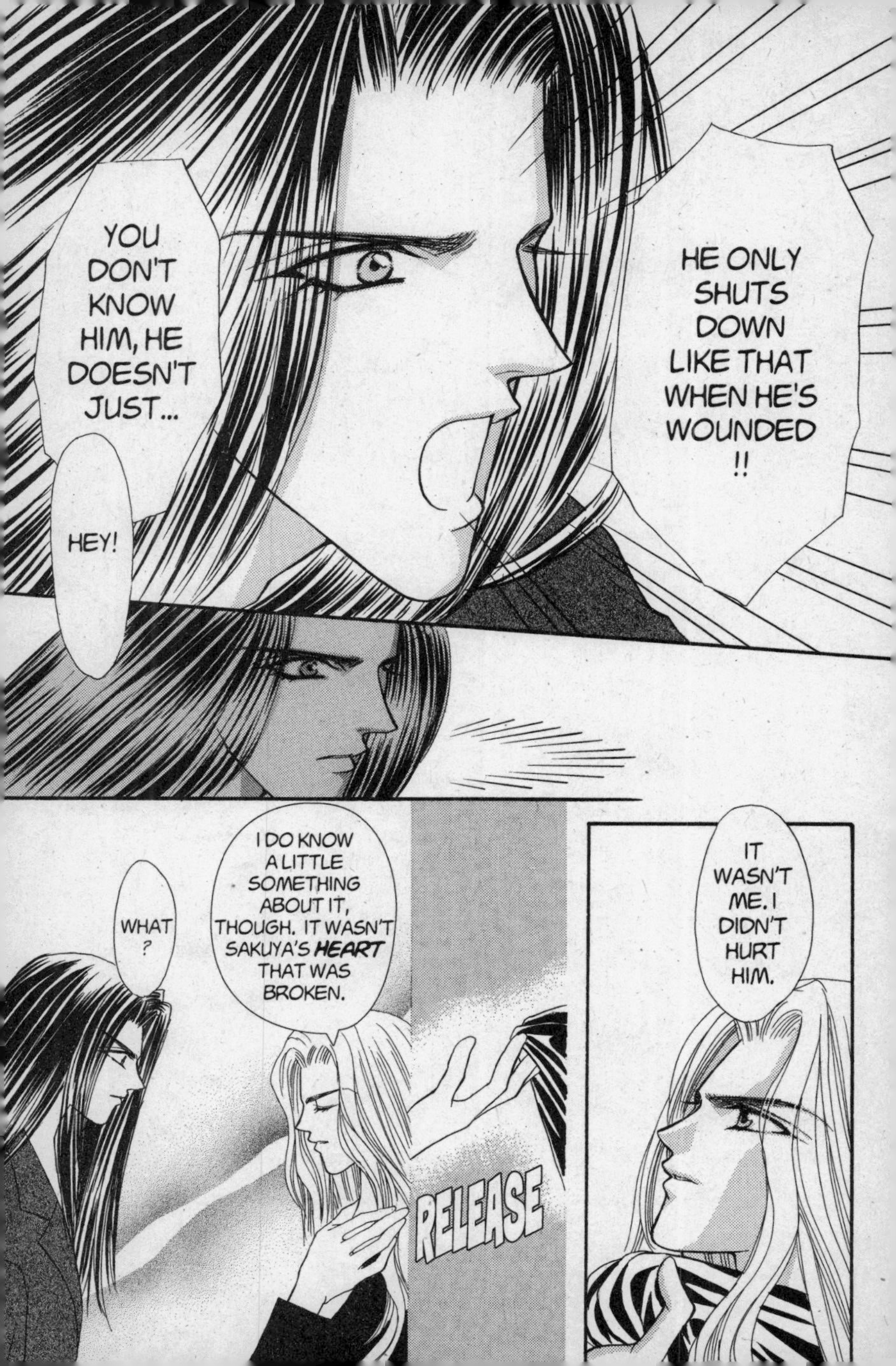
HE ONLY SHUTS DOWN LIKE THAT WHEN HE'S WOUNDED !!
YOU DON'T KNOW HIM, HE DOESN'T JUST...
HEY!
IT WASN'T ME. I DIDN'T HURT HIM.
I DO KNOW A LITTLE SOMETHING ABOUT IT, THOUGH. IT WASN'T SAKUYA'S *HEART* THAT WAS BROKEN.
WHAT ?
RELEASE

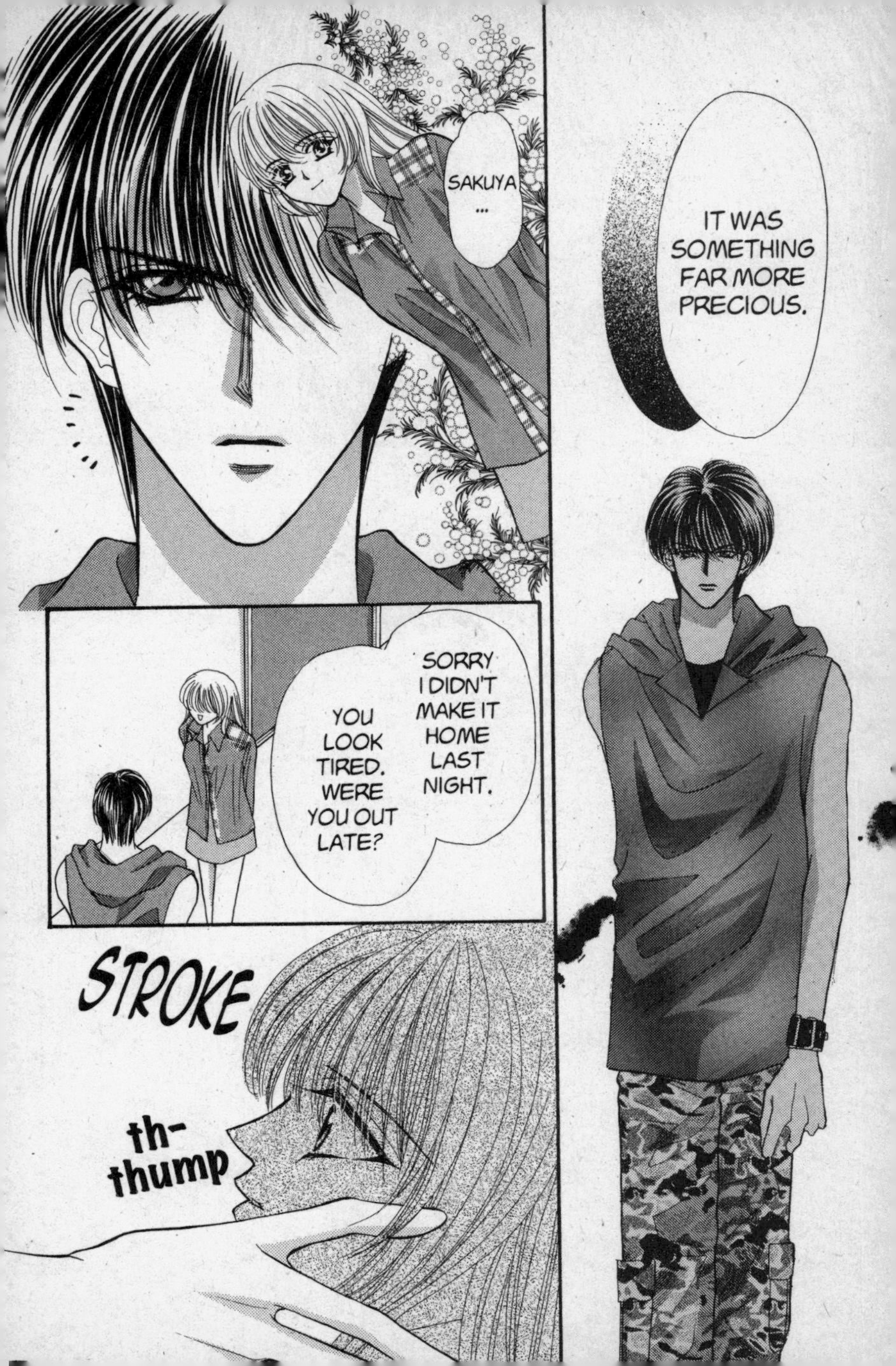
IT WAS SOMETHING FAR MORE PRECIOUS.
SAKUYA ...
SORRY I DIDN'T MAKE IT HOME LAST NIGHT.
YOU LOOK TIRED. WERE YOU OUT LATE?
STROKE
th-thump

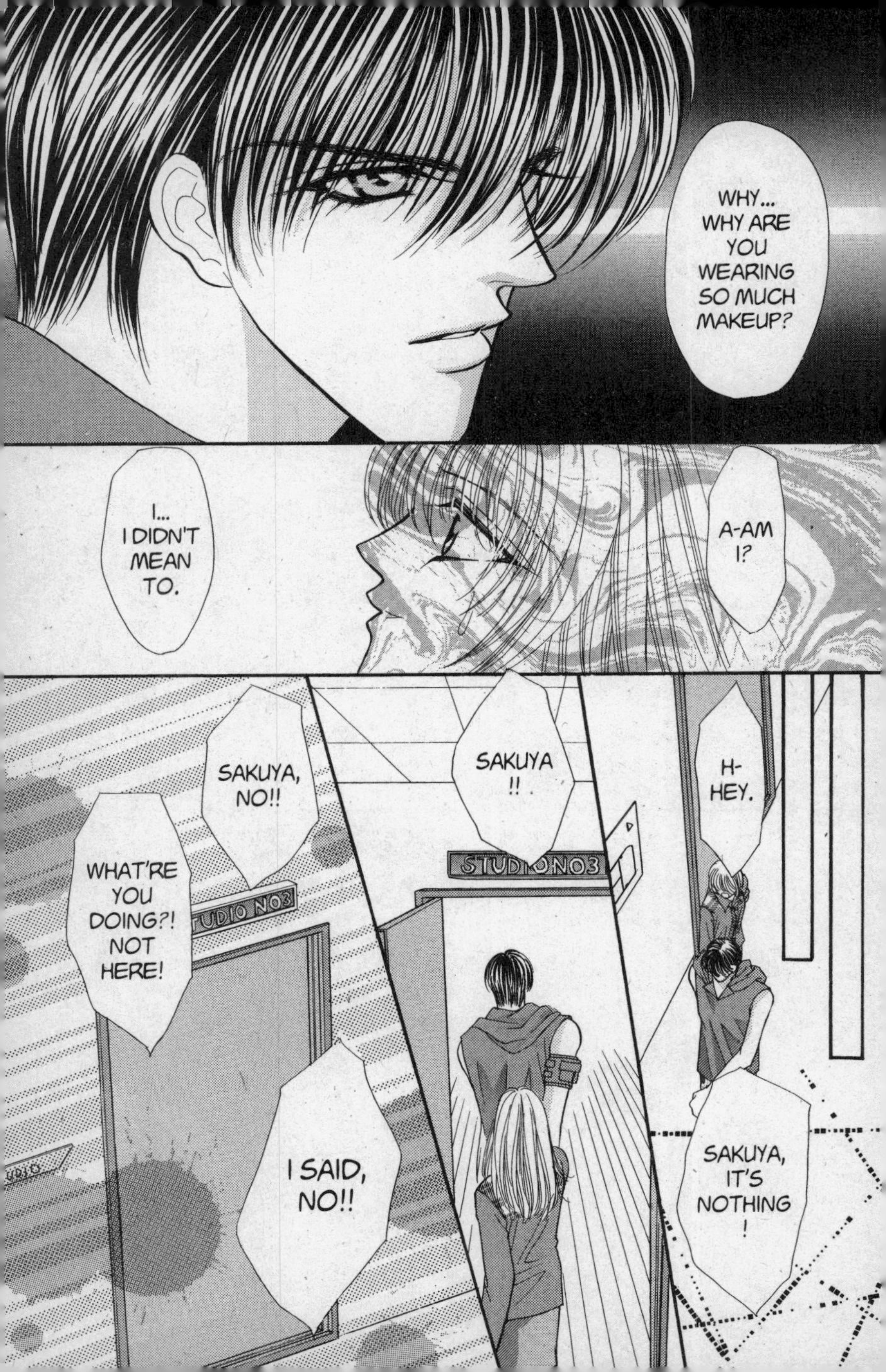
WHY... WHY ARE YOU WEARING SO MUCH MAKEUP?
A-AM I?
I... I DIDN'T MEAN TO.
H- HEY.
SAKUYA, IT'S NOTHING!
SAKUYA!!
STUDIO NO3
SAKUYA, NO!!
WHAT'RE YOU DOING?! NOT HERE!
I SAID, NO!!

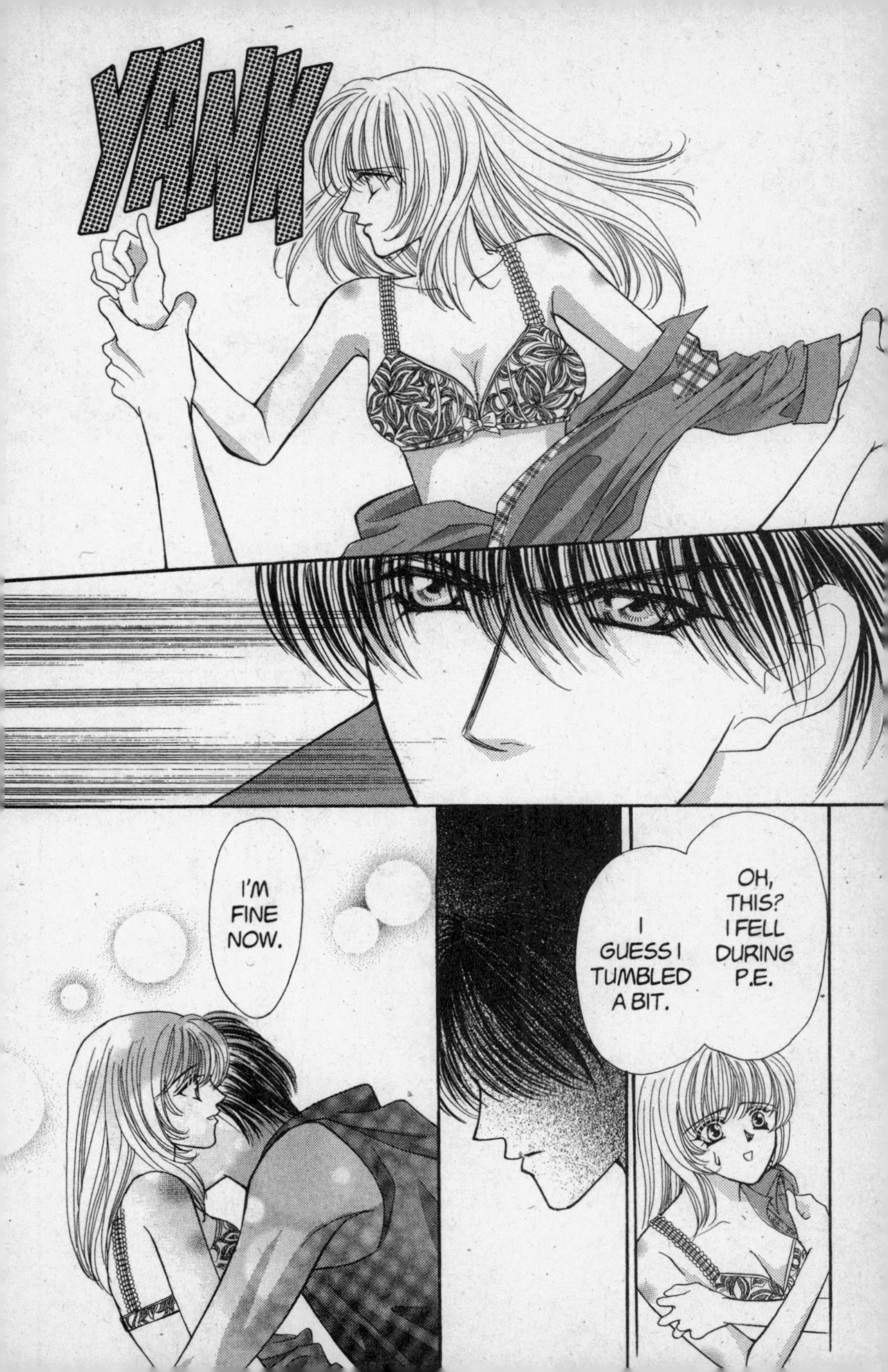
YANK
OH, THIS? I FELL DURING P.E.
I GUESS I TUMBLED A BIT.
I'M FINE NOW.

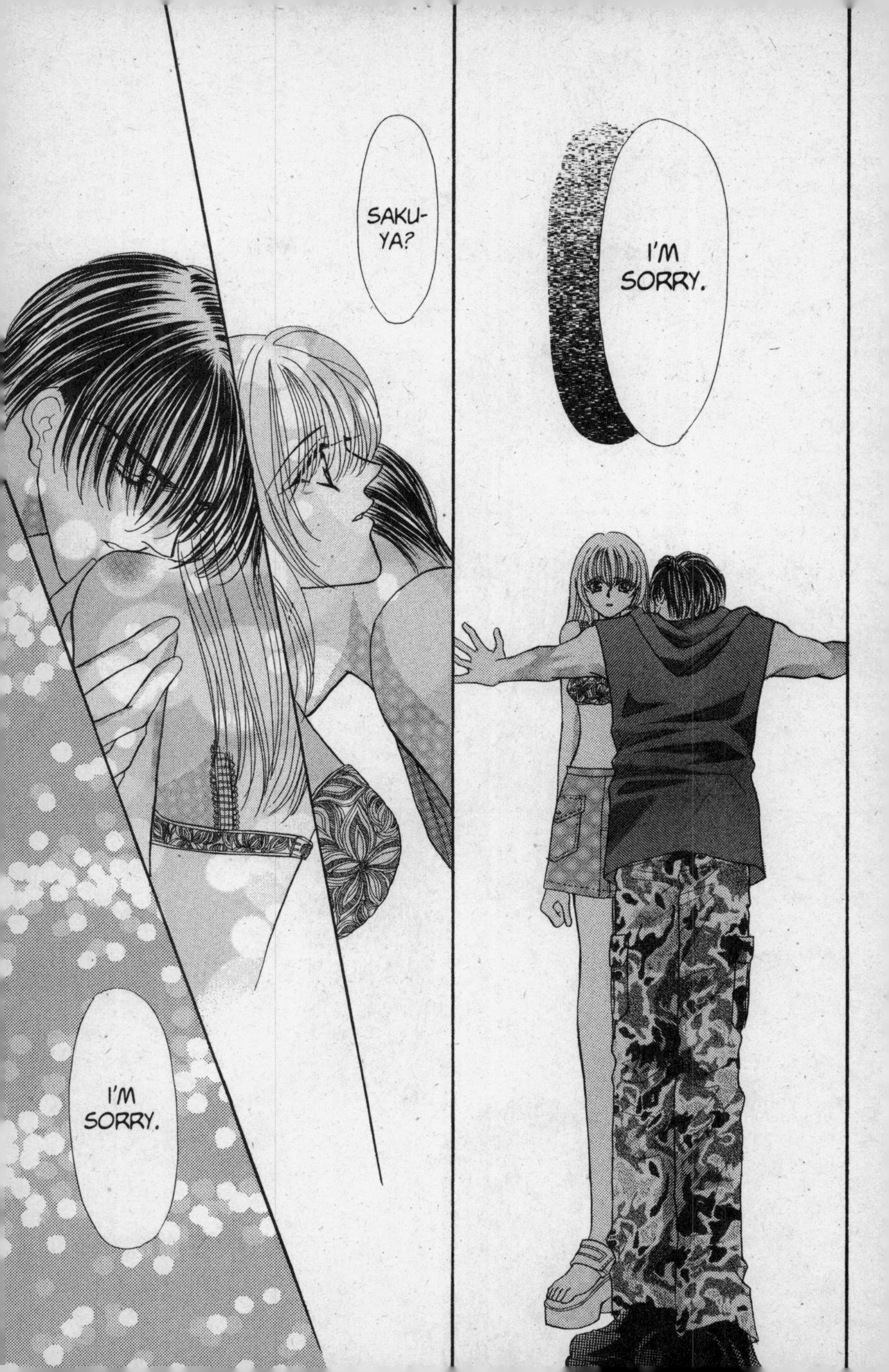
I'M SORRY.
SAKU-YA?
I'M SORRY.

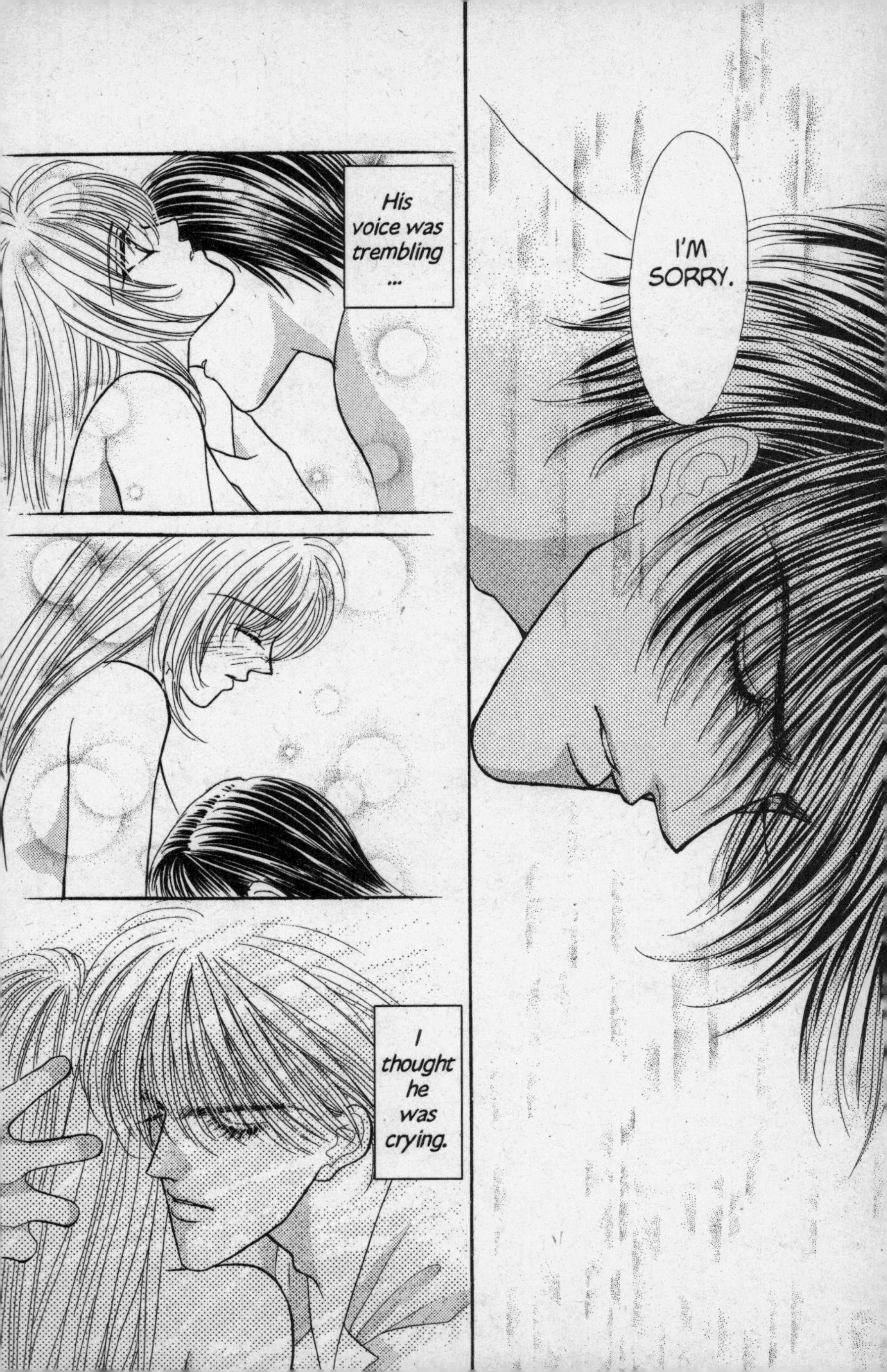
I'M SORRY.
His voice was trembling ...
I thought he was crying.

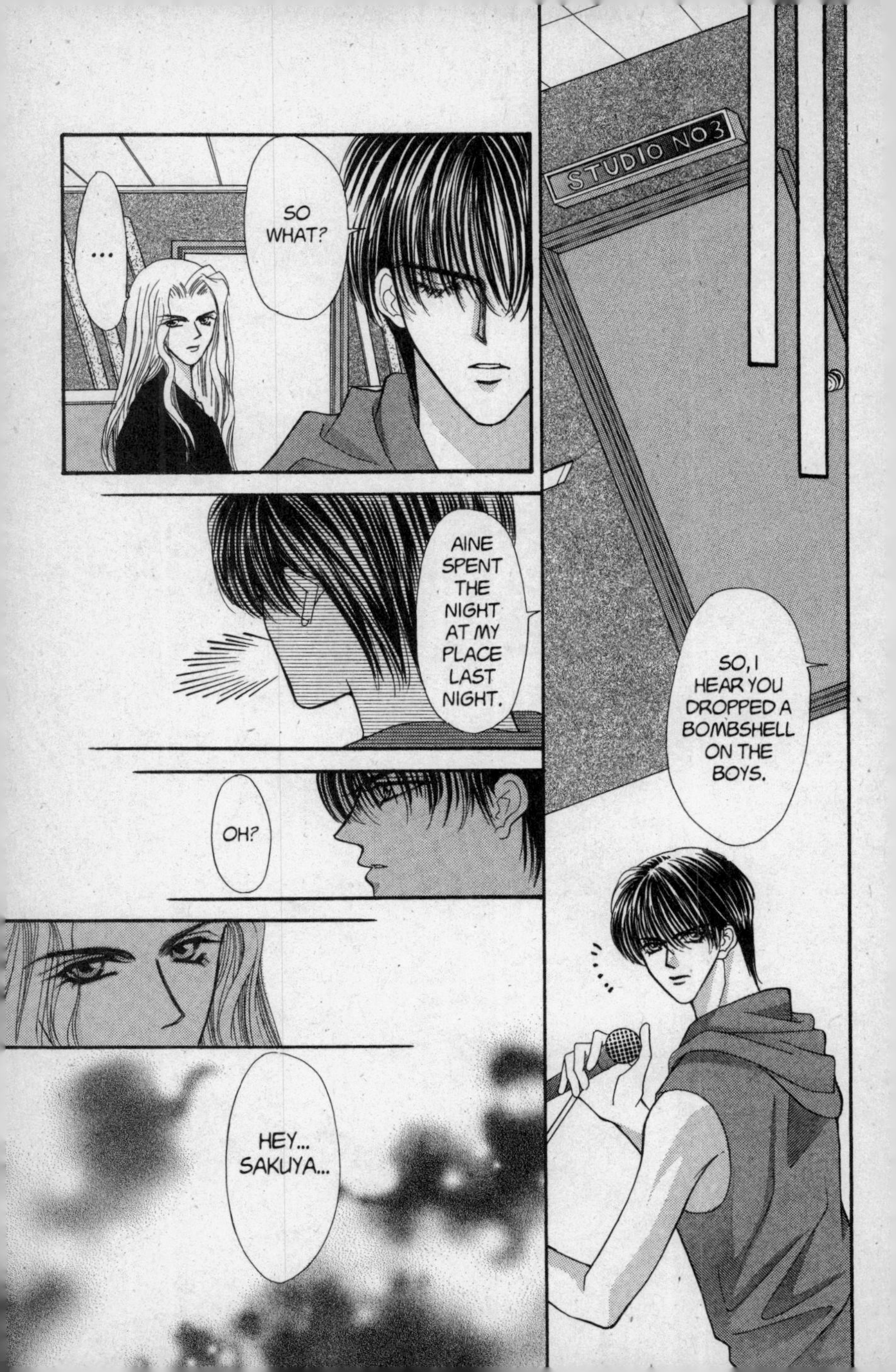
STUDIO NO3
SO, I HEAR YOU DROPPED A BOMBSHELL ON THE BOYS.
SO WHAT?
...
AINE SPENT THE NIGHT AT MY PLACE LAST NIGHT.
OH?
HEY... SAKUYA...

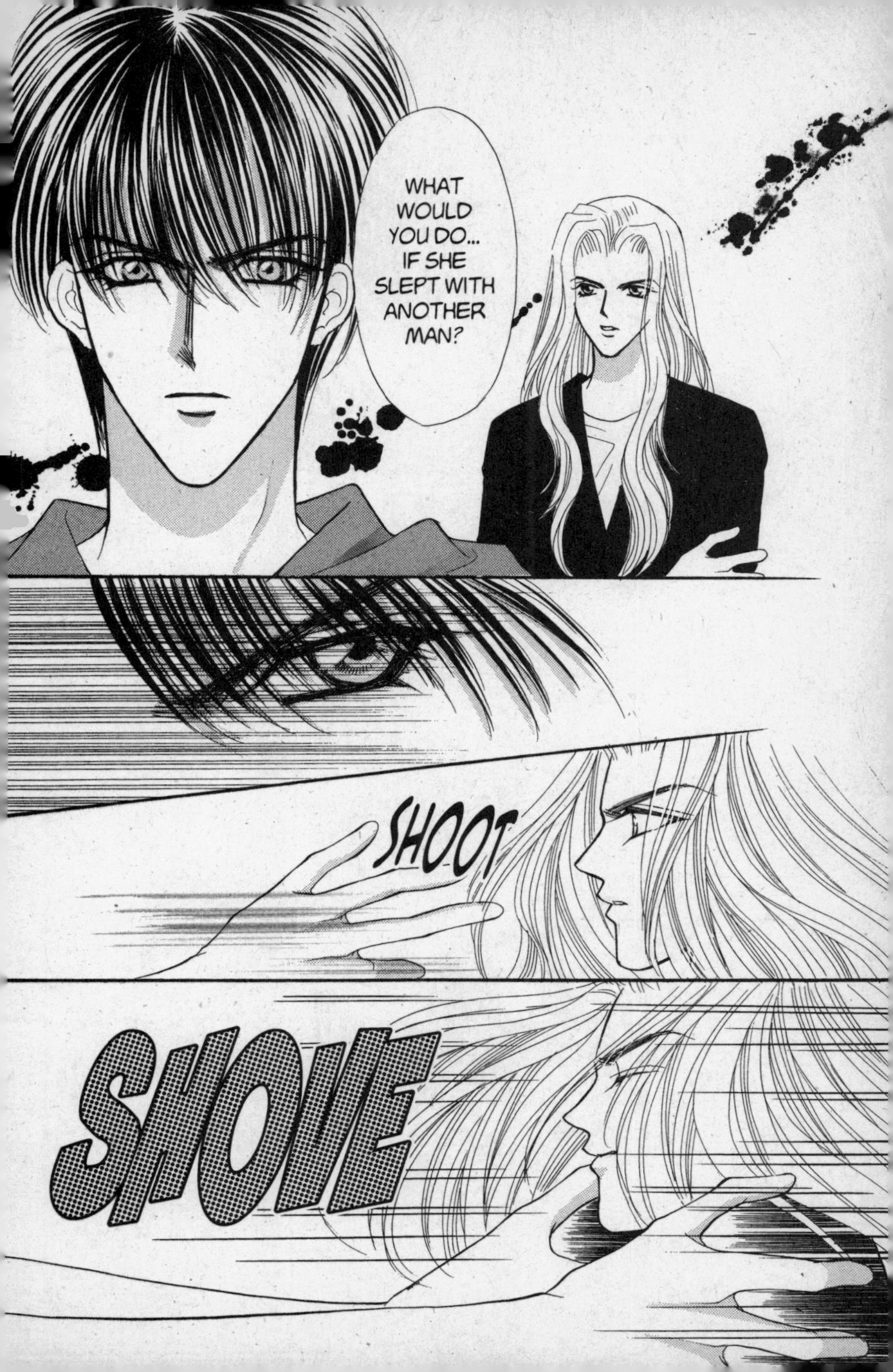
WHAT WOULD YOU DO... IF SHE SLEPT WITH ANOTHER MAN?
SHOOT
SHOVE

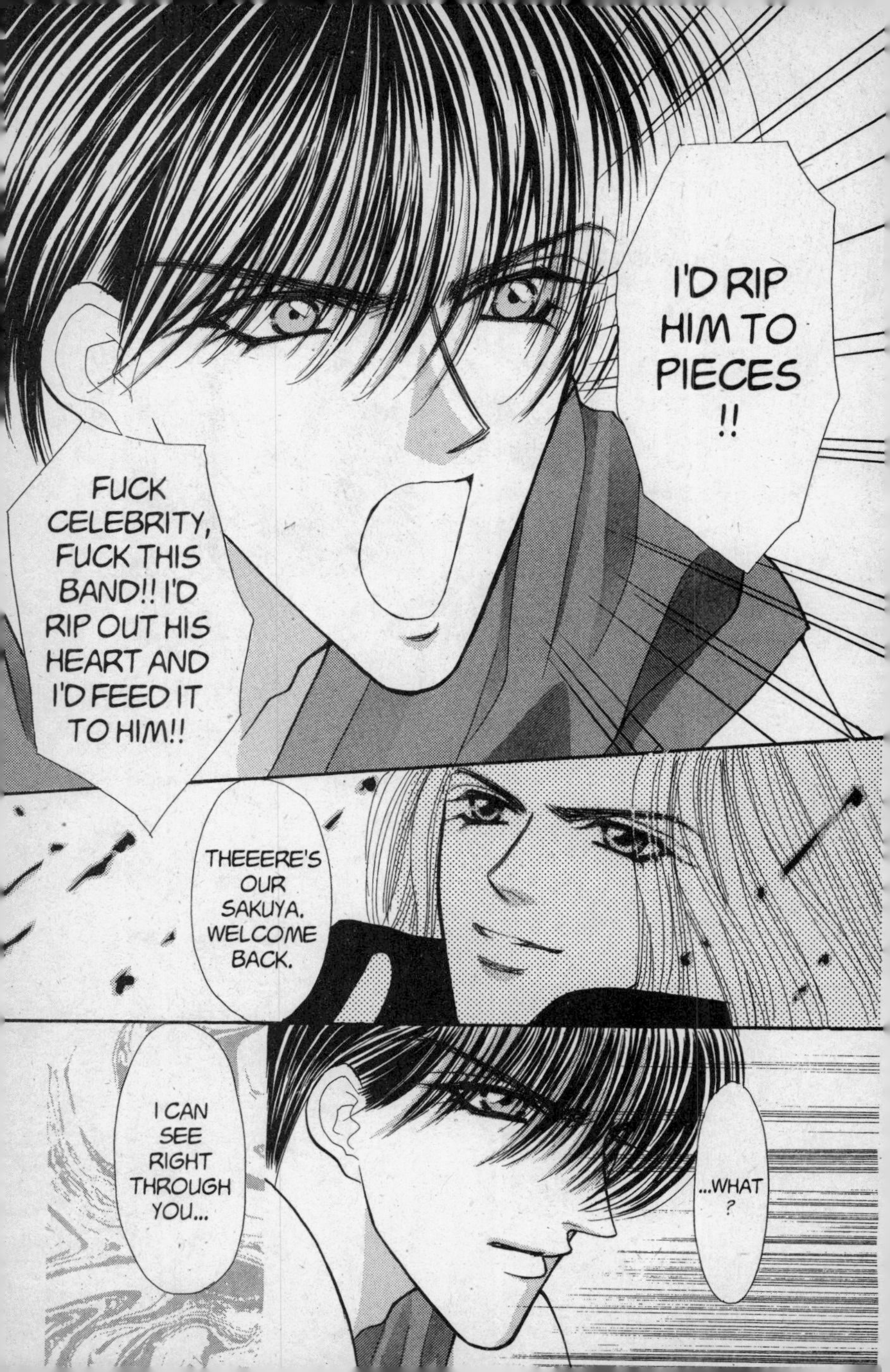
I'D RIP HIM TO PIECES!!
FUCK CELEBRITY, FUCK THIS BAND!! I'D RIP OUT HIS HEART AND I'D FEED IT TO HIM!!
THEEERE'S OUR SAKUYA. WELCOME BACK.
...WHAT?
I CAN SEE RIGHT THROUGH YOU...

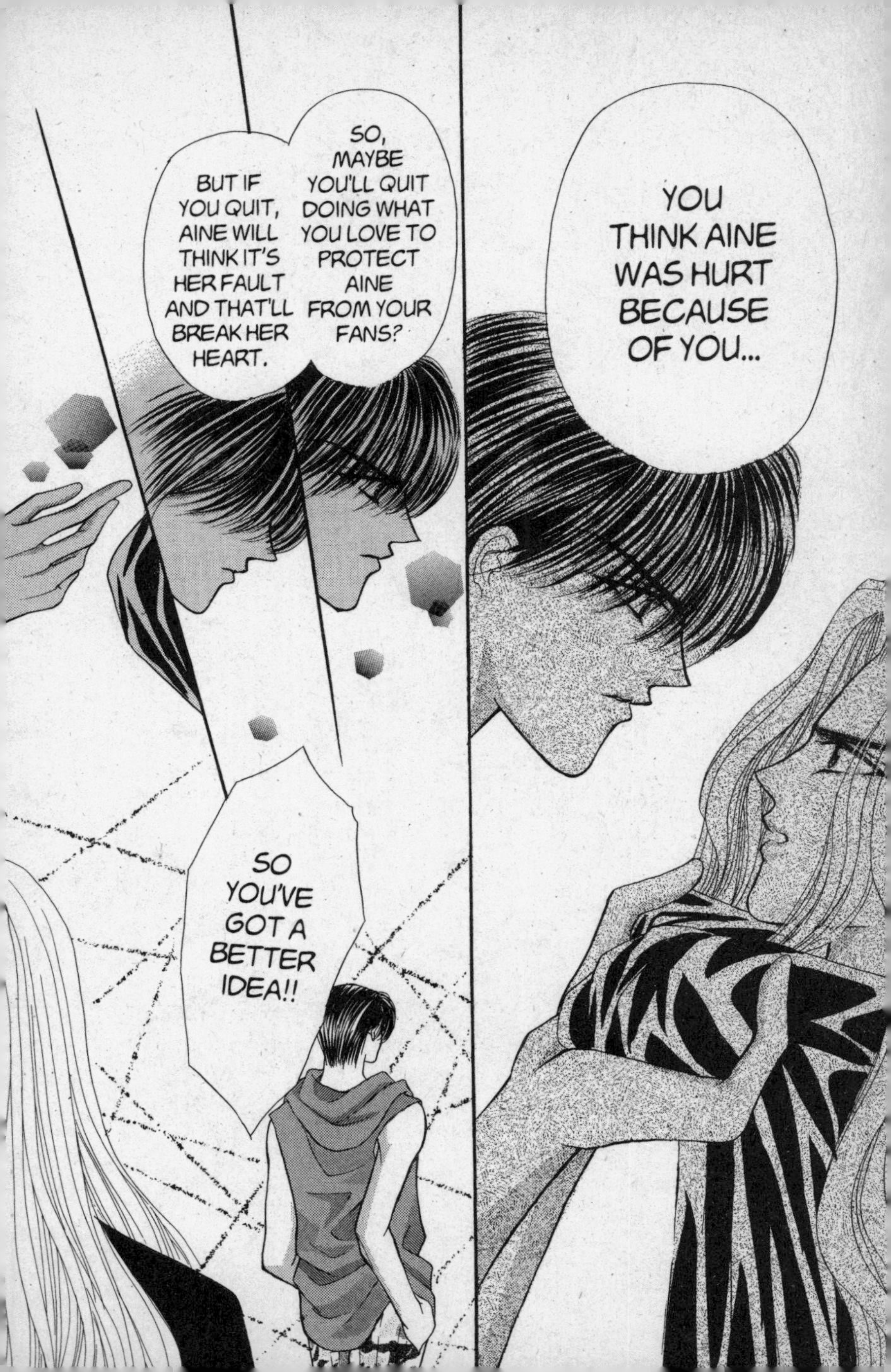
YOU THINK AINE WAS HURT BECAUSE OF YOU...
SO, MAYBE YOU'LL QUIT DOING WHAT YOU LOVE TO PROTECT AINE FROM YOUR FANS?
BUT IF YOU QUIT, AINE WILL THINK IT'S HER FAULT AND THAT'LL BREAK HER HEART.
SO YOU'VE GOT A BETTER IDEA!!

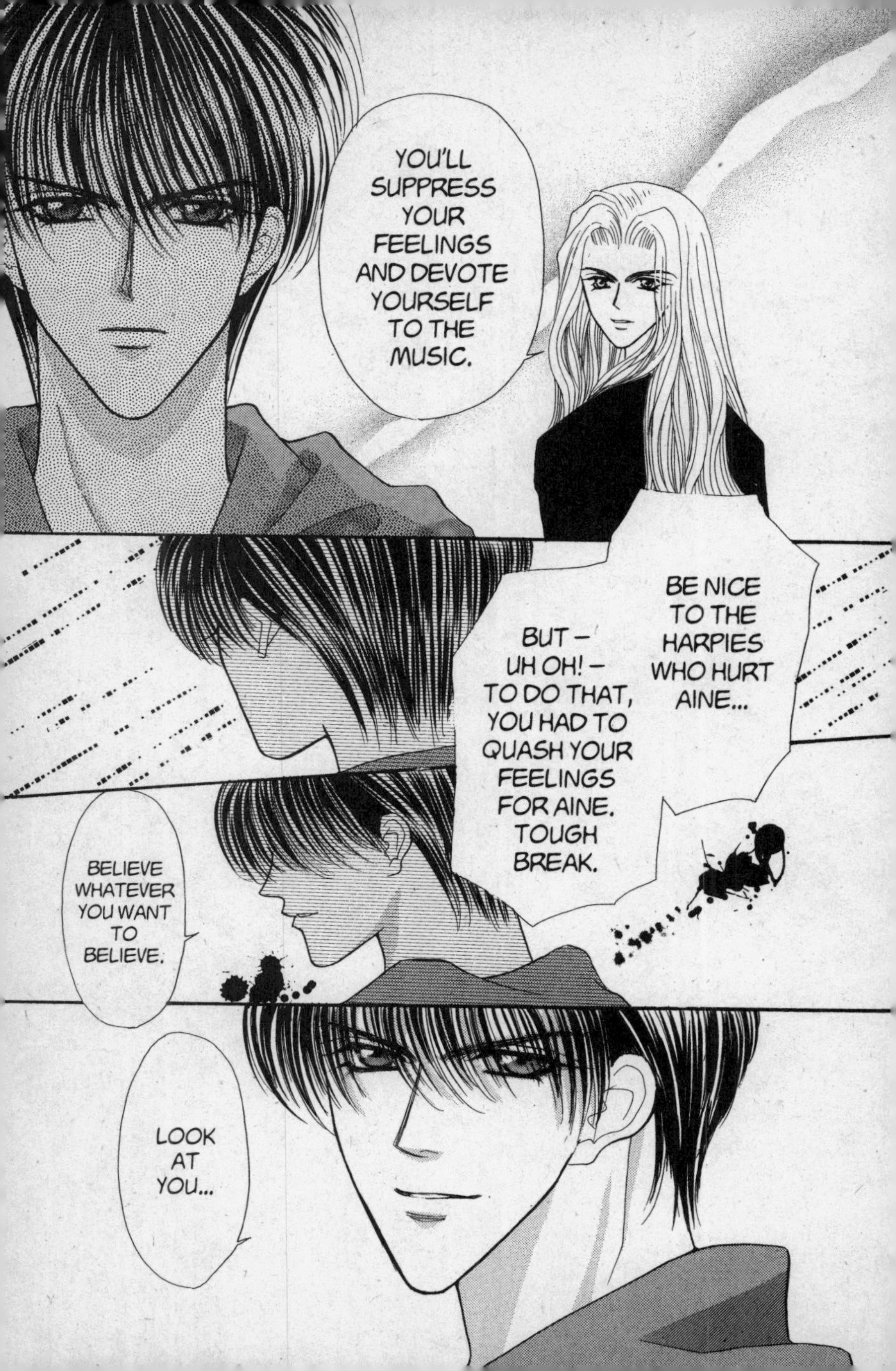
YOU'LL SUPPRESS YOUR FEELINGS AND DEVOTE YOURSELF TO THE MUSIC.
BE NICE TO THE HARPIES WHO HURT AINE...
BUT – UH OH! – TO DO THAT, YOU HAD TO QUASH YOUR FEELINGS FOR AINE. TOUGH BREAK.
BELIEVE WHATEVER YOU WANT TO BELIEVE.
LOOK AT YOU...

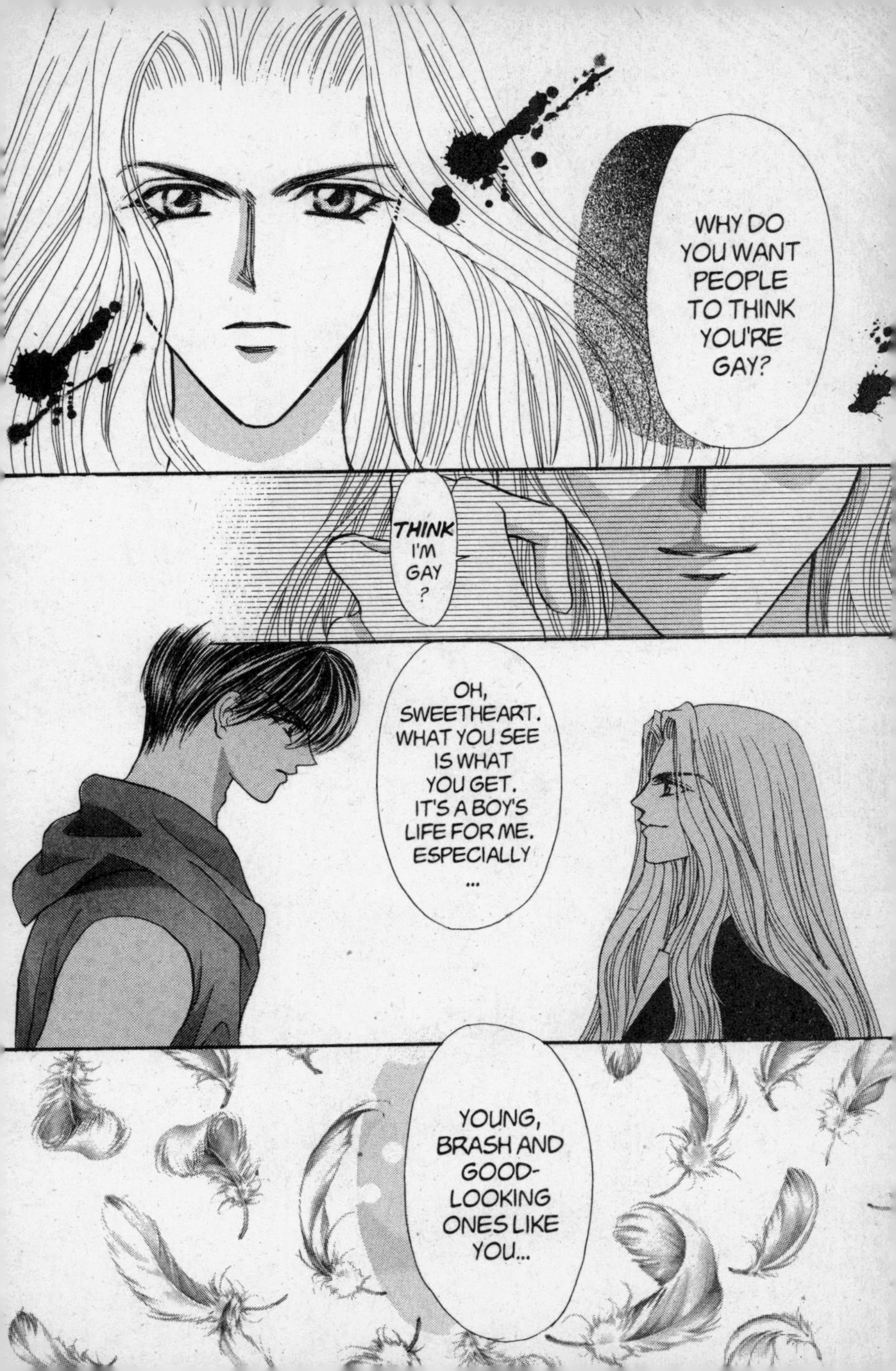
WHY DO YOU WANT PEOPLE TO THINK YOU'RE GAY?
THINK I'M GAY?
OH, SWEETHEART. WHAT YOU SEE IS WHAT YOU GET. IT'S A BOY'S LIFE FOR ME. ESPECIALLY...
YOUNG, BRASH AND GOOD-LOOKING ONES LIKE YOU...

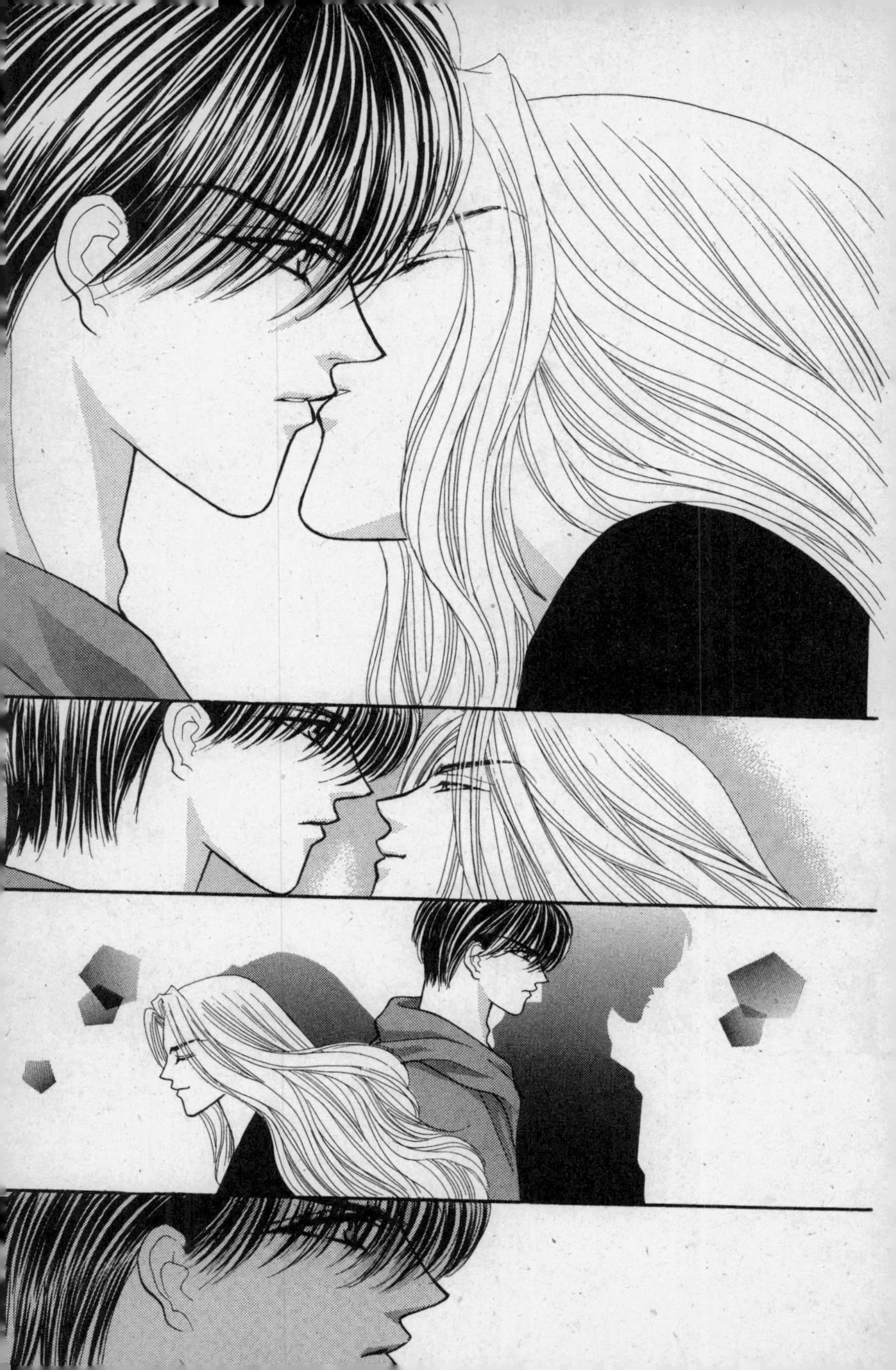

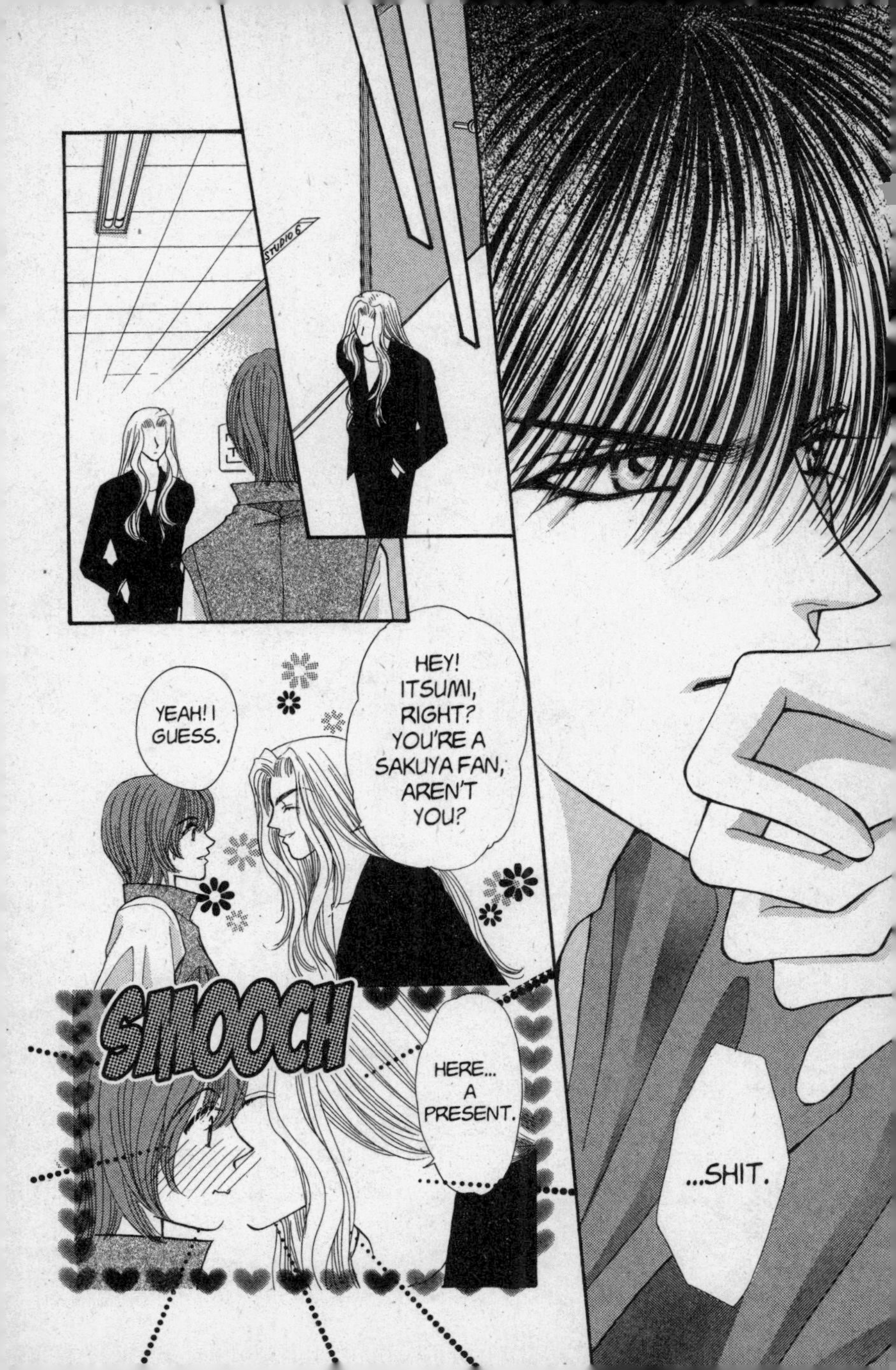
...SHIT.
STUDIO 6
HEY! ITSUMI, RIGHT? YOU'RE A SAKUYA FAN, AREN'T YOU?
YEAH! I GUESS.
SMOOCH
HERE... A PRESENT.

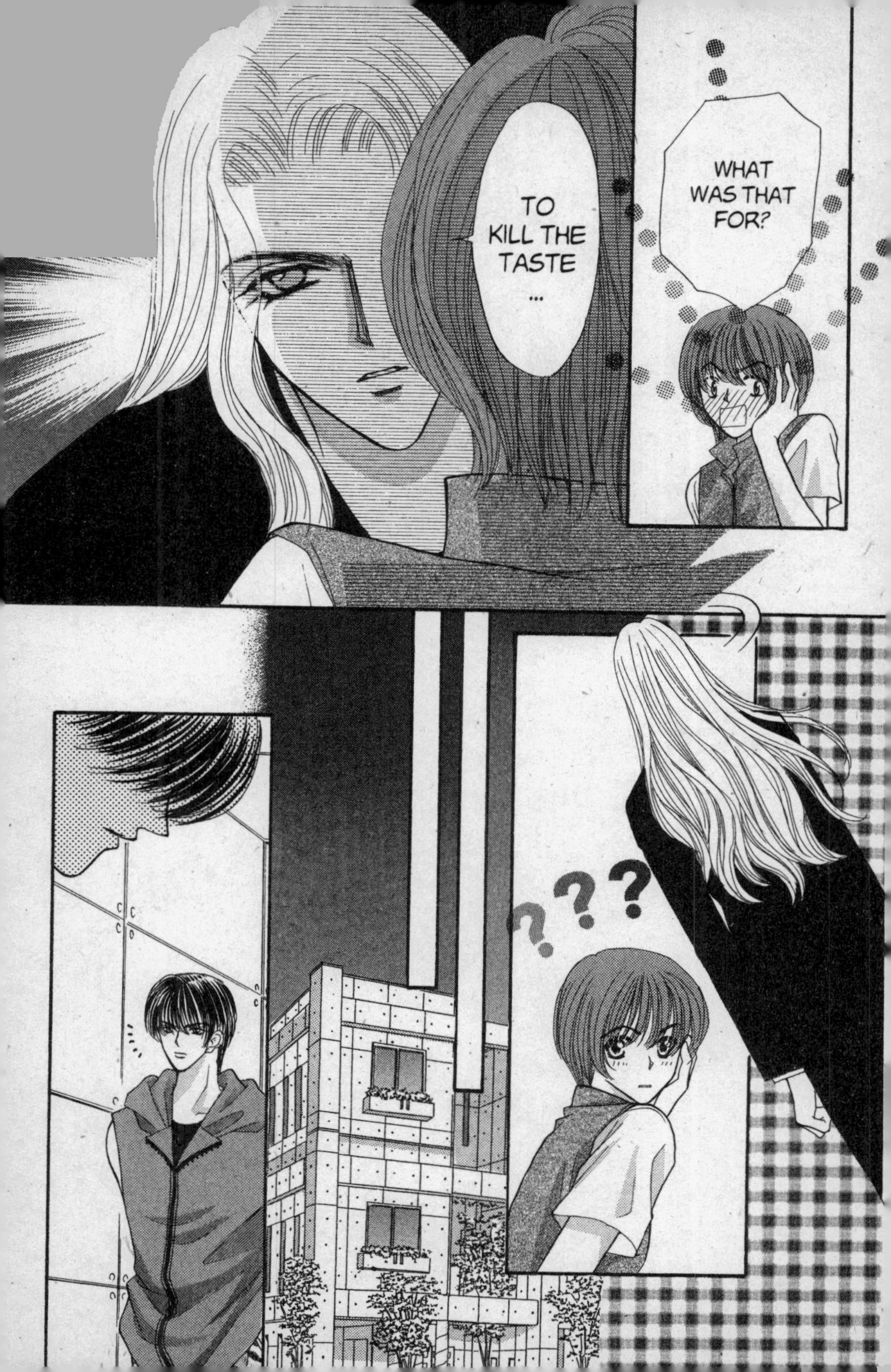
WHAT WAS THAT FOR?
TO KILL THE TASTE ...
???

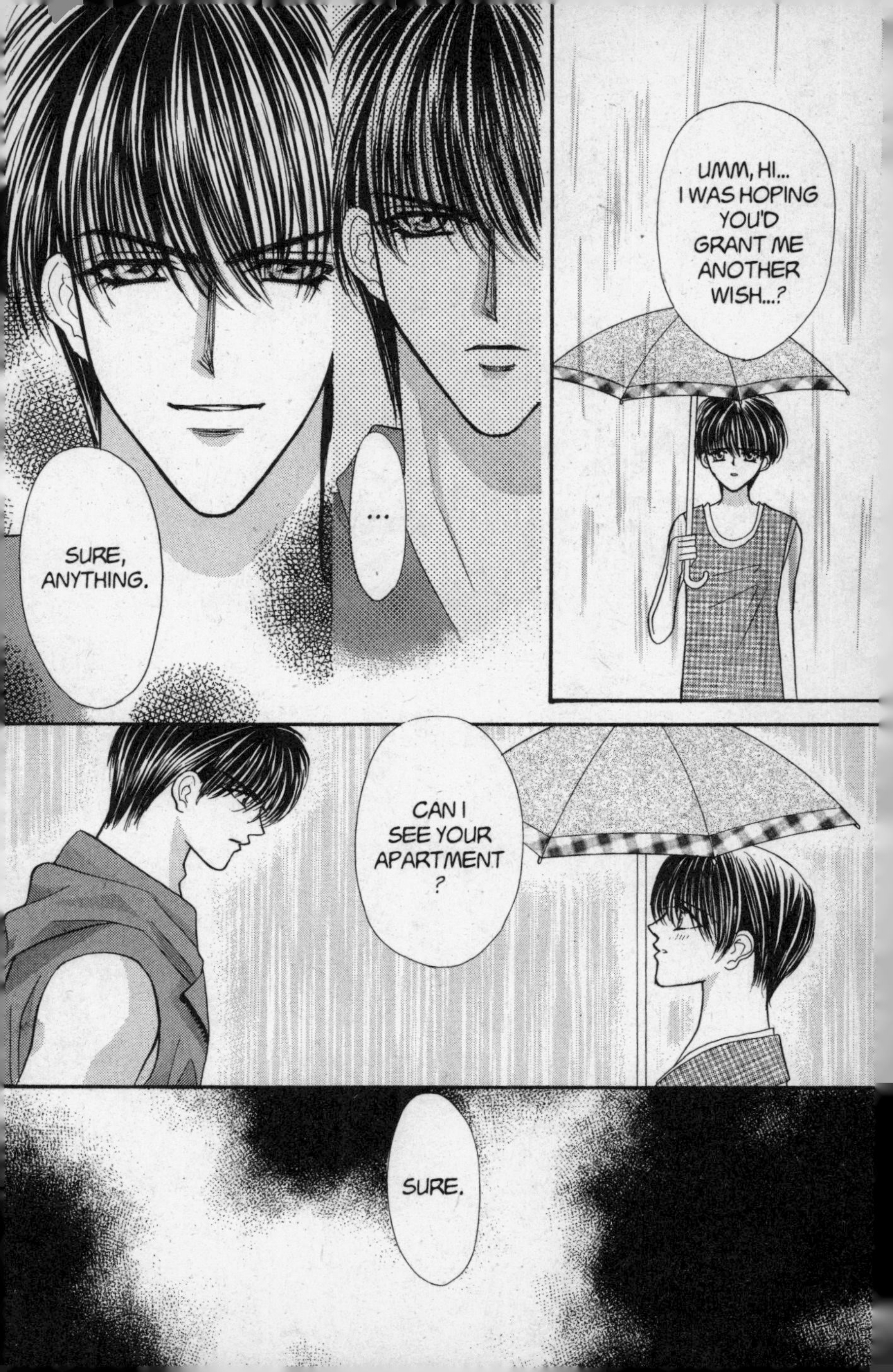
UMM, HI... I WAS HOPING YOU'D GRANT ME ANOTHER WISH...?
...
SURE, ANYTHING.
CAN I SEE YOUR APARTMENT ?
SURE.

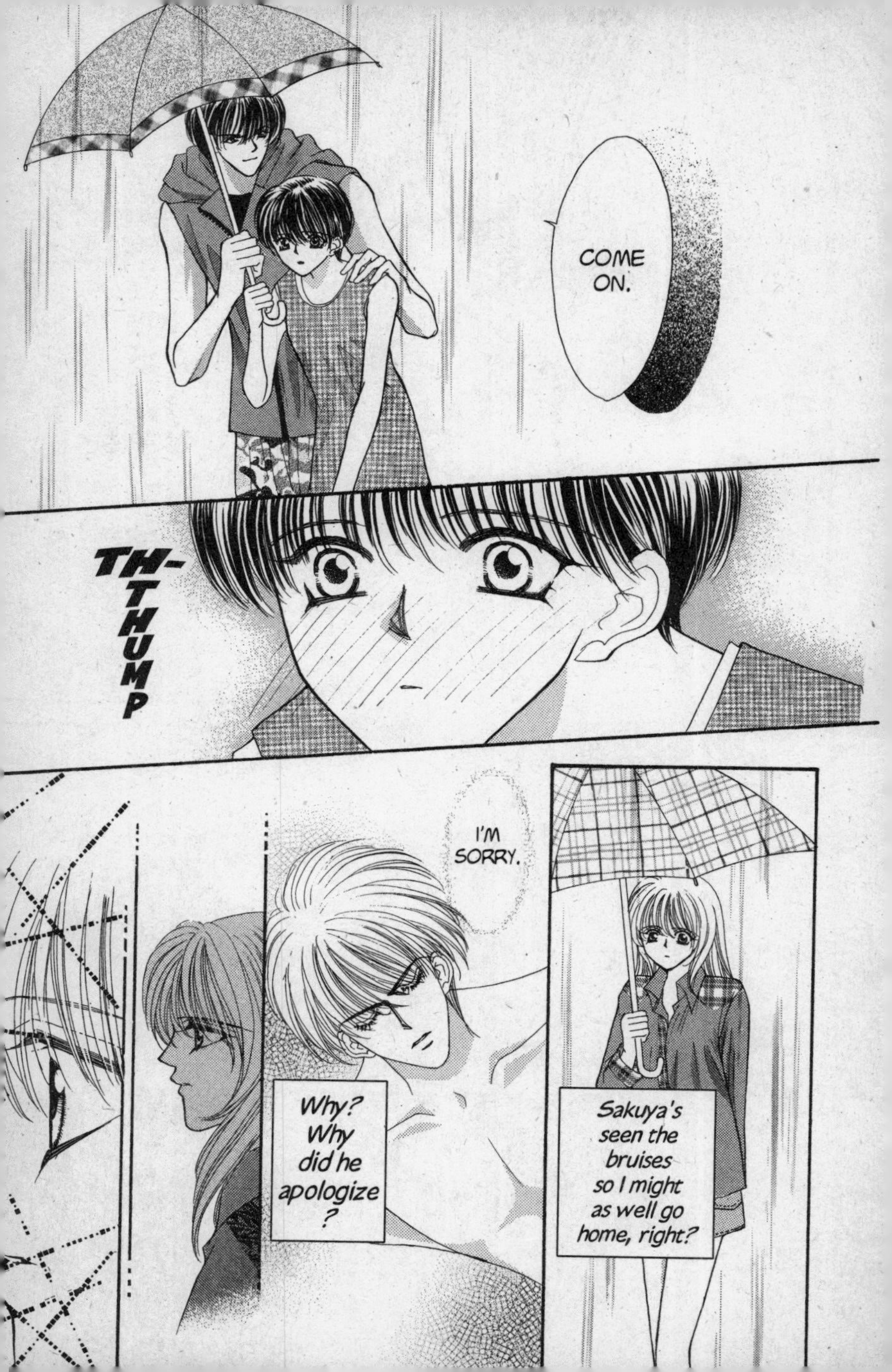
COME ON.
TH-THUMP
Sakuya's seen the bruises so I might as well go home, right?
I'M SORRY.
Why? Why did he apologize?

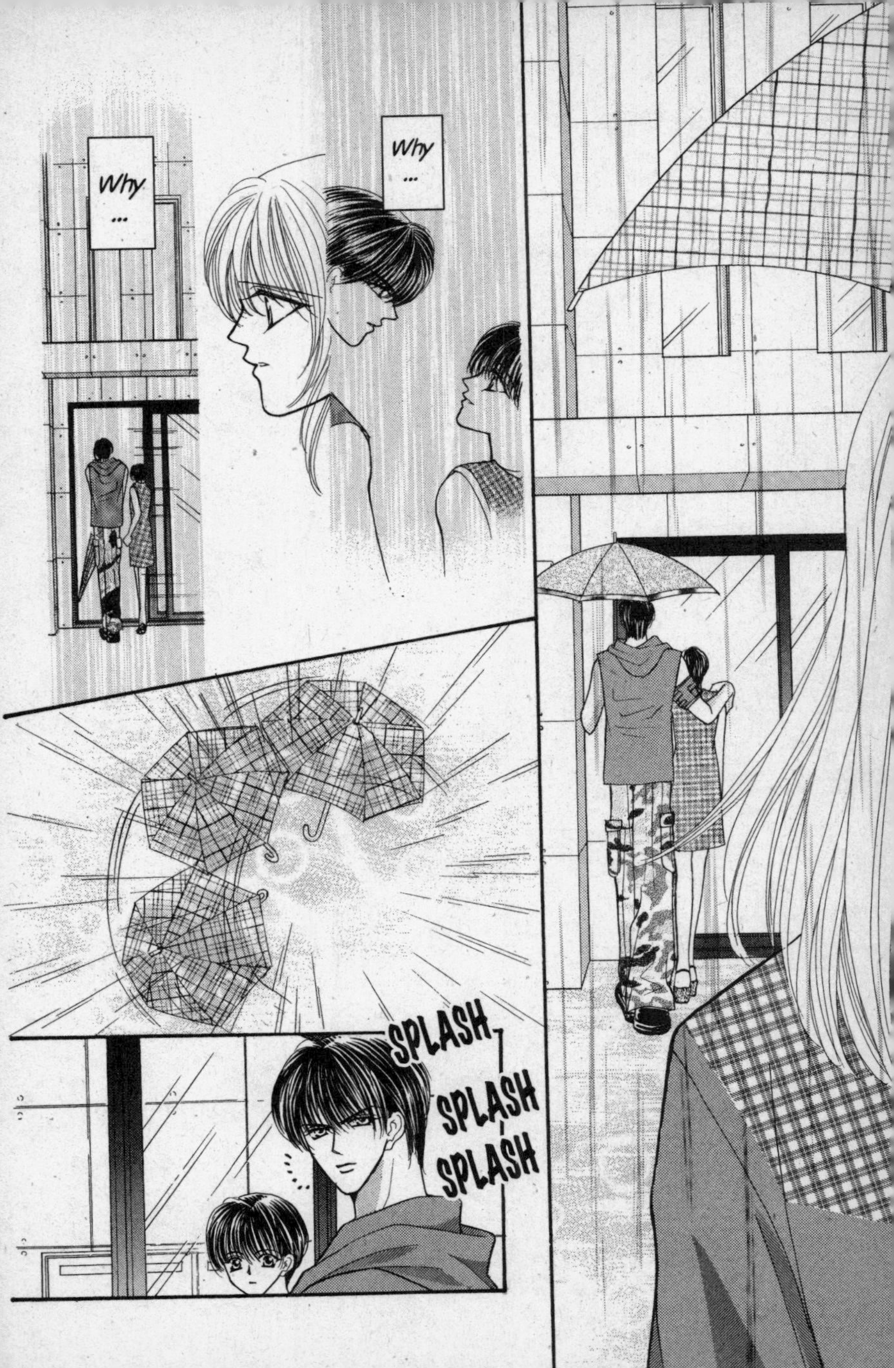
Why ...
Why ...
SPLASH
SPLASH
SPLASH

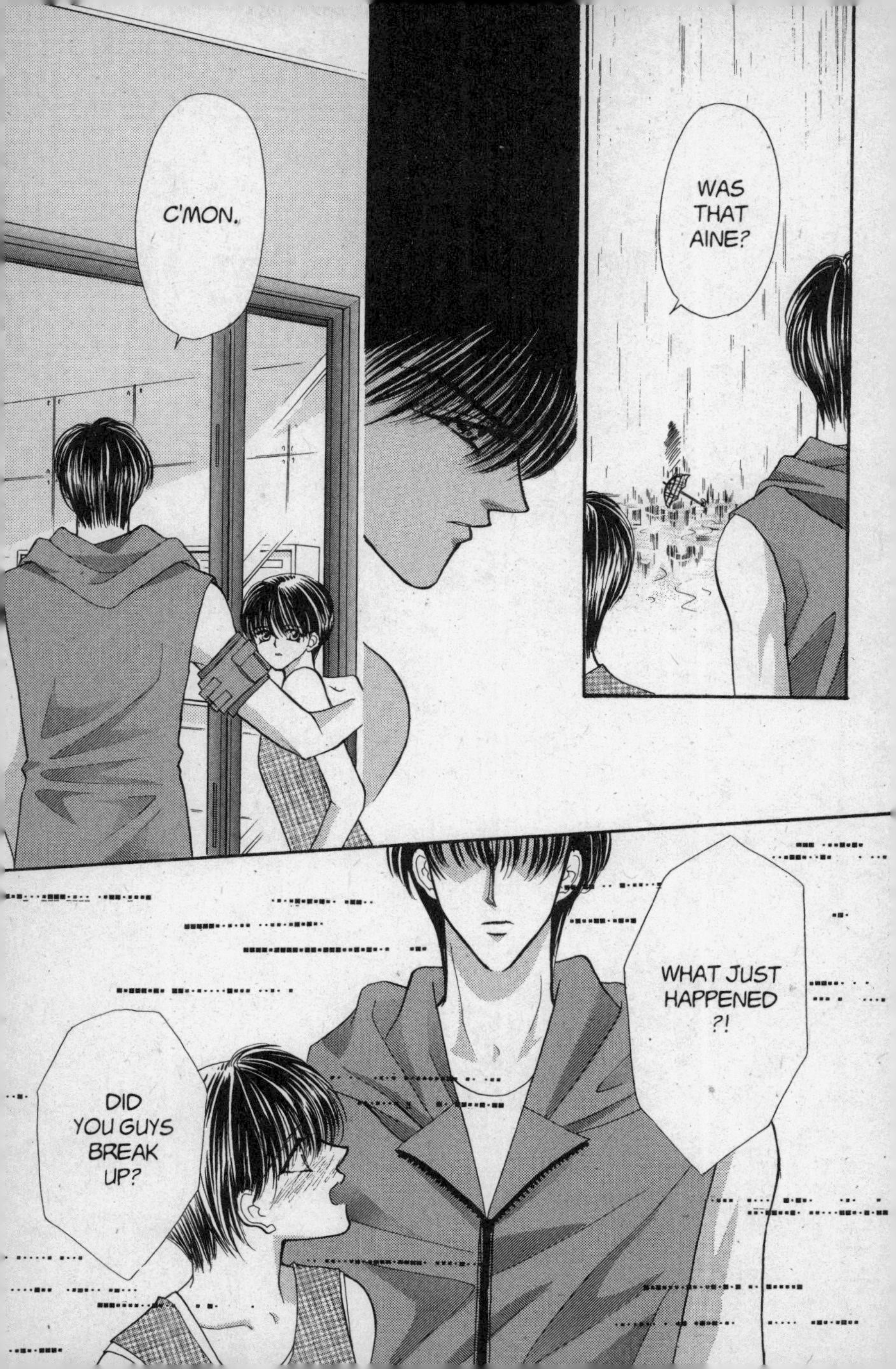
WAS THAT AINE?
C'MON.
WHAT JUST HAPPENED ?!
DID YOU GUYS BREAK UP?

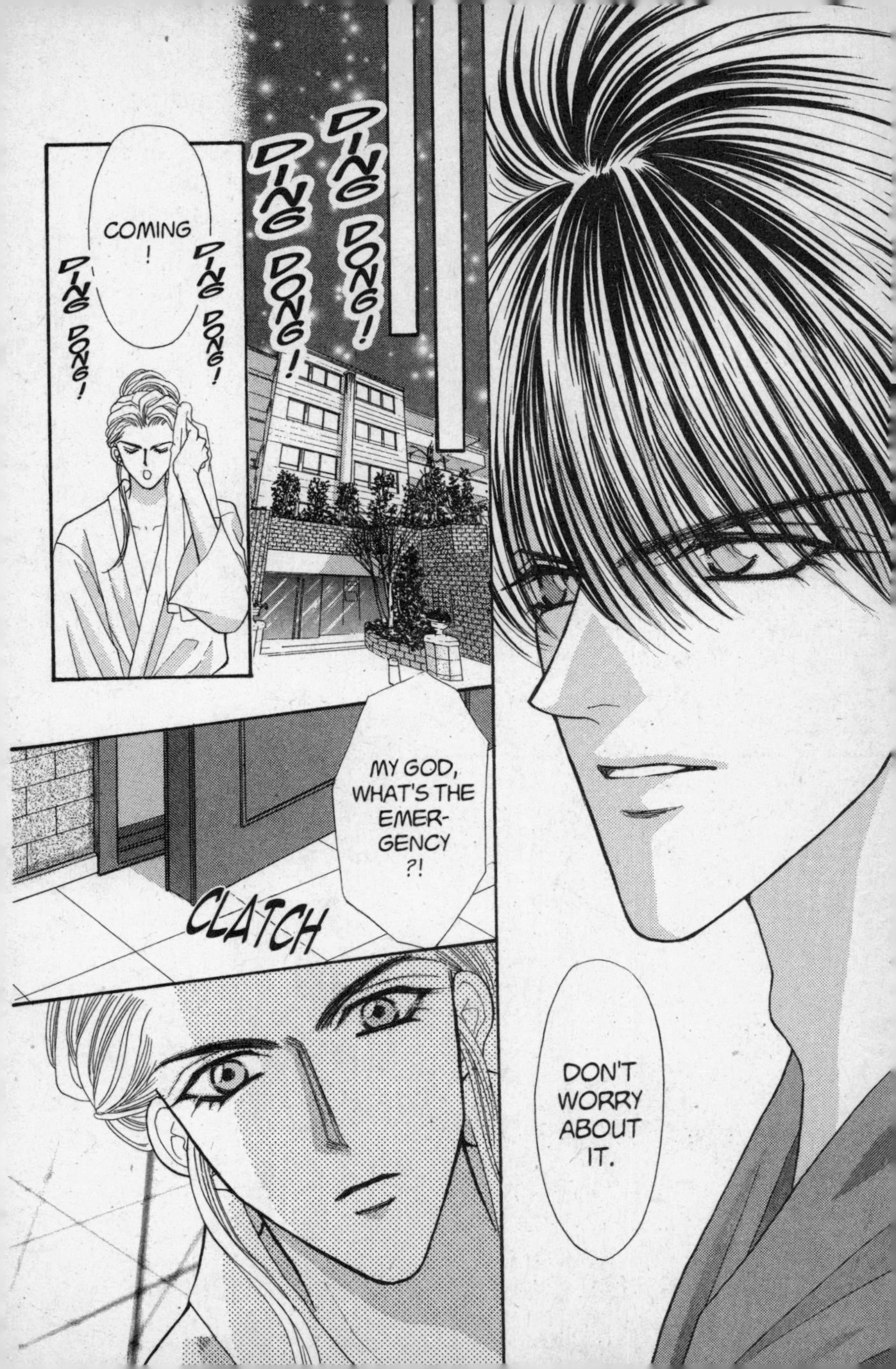
DON'T WORRY ABOUT IT.
DING DONG!
DING DONG!
COMING!
DING DONG!
DING DONG!
MY GOD, WHAT'S THE EMERGENCY?!
CLATCH

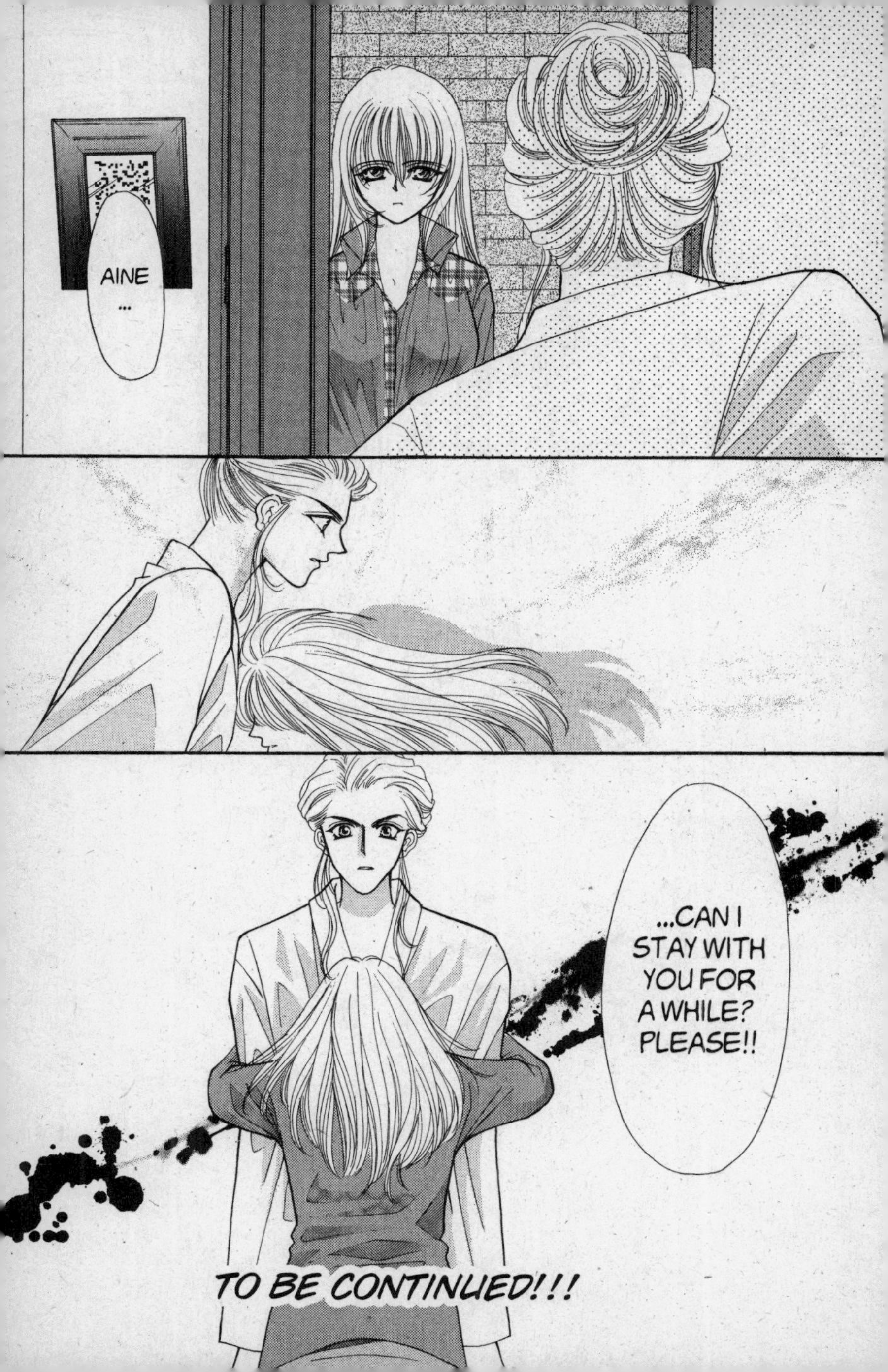
AINE ...
...CAN I STAY WITH YOU FOR A WHILE? PLEASE!!
TO BE CONTINUED!!!

Satanic Verses,
column by Kelly Sue DeConnick

I'm With The Band

O, Povero Sakuya! How harrowing it is to be a rockstar. How he doth suffer the drama. The love of his fans, it's destroying him—destroying him, I say! How does he manage? What complex rockstar coping mechanisms must he employ? Anxious for answers, I turned to my favorite real-life rockstar for the inside scoop. Former-Soul Coughing-front-man, now-solo-artist Mike Doughty broke the code of silence and gave me the lowdown on what life is like in the idol's inner circle:

KSDC: Is it true that virgins write the most sensual lyrics?

MD: Yes, but they're generally about unicorns.

KSDC: Sakuya dislikes "guys who try to step to [him]." How do you feel about guys who try to step to you?

MD: In truth—they kinda turn me on.

KSDC: What's your blood type? Shoe size? Favorite movie? How long does it take you to get ready in the morning?

MD: I don't know my blood type. Shoe size is nine. Fave movie is *All About Eve*. About four hours.

KSDC: So—for real—how often do you have to protect your girlfriends from hoards of jealous fans? Do they carry knives?

MD: Whew, VERY often. Who has knives? The fans? The girlfriends definitely have knives. Hoo boy.

KSDC: When you play secret shows for your die-hard fans, what name do you use? Is it Ythguod Ekim? (Because that would be totally rad.)

MD: I had to read that a bunch of times to realize that name's not a first cousin of Muad'Dib. Actually I have a whole second career in avant-jazz under the name "Mandy Moore." Sssh!

KSDC: Do you and your band have a plan in place for the inevitability of your being kidnapped and tortured by your half-brother, the jealous American mogul?

MD: I have a plan—well, it's more like a to-do list. As for my band—I'm getting the impression that they don't really care if I get kidnapped by my half-brother the jealous American mogul. Callous!

KSDC: If someone in your band were, say, in love with his stepsister—would that technically be incest?

MD: Oh, no no. Half my drummer's harem is second cousins.

KSDC: Sakuya wore a strangely appliquéd blouse to rescue Aine from Tomoyuki's clutches. What do you wear to woo girls out of windows?

MD: Boxer briefs.

KSDC: Which outfit are you hottest in: a) your school uniform; b) your tight black sweater; c) that marabou feather robe thing; or d) a towel.

MD: I actually like to wander around in a towel, looking rather like King Kamehameha. Girls love that look, too.

KSDC: What's it like to whisk women away on your private jet at a moment's notice?

MD: Well, it's an exquisite feeling, of course. Although it's not really a moment—it takes a half hour or so. Less time for the hovercraft.

KSDC: Do you stock said private jet with exotic aphrodisiacs? What kind?

MD: Yes. Cheetos and Gatorade. Don't laugh! It works.

KSDC: We understand that as young men, nascent rockstars often sell themselves to soap opera actresses as love toys. What are the pros and cons of this approach?

MD: You know, at this point I'm beginning to wonder how you got all this inside information on me. You're really freaking me out, pal.

…For more on Mike, see MikeDoughty.com. For his latest album, *Haughty Melodic*, see iTunes or your favorite record retailer.

My backstage pass in hand, a bitter taste in my mouth and my copy of *Skittish* cleaved tight to my aging bosom, I remain,

Yours,

Kelly Sue DeConnick
May 2005

Kelly Sue DeConnick is responsible for the English adaptation of *Sensual Phrase*. She also works (or has worked) on the titles *Descendants of Darkness*, *Kare First Love*, *Sexy Voice and Robo*, *MeruPuri*, *Doubt!!* and *Blue Spring*. She lives in Kansas City and can be contacted c/o VIZ Media.

EDITOR'S RECOMMENDATIONS

More manga!

If you like

Sensual Phrase ™

here are three more books the editor thinks you'll enjoy:

Yami no Matsuei © Yoko
Matsushita 1996 /
HAKUSENSHA, Inc.

Descendants of Darkness
Welcome to the world of shonen ai...a place
where boys love boys. Artist Yoko Matsushita
has created a funny and sexy series about the
bureaucracy of love and death.

© 2002, 2003 Iou KURODA /
Shogakukan Inc.

Sexy Voice and Robo
Today, Nico is a 14-year-old telephone-dating
call girl. But tomorrow, who knows? She might
be a fortuneteller or a spy. Don't miss this
award-winning effort from Iou Kuroda.

© 1989 Naoki YAMAMOTO /
Shogakukan Inc.

Dance Till Tomorrow
An erotic comedy from the pen of Naoki
Yamamoto. Arguably the most sexually explicit
manga ever published by VIZ Media.

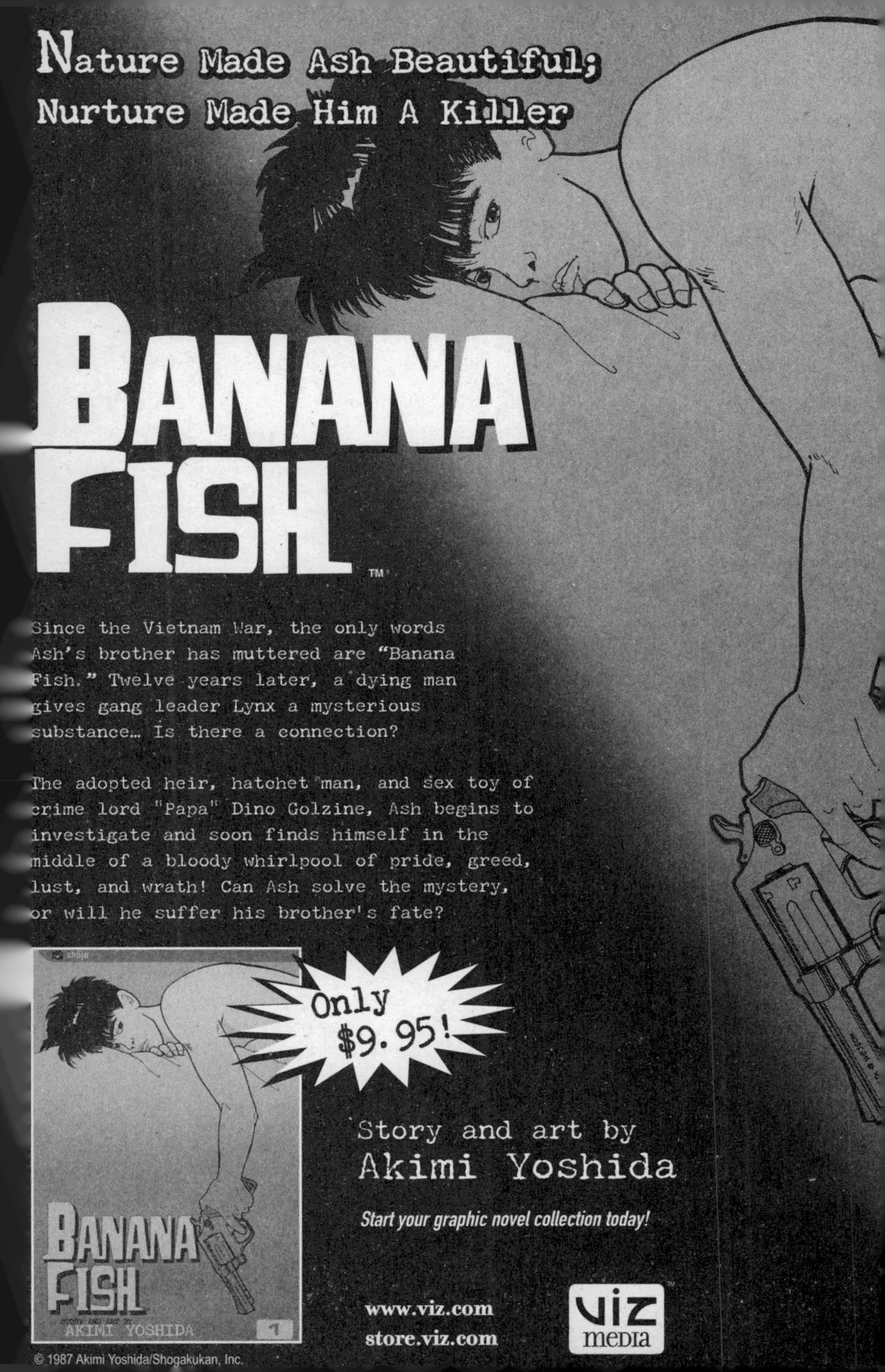
Nature Made Ash Beautiful;
Nurture Made Him A Killer
BANANA FISH™
Since the Vietnam War, the only words Ash's brother has muttered are "Banana Fish." Twelve years later, a dying man gives gang leader Lynx a mysterious substance... Is there a connection?
The adopted heir, hatchet man, and sex toy of crime lord "Papa" Dino Golzine, Ash begins to investigate and soon finds himself in the middle of a bloody whirlpool of pride, greed, lust, and wrath! Can Ash solve the mystery, or will he suffer his brother's fate?
Only $9.95!
BANANA FISH
AKIMI YOSHIDA
1
Story and art by
Akimi Yoshida
Start your graphic novel collection today!
www.viz.com
store.viz.com
VIZ MEDIA
© 1987 Akimi Yoshida/Shogakukan, Inc.

Every Secret Has a Price

Hatsumi will do anything to keep a family secret — even enslave herself to her childhood bully, Ryoki. Forced to do what he wants when he wants, Hatsumi soon finds herself in some pretty compromising positions! Will Azusa, her childhood friend and current crush, be able to help? Or does he have an agenda of his own?

From the top of the Japanese manga charts, HOT GIMMICK is now available for the first time in English.

Start your graphic novel collection today!

Only $9.95!

www.viz.com
store.viz.com

© 2001 Miki Aihara/Shogakukan, Inc.

The Power of a Kiss

Soon after her first kiss, Yuri is pulled into a puddle and transported to an ancient Middle Eastern village. Surrounded by strange people speaking a language she can't understand, Yuri has no idea how to get back home and is soon embroiled in the politics and romance of the ancient Middle East. If a kiss helped get Yuri into this mess, can a kiss get her out?

RED RIVER

Start your graphic novel collection today!

ONLY $9.95!

www.viz.com
store.viz.com

VIZ MEDIA

© 1995 Chie Shinohara/Shogakukan, Inc.

All New SHÔJO Graphic Novels!

shôjo

Starting at $9.95!

The latest volumes now available at store.viz.com:

Angel Sanctuary, Vol. 11
Banana Fish, Vol. 11
Basara, Vol. 15
Boys Over Flowers, Vol. 15 *
Hana-Kimi, Vol. 9
Happy Hustle High, Vol. 4
Hot Gimmick, Vol. 10
Kare First Love, Vol. 6
Sensual Phrase, Vol. 11

* Also available on DVD from VIZ

www.viz.com

Tenshi Kinryou Ku © Kaori Yuki 1994/HAKUSENSHA, Inc. BANANA FISH © 1987 Akimi YOSHIDA/Shogakukan Inc. BASARA © 1991 Yumi TAMURA/Shogakukan Inc. HANA-YORI DANGO © 1992 by Yoko Kamio/SHUEISHA Inc. Hanazakari no Kimitachi he © Hisaya Nakajo 1996/HAKUSENSHA Inc. HAPPY HUSTLE HIGH © 2004 Rie TAKADA/Shogakukan Inc. HOT GIMMICK © 2001 Miki AIHARA/Shogakukan Inc. KARE FIRST LOVE © 2002 Kaho MIYASAKA/ Shogakukan Inc. SENSUAL PHRASE © 1997 Mayu SHINJO/Shogakukan Inc.

NOTE: Cover art subject to change.

LOVE SHOJO? LET US KNOW!

☐ Please do NOT send me information about VIZ Media products, news and events, special offers, or other information.

☐ Please do NOT send me information from VIZ' trusted business partners.

Name: _____

Address: _____

City: _____ **State:** _____ **Zip:** _____

E-mail: _____

☐ **Male** ☐ **Female**   **Date of Birth** (mm/dd/yyyy): ____ / ____ / ____   (Under 13? Parental consent required)

What race/ethnicity do you consider yourself? (check all that apply)

☐ White/Caucasian   ☐ Black/African American   ☐ Hispanic/Latino

☐ Asian/Pacific Islander   ☐ Native American/Alaskan Native ☐ Other: _____

What VIZ shojo title(s) did you purchase? (indicate title(s) purchased)

_____

What other shojo titles from other publishers do you own? _____

_____

Reason for purchase: (check all that apply)

☐ Special offer   ☐ Favorite title / author / artist / genre

☐ Gift   ☐ Recommendation   ☐ Collection

☐ Read excerpt in VIZ manga sampler   ☐ Other _____

Where did you make your purchase? (please check one)

☐ Comic store   ☐ Bookstore   ☐ Mass/Grocery Store

☐ Newsstand   ☐ Video/Video Game Store

☐ Online (site:_____)   ☐ Other _____

How many shojo titles have you purchased in the last year? How many were VIZ shojo titles?
(please check one from each column)

SHOJO MANGA

☐ None
☐ 1 – 4
☐ 5 – 10
☐ 11+

VIZ SHOJO MANGA

☐ None
☐ 1 – 4
☐ 5 – 10
☐ 11+

What do you like most about shojo graphic novels? (check all that apply)

☐ Romance
☐ Comedy
☐ Other _____

☐ Drama / conflict
☐ Real-life storylines

☐ Fantasy
☐ Relatable characters

Do you purchase every volume of your favorite shojo series?

☐ Yes! Gotta have 'em as my own
☐ No. Please explain: _____

Who are your favorite shojo authors / artists? _____

_____

What shojo titles would like you translated and sold in English? _____

_____

THANK YOU! Please send the completed form to:

NJW Research
ATTN: VIZ Media Shojo Survey
42 Catharine Street
Poughkeepsie, NY 12601

Your privacy is very important to us. All information provided will be used for internal purposes only and will not be sold or otherwise divulged.

NO PURCHASE NECESSARY. Requests not in compliance with all terms of this form will not be acknowledged or returned. All submissions are subject to verification and become the property of VIZ Media. Fraudulent submission, including use of multiple addresses or P.O. boxes to obtain additional VIZ information or offers may result in prosecution. VIZ reserves the right to withdraw or modify any terms of this form. Void where prohibited, taxed, or restricted by law. VIZ will not be liable for lost, misdirected, mutilated, illegible, incomplete or postage-due mail. © 2005 VIZ Media. All Rights Reserved. VIZ Media, property titles, characters, names and plots therein under license to VIZ Media. All Rights Reserved.